MAJOR COTTERELL
AT ARNHEM

A WAR CRIME AND A MYSTERY

JENNIE GRAY

For Shubbs, devoted brother of Anthony Cotterell, who contributed so much
to this book but sadly did not live to see it published.

One could only understand Anthony at all well by keeping always in mind that
he was a writer. He was that more than anyone I ever met.

Ernest Watkins, autobiography

The battle for Arnhem contains all the ingredients of a classical tragedy, both
from a civilian and military point of view.

Piet Kamphuis, *Holland at War Against Hitler*

Back cover image of captured British airborne soldiers from *Retake Arnhem Bridge: An Illustrated History of Kampgruppe Knaust, September–October 1944*, by kind permission of R.N. Sigmond Publishing

First published 2012
by Spellmount, an imprint of

The History Press
The Mill, Brimscombe Port
Stroud, Gloucestershire, GL5 2QG
www.thehistorypress.co.uk

© Jennie Gray, 2012

The right of Jennie Gray to be identified as the Author
of this work has been asserted in accordance with the
Copyrights, Designs and Patents Act 1988.

British Library Cataloguing in Publication Data.
A catalogue record for this book is available from the British Library.

ISBN 978 0 7524 7980 4

Typesetting and origination by The History Press
Printed in Great Britain

CONTENTS

DRAMATIS PERSONAE

Surname	First name	Rank/title	Role	Description
Adam	Sir Ronald	General	ABCA & War Office	Adjutant-General of the British Army, ultimately responsible for *WAR*
Beattie	Edward		American war reporter/PoW	As PoW, taken to Berlin to meet Nazi hierarchy – possible parallel to Anthony's treatment
Braden	Unknown	Dr	German Military in Holland	Travelling in the car with Etter when they came across the Brummen shooting
Briggs	Bernard	Captain	Airborne Forces	On the truck at Brummen
Cairns	John	Lieutenant	Airborne Forces	On the truck at Brummen, cared for Anthony after he was shot
Conroy	David	Major	Search Bureau	Key part of the search for Anthony
Cotterell	Geoffrey		Family	Brother of Anthony
Cotterell	Graham		Family	Father of Anthony and Geoffrey
Cotterell	Mintie		Family	Mother of Anthony and Geoffrey
Etter	Gustav	Oberleutnant	German Military in Holland	Wehrmacht Intelligence Officer, prevented further shooting at Brummen
Finlay Wilson	R.	Lieutenant	Airborne Forces	On the truck at Brummen
Fritzsche	Hans	Dr	German Propaganda	Chief of the Radio Division of the Ministry of Propaganda under Goebbels from 1942
Frost	John	Lieutenant-Colonel	Airborne Forces	CO of 2nd Battalion, 1st Parachute Brigade
Gough	Freddie	Major	Airborne Forces	CO at the Arnhem bridge after Frost wounded, senior British officer at Brummen

Hibbert	Tony	Major	Airborne Forces	Brigade Major of 1st Parachute Brigade HQ, escaped at Brummen
Kamp	Gerrit	Sergeant	Netherlands War Crimes Commission	Military policeman, key figure in search for Anthony
Kinsleigh	H.P.	Captain	War Crimes Group (NWE)	Chief investigating officer, Team 3, Field Investigation Section
Korteweg	Anton	Dr	Dutch in Brummen	Attended to the wounded after the Brummen shooting
Lathbury	Gerald	Brigadier	Airborne Forces	CO of 1st Parachute Brigade
Lathe	Heinrich	Dr	German Military in Holland	Doctor at No. 12 Rozenhoflaan on the night of 23 September 1944
Matzke	Rudolf	Unterscharführer	German Military in Holland	SS guard, accused of murdering the British prisoners at Brummen
McCracken	Ernest	Private	Airborne Forces	Shot at Brummen, died the same day
McNabb	Trevor	Lieutenant	Airborne Forces	Shot at Brummen, died four days later at St Joseph's, Enschede
Pool	Janie		Family	Aunt of Anthony and Geoffrey
Reade	A.E.E.	Major	War Crimes Group	Legal Section of War Crimes Group (NWE) at HQ, BAOR
Saniter	Erich	Dr	German Military in Holland	Doctor at No. 12 Rozenhoflaan on the night of 23 September 1944
Schmidt	Paul	Dr	German Propaganda	Chief of the Press Division of Ribbentrop's Foreign Office
Shubbs			Family	Family petname of Geoffrey
Staubwasser	Anton	Obersturmführer	German Military in Holland	Chief Intelligence Officer of Model's Heeresgruppe B, superior officer of Etter
Tannenbaum	Albert	Lieutenant	Airborne Forces	Shot and seriously wounded at Brummen, survived
Taubert	Eberhard	Dr	German Military in Holland	Propaganda chief in the Netherlands, in charge of Radio Hilversum under Goebbels
Tigges	Ernst	Dr	German Military in Holland	Soldier-Journalist providing news for Radio Hilversum
Tjeenk Willink	Aps		Dutch in Brummen	Mother of Dick, hid Tony Hibbert after shooting, key helper in search for Anthony

Tjeenk Willink	Dick		Dutch in Brummen	Son of Aps, hid Tony Hibbert after shooting, key helper in search for Anthony
Urquhart	Roy	Major-General	Airborne Forces	CO of 1st Airborne Division
Watkins	Ernest	Captain	ABCA & War Office	Worked for Anthony on *WAR*, took over as Major after Anthony's disappearance
Watts	Stephen	Captain	ABCA & War Office	Worked with Anthony on *WAR* until early 1943

PROLOGUE

Brummen, Province of Gelderland, Holland, 23 September 1944

It was a warm afternoon and the weather was beautiful, with the fine clear light often seen in Gelderland as autumn approaches. In Brummen, the Dutch were going about their usual Saturday business and the German occupiers were likewise going about theirs. Village children played in the sunshine whilst their adults shopped in the small marketplace. But beneath the calm surface of an apparently ordinary day there lay an immense trembling excitement. It was 23 September 1944, exactly six days since the largest airborne attack in history had been launched by the Allies on Dutch bridges at Eindhoven, Nijmegen and Arnhem.

Brummen lay a mere eight miles north-east of Arnhem on what was now one of the main routes to Germany. From Sunday until Wednesday night, the villagers had heard the thunderous din of a battle fought as fiercely as that for Stalingrad. They had seen the black clouds of smoke rising from the ruined town and had heard stories of the desperate struggle. Hopelessly outnumbered, a small British force had fought on at Arnhem bridge until the early hours of Thursday morning. Then the incessant thunder of the guns had faded, though it could still be heard from a little farther down the Rhine at Oosterbeek, where the British general, Urquhart, and his men were holding out.

From first light on Monday, straggling groups of refugees from Arnhem had been passing through the village. Some had found shelter there; others had continued on their way. But with the battle lost, a far more dramatic exodus had started – the victors were moving their prisoners to Germany. The villagers had already seen several batches of prisoners driven past in lorries, or marched through under armed guard. After four years of German occupation, the airborne soldiers were an astonishing sight. Although the British had lost the battle, the villagers still saw them as liberators, close to heroes of legend in their valour. The soldiers' red berets were very striking, as was their smiling courage in the face of adversity. They were singing or whistling 'It's a long, long way to Tipperary', the archetypal song of the European resistance, which was sometimes quietly echoed by the villagers to show where their sympathies lay. Other villagers waved a scrap of material in the Dutch national colour, orange, or surreptitiously made the illegal V-Victory sign.[1]

At around 6.00pm a solitary German army lorry, travelling at high speed and without escort, arrived in Brummen. In the driver's cab sat the driver and two Waffen-SS men. On the running board, armed with a sub-machine, was another SS guard. The back of the lorry had wooden side-boards and tail-board, but the usual tarpaulin cover had been removed and the passengers could be clearly seen. Two Luftwaffe guards were sitting by the tail-board, armed with pistols and rifles. They were guarding some thirty British airborne soldiers, almost all of them officers, who were having to stand because space was so limited. A couple of the officers had found an uncomfortable perch on the metal roof of the driver's cab. One of these was a 27-year-old Major, slight in build and strikingly good-looking, with dark brown hair, a pale complexion, and brown-green eyes.

The truck came down the side of the marketplace and turned left into the sharp bend of the road to Zutphen. Owing to the combination of the bend and the crowd of villagers, the speeding vehicle was forced to slow right down. Two of the SS guards jumped off, apparently to deal with some villagers who were making the V-Victory sign. As they did so, Dutch onlookers suddenly noticed that two British officers were making an escape attempt. One jumped off to the left of the lorry, the other to the right. The second man stumbled and fell as he landed but was up immediately, running for his life in a hail of bullets. By a thoroughly unlucky chance, another German lorry had just appeared from the opposite direction and its driver alerted the first lorry that it was losing its prisoners. SS soldiers jumped down from the second lorry and opened fire. In a split second, the peaceful scene in the marketplace had degenerated into a maelstrom of chaos, violence and bloodshed. The civilians fled in horrified panic. On reaching the safety of home, some watched the scene from behind their curtains. They saw the truck with the remaining British soldiers move out of the marketplace around the sharp bend into the Zutphen road. The truck stopped with a jerk by the Post Office, a large handsome building which stood in a quiet and pleasant street.

The prisoners had lost their balance and had been sent sprawling when the truck stopped. None of them were trying to escape, yet firing was still going on. Then as suddenly as it had all started, everything seemed to stop. Events had happened so quickly, had been so terrifying and confusing, that, as yet, none of the Dutch were sure exactly what had happened. But one nightmare thing was obvious – an SS soldier had been shooting into the now stationery truck with a sub-machine gun at point-blank range. Only the jamming of the gun or the emptying of his magazine had prevented a mass execution. He was fumbling with his gun now, trying to make it work. Another SS soldier joined him and began taking pot shots at the prisoners with a pistol.

Only a few seconds more might have seen them murder everyone in the truck. But then, as if by a miracle, a third German vehicle chanced upon the scene, a Volkswagen staff car from Field Marshal Model's Heeresgruppe B. In it was travelling a Wehrmacht officer, on his way to interrogate prisoners. Critically, the Wehrmacht officer outranked the SS guards at the scene. He took immediate charge of the situation. Witnesses would remember him shouting at the SS, 'What are you doing? These are British officers, not Russians.'

All the prisoners who could move were ordered to get off the truck, and made to sit on the side of the road, cross-legged, with their hands on their head. The dead were removed, placed on the ground in front of the prisoners, and then – and only then – were the wounded taken off the truck. Amongst them was the dark-haired Major who had been sitting on the driver's cab. He was seriously hurt, but conscious and lucid. Though the Brummen villagers did not know it yet, his name was Anthony Cotterell.

PART ONE

BECOMING A SOLDIER: MARCH 1940 – JUNE 1941

I

THE COTTERELL FAMILY

nthony Cotterell was not a professional soldier, he was a conscript. Nor could the British Army turn him into a professional soldier once it owned him. First as an ordinary infantry private, then as a very junior infantry officer, he failed to fit the military roles for which the Army had trained him. He got the lowest pass grade achievable on his officer training course, and in subsequent postings proved something of an absent-minded liability to his commanding officers. But what he could do for the Army was write. By the time of the battle of Arnhem, he was one of the Army's top journalists, an ambitious young man becoming famous not only in military but in civilian circles. He went to Arnhem not to fight but to record the extraordinary airborne drop of some 11,000 soldiers in an operation which was confidently expected to end the war by Christmas. Instead, the operation turned into a colossal military disaster. Amongst the thousands of prisoners taken after the battle was Anthony.

The path which led Anthony to Brummen had begun on 9 March 1940, when his call-up papers arrived at his family home in Wanstead. It was the period of the Phoney War, when, despite a few alarms and excursions, life was continuing much as it had done pre-war. Anthony, then only 23, but already a feature writer on the *Daily Express*, had come home for the weekend as he always did. His family was small but close-knit, consisting of his parents, Graham and Mintie, and his only sibling, his younger brother, Geoffrey, who was trying to become a novelist.

On the morning that he received the call-up letter, Anthony's immediate preoccupation was how on earth he was going to break the dreadful news to his family. Although the letter had been expected for weeks, everyone was hoping against hope that it would be delayed for a very long time. Mintie was in a deep state of anxiety about both her sons, for Geoffrey was also on the verge of being called up. Like all her generation, Mintie remembered the slaughter of three-quarters of a million British men in the trenches of the Great War, and was haunted by the nightmare that it might all happen again.

She also had a less serious concern – she feared that army life would coarsen Anthony. This was not a view shared by his caustic *Daily Express* friends, who quipped that Anthony would coarsen the Army.[2]

The Cotterells' family home, Ham Frith, stood opposite the Green at No. 1, Grove Park. Wanstead had once been a favourite haunt of Tudor grandees, attracted by the rich hunting in nearby Epping Forest, but their rural idyll had long ago been destroyed by the creeping growth of London. One of the few remnants of Wanstead's golden age, the Green was a meeting place for people with dogs. It was dotted about with a few ancient trees of which the locals were extremely proud: 'They regarded the trees as the innermost outskirts of Epping Forest and as a satisfactory substitute for the countryside.'[3]

Ham Frith was a very large red-brick house, built around 1900, with something of the Arts and Crafts style in its architecture. Handsome, spacious and airy, it smelt evocatively of wood and polish. Several of its furnishings were of good solid oak, carved in the fashion of the Middle Ages as interpreted by commercial disciples of Burne-Jones and William Morris. There were brick fireplaces, leather armchairs, brass candlesticks, and bits of Arts and Crafts-style pottery which had come from Mintie's old family home in Plymouth. Because of the family's love of music, there were two grand pianos, one in the drawing room and one in the back room. A one-storey extension, with a wall composed almost entirely of windows, overlooked the large, beautifully kept garden.

Both Anthony's parents had made their own way in life. Mintie's family, once wealthy, had fallen on hard times after the early death of her father, and before her marriage she had worked occasionally as a singer and a pianist. Graham had come from a respectable but impoverished middle-class background. He too had been a pianist, good enough to contemplate turning professional, but instead had chosen the more prudent path of dentistry. His local surgery was in Ham Frith itself. With its treatment room, X-ray and telephone room, dental assistant's room and waiting room, the surgery took up about half of Ham Frith's ground floor. Graham also had a very prestigious practice in London, in Cavendish Place, between Regent Street and Harley Street. In addition, every Saturday he held a free surgery at Queen Mary's Hospital for the East End, in line with the medical tradition of services to the poor.

Graham had a very dry sense of humour. On Mintie's side of the family, there were two elderly spinster aunts named Pop and Mil, still living in Plymouth – 'dried-up, poor old things, who lived very simple lives'. After they died, someone observed of them piously, 'All they wanted was the air to breathe,' at which Graham snorted, 'And that's all they bloody well got!'[4]

Attractive, sociable, cynical, and very generous, Graham was not short of female admirers. He and Mintie had a strong but occasionally tempestuous marriage owing to his tendency to have affairs. Mintie was a feminist in an unobtrusive way, who once told Anthony's cousin, Rosemary, that she should never support men against women.[5] Strong-willed and passionate, Mintie had been ravishingly pretty in her youth and was still very elegant and charming, with dark hair and delicate features. Geoffrey took after Graham, but Anthony was very like his mother, a masculine version of her fine-boned feminine beauty. He and she shared the same birthday of 19 December. Although they had occasional clashes of will, they were very close to one another and she adored him.

Anthony's bedroom was at the front of the house, overlooking the Green. He had never really moved away from home and family, and the room had been preserved for him by his parents almost unchanged since boyhood days. The arrival of the call-up letter decisively ended the life he had led for the last six years, ever since he had abandoned his medical and dental studies at Guy's Hospital in order to follow his dream of becoming a journalist. He was now about to enter an entirely new way of life, one for which he was unfitted by tastes and character but which he was absolutely determined to make the best of. Weeks earlier, he had decided – with characteristic brio – that he would write a best-selling book about his conscript experiences. Now that the call-up letter had arrived, he immediately began to make notes for the book. It would be published ten months later under the title *What! No Morning Tea?*, and it would indeed become a best-seller.

What! No Morning Tea? begins at the very moment that Anthony received his call-up letter. The book's unconventional tone, which would be anathema to conventional military types, is immediately evident in the first few paragraphs:

> I was just putting the lead on the dog when our maid Daisy gave me the letter.
> I took one look and knew. This was it. And it was.
> A railway voucher, a postal orders for 4s, and some orders.
> For the first time since I left school someone was giving me orders which I couldn't walk out on or argue about. [...]
> I really laughed. The whole thing was so awful, it was funny. Everything you had ever worked for was sent up in smoke by that halfpenny circular. Every hope, every plan.
> Not that I had anything in particular against the Army. But I was comfortable and I didn't want to be disturbed. An unconscientious objector.[6]

The call-up letter gave Anthony less than six days to put his affairs in order – he was to go into the Army on the following Friday. Needing to be alone to digest the appalling news, he took Sam, the dog, for his accustomed Saturday walk on the Green. He stayed out for more than an hour, walking about and thinking.

> I wasn't thinking about the amputation of good-bye, or the blow of throwing up a life that was being quite kind to me. The thoughts jumping through my mind were whether I should take hair-cream and what time I should be free at nights. Then I couldn't get there by 12 noon. That would mean catching a train before 8am, and I never get up before 9. I must wire them to say I shall be arriving later.
> My God, no. I must not wire them to say I should be arriving later. That day is done. From Friday on I get there just when they say. 'They' had come into my life again.[7]

By the time he returned to Ham Frith, Anthony had decided not to say anything about the call-up letter but to carry on exactly as if nothing had happened. That way nobody would be upset, and he and the family could enjoy his last weekend at home. At some point during the following week, when he was back in London, he would ring his mother and tell her that he was going to Brighton at the weekend when in reality he would be going to his training camp. He would write and admit the truth only once he was in the Army. The sole exception to the news blackout would be Geoffrey.

Back at Ham Frith it was lunchtime.

> Naturally the big topic at lunch that day was when I should be called up. The subject was quite unchangeable.
> 'It can't be long now,' said Mother. 'I don't know what I shall do when it does come. I don't know. I really don't know. I lie awake at nights shuddering at it. My God, I never thought this would ever have to happen again.'
> 'Ah well, there you are,' I said.
> 'Perhaps you'll get another month or two.'
> 'That's right,' I said.
> It was just like every other Saturday afternoon.[8]

After lunch, his uncle and aunt, Ivor and Jane Pool, arrived. Jane, usually known as Janie, had no children of her own, and was very close to her sister Mintie and her nephews. A brilliantly gifted pianist, Janie had once been a child virtuoso, but the death of her and Mintie's father had destroyed her hopes of a glittering musical career. As a young woman, Janie had earned money by playing in the small orchestra of a café popular with First World War naval officers. Amongst those officers had been Graham, who had at first found her rather attractive and paid her much attention until he met her much younger sister, Mintie. Besides being incredibly beautiful, Mintie had a captivating, bubbly, flirtatious manner. Inevitably Graham married her rather than the sweet-faced but older and more serious Janie.[9]

Janie's marriage to Ivor took place almost on the rebound. Ivor was a soldier and extremely good-looking, but he was never to have Graham's success in life. After the war, he became an engineer for the Post Office, obsessed with inventing gadgets which were always going to make his fortune but never did. The marriage was disconnected and unhappy. Ivor grew profoundly jealous of Janie's musical brilliance and independence, and spoke of her with spiteful disparagement in front of other people. A tangential gleam of the situation between husband and wife appears in Anthony's description of the archetypal family weekend at Ham Frith:

> Week-ends in our family have always been rather stylised affairs, with the same people being punctually unpunctual for the same things.
> Aunt Jane and Uncle Ivor always came out on Saturday after lunch. They had hardly missed a weekend for twenty years. For twenty years Ivor had come in and said that Jane had ruined his afternoon by not being ready at the proper time. For twenty years Ivor had driven out from town like the fire brigade to get to his golf, and then when he got there, wasted half an hour playing games with the cat, the dog or the parrot. Different cats, different dogs, different parrots, but the same games.

This ordered way of life was on the verge of coming to an end. Not only were Anthony and Geoffrey about to be conscripted, but Janie was shortly to volunteer for war service with the Entertainments National Service Association (ENSA). Her marriage with Ivor would end, and she would spend the next five years on the road. In May 1945, ENSA would take her to Holland just after the Liberation, where she would make the first on the spot enquiries in Brummen about the shooting.

Writing of this last old-style weekend at Ham Frith before everything changed forever, Anthony gently mocked his own pedestrian ways.

> My week-end routine was always the same. Golf lesson Saturday morning, pictures in the afternoon, take the dog for a walk after dinner, get up late Sunday morning, play golf with our pro, Allan Dailey, after lunch.
> The funny people I met up in London used to tell me I ought to get away for a change at week-ends, but I enjoyed things my way. And at home I got things my way. I enjoyed it far more than having a change spending too much money on too many drinks somewhere in the country.
> I tell all this not only for personal advertisement but to indicate the rather pedestrianly routined sort of young man I was on entering the army.[10]

On this particular day, everything went off as it usually did. Ivor played for a while admiringly with the new kitten, Dietrich. Then he, Graham, and Graham's friend Mr Townley, went off to the nearby golf club as they always had done on Saturday afternoons, seemingly since time immemorial. As Graham was leaving, Mintie said 'Don't you be late back from that club,' knowing perfectly well that he would be. Anthony lit his Saturday afternoon cigar and settled down in a chair by the fire; Geoffrey played dance music on the gramophone. Time flew gently. At 4.00pm the two brothers, their mother and aunt had a cup of tea, and then drove to the pictures at Ilford as they had done for years on Saturday afternoons. Anthony found it sad to be doing it for the last time.

The picture ended at about 8.00pm. They emerged into a blacked-out night, lit only by the intermittent flaring glares where men were working on the tube railway extension.

> Father and Ivor were home before us. We had a couple of drinks and then sat down to dinner. It was the last beef-steak pie before meat rationing. I went down to the cellar and got our Saturday night bottle of red wine.
>
> We had our invariable argument about sex, about local personalities, and about how to run a house.[11]

The argument, though heated, would not have been a serious one. The family were very close, and their tenderness for one another was expressed in their various pet-names. Mintie's Christian name was Millicent, but to Janie she was always Mintie whilst Janie to her was always Judy. Anthony was called 'The Count' when Mintie and Geoffrey discussed him, whereas when Mintie and Anthony discussed Geoffrey he was always 'Our Young Friend'. On an everyday basis, Anthony was 'Tone' and Geoffrey was 'Shubbs'. This latter name came from the first time that Anthony, then three years old, had seen his tiny infant brother, and with his incredible precocious intelligence had pronounced, 'I name this little thing Shubbles'.

Anthony did not break his silence about the call-up letter either during the evening meal or in the various quiet middle-class amusements of the following day. After years of the rigours of public school, he was too fine an actor to betray his personal secrets and no one in his close family guessed a thing.

For six years Anthony had attended King's School, Rochester, as a scholarship boarder. The school had been his own choice, not that of his parents, and it was he who had arranged the scholarship, worked for it, and won it. A hugely prestigious and ancient institution, King's School had taught him the accent and manners which could only come from such a privileged education. It had also, however, taught him the darker arts, in particular how to tell barefaced lies without the slightest feeling of shame. Like many of his contemporaries, Anthony was about to discover that public school had been an excellent preparation for army life. As a conscript, he would comment that there could be 'no less ardent old school boy than I' whilst acknowledging how well he had been taught: 'From the point of view of personal happiness give me the Army every time, but if you have been to [a public school] the Army discipline and atmosphere comes quite naturally.'[12]

The weekend routine at Ham Frith always concluded with Anthony packing his suitcase late on Sunday night for the return to London by train on Monday morning. On the last night that he slept in his old bedroom before going into the Army, he sat down upon the bed and in his usual hyper-observant way recorded the following:

> It was like the last night of the holidays. Only the tuckbox was missing. For the room was still essentially a schoolboy's. *The Wonder Book of Why and What* and the bound volumes of the *Model Railway Magazine* were still on the shelves. There were none of the appurtenances of young manhood. No pipe-rack, no tobacco jar, no photographs of young women. The brown Jaegar dressing-gown on the door was still marked A Cotterell, School House. Time had marked time.

By breakfast time my Sidney Carton complex was at boiling point. I was bathed in self-satisfaction; bidding silent farewells to everything in sight, even the lavatory.

Mother was up in the bathroom rummaging with the laundry when I said my usual good-bye. She looked up a minute. 'Oh, good-bye darling. Take care of yourself. I worry, you know.'[13]

Still pretending that everything was normal, he kissed her goodbye affectionately and left to catch the train to London.

2

FLEET STREET JOURNALIST

O n arrival in London, Anthony headed for the *Express* offices in Fleet Street, in the
heart of the press district. Number 121-128 Fleet Street had been specially built for
the *Express* in the early 1930s. Designed in the ultra-fashionable Art Deco style, it
reflected the newspaper's ethos of being bright, young, dynamic, and risk-taking. The
exterior was covered with black Vitrolite and clear glass interspersed with chromium strips, but
it was the interior which was the most remarkable, in particular the magnificently exuberant
entrance hall. Mythical figures representing industry looked out over an expanse of marble and
gilt, whilst from the opulent ceiling with its shining zigzag cornice there hung an immense
silvered lantern. There was a Moorish influence, all mixed up with a lot of other flummery, and
the whole dominated by Epstein's head of the proprietor, Lord Beaverbrook.

Writing of his last Monday there, when he knew that he might be leaving the place for ever,
Anthony gave his own, very characteristic description of it:

> Downstairs in the musical comedy entrance hall I gazed pensively for a moment at Epstein's
> head of Lord Beaverbrook. I never pass it without recalling the story told of little Maude
> Mason, the schoolgirl whose patriotic essay was mentioned in the House of Commons. With
> commendable public spirit the *Daily Express* took Maude to Parliament so that we, the people,
> might know what she thought about it. They brought her back to the office to be interviewed,
> and while going upstairs she is supposed to have leaned over the banisters and been sick on
> Lord Beaverbrook's head.[14]

Anthony went upstairs to where he worked in a corner of the second floor. It was around
11.00am, an early hour for a London journalist to be at work, and not all his colleagues had yet
arrived. There was a review copy of a book about career choice on his desk, one problem, as he
observed to himself sardonically, that he did not have.

Anthony's desk was near that of the cartoonist, Osbert Lancaster, who had recently quipped
that Anthony's departure for the Army would 'inevitably be tinged with farce' and that the
only tears, apart from Anthony's, would be 'caused by laughter'.[15] Other staff such as Miss Coe
(who would kindly write to Anthony at conscript camp to give him all the latest office gossip)
had been somewhat more sympathetic, but the *Daily Express* workplace culture was so vivid,
cruel and worldly that it tended to drown out the quieter, kinder voices.

When Anthony had joined the staff in April 1936, the *Daily Express* was approaching its
zenith as the most exciting and influential newspaper in Britain. Its owner, Lord Beaverbrook,
dominated both the newspaper and political worlds. A close friend of Winston Churchill, his
genius for organisation, motivation, and publicity would lead to him being created Minister of
Aircraft Production in the summer of 1940, a position which he would make a huge success of. A
political intriguer and master propagandist, Beaverbrook had acquired the *Daily Express* in 1916
when it was in serious financial difficulty. He had utterly transformed it. By 1937 the paper had a

staggering daily circulation of 2,329,000. In October 1938, sales topped two and a half million for the first time.[16] It was the perfect milieu for an ambitious, hard-working youngster like Anthony.

Before he had been taken on the staff, Anthony had worked for some months in the newspaper's library as a general dogsbody, soaking up the ethos of the place. He had also contributed to the paper on a freelance basis, providing fodder for the gossip columns and imitating the style of 'William Hickey', the column written by one of the paper's star journalists, Tom Driberg. Anthony's anonymous contributions had become so numerous that he was soon earning around £1,000 a year, a colossal sum for a young journalist who was just starting out. The newspaper cut its expenses in half when it gave him a permanent job on a reporter's salary.

As a new conscript, Anthony wrote – in a very temporary mood of intellectual abasement – that he enjoyed cleaning the windows of his army hut because it was 'wonderful not having to think of anything original'. But far more characteristic was his intense love of and involvement in the whole business of words and ideas. He also loved the lifestyle that money brought, which was much drinking and eating out with friends and family, and weekly visits to the theatre or cinema. At a time when a new conscript's wages (if he was a single man) were a mere 10s a week after deductions, Anthony would take a colossal drop in salary through being conscripted into the Army.[17]

Anthony had enjoyed himself on the *Daily Express* and had had a very good time – 'All sorts of jobs: some fascinating, mostly interesting, and plenty daft'. One characteristic assignment was being sent to Great Tey in Essex to ask every man and woman in the village ten questions on their political convictions. Never one to neglect a skill acquired by much hard work, Anthony would later conduct similar *vox populi* surveys in the Army. Other memorable journalistic feats included 'spending a week in London with the Average Man; spending two weeks with the Typical British girl (spending being the operative word), and ten days with Britain's Happiest Married Couple'. Then there was the week in Ashton-under-Lyne, Beaverbrook's old parliamentary constituency. Once again Anthony was conducting a survey:

> A miniature social survey, comparing moral, mental and physical conditions in 1913 and 1938. This was not for publication but for Lord Beaverbrook's private reading [...] With my expenses for cars and hotel, and salary it must have cost about £50. It couldn't have taken him more than ten minutes to read. How the rich live.[18]

The *Daily Express* employed many of Britain's top journalists, including Paul Holt and John Rayner. Holt was famous for the acidity of his pen. The *Daily Express*'s editor, Arthur Christiansen, would describe Holt as 'a £2000 a year hornet-of-a-journalist, whose sting was lethal, even in that era which was pretty tough and hard-hitting'.[19] Rayner was raffish and elegant, a man of the world, who though married had affairs with delectable actresses like Vera Zorina, the star of the 1938 film *The Goldwyn Follies* and the 1939 film of the musical 'On Your Toes'.

As a 19-year-old cub reporter, Anthony greatly admired Rayner, and his influence may perhaps be seen in the studio photograph of Anthony taken in 1936, the year that he joined the *Daily Express* staff. Beautifully lit like a film noir scene, the image shows Anthony with the collar of his overcoat theatrically turned up, looking exactly like a film star.

Rayner and his type were part of a very glamorous world in which Anthony mixed for a while. There was a certain culture of sexual licence at the *Daily Express*, and Anthony, as an extremely good-looking youngster, undoubtedly came in for his share of it. Once or twice, Geoffrey joined him at the many glitzy parties to which Anthony was invited, at which ultra-sophisticated people like Noel Coward held court and set the style. Anthony loved dipping into this glittering, brilliant, febrile world, but when war broke out his contact with it became more peripheral. He was too intelligent, too hard-working, and too fond of home comforts to be star-struck. Yet for a while it must all have seemed incredibly seductive.

Since the outbreak of war, various excesses on the *Daily Express* had been toned down. The paper, though still vibrant, was constricted by wartime regulations. Censorship had come in, together with paper rationing. The paper had dropped immediately from twenty-four pages to twelve, then to eight, then to six. By September 1940, it would be a mere four, which it remained for the rest of the war. Compression was vital, and prolixity the ultimate sin.[20]

On his last day in the *Daily Express* offices, Anthony looked over the article which he had been working on the previous week. It described his view of wartime journalism:

What is this newspaper?

It is a man running to a telephone in Amsterdam, bending over a tape machine in New York, sheltering from bombs in Helsinki, sending a cable from Shanghai, looking for a war in France.

Work. Speed. Movement. Action. These are the ingredients. So hurry. Quick. No time to spare. For in a few short avalanching hours today will be yesterday. And yesterday's crop of headlines are as cold as yesterday's mashed potatoes.[21]

After half-heartedly contemplating finishing the article, Anthony put it back in the drawer – 'the subject of newspaper production in wartime didn't have any point any more.'

By now it was 11.30am and people were beginning to arrive. He went to see the Features Editor to ask for a few days off as he was expecting to be called up very soon, but left out the vital point that actually he was going into the Army that Friday. Leave having been granted, he went back to his desk, picked up his hat, and glanced around the office one last time. Miss Coe was going through readers' letters; Mr Gask was looking at the American papers for ideas; Lucy Milner was scanning a fashion drawing; John MacAdam was dictating to his secretary. 'Well, well; just like old times,' Anthony wrote as the epitaph to his dream job.[22] And then, without fuss or farewells, he left the building, and walked back into the hubbub of Fleet Street.

His next act was to go to a barber. The Army required a butchery job, maximum hair length: one and a half inches. Anthony noted that there was 'another candidate for military honours in the next chair' who was practically in hysterics – 'Oh dear, you're not to take any more off. I won't have it. I don't care what they say. It's indecent. I feel absolutely undressed.'[23]

The next three days were pleasant in a lugubrious sort of way. Anthony spent money lavishly, having a few drinks with everyone he knew, and re-visiting all his usual restaurants and bars. He had 'some sentimental evenings which were all the more poignant because my companions didn't know what I was being sentimental about'. On the last Thursday 'before the end of the chapter', he went to Scott's at lunchtime to meet his brother, Geoffrey. By chance, Anthony's closest friend on the *Express*, Harold Keeble, was also there, sitting a few tables away. Puckish in appearance and manner, Keeble was also witty, kind, honourable, and a brilliant journalist. He had just signed a contract with the *Sunday Express* which added £1,250 a year to his already extremely substantial salary. Anthony tried hard not to think about it.

Only a year or so earlier, he and Keeble had been collaborators on a mad project which they had dubbed 'A School for Matrimony'. For five or six weeks they met two or three times a week for dinner at Kettner's to talk over their grand plan. Their idea was for a correspondence course on proposal, engagement, wedding, reception, and matrimony. Each lesson was to be in a bulky cellophaned box containing a series of sealed envelopes and gadgets, the gadgets having nothing to do with sex as Anthony and Keeble had decided strictly against the physical in favour of the psychology of marriage. 'There would be charts and graphs and lists of rules and quiet homely talks', as Anthony described it in an undated private paper.[24]

It is difficult to say quite how seriously they took this hare-brained scheme, but it certainly appears that they expected to make a fortune out of it. Eventually it petered out, but, reluctant to waste the hours of work, Anthony turned it into a book called *The Expert Way of Getting Married*. Appearing in 1939, the book was a damp squib, a nothingness, its voice drowned out by the catastrophe which was by then engulfing Europe. Only a year after its publication, Anthony was describing it as 'an odd little book', which suggests that he was already disowning what must have come to seem a rather embarrassing creation.[25] It is almost unreadable now except as a period piece. Awash with cod psychology, it is only redeemed by the occasional very funny quip, such as 'Barbara Hutton's wedding receptions have been successful. There are forty million reasons why. Each one a dollar.'[26] Apart from the jokes, however, it is almost impossible to believe that the book was written by Anthony. It was a thoroughly unpromising beginning to his eventual total of seven books.

Anthony did not dwell long on the diametrically opposed prospects that he and Keeble were facing. Geoffrey had arrived, bringing Signe, Anthony's Swedish girlfriend, a spectacularly beautiful fluffy blonde of the Marilyn Monroe type. Signe was a model, who had been the star of a very artistically posed and beautifully lit nude book by the well-known photographer, John Everard.[27] Sweet-tempered and placid, Signe got on well with Anthony's mother despite a froideur having being cast over their relationship by Mintie's accidental discovery that Signe and Anthony were having sex in his tiny London flat. Born in the Victorian era, this was not something which Mintie could ever condone.

Anthony had initially been very much in love with Signe, but the relationship was to peter out once he was in the Army. He was not the romantic type, being very self-sufficient, and his driving ambition prevented him from wasting much time on girls. One of the barometers of his journalistic success was the number of letters he received each day. Each day would bring at least a handful, but his highest total was 409. Once he got twenty-nine proposals of marriage, but neither these nor Signe could tempt him to settle down.[28] Something of his attitude to imprudent early marriages can be seen in an anecdote dated around November 1940:

> I became very friendly with a young man who had just got married on what seemed to me a rather unsteady financial basis. I am all for love, but not on the kind of dole which most of us have to put up with in the Army. He had a considerable, if not original, intelligence [...] If he worked hard and cultivated the appropriate people he would do very well a little later on. But, of course, like any young man of some spirit he wanted to eat the apples now. I lent him a book, *Love in Our Time* by Norman Collins, which described how a young man who got married on a modest income was gradually obliged to [...] settle down to a very ordinary married life.[29]

Anthony, who could be something of a tease, added a trifle disingenuously, 'I thought this young man would enjoy reading the book, but it frightened the life out of him; he accused me of trying to upset him'. Anthony had no intention of marrying in haste and repenting at leisure; he wanted to make a name and a fortune first.

As soon as Geoffrey saw Anthony at Scott's, he noticed that his hair had been cut very short.

'Are you for the jump?'

'Yes, tomorrow.'[30]

For Geoffrey, too, the day of reckoning was looming. He would follow Anthony into the Army a month later, on 18 April. As always in their relationship, Anthony was taking the lead; once he was in the Army, he would send Geoffrey useful tips by letter on how to make life as a raw conscript more endurable.

That Thursday, anyone seeing Anthony and Geoffrey at the table at Scott's would have known at once that they were brothers, even though Geoffrey was considerably taller and there was something a little shambolic about him which was totally missing in Anthony. Though Geoffrey took after their father whilst Anthony was more like Mintie, they had a strong facial resemblance, and an easy rapport and identical subversive sense of humour. No matter how long they had been apart, as soon as they met they instantly fell back into their old symbiotic ways.

They had always been very close. As children, Anthony had been the daring one and Geoffrey had trailed after him, sometimes terrified out of his wits but unwilling to be left out. It had always been Anthony who lit the fireworks on Guy Fawkes Night, or did anything which carried any hint of physical danger. Anthony protected and defended Geoffrey, and had done so all his life. Once, when Geoffrey was just learning how to write, Anthony, who cannot have been much more than seven years old himself, wrote carefully at the top of a blotched letter that Geoffrey had composed with much labour, 'Excuse his scribble but he cannot help it' and signed it with his initials, J.A.C.

For a long time Geoffrey had been quite literally in Anthony's shadow, but in his teens he had suddenly shot up and now towered a good five inches over him. In his novel, *Then a Soldier*, Geoffrey gives a partial portrait of himself as Robert Halbrook.[31] He has made Robert short and 'almost very good-looking, after the style of a woman's magazine advertisement', as well as altering various traits of character, but there are a number of striking parallels. If asked what his job was, Robert, exactly like Geoffrey, tended to say that he was a journalist because this was much easier than trying to explain what he really did. Robert finally told a fellow conscript that he was not suited to journalism, 'Too much work ... Too much perseverance required.' He then admitted the awful truth that he wrote pulp fiction, 'romances with a capital R and plenty of slick action for factory girls to read. Five quid a time.'[32] In real life Geoffrey worked very hard at writing pulp fiction, lurid stories which more often than not were rejected. It was a hard apprenticeship for his eventual career as a best-selling novelist.

Because Geoffrey loved and admired his brother greatly, he did not suffer from jealousy about Anthony's successes and was perfectly happy to take advantage of them if the opportunity arose. One such episode had occurred four years earlier in 1936, whilst Geoffrey was in Berlin for several months, learning to speak German fluently. Anthony, who had just been given a permanent place on the *Daily Express* staff, sent him one of his new business cards. That June, Geoffrey conned his way into Hitler's extravagant Olympic stadium, which was still being built, by flourishing Anthony's business card. Its impressive appearance belied its flippant credentials, for it read:

April 1936

Mr Anthony Cotterell
This name makes news
Time marches ON

Daily Express
Fleet Street EC4   Phone Central 8000

It was also at this time that Geoffrey wrote a bogus letter to the *Daily Express*, purporting to come from five devoted readers, Englishmen living in Berlin. It gave a list of their favourite correspondents, beginning with Paul Holt and ending with Anthony Cotterell, and it ended with great correctness, 'Thank you for your newspaper'. To complete this masterpiece, Geoffrey forged five different signatures. The *Daily Express* was completely taken in and the letter duly appeared in the paper. Mintie was in on the joke. When Anthony rang her up, and said 'Have you seen the paper this morning? They're rather pleased with it,' she broke down in giggles and revealed the plot. On the other end of the phone, she heard Anthony collapse in laughter.

At the brothers' last lunch together before Anthony went into the Army, they firmed up the details of another small practical joke. As soon as Anthony had an Army address and service number, Geoffrey was to go to Selfridges and get mourning cards printed with black borders. In the top right corner would be Anthony's Army details, in the centre the words: 'Anthony Cotterell

– Not Lost but Gone Before'. The joke was barbed because so many of Anthony's associates were also in danger of being called up. The cards would be sent out to a long list of contacts.

Some two weeks later, whilst at initial training camp, Anthony would open the *Daily Express* to find that Tom Driberg's alter-ego, William Hickey, had given him a paragraph about the mourning cards. Anthony was very pleased. The certainty that he had not been forgotten greatly cheered him up, and he recorded in his diary mockingly, 'What an amusing fellow I am'.[33]

After lunch with Geoffrey and Signe, Anthony went shopping for three absolute essentials: a brandy flask, its contents, and a thermometer. The latter was because he was prone to catching every passing infection and liked to monitor the incubation of his illnesses. Thus suitably equipped for life in the Army, he went back to his tiny flat in Russell Court, Bloomsbury. The flat was for little more than sleeping in from Monday to Friday, or for the occasional visit of Signe. Anthony kept the hours of a *Daily Express* journalist, getting up at 9 or 10.00am and going to bed around 1.00am. He ate out most of the time and was not remotely domesticated. He had a charlady, Mrs Weller, who was supposed to keep the place clean but did not. She was a very quick worker: 'In and out, up and down, you couldn't expect her to catch everything.' There was one particular ledge he always meant to tell her about, which had remained undusted since his arrival in late 1937 and remained resolutely undusted when he left.[34]

Anthony was not a practical person with his hands and one of his basic dictums was 'In small things [...] act or rather inact on the principle that if you do nothing other people do it for you'. His casual standards of tidiness and cleanliness would be blasted by the obsessively meticulous sergeants and senior officers he was shortly to come across in the Army. Commenting on the assiduity with which he, as a conscript, now polished his boots, he wrote of his methods of boot-cleaning in his former life, 'I used to put them on and clean them on the opposite trouser leg, and get the trousers cleaned instead.'[35]

The flat was so small that he found it difficult to make the quintessential drama out of clearing it up.

> I thought this was the proper thing to do. People always talk about clearing up things before going away. But perhaps I was living a very simple life, for really there didn't seem to be anything much to clear up. Or nothing that couldn't wait.[36]

The day was drawing to a close. He rang Mintie with his pre-prepared lie about going to Brighton. Then he played dance records and had a few drinks. He paid one or two calls and went to bed at 2.00am. His life as a Fleet Street journalist was over.

3

CONSCRIPT LIFE

After very little sleep, Anthony got up early in order to reach Waterloo Station for the 8.30am train. During his time in the Army, he would often write about the appalling hours of rising and the unsatisfactory nature of the sleeping arrangements. The Army never cured him of his preference for sleeping late in a comfortable bed. In Normandy after D-Day, he would jot down a hilarious grumble about the discomforts of sleeping in a war zone. But for now his problems were far more prosaic. He washed, dressed, skipped breakfast, and set off for the station on the other side of London, trying to meet the first deadline of his new life.

In the diary which eventually become *What! No Morning Tea?* he would entitle this first day 'Friday: Off the Deep End'. His intention was to keep daily notes, and for this he had bought a tiny ringed binder with punched paper sheets which would exactly fit the leg pocket of his Army trousers (the type of notebook he would use throughout his Army career). The one bright spot, as he saw it, in his forcible induction into the Army, was that he was in the first group to be called up under the National Service Act. As a friend and colleague would later observe, this gave Anthony a great deal of satisfaction: 'the Government was giving him the chance to cover at first hand an event of the greatest interest to the public, and this he was prepared to exploit to the full.'[37]

At Waterloo station, whilst waiting for the train to arrive, he observed the many young men who were clearly in the same situation that he was. They carried small suitcases and had an air of nervous tension, bravely concealed. There was no one there to wave him goodbye, but he silently watched other people's leave-takings. The parting of one family – father, mother, sister and brother – moved him perhaps more than he wished. He noted in his diary 'the death-house intensity of the mother's last-minute kiss' as she reluctantly parted with her adored son.

On the train he ate a plum, a pear and an apple for breakfast, but did not touch his full brandy flask, mainly because he did not feel like drinking but also because of the complications of etiquette – should he share it round or keep it to himself? He felt 'melancholy rather than miserable; but not much of either: and surprisingly no physical excitement'. The last phrase referred obliquely to the tingling nerves and digestive disorders which always affected him at dramatic moments in his life.

After a four hour trip, the train arrived at Dorchester. Anthony wrote:

> About 200 got out of the train. We were led off by an N.C.O., shambling down a subway like convicts, and watched by other passengers with the same fascinated horror that people watch convicts.[38]

After ten minutes march, they arrived at the barracks. The rest of the day would be taken up with the minutiae of registration and kitting out. Anthony recorded everything: from the type of huts and how many men lived in them (wooden barracks huts, twenty-four occupants); to what you drew from the stores (four blankets, a large china mug, a knife, a fork and a spoon). He also noted the new clothes that he was given, especially the enormous heavy boots which would shortly cause him serious trouble, operating on his shins 'like a nutmeg grater'. A less painful sartorial addition was the side cap, but this too brought problems:

> You walk like a juggler, every minute afraid it will fall off. It takes weeks to get the knack of wearing it at the proper angle: you have to 'walk beside it'.[39]

His first Army meal was endured – stewed meat, potatoes, beans, and bread passed down the table from hand to hand, followed by a pudding of stewed apples in gelatinous custard. Anthony, who was fond of eating well, wrote that in the face of this dramatic change of life, normal critical standards were 'almost completely suspended', a philosophical take on Army grub which would not last for very long. For tea they had bread, butter and a hunk of fish, 'no decadent dickering about with plates however'. Anthony ate his squashed up into a monster sandwich, already resolving to eat out as much as possible.

Having made up their beds, the men were allowed to do what they wanted for the rest of the day though they had to be back at the hut by 11.15pm, one hour after lights out. Beginning a pattern which would endure throughout his Army career, Anthony left the camp and went off to look for civilisation elsewhere. On this first night, somewhat unambitiously, he went to the local YMCA. The two women helpers were inept at the job. Anthony wrote in his diary, 'They would have been more at home in a cathedral-shadowed tea-shoppe. But then so would I.'[40]

That night he slept well despite the hardness of the bed and the lack of sheets. He woke once or twice:

> The snoring was something awful, and one or two were talking in their sleep. 'It's raining, it's raining,' one of them said. Fortunately these manifestations died down after the first few nervous nights.[41]

Reveillé the following morning was at 6.30am. The first full day in the Army had arrived with its sense of being a new boy, of being gauche and inept and not knowing the ropes. After breakfast, Anthony and his fellow conscripts were marched to the barrack square to watch men who had been in training at the camp for four weeks, and found them most impressive. Their sergeant told them they wouldn't think anything of it in a month or two, and marched them off to draw their rifles. They were also given their Army numbers, and heard all the regulations which were to govern their lives from then on.

> 'It'll take a long time, so you may as well make up your mind to it,' the Company Commander said. It took him fifty-seven minutes dead. In that time he told us the penalties for every crime from rape to treason, from cowardice to cruelty to animals.[42]

Once again the authorities were generous with free time, and after lunch on the Saturday all were released for the rest of the day. Anthony headed into Dorchester. At one point depression nearly overwhelmed him.

> People are very kind to soldiers. In a way their sympathy is the most depressing thing of all. I went into a grocer's and asked what would be a good thing to buy for a snack over the weekend. He sent me to buy a loaf and made me a whole lot of sandwiches, throwing the butter in for free. I am not sure I altogether like the idea that because you are a soldier you must be down and out; still, it was a nice gesture. [...]

I came back and sat on my bed, writing this. I felt rather low. I could have rung home, but I thought that would only make me lower [...] I knew that a drink would cheer me up, but I was too melancholy to get it. The only other man left in the hut didn't drink. Finally I went off by myself, practising salutes along the lane into the town.[43]

He went to a pub, had a double whisky, then on to the Soldiers' Institute for some sausages, mash and cocoa, then back to the pub for another double whisky. Later he noted in his diary: 'It cheered me up. But everything that cheered me up cost money. I spent about 10s during the afternoon, an expenditure about as much out of the average conscript's reach as polo.'[44]

Despite his elitist education and four years' immersion in the bright, intolerant office culture of the *Daily Express*, Anthony had retained a natural sensitivity to other people's troubles. His observations on the financial plight of the average conscript would always be kindly, if somewhat tinged with horror. Soon he would observe his fellow conscripts becoming ever more strapped for cash. The parcels and postal orders sent by friends and relatives dwindled as the novelty of the loved one being in the Army wore off. Faced with the reality of living on 10s a week, most of the men spent their spare evenings in the hut because it was no fun walking the streets with no money in their pockets. If the military day ended early, this only meant more empty hours to kill, constantly asking what the time was and deploring how early it always seemed to be.

The conscripts' biggest single expenditure was on cigarettes, taking precedence even over drinking, not a choice which Anthony would ever be faced with. Drink helped him forget his troubles for a while, but a major part of the attraction was that pubs, hotels and restaurants gave him a temporary respite from military life. It was only rarely that he found his butchered haircut and standard-issue uniform made a difference to how restaurant staff treated him. However, one such incident, which made him absolutely livid, occurred during his very first week in the Army. He had gone for lunch at the Royal Hotel in a nearby seaside town, and the head waiter made a great performance about fitting him into the empty restaurant.

I sat there fuming. My God, you give up everything to risk your life. And that's the gratitude. Last week it would have been 'Yes, sir' and 'Oh, sir' and 'Are they looking after you, sir?'

I approached the head waiter on the way out. I was heavily sarcastic. 'Not quite so many as you were expecting, eh?' I said.

He smirked.

'I got the impression you were excluding me as a matter of policy,' I said.

'Oh no, sir,' he said.

'Well, I was rather interested because I am writing a book on my experiences as a soldier, and I am always delighted to find an opportunity of giving a place unfavourable publicity.'

He gabbled excuses. I left feeling that I had struck a blow for democracy. Not much of a blow. But a blow.[45]

In these first few weeks in the Army, he was very sensitive to how civilians perceived him, noting amongst other things the look of horror on some workmen's faces when they saw the simulated savagery of bayonet practice. The sergeant was screaming at the conscripts, 'Go on, kill him, he's after your guts,' whilst Anthony and his fellows were supposed to utter 'orgasmically murderous screams' as they plunged the bayonet into the sack. Most of the conscripts, Anthony wrote, sounded hurt rather than hurting as they uttered their embarrassed cry of blood-lust, but all the same the workmen's reactions were very disconcerting.

On Sunday, 17 March, Anthony wrote his letter home, finally confessing to his mother and father where he was.[46] Handwritten in scrawled pencil on ruled notebook paper, the letter is rambling but rather touching because it is so unpremeditated.

DORCHESTER

Dear Mother and Father

This is a mad sort of letter. I don't quite know how to start.

But the point is this. That I am in the Army now. I came here on Friday by the 8.30am train and here I stay for eight weeks. After that, if I am reasonably lucky, I go somewhere else to train for a commission. This is apparently a regular routine, and incidentally there seems no reason why it shouldn't work in the case of Shubbles [Geoffrey] especially if he reads the manual of Elementary Drill (All Arms) HM Stationery Office.

The reason I didn't tell you I was going beforehand is simply that I thought it would save a lot of lumps in the throat on both sides if I didn't.

I had the letter on the previous Saturday, and decided that to publish it would only spoil the weekend.

I told no one at the office and that was much more satisfactory too.

It was undoubtedly one of the most dignified and romantic exits.

And now let me tell you what has happened so far.

Arrived Friday about 12.30. About a hundred others. Atmosphere democratic to a fault. Medically examined and shown to huts. These are centrally heated. The beds have hard mattresses and under-sized cylindrical pillows. You get four blankets which you can use as you will. Personally I slept well though some I believe did not.

I have a corner bed. (When you are led to the huts, Shubbles, get in front of the herd so you can get one too.) We were fitted up with battle dress and boots, also long pants, shirts, pullover, braces, socks.

We had to put these on immediately. The worst thing was not the boots but the cap; it seemed quite impossible that it would ever stay on.

We were free at 5.30, allowed to go anywhere until 11.15pm. [...]

Incidentally the food is absurd. I have read many complaints that the Army cooks ruin good food. To my mind it is the Army food that ruins the cooks.

Added to which there isn't enough of it.

Fortunately there are plenty of places to eat out in Dorchester. I am writing this at the place where I had lunch. A good lunch, the bill for two with half a bottle of wine being about ten shillings.

Ten shillings being easily one week's pay. (The other 4s are saved for you presumably to provide for the purchase of a wreath.)

It is essential that Shubbles should have at least 25s a week above Army pay. It makes all the difference in the world to be able to go and sit somewhere comfortable. [...]

You get a weekend leave after three weeks. What arrangements do I have to make with Barclays Bank? Will you send me £3 to arrive about the weekend?

By the way I am now Private 5729633, that's me, Private 5729633. [...]

Did I say we had hot water to wash in? You can wear pyjamas but for my part I find it quicker to sleep in shirt and pants.

There are shower baths but you soon lose interest in non-essentials.

Fortunately the pictures are open on Sundays. There are two cinemas, one modern.

So there we are eh?

Yrs

Private 5729633

P.S. Send six handkerchiefs

Later Monday. We had elementary Arms Drill this morning and very strenuous P.T. this afternoon. I have just had a bath at the hotel here.

Anthony's usual brotherly care for Shubbles – Geoffrey – is very apparent in the letter. His thoughtfulness extended to remembering that Geoffrey had no savings and would need subsidising by his parents if he was to have any chance of a civilised conscript life.

The letter also shows how firmly Anthony was already set on the course of escaping as often as possible from military life. Going off to a hotel, even if only to pay a shilling to take a bath, would become a fixed habit. Until he began his second literary career as a commentator on Army affairs, he would finance these life-saving indulgences out of savings from his first literary career as a journalist. In 1944, he would define his principle of thrift up until March 1940 as having been 'to save enough money to enable me to live for a year at exactly the same standard as I was living at the point when fired, maimed or conscripted.'[47]

Anthony would write home very frequently in his first weeks as a soldier. One undated note simply reads, 'Dear Ma: just a line to say I love you. P.S. I have just been vaccinated.' He wanted to reassure his mother that he was all right, but at the same time, for his own sake, he very much needed to keep up the contact with home.

He used his memories of boarding school to help with adaptation to army life. On the occasion in which the conscripts had to rehearse for the correct procedure on pay day, he wrote:

> One by one we marched down the hut, halted, turned right, saluted, held up the left hand for the imaginary money, saluted again, turned left and marched on. I think I was the most successful performer. Simply, of course, because of the unhappy afternoons I spent at school. But whereas at school I was the sniggerer at the back, here I was the zealot out in front.[48]

The real payday would come later that week, and was held – of all places – in the lavatory.

Anthony had been out of school for six years now, but the memories were still resonating. Getting in after lights out one night and finding two letters on his bed, he got under the blankets and read them by torchlight, commenting sardonically in his diary afterwards, 'Greyfriars days'. Greyfriars was the famous fictional school of Billy Bunter.[49]

Schoolboy humour was often the best way of keeping up one's morale. Anthony, whose extremely youthful and innocent-looking face was the perfect mask, possessed a consummate genius for ridicule. His saluting technique having come to perfection, one night he followed a young subaltern (a very junior officer) about Dorchester, saluting him every five yards to make him salute back. Anthony recorded without the slightest shame, 'He didn't know where to look. Simple pleasures are the essence of army life.'[50]

The physical regime was strenuous in the extreme. Anthony hated physical games, 'especially those with a tendency to physical injury'. Football he described as 'a little too bustling for my tastes'. As for the PT instructors, they were a breed apart, 'muscles rippling with sheer self-satisfaction'. One of these men asked Anthony what he had done before joining the Army. '"Journalist, sir," I said brightly. "Mn," he said as if that explained everything.'

Later in the day, the man added insult to injury by telling Anthony, 'I thought you were a clerk with self-indulgent tastes' and declaring that being in the Army would do him all the good in the world. Anthony, who had not lost his fire, at once retorted: 'No doubt. But I shall revert to the same life I lived before the war immediately if and when I leave the Army. So what will be the good?'[51]

Nonetheless, being a scrupulously accurate observer, he noted after a few days that his conscript group were looking better in every way. They were fitter, stronger, more confident and alert; their posture had improved immensely, and they were marching instead of slouching. He also discovered a strange and unexpected benefit to physical fitness – you could drink an enormous amount without getting a hangover.

Adaptation to the Army and to the relentlessly communal life continued apace. He was now living with people who were for the most part very uneducated and not very bright. Writing without malice (though often with barely concealed exasperation), Anthony collected many instances of stupidity, some large, some small, like a man asking if aloof was spelled o-l-o-f-f. Loud inane conversations, mouth organs, ukuleles, banjos, accordions, and communal singing all make their appearance in his diary; at times the racket was such that it was very hard to concentrate on his writing. Everyone swore a great deal: 'Just one word. I don't quite know how not to say it. It starts with the sixth letter of the alphabet.'[52] Anthony added that the non-stop use of the adjective slowed down conversation. But for the most part there was an atmosphere of live and let live, a forbearance bred of common misfortune. No one seems to have minded Anthony 'scribbling' all the time; no one came and peered over his shoulder and asked 'fool questions'. The notebook in his trouser leg was not commented upon either.

In the hut there were four married men, and seven who were engaged. Anthony noted that married men had a contempt for the sexually inexperienced. As the novelty of army life wore off, talk about sex and romance was increasing. Married men yearned for their wives, and the unmarried men for the girls back at home who had the considerable mystique of distance. The local girls were sometimes deemed too forthcoming and not respectable enough. Anthony thought this point of view ridiculous; his own opinion was that the majority of the local girls were 'respectable to the point of perversion'.

Though he sometimes found his hut mates irritating, knowledge of their common plight helped to make things bearable: 'It is strange to be in contact with men who one and all have had their lives ripped to pieces. Strange how little they complain.'[53] Anthony did not complain either. Nor would his family have liked it if he did. One of the letters which Anthony had read under the bedclothes by torchlight was from his favourite uncle, Mintie's brother Alec Crews, whose family nickname was 'Meggs'. Meggs had been in the Army in the First World War and had recently volunteered for this one. His letter, which arrived on 10 April, thanked Anthony for the mourning card he had sent – 'this is the first communication I have ever had from you' – and continued: 'What a game. So they roped you in at last. Well it's no good belching against thunder. So let's get on with it and hope for the best.'[54]

'Letters from home mourn me for dead,' Anthony wrote, referring to his family's initial response to his letter announcing that he was in the Army. But they adapted quickly, and by his second week he was writing facetiously. 'I have just rung up home. It was disappointingly matter-of-fact. None of the heart-wrung atmosphere one had been taught to expect.'

He would, however, be absolutely delighted when his family shortly started to visit him. The Army would never cure Anthony of hankering after his old, comfortable and happy way of life, though once Anthony had cured the Army of expecting him to be a conventional soldier, he did discover many ways of making the loss more tolerable.

4

THE ANTELOPE AND OTHER UNMILITARY ACTIVITIES

O n Friday 29 March, Geoffrey came down to visit Anthony for the first time. It was two weeks since he had seen his brother, and, as Anthony reported, 'he could not get over how much better I looked'. Anthony asked Geoffrey to note down the changes he saw in him, and Geoffrey wrote the following piece:

I had last seen Anthony at the cab rank just outside the BBC where we said good-bye. He was negligently dressed in a pale green light overcoat, a brown trilby and an indeterminate though well-cut suit. His complexion was the kind of weak ivory of a journalist in work. He was smoking a cigarette and getting into a taxi.

A fortnight later I whistled outside the door of a hotel bathroom, and it was opened – somewhat suspiciously – by Private 5729633. He was not a precious sight. He was preparing to get into a bath, hardly seeable for steam, and he was half dressed in khaki trousers, a thick sweater and boots, very big boots.

I said half dressed, but seven eighths was about the right figure. He took off rolls of thick underwear, both his own (rather discoloured) and His Majesty's, one after another until at last all was off, an impressive pile in the corner. Then I saw his face was very red, like a farmer's boy. I thought it was the heat of the steam. But when he had put all the layers on again I realised that this was Anthony's new complexion.

He was chatting happily, he had had a big day, they had made him the corporal's deputy. Looking at him carefully, at the short ruffled haircut, at the boots, the unattended, if clean hands and the new complexion – above all, the new complexion, I was suddenly reminded of a photograph of him in his last year at school. It was quite astonishing. He was exactly like it. Yes, he looked as if he had lost five or six years, and he didn't seem to mind very much.[55]

Anthony had just been made acting NCO for his hut. This was not such an exalted honour as it seemed at first – Anthony would later discover that six men were picked from each platoon for training as NCOs and tried out in turn. However, it was a start. Anthony was determined to become an officer. Officers had 'a sort of film star status', they lived in a realm high above that of the common soldier, and Anthony was most keen to impress the authorities that he was officer material.

Geoffrey was staying in Anthony's usual Dorchester haunt, The Antelope, an old coaching inn with a handsome bow-windowed facade. After enjoying Friday evening together, the brothers arranged to meet again there the following day for lunch. On Saturday morning, therefore, Anthony had to charm the corporal in charge into letting him off potato-peeling duty, and, having done this in his most winning manner, 'slimed off'.

A good lunch, preceded by a small incident. I was leaning on the bar talking to Geoffrey about my experiences as an NCO and as I said: 'So I said firmly ...' the landlady burst out laughing. 'Why YOU couldn't ever be firm,' she said.[56]

After lunch, Anthony dozed in the lounge until tea time while Geoffrey read what his brother had so far written about conscript life. When Anthony awoke, he returned the favour by reading one of Geoffrey's stories in the *Daily Mail*. They went to the pictures, had dinner, and Anthony returned early to the barracks at 10.00pm, 'my idea being to attend to lights out. I didn't want to be absent from any function so soon.'

As acting NCO, Anthony would become something of a martinet, though very willing to ridicule himself privately for this. He was such a rara avis that the majority of his hut mates seem to have accepted his despotism with something like a tinge of semi-affectionate pride. Anthony's intellectual calibre was so dazzling that when he turned it on at full power, there was nothing someone less literate and articulate could do except subside into deflated silence. Anthony described in detail one particular challenge to his authority:

One or two people started singing and beating time on the iron bedsteads. It developed into a crescendo.

'Shut up,' I shouted.

They did. Except the footballer, who went on tapping mildly.

'I told you to stop that,' I said.

One or two then complained that there was nothing to stop them singing or tapping.

I said, 'I suppose I shall have to make a test case to get some response to my orders. I don't want to victimise you, but I shall have to.'

'But you can't stop me tapping me foot.'

'The question is that you are making a challenge to my authority. I am telling you to stop doing something which I prohibited because people were doing it too much.'

A voice: 'Ask the sergeant if we bain't allowed to tap our feet.'

'Ask him by all means, But I think you will find that he and the rest of the hierarchy will support me.'

There was a silence.

Someone said, 'Go on, sing, boys,' but no one did.

There were murmurings of 'He knows no more'n us,' and 'Are we a lot of kids?'

I stood up and pacing nervously up and down, said,

'In deference to the exquisitely witty Mr Stockley and others, I should like to make it clear that I am not trying to stop you singing, playing musical instruments or otherwise making fools of yourselves. I merely prohibited a man from doing something other people had been doing too much.'

This was a complete success. There was dead silence for more than a minute broken by an admiring, 'Hasn't he got a big mouth?'[57]

A couple of days after this – and sundry other altercations with the 'tough guy funny men' who were trying to bully their weaker fellows into mutiny – the platoon went trench-digging. Anthony's enemies were infinitely better at this than he was:

They knew how to dig trenches and I didn't. But after shouting 'Get on with it, Cotterell. Bend thee back. Get down to it, man' etc, for some minutes, they started helping me. Telling me how not to waste my strength taking unnecessary swings with the pick and so on. Extraordinary after the black hatred their faces had registered when I ordered them about.[58]

Anthony discovered that he had been given a nickname, Lord Haw-Haw, a reference to his posh public school accent and manners rather than a slur on his patriotic character. Lord Haw-Haw was the nickname of the Anglo-Irishman William Joyce, who was becoming infamous for his radio propaganda broadcasts on behalf of Goebbels' Propaganda Ministry.

Though he did his best to muck in, Anthony would always remain apart from his fellow conscripts; there was something exotic about him that they clearly recognised. As did Anthony himself, commenting with typical self-mockery, 'compared to most people, I am a wilting hothouse plant'.

In the fourth week of Anthony's training, the war, which had been jogging along quietly for seven months, suddenly took an extreme turn for the worse. On Tuesday 9th April, Anthony wrote in his diary:

> Rumours all day about the Germans invading Holland, Denmark and Norway. But hardly the slightest interest [to be seen in his fellow soldiers]. The morning papers had nothing and there aren't many radios.
>
> But after lunch – just now – Padbury came running in to say that Hitler had gone into Denmark and Holland and was at war with Norway. The atmosphere electrified for several minutes.
>
> Comments: 'It won't be long now.'
>
> 'I'm going on the bottle tonight.'
>
> 'No more Maginot now; it'll be you or him.'
>
> 'I don't bloody well care.'
>
> 'I'll buy a paper tonight to have a look.'
>
> But a few minutes later it had completely dropped out of the conversation. There were nineteen in the room; four were reading papers, three were writing letters, two were singing 'I'll pray for you,' the rest were sleeping or cleaning their buttons.[59]

Eventually the news was confirmed that that it was only Norway and Denmark which had been attacked. It would be another month before Germany invaded Holland.

Despite the dire implications for them personally, none of Anthony's fellow soldiers seemed particularly worried by the escalation of hostilities. Although British troops would soon be part of the desperate fighting in Norway, no one in the hut seemed anxious that they might form part of the force. This apathy and unconcern about affairs which directly affected them would be seen again on Friday 10 May, when the war entered its most dangerous period for Britain. On that particular day the real focus of attention was not on the dire situation across the Channel but on the local pub and the end of term party.

Anthony was glad to have a break from soldiering at the end of the fourth week. His mother Mintie came down on Thursday, having arranged to spend the weekend in Dorchester. She was staying at Anthony's second home, The Antelope. On the Friday evening Anthony was sitting in the hotel lounge with her having a drink when, to his delighted surprise, in walked Geoffrey. He had sent Mintie a telegram only an hour or so earlier, 'Coming to dinner because I am so hungry'. Geoffrey had just got his call-up papers – he was due at his camp in a week's time.

That evening the three of them decided that they would all go to the cinema the following day as had always been their Saturday afternoon custom. Aunt Janie would be sadly missed, but otherwise things would be as they always had been.

After Saturday lunch at the Antelope, however, Anthony began to feel seriously unwell. The cinema outing went ahead, but by now he felt too ill to enjoy it. Once back at the hotel and feeling worse than ever, he decided to rest until late evening. He would then go back to the barracks to sleep, and come back the following day if he was feeling better.

All the emotional pressures which had been boiling inside him, all the stresses and tensions of his first four weeks in the army, could now, for a few hours, be completely forgotten. He wrote:

I flopped down on Geoffrey's bed, fully dressed, boots and all. Mother covered me with the eiderdown, her fur coat, Geoffrey's overcoat, and my greatcoat. She drew the curtains and tiptoed from the room.

It was release to relax. The urge to resist, the indignation, the sense of injustice faded. Fever and weakness swept over me like clouds round a mountain.

After a short sleep, he woke up perfectly relaxed. But his temperature had risen to 101.6 degrees. Hoping to get a doctor's sanction to stay at the hotel, he and Geoffrey tried to contact a civilian doctor Anthony had met (and doubtless charmed) at the pub, then the head doctor at the barracks at his private house, but could get hold of neither. Mintie's comment was that it was pretty naive of Anthony and Geoffrey to try to find a doctor on a Saturday night 'with contract bridge still legal'.

Finally Mintie herself went up to the barracks. She was in her late forties but still very charming and attractive; it was obvious she would be a far better emissary than Geoffrey. The hardened NCOs at the barracks were secretly just as homesick as everyone else – they would be unable to resist such a sweet doting mother, who if necessary could come over all fluffy-headed to defuse any possible trouble for Anthony.

A soldier was now sent back to assess Anthony's condition. The soldier, in a very kindly way, asked if Anthony could walk back to the barracks, leaning on him. Anthony said that he supposed that he could but that he did not want to unless it was absolutely necessary. The soldier then told him to stay where he was. That night Anthony slept beautifully in the luxurious silence and solitude of the hotel bedroom. To add to the elements of farce about this whole episode, a Royal Army Medical Corps doctor came up from the barracks in the middle of the night to inspect him but could not find the right room and so went away again.

In the morning, Mintie once again went up to the barracks to report on her son's progress back to health. On her return to the hotel, she said that everyone had been charming – 'Us don't want to hurt y'lad,' the honest warriors had beamed.

A doctor finally arrived, and having examined Anthony, and found not a great deal wrong with him, nonetheless told him to stay at the hotel until the following day and follow a diet of 'slops, custards, dry toast, stale bread'. Mintie was slightly confused by the doctor's civilian clothes, and asked:

'But will it be all right with the Army?'

'Well, madam, I am the Army.'

The rest of the day was splendid. His malaise producing a gently pleasant weakness, Anthony talked with his mother and brother, or read short stories and the comic strips from American Sunday papers. All the old blessings of his former life encircled him; it was the most delightful respite from military life.

The doctor reappeared on Monday, his visit being of the shortest duration; as Anthony wrote, 'he practically met himself coming out'. He advised Anthony to potter about a bit at the hotel, stay the night, then go back to the barracks for sick parade at 9.00am on Tuesday. Anthony had another leisurely day, a bath, lunch in bed, took tea out, worked on his book until dinner, had a good dinner, and then another luxurious night. To add spice to it all, before supper he met a fellow writer in uniform, Alec Waugh, the brother of Evelyn Waugh, and at that time a well-known name. Anthony had a brandy with him and his fellow officer in The Antelope's bar.

The blissful interlude could not last. On Tuesday Anthony was back in barracks, the prescription: tonic three times daily and attend sick parade for at least seven days, known as Attend B.

The whole episode led to a great deal of amusement at Anthony's expense. The sergeant at sick parade could not resist poking fun; when ushering Anthony in to see the Medical Officer, he described him as 'The man from the hotel, sir', as if announcing a comic turn. A couple of weeks later, when Anthony was at sick parade again, the sergeant used the same phrase and 'looked as if he expected me to sing and dance'.[60]

But ridicule meant nothing – the stay at The Antelope had been utterly delightful. On Wednesday 17 April, Anthony wrote home:

Dear Mother

Everything has worked out rather well. I saw the doctor again this morning. He put me on 10B for 'at least a week'.[61] This means doing nothing very much, so it will be a good opportunity to get on with my bit of typing. I can read up what I am missing in a book.

I met Alec Waugh in the hotel. He and his companion were full of surprise and admiration at the way I had managed to be allowed to stay at the hotel.

I am still a bit feeble, but I think I shall be perfectly well in a day or so.

So young Geoffrey is going off to war. You must be worried sick. We can only pray he returns safely, and that he doesn't get run over.

Thank you for coming down mother. Thank you very much.

Yrs Anthony

The following day he wrote again, sympathising with Mintie for the loss of Geoffrey's company:

Dear Mother

Here is a little letter to cheer you up in your bereavement. I am sorry there was no stamp on my last letter but I didn't have time to get one without missing the post. I am still pretty debilitated, but I think I shall be alright after the weekend. The Sergeant is allowing me to sleep in his room during the afternoons.

He said to me yesterday, 'You won't be here much longer', meaning the OCTU, but of course 'not much longer' means about two months.

At a conference yesterday the question was discussed of providing somewhere for soldiers to receive their parents.

'Oi know,' said the Sergeant Major, 'Take 'em down The Antelope and go sick.' Admirable publicity.

Oh well all the best, Mum.

P.S. Please send my cheque book.

5

DEPRESSION

Only a week later, Anthony was ill again – but then so was just about everyone else in his hut. They had begun their TAB inoculations which were infamous for producing extreme reactions. In anticipation of this, they had all been placed off duty for 48 hours. Four hours after the injections, the hut was awash with what Anthony called 'Crimean scenes'. He went to bed fully clothed, a policy he continued for the next two nights, commenting: 'The simplification thus effected is enjoyable. If you leave dirt alone to accumulate it doesn't bother you for some days.'

After two days, he was still very unwell. He reported sick and rather unofficially stayed in bed whilst the others in the hut went up for breakfast. 'A very tall thin fellow had also reported sick. He looked as if it would have saved time to report dead straight off.'[62]

Gradually Anthony recovered, and by the Saturday of that week was applying for a Signallers course, lasting three months, on the grounds that it was 'easier on the feet'. He still hoped for transfer to officer training but there was no sign that this would happen soon. In fact, he would have to wait for another two months.

The relentless communal living, and total lack of privacy and autonomy, sometimes came close to being unbearable. What Anthony found hardest was the unremitting pressure from NCOs and officers, who expected unquestioning obedience and absolute conformity to high military standards. He would write of this with typical cheerfulness, 'You have to get used to having your appearance and arrangements scrutinised. They inspect everything. I have never been looked at so much in my life.' Four years later, he would refine this description of a conscript's life to: 'You are inspected, expected and suspected every minute of the day'.[63]

Every so often there were small glimmers of hope about what he felt in his worst moments was a hopeless situation. He was prepared to exploit all possible opportunities to improve things regardless of how unpromising they might seem. On 2 May, he received a letter from Marie Stopes, the eminent campaigner for birth control and sexual health. He had never met her, though he had once interviewed her on the telephone and 'she told me to marry without delay'. Marie Stopes wrote to Anthony that she was collecting 'a few specially bad cases of square pegs in round holes so that I can go and stamp at high authority'. She said that he sounded like a pretty bad case; would he like her to raise his case, or would he prefer to be left in status quo? Anthony wrote back the same day, saying that the one status he didn't wish to be left in was quo.[64]

The following week his training course ended. In reorganising his diary to make the most effective use of material for *What! No Morning Tea?* Anthony accidentally muddied the chronology by moving a conversation back one week. Of this last week of training, he wrote:

We did nothing until lunch time. There was a great atmosphere of complacence. Some even started talking politics, a sure sign of happiness not to be engrossed with the usual domestic concerns of military life. 'I tell you Churchill wasn't given a chance until last week. I can prove it. Look here, it says so in the *Daily Mirror* here.'

One of the country boys spoke up. 'Oi 'ope 'e doan't go into Belgium,' he said, it being some days after he had [...]

'Oi dunno 'bout Mr Chamberlain. Poor man, 'e worked hard, Oi wonders if Mr Churchill'll do better.'

'Ah,' I said, 'It's no use locking the stable door after the horse has gone.'

'Ah,' he said.[65]

It was actually on the following day, 10 May, that the Netherlands and Belgium were invaded, Chamberlain resigned, and Churchill took his place. Throughout the book Anthony left dates deliberately vague in order to make its message more universal. For the same reason, he did not emphasis these world-shaking events; he relegated them – exactly as his fellow conscripts had relegated them – to the background of the end of course party.

The party duly took place. In recognition of his supreme gift for words and knack for using phrases which nobody understood, Anthony was the one chosen to get the present for their sergeant and to make the speech of thanks that accompanied it.

Before they all went their separate ways to their own particular wartime fate, the platoon had their photograph taken with their sergeant; Thirty-two conscripts grouped together on a dull day on a featureless patch of grass and stared, smiled or scowled at the camera. At the very back, half obscured, as though he had darted there at the last minute, Anthony can just be seen grinning.[66]

When he edited and reorganised his conscript diary to make the finished book, Anthony made sure that *What! No Morning Tea?* ended on a very up-beat, ebullient note. He deliberately sought out all the positive things about his training and listed them carefully for the future conscripts whom he hoped would be reading the book:

Army life has all the bad points of life in a large family and a whole lot more bad points of its own. But it also has some of the good ones. They may order you about all the time and you are bound to obey any order, but they in their turn are bound to look after you all the time.[67]

He intended his book to be marketed as a guide to what new conscripts could expect of army life. When *What! No Morning Tea?* was published some months later, the jacket blurb would indeed emphasise this, saying that every man who was going to be called up would want to read it, as also would 'the parents, wives and sweethearts both of conscripts and those about to be conscripts'. Anthony knew that he had been amongst the first of a massive social mobilisation, in which well over 2 million men would be conscripted into the Army.[68] No one else had written anything comparable to his light but informative take on conscript life, and he had great hopes that the book would sell extremely well.

What! No Morning Tea? was written with great wit and panache. It was short, vivid, and highly entertaining. Anthony wrote of himself with cheerful lack of respect, unashamedly describing his laziness, incompetence, resentment, ambition and deceitfulness, but all in such a winning and amusing way that the reader could not help liking him. He also showed no particular awe of his superiors. On the verge of leaving his training camp, he was inspected by a very young officer:

'Are those your only pair of trousers?' he said.

'Yes, sir.'

'Did you sleep on them or in them?' Every fibre in my brain urged me to point out that his own front trouser buttons were undone. But eight weeks' training told. I said nothing.[69]

The book ends with Anthony leaving the training camp as he moves to the next stage of his army life. As he and his fellow soldiers march down the road, he reflects that it is 'goodbye to a chapter' and glances back sentimentally to make his farewell, only to be bawled at by the sergeant, 'Keep your blasted eyes front'.

Keeping a diary of his military life had proved so useful that Anthony immediately began another one. It too would be made into a book, *An Apple for the Sergeant*, but this one would not be published for another four years.[70]

This second diary began with his move to another camp in Dorchester, where he was to be trained as a Signaller. He had won the place against a fair degree of competition, for others in the platoon had also realised that becoming a specialist would involve 'much less marching and tedious physical exercise' than being an ordinary rifleman. Private Daly, a distant relative and the nearest thing to a friend that Anthony had found in initial training, had also won a specialist's posting but to another unit. They lived in different quarters but met when off-duty. A third man, Private Baker, now also became a friend and often joined them on outings. He was a fellow signaller with whom Anthony partnered up in the absence of anyone more intellectually exciting.

The war in France was going horribly wrong; but, as Anthony wrote, he and his group were more interested in their own progress in Morse code. Despite his initial feelings of horror on seeing a classroom of students learning Morse code, Anthony discovered to his surprise and 'complacence' that he could pick it up very easily. Four years later he would note: 'It is the only military activity for which I have shown more than mediocre aptitude'.

At the beginning of the course, Anthony and Baker shared a tiny, rickety, vermin-infested room in a converted barn in Dorchester. The window looked out on a small pretty garden, beyond which was a glimpse of the River Frome. After the communal life of the barracks hut, it was absolute bliss. They even became slightly house-proud, buying a small white wooden cupboard from a second-hand furniture dealer for 5s. They scrubbed it out and placed it, still wet, between their beds, then took it out again and cut its legs short because it was too tall.

They very much enjoyed their secluded bolt-hole with its unaccustomed privacy and seclusion. You could even read after lights out, so long as you listened for the sounds which indicated the sergeant next door was going to blow his candle out – then you hastily blew out yours so that no tell-tale gleams would shine through the holes in the walls.

The only drawback was the hyperactive rodent life, particularly at night. The creatures would run away temporarily when Anthony banged his boot on the floor, but they very soon returned, attracted by the Army bread which was stored in the room in a packing case. Anthony tried not to take any notice of them, 'for presumably in France, where we all expected to be consigned in the near future, I would live with mice and rats for years'.[71]

The usual inanities of army life featured in their new posting. Amongst these was the classic episode with the palliasses. On the morning of their arrival at the new billets, they were marched off to stables in another part of Dorchester to fill their palliasses with straw. In the afternoon, half-way through their first Morse code class, a young sergeant came in with an order that they were to interrupt their class and empty the palliasses.

> 'But we've only just filled 'em,' said someone. 'You don't interest me,' said the sergeant. We collected the palliasses from our beds, fell in outside, and marched across the town to the stables, where we emptied the straw into the same barn from which we had collected it [...] The absence of straw in our palliasses became sharply evident when we went to bed. [...]
>
> The following morning we were marched with our empty palliasses round to the stable again. We filled them with the same straw with which we had filled, and subsequently emptied, them yesterday. It didn't appear to be any better or worse for its night in the stable.[72]

This sort of thing amused and infuriated Anthony in about equal measure. He would note many instances of Army inanity in his diary; they always made very good copy. The simple act of writing them down was also therapeutic. Writing made a tremendous difference to his equanimity and lent point to many maddeningly pointless things.

In an undated letter, written to Mintie around this time, Anthony gives his address as White Hart Billet, Dorchester. Referring to the worsening war situation, he ended the letter rather flippantly, 'We are all confined to Dorchester since Saturday to deal with parachute troops and/or riots. Well, well. Yr loving son Anthony.'[73]

A second undated letter followed, which enclosed the photograph taken of his former platoon at the end of their initial training. The letter shows not only how he looked upon his own letters as raw literary material, but also how much he relied on his mother to do things for him.

Dear Ma

I hope you are well and not worrying too much about Dad. How many has he brought down so far? [74]

Will you send me a pair of pyjamas, winter weight and full size? Have you catalogued my articles yet? Have you tried for a suitable cuttings book? The point being that I want to go through them and copy one or two oddments out. What has become of my tuckbox? It would come in handy. Please send the letter I sent you telling you that I was in the Army.

Monday: Thanks for your letter. We have spent the day firing the Bren gun out at Weymouth. I was in deadly form.

The last few days have been marred by one incident. The theft of £3 from my wallet the night before transferring to 'S' company. I forgot to mention it last time. Enclosed is a happy snap taken before our transfer.

Love Tone[75]

The literary material contained in the family letters was looked upon as a valuable resource, not only by Anthony but by Geoffrey.[76] The letters were always kept for possible future use. In an undated note, written when Anthony had become an officer and his men had become a form of unpaid labour, Mintie wrote:

I am forwarding letters as per request from Shubbs. He says will you please keep them carefully as I have. Have your men type a carbon copy of them. This is important. 'Do unto others etc' and don't forget all your letters are my property carefully preserved, will you.[77]

The luxury of commanding Army typists lay in the future. As a lowly private in Dorchester, Anthony did his own typing. He worked hard on the text of *What! No Morning Tea*, which he would soon start to send out to publishers. He expanded some incidents and crossed out others, carefully hammering the thing into shape. He sometimes wondered what was the point of all this work on something which 'apart from its literary demerits, looked like being profoundly outdated by the fall of France, which was now taking ominous shape'. At times he must have experienced a sinking feeling that the book would never be published, or – perhaps even worse – that it would become a damp squib like his first book, *The Expert Way of Getting Married*.

Sometimes he worked on the diary or on the typewritten text which succeeded it in the familiar comforts of the Antelope Hotel. The drawback there was a gossipy old porter 'who liked to tell me all he knew'. Anthony was well on the way to becoming part of the Antelope family. When he passed through Dorchester the following year as an officer, the hotel receptionist would regale him with all the latest gossip, how the doctor did not come in any more because he was married, so was the dark girl from the local restaurant, Judge Jeffrey's, but Miss Gillespie, the manageress at Judge Jeffrey's, was still around – as Anthony commented, 'she must be on the inventory by this time'.[78]

Things were so comfortable at the White Hart Billet that naturally they had to change, and Anthony's platoon moved to new quarters which were spartan in the extreme. Dramatic variations in living conditions were a feature of military life, as was the type of food, either quite good or absolutely terrible. Anthony was reasonably stoical about it, and did not dwell upon the exchange of a pleasant way of life in Dorchester for a primitive camp of wooden huts in a field. There was only one tap in the camp, surrealistically placed all by itself in the grass. It was constantly surrounded by men waiting to use it, standing in an ocean of mud.

One minor improvement on the Dorchester billet was that there was a proper dining hut with table and benches, instead of having to eat in the room in which they also worked and slept. However, as they queued up for dinner on the first day and it started raining, Anthony realised that the dining hut had 'no roof, nor any glass in the windows, nor any door in the doorway. It was more of a gesture than anything else.'

His parents came down to see him, staying at The Antelope, and they spent their time together going for walks or sitting too long over afternoon tea, either at the hotel or at Judge Jeffrey's. Anthony found these occasions, particularly when Baker or Daly also came to tea, 'almost rejuvenatingly' like the times when his parents used to visit him at boarding school:

> Baker and Daly were exactly like two guest schoolboys. The esoteric nature of our conversation, the preoccupation with administrative details, the concern to propitiate petty functionaries, the fear of getting back late, and the schoolboy appetites in the teashop were all exactly the same.[79]

Even the banter was similar. The walls of Judge Jeffrey's Olde Worlde Restaurant were hung with ancient weaponry such as allegedly eighteenth-century muskets. Daly said they were almost the same type that he and the others had just been issued with. Baker said that they would be getting bows and arrows next, to which Daly quipped, 'Bows perhaps; arrows I doubt'. The joke was all too topical – there was a dire shortage of arms in the kingdom.

His parents had brought news of how Geoffrey was getting on, having visited him at his training camp. Geoffrey's start in the Army had been even more inauspicious than Anthony's. He would later fictionalise his experiences in his novel *Then a Soldier*. This described a batch of new conscripts who had arrived at their camp in torrential rain which had soaked them to the skin:

> The warm food certainly had a bracing effect on them, but it also released them from the numbed wetness which had been their principal feeling up to now, and they became more conscious of the general discomfort they had come into. They started quite suddenly to remember home again. The conscript's misery, passing on from Caesar's levies and the uncountable hundreds of thousands who had been pressed into service under the Tsars and the Prussians and the Habsburgs, reached them too. The little town of army huts now showed itself [...] Jackie was just rationalising to himself the idea of life in a communal hut, when he noticed that there were some tents on the hill.
> He was not alone in this observation.
> 'Holy Mother!' groaned the man next to him.[80]

Geoffrey slept his first night in the Army in just such a tent, with earth for the floor and the rain rivuletting across it.

The following days would see Geoffrey experiencing the same shocked revolution of attitudes as Anthony; he would note of the Colonel of the regiment and other very senior officers that they who had seemed 'comic opera figures from outside the Army were now immense in their real grandeur'. These potentates wielded a life-and-death power over one's fate. Even relatively junior officers lived in a separate universe. A scene in the novel dramatises this to great effect when at a pub an officer asks Geoffrey's alter-ego, Robert Halbrook, and his companion to play darts for charity:

> The officer, who was in charge of a lonely, wet, miserable Bofors gun site four miles outside the town and would have had a long conversation with the hotel cat for the sake of talking, was not aware that he had made the evening for Jackie and Robert. But this was quite natural. The sudden jerking change from civilian to army life, from a life of reasonable ease and comfort to one in which you assume slave status [...] cannot help upsetting your sense of proportion. An officer asking you to play darts, if only with the idea of helping charity, is like Churchill and Shaw dropping in for a quiet chat some evening.[81]

Both Mintie and Graham found it impossibly hard to deal with the possibility of their cherished sons being turned into cannon fodder. But they were also very concerned with the more immediate problems which both sons were facing. On this latest visit to Dorchester, Anthony guessed that his parents imagined 'I must be leading a paranoiac and hypersensitive existence with bullies continually twisting my arm, and vicious clods jeering at me, encouraged by brutal and dehumanised sergeants'. They appeared 'pathetically relieved' at the comparatively civilised form of Anthony's new way of life. Anthony very much wanted his parents to feel happy, so he tried to look contented but succeeded only in 'registering jibbering idiocy'. Nonetheless, with a visit to the cinema with Baker and Daly, all appeared to be going well. That was until his parents drove him back to the camp, fairly late after dinner.

'"Good God!" said Father.

"Oh, how awful!" said Mother.'

To them the camp looked gloomy, primitive and horrible in the twilight. Anthony wrote that he had not really had a chance to look at it in quite that way; he saw it as 'the Headquarters of the military organisation in which I was immersed up to the neck'. He regarded its accommodation without enthusiasm but took its primitiveness for granted.[82]

Just as in the old school days, before his parents left to go home, his father Graham very sweetly asked him if he needed any money.

Once his parents had gone, and he faced the vista (if he was lucky and not killed or maimed) of endless years in the clutches of the military, Anthony began a slow descent into depression.

Certain aspects of military life had initially seemed funny, interesting, and a bit like a holiday; his attitude was buoyant and he wanted to do well because it increased his chances of being accepted for officer training. In the first few weeks, amused by the newness of it all and the excitement of writing his book on conscript life, he had managed to fight off the ever-threatening melancholia. Now the impetus which had carried him so well began to falter and he started to find army life very tough indeed. Very unusually for Anthony, an element of self-pity crept in.

> I regarded my conscription as a human drama of the first importance and depth. I saw myself as an unhappy marionette fighting bravely to survive. The whole thing seemed to me extremely poignant. It probably wasn't quite the right approach to a career in the Armed Forces.[83]

One of his major problems was that, apart from Morse code, he had no aptitude whatsoever for any of the tasks which the Army set him. He was unathletic, uncoordinated, absent-minded and forgetful; he had 'an unholy knack' for appearing ridiculous in military situations. His superlative gift for writing had not the slightest relevance in his present circumstances. Nobody knew that he had once been a highly paid journalist on a top national newspaper, and nobody cared. Once, when he was yet again being reprimanded for being slow and clumsy, with boots and cap badge which did not shine with regulation brightness, a sergeant helpfully pointed out to him that the Signals technical training 'might help me to a more remunerative job in after-life'.

Dinner one evening at a delightful house near Weymouth brought back memories of his old life all too strongly. The luxuriously equipped bathroom, the books and bottles, the gramophone records and manicured hands, the scent and the gentle cultured voices – all these were balm to his senses. He did not name names but clearly there was someone there whom he liked very much. 'Women are a great idea. You don't realise how arid a barrack room is until you are reminded that the other kind of life still goes on.'[84]

Back at the camp, he felt helpless and that he had lost all power to control his own destiny. When *What! No Morning Tea?* was turned down by a publisher whom he had expected to take it, an almost paralytic depression descended:

> Time went by. The weather got warmer. You could read in the fields in the evening very pleasantly. It sounds delightful in retrospect – healthy, simple and happy, but, of course, no state of human affairs is without its complications. My diary, *What! No Morning Tea?*, over which I had worked and worried so hard, was sent back rejected by Mr Allen Lane. Writing in all its forms is a heart-aching business. The thing you have just written and, after the usual maddening interval, had turned down, looms over your personal horizon reeking of all the straining effort that, for the moment, looks like being wasted. Depression is a kind of almost physical numbness of the brain, an emotional state that practically paralyses the processes of rationalisation which normally reconcile us to our shortcomings. There is nothing you can do about it because there is nothing you want to do about it. Subsequently I sent the book to an agent, who also returned it with a reader's report to the effect that it was a very ordinary account of recruit training in the Army, and since so many people were also undergoing it the experiences described in the book were well-known enough for them to have no commercial market value. I am happy to say that, at the time of writing, this agent is in gaol, where I wished him at the time.[85]

Meanwhile Britain's fortunes in war had reached rock bottom. On 15 May, the hopelessly outmatched Netherlands had surrendered. The fighting in France went catastrophically badly. The evacuation of the British Expeditionary Force, the BEF, from Dunkirk began on 26 May. Two days later, Belgium surrendered. On 17 June the so-called Armistice was concluded by the Germans with the Pétain government in France. Within the space of little more than a month, the entire outlook of the war had changed and British war strategy lay in ruins. A few miles of sea was now all that divided a seemingly omnipotent enemy from British soil.

Geoffrey's fictionalised account of the critical times of June 1940 vividly describes the scene at his camp:

> At three o'clock they were all called out. Something was up. The NCOs stood in self-important little groups [...] There was an impressive quietness. After an interval, Major Lomax, followed by four second lieutenants, the troop officers, strode quickly into the middle of the square. [He] looked slowly round the faces of his men. He wore, he hoped, a look of cold, grim determination. He sniffed. He stood with his feet apart, Mussolini style, and he kept beating his leg with his stick. The troops were overawed.
>
> 'As you may know,' said Major Lomax, 'the country is in a serious position. The battle in France, for the moment, has gone against us. Our backs are to the wall. Well, it is when our backs are to the wall that we British show our teeth to the best advantage.'[86]

Rigorous martial training occupied the next few days. Then two lorries suddenly arrived at the camp, full of Dunkirk evacuees – unkempt and exhausted men in odd combinations of clothes as if they had been shipwrecked. Within a few minutes, Twenty more lorries arrived, disgorging hundreds of similarly dishevelled soldiers.

For a few seconds they stared at them as if they were inhabitants from another world. Then one of the men called over to them.

'Where is this, chum?'

'Canderbridge.'

'Where the hell's Canderbridge?'

'Somerset. Who are you?'

'I've forgotten,' the man said. Then he grinned at them. He was wearing an officer's coat, a blue shirt, khaki trousers and gum boots. 'I'm in the 6th South Staffs. We're just back from France.'[87]

In his notes home, Anthony adopted a flippant tone about the crisis and even about the Dunkirk evacuees. In a very brief letter, not even signed, he wrote:

Dear Ma

Great apologies for not writing. Trunk calls hours delays. We are kept in digging trenches all day and nursing BEF survivors.[88]

Another undated note from the same period read:

Dear Ma

Do I detect a trace of bitterness in your last letter? I really am sorry to have been casual but if it is any consolation I have been casual with everyone else. This last week has been a little difficult. Not only with moving and trench digging but in rehearsing the part we would play in the event of invasion. We have spent the entire weekend travelling round the country in motor coaches. Not too bad except that owing to all the junk we have to carry you can't sit down properly.

For the last three, no, four nights I have tried to ring you up but there was a delay of hours, caused by the BEF, one and all of whom is phoning home [...]

I was put on a charge for popping out on Saturday night to phone you and also, let me confess, to get a little drink, while I was on fire picquet. So far there have been no developments.[89]

Unknown to Anthony, two men had escaped from France with the BEF who, four years later, would have the most immense influence upon his life. The first was Freddie Gough, who would be his commanding officer (CO) on the truck at Brummen. The second was Tony Hibbert, the man whose escape from the truck in Brummen marketplace would be the immediate catalyst for the shooting.

6

OFFICER TRAINING

At the end of June, at very short notice, Anthony received his posting to his Officer Corps Training Unit, or OCTU. Ever since being conscripted in March, he had held great hopes for a better life as an officer, but in the event he was to find it in some ways even more painful than being a private. Living conditions would be markedly better, but his inaptitude for military life would become ever more glaringly and humiliatingly apparent. Had it not been for the success of *What! No Morning Tea?*, it is hard to know where he would have ended up or what the Army would have done with him.

168 OCTU was at Aldershot, a place with several cinemas and many shops, pubs and restaurants. But, as Anthony wrote, it was all fiendishly overcrowded; 'everywhere was thick with troops'. He took an immediate dislike to the place because it was so saturated with military life:

> When we arrived we had to queue up to give our names, numbers and previous occupation to a row of officers. [The Platoon Sergeant] issued us with dozens of training pamphlets and note-books. I looked through them in a sort of dulled despair. He told us the most horrific stories of how much work we had in front of us. Everybody believed and improved on these stories. It seemed quite feasible; the whole atmosphere of the landscape for miles around was strictly regimental. It seemed unlikely that any tolerable human life could emerge from such a set-up.[90]

The Commanding Officer of 168 OCTU was Lieutenant-Colonel R.C. Bingham. In January 1941, three months after Anthony had moved on, Bingham was to become infamous for a letter which was published in *The Times*. In it, Bingham stated that officer shortcomings were directly due to commissioning men who did not have 'the old school tie' instincts for leadership and for taking responsibility for their troops. He was referring to middle- and lower-class men who, he considered, did not have the instinctive *noblesse oblige* which the public schools bred. His comments sparked off such an immense furore that Bingham lost his post.[91]

Anthony's detailed account of his first experience with Bingham certainly sets the scene for Bingham's subsequent notoriety:

> We were marched down to a big wooden lecture hall to hear an opening address by our Company Commander, who was tall, broad and fearsomely military. There is nothing more forbidding than a face hidden behind a fine military moustache; it makes it so difficult to detect any sign of human sympathy. The Company Commander told us that we were no longer ordinary private soldiers; we were now potential officers, and perfection must therefore be our standard, particularly when walking out after duty. There must be no familiarity with other ranks, though, of course, it would be advisable not to carry this to any ridiculous lengths. However, we were subject to the same discipline as the ordinary private soldier, and in fact this would be even more rigorously applied. We should find that there were bars set aside for officers and cadets and we were advised to keep to these particular bars.

He also warned us that there were women in Aldershot, some of whom were not above reproach. Personally he couldn't understand any man who had the chance to hold the King's Commission losing his head over women; but there it was. There were also a large number of tailors' representatives in the town who would attempt to lure our custom with specious promises and beer. There were cases of men who had ordered their uniforms on the strength of their outfitting allowance and had then failed the course. You couldn't, in fact, be too careful.

'Four grades of cadets are turned out here,' said the Company Commander: 'Grade A, first-class chaps, above the average – any Battalion proud to have them; Grade B, good chaps and good value for anybody – any Battalion very pleased to have them; Grade C, good fellows, men you could trust, but perhaps not quite so quick as the others; nothing against them, of course, probably tried very hard but they hadn't quite got that little extra. Yes, all those three grades are very good chaps. And then,' he said, with a tinge of disgust, 'there's Grade D.'

I was sorry he didn't say much about Grade D, because I had the feeling, rightly as it transpired, that that is what I would turn out to be. I was the only one in our Company.[92]

Anthony knuckled down to his new life, but soon discovered it to be 'a pretty horrible one'. He found the hotly competitive atmosphere very difficult to cope with, particularly living with the swots who strained so hard to ingratiate themselves with their instructors. He had the good grace to admit that part of his bitterness was caused by jealousy, for he was proving absolutely hopeless at just about everything they tried to teach him.

They used to take us out and station us in front of a piece of landscape and tell us to draw a panorama sketch map of it. While all the others were deftly summarising the topographical features I would laboriously, with dropped, hopeless jaw, produce the kind of thing I could have done equally well at the age of six.[93]

A letter to Geoffrey told something of his discomfort, and that as usual he was disassociating himself from the place by taking refuge in writing:

Well we have settled in now and everyone is pulling together. The course is a little too practical for my liking, but there you are. Gone to Aldershot, the town with the lowest collective IQ on earth. We had a lecture on discipline from our own Colonel Bingham who is just like the men in *Esquire*. They are all like that. It is phantastic. I shall always remember that lecture. Laugh, I nearly died. You ought to meet Lieutenant Cook, our platoon commander. In appearance a cross between Emrys Jones and Cesar Romero but sprung from the ruling classes.[94] This morning he came in looking worried. 'Here, I say, have you all heard about this dashed idea for sort of suicide squads to harry these Hun tanks. Platoon from each unit pledged to harry the dashed beggars down eh? Well dammit its not so bloody funny let me tell you because we've been chosen for the job. Bicycles they're going to give us. Bicycles mind you against dashed great tanks. If any of you fellers have any ideas about how to beat these things with dashed bicycles I'd like to have them. I'm supposed to work out some ideas but frankly I can't think of a single dashed one.'

There is an ominous silence about my book.[95] But you know I have long since come to the stage when disappointments have lost their power to disappoint. It's not that I don't care but I am really getting used to reverses. And incidentally I may say, to successes.

I have just been reading my diary of early days on the *Express*, the one that Mother saw. It is entirely fascinating. Now my idea for my next book is this. To write a Johnson-Boswell biography of a thoroughly decent Langman Junior type, a man who went to a small public school, then qualified as a dentist, started a suburban practice, and joined up on the outbreak of war. Say he was killed by a bomb bursting in his surgery and the book[96]

At this tantalising moment the page ends and the rest of the letter has been lost. Langman was a member of the Wanstead golf club which was close to the Cotterell family home; he was a deeply conventional man, though as Anthony said 'thoroughly decent'. Anthony never went anywhere with this novel, one of several he planned during the war years, and at least one of which he made a serious start on.

Ever since being conscripted, Anthony had been contributing articles to magazines and newspapers which he was supposed to first submit for the approval of his Commanding Officer. He now had a new article on officer cadet life, but judging that the text might fall foul of Colonel Bingham, he decided to get it published anyway and then improvise a way of dealing with the fall-out. The story of how he did this was written down by Stephen Watts, who was to work with Anthony from mid-1941 onwards:

> The day [the article] appeared in print he presented himself at his company office clutching a copy of the paper and doing his best to look pale and worried. Anthony was naturally pale and especially in battledress he looked disarmingly young and innocent.
>
> He requested that the Sergeant-Major take him before the CO. The interview with the formidable Colonel Bingham went something like this:
>
> AC. 'Sir, a terrible thing has happened.'
>
> CO. 'Well, my boy, what is it?'
>
> AC. (*rather breathlessly*) 'Sir – I was a journalist in civilian life. I wrote an article about officer training, sir, and I knew I had to submit it for your approval, sir.'
>
> CO. 'Yes, my boy, quite right.'
>
> AC. 'But, sir, I had no typewriter and my handwriting is very bad, sir, and I did not want to waste your time, especially as the article might not be accepted. So I sent it to the paper, sir, with a letter saying if they wanted to use it would they send me a proof first so that I could submit it for your approval. But (*producing the paper*) look what they've done, Sir. They've gone and printed it.'
>
> I am sure that at this point Anthony sounded distraught at this heinous breach of King's Regulations into which his good intentions had led him. The response was exactly what he had foreseen. Colonel Bingham was fatherly, stern yet sympathetic. He knew what these newspapers were, he said; such behaviour was typical. He understood. In future if Cadet Cotterell thought of writing anything for the Press he should come and see him (the CO) first and he would give him the benefit of his advice.
>
> And Cadet Cotterell, having said a fervent 'Thank you, sir,' marched out of the Orderly Room, exonerated without being charged, under the wing instead of the lash of the feared Colonel Bingham.
>
> Attack, Anthony murmured, unoriginally but aptly, is the best defence.[97]

The article had appeared in the *Daily Express*, which remained a significant part of Anthony's writing life. Occasionally other things occurred which were a link back to his glory days in Fleet Street. One evening at the OCTU, he came across a queue of men in civilian clothes, the last remnants of the direct commissioning system – straight from civilian life to officer training. Amongst the group he noticed John Grime and Geoffrey Cox from the *Daily Express*. Grime had been the dramatic critic. Cox had won a great name for himself as a war correspondent, 'but he didn't look like a man with a great name at the moment'.

> They were both pathetically pleased to see a familiar face, and treated me with more than usual respect, perhaps afraid that I might twist their arm or report them to the prefects. Also in the queue I noticed a man who is quite noted as a divorce lawyer. Standing in the queue he looked quite incapable of conducting his own affairs, let alone anyone else's.[98]

At moments like this, Anthony appeared at an advantage to other cadets, but for the vast majority of the time the reverse was painfully true. He did not do at all well at OCTU. He wrote that it was like a hotted-up version of his recruit training, but with the added nervous strain of living up to much higher standards. There was none of the old slap-happy approach; instead everything was grim, dutiful and humourless. 'Of course, this can't last long in any situation. You find your level in the back row of the squad and adjust yourself.'

His lack of engagement simply increased the flippancy with which he regarded the war. As the invasion panic increased, he and his fellow cadets were co-opted into heavy work, digging a tank ditch and constructing wire fences which they sarcastically dubbed the Bingham Line in honour of their Commanding Officer. They had also been allotted an operational role, which was to defend the neighbourhood against attack. Anthony wrote: 'One of our main concerns about the German attack was that if they were going to do it they should do it quickly and enable us to leave the OCTU.'[99]

Meanwhile, his poor aptitude was starkly represented by the reports on his progress written by the Company Commanders:

1st Month [written by Lieutenant A Cooke, Commanding 'A' Company]
Quite satisfactory. Does his best and is reliable. Average.

2nd Month [same officer]
I feel that he tries his best, but by nature he is inclined to be vague. He has progressed. More confidence needed.

3rd Month [writing semi-illegible but looks like a Captain M.A. Graham]
Still trying but needs still more confidence and concentration. When he has acquired these he should do well.

4th Month [same officer]
Rather disappointing. He has still got to overcome his vagueness of manner which is reflected in his work. He must also improve his knowledge of tactics.

The epitaph on his training course was written by Bingham himself: 'He will be quite useful after some practical experience of regimental life and routines.' Anthony appended his initials to this humiliating verdict. His course grade was D, the lowest one could get and still pass.[100] For the man who had won a scholarship to Kings School, Rochester, a scholarship and Governor's Exhibition to Guy's Hospital in London, and, at the age of nineteen, a coveted staff writer's job on Britain's top newspaper, it was nothing short of total, abject failure.

Anthony's course had begun on 29 June and ran until 12 October against a war background of increasing ferocity. The Battle of Britain had been won by the RAF, but on 7 September the Blitz began. Wanstead was close enough to London to be very seriously affected, and Anthony's constant concern over the coming months would be for his mother and father. Ironically, he and Geoffrey, though soldiers, were now much safer than the civilians because they did not live in metropolitan areas. Geoffrey, who was also hoping for officer training, was at present guarding a Midlands aircraft factory. His duties in order of national importance were: to fight and destroy any paratroops who chose to land in the neighbourhood; to stop anybody trespassing in the vicinity of the factory; and to prevent the local farmer's sheep from getting in everywhere, which was the only part of the job which ever happened.[101]

Anthony's letter to his Aunt Janie written just before he left OCTU that October reflects the extraordinary circumstances of the time:

I was glad to hear you had a safe journey home but what are you talking about? Under the circumstances I thought I would write to report that all is as well here as it can be here. We have two warnings a day when the planes pass over towards London but they haven't yet dropped anything here. Funny isn't it? I must say I got a laugh at reading they had hit another newspaper office. [...]

And how are you all at home? We don't go in shelters here thank God, partly because there are none.

Lottie Lamour the current star at the Theatre Royal here tells me that they nearly destroyed East Ham Palace last week. I shall emphasise that Lottie and I are only friends, owing to her awful teeth. Remember me to father.

Love Tone

P.S. I have been quite unable to get you on the phone.[102]

Both Anthony and Geoffrey wrote an account of going home in the Blitz. Anthony's was factual and concerned one specific weekend. Geoffrey's was fictional and probably an amalgam of more than one visit. Neither are dated, but can be placed around January-February 1941.[103] Anthony wrote:

I went home on a Friday. It was nearly a year since I had gone away to war. But instead I was going home to war. The train out from London was late. But, then, it always was. There was the same old porter wheezing along slamming the doors, unchanged except for his tin hat.

The main street was empty. I passed no one but an ARP warden and a policeman. Up above, things had been quiet, but now they were hotting up. The barrage was on and in the flashes you could see the ruins of the row of shops which Mother had written to say had been destroyed.

Home looked just the same. I pushed open the door and walked into the dark, empty hall. 'Come on down, we're in the cellar,' Mother called up.

I walked downstairs into a new way of living. Mother and Father were in the coal cellar, both in bed and fully dressed. And in a third bed there was Mrs Long, wife of the doctor across the road. Their house had been destroyed by incendiary bombs, her children evacuated and her husband was the head ARP doctor, so if he got any sleep he got it round at the squash courts, which were now the ARP Headquarters. So she slept in our cellar.

The cellars were a superb ready-made refuge, which would have survived everything except a direct hit. Steps under the main staircase led down to a tiny passageway, 15ft x 4ft, off which ran two narrow compartments. In these were six camp beds, a hoard of old trunks and school tuck boxes, and the family's stores of tinned food, beer, wine, sherry and whisky. Mintie had done her best to make the place homely. Besides each bed lay a book, or some *Picture Post* or *Lilliput* magazines. The whitewashed walls were draped with some old chintz coverings. In its own way, it was both cosy and comfortable.

Anthony's account continued:

Mother got up to get me something to eat. 'It's lovely to see you, darling,' she said placidly. The kitchen walls were shaking as the guns barraged around us and a German aircraft droned overhead.

'Aren't you frightened?' I said.

'Well, I was at first. I was afraid to come in here alone, but now I don't mind.'

Father came in to watch me eat. He had been outside scouting around. 'I thought I heard something hit the roof, and you've got to watch out for those small incendiary bombs,' he said.

'What are your reactions to all this?' I asked him.

'Horror and terror,' he said. 'But the funny thing is you worry more about your house than yourself.'

The following day Geoffrey arrived on weekend leave. In his novel *Then a Soldier*, he would describe Robert Halbrook and his friend, Les Pawley, getting off their train and going straight down to the tube at Euston, where they saw the incredible scene of 'the thousands of improvised beds, the hastily collected private belongings which seemed grotesquely out of place'. They watched it all speechlessly. 'They had only heard about it vaguely and they never quite believed that it really could be true ... Each tube station they passed through was the same, crowded and fantastic and exciting.' Those trying to sleep stared at the passers-by 'with a kind of hostility'. Quarrels were going on over space, not only on the platforms, but on the stairs and every usable corner.[104]

Robert, Geoffrey's fictional alter-ego, was going to Watham Heath, the fictional equivalent of Wanstead. The journey ran via Bethnal Green, Stratford, and Leytonstone. When his train finally pulled out of Liverpool Street, Robert found the surrealistic nature of the experience extraordinary.

It was odd to look out at the familiar shapes of the buildings, to reflect that only half an hour before they had been the scene of a battle. When you considered the years you had made this journey, until the stops were so familiar to you that you did not have to look up to know where you were, it was crazy.

Robert arrived at Watham Heath in the starry darkness of an intense blackout. As he walked home to the fictional counterpart of Ham Frith, an air raid began. The guns of the local Ack-Ack were very nearby and deafeningly loud, but beyond the noise they made he could just hear 'a queer, regular little tinkle'. At first he thought it must be tiles falling from roofs, or glass. Then he realised it was shell splinters. 'His tin helmet, webbing, rifle, were all merely theatrical make-up. All he cared about was getting back, sheltered from the storm.'[105]

Both Anthony's and Geoffrey's accounts tell of a local elderly lady named Miss Howard (or, in *Then a Soldier*, Mrs Elliott) who had refused to use a shelter. Miss Howard and her house did not exist anymore. The dangers were extremely real, but what both the brothers were amazed by was the astonishingly blasé behaviour of the civilians – Mintie, Graham, and their Wanstead friends. Geoffrey's fictionalised account describes them all as wearing extraordinary clothes, the women in siren suits with their hair done up in a scarf (the quintessential and rather modish war outfit), and the men in old dirty clothes, suitable for scrambling about in when one was watching for incendiaries. All seemed actually rather happy with the shake-up of their comfortable routine middle-class life; the women in particular, after years of being confined to domestic life, at last had a public-spirited job of work to do. The calm at home during a bombing raid seemed almost lunatic. Despite the continuous anti-aircraft gunfire, the occasional crumping of a bomb, and the house shaking with the fantastic detonations, it was like being in 'a safe, serene madhouse in the middle of an inferno'. Robert, Geoffrey's fictional alter-ego, later realised that far from being mad 'they had all developed the mentality of a front line fighter, the panickless common sense which makes a hell bearable'.

On the last day of their visit, Anthony and Geoffrey played golf with their father and his friend Mr Townley. Anthony wrote:

The only difference was that the guns were going off intermittently; and as Father was playing out of the bomb crater at the sixth, Mr. Townley pointed up and said, 'Look, there's a dog-fight going on.' But though Geoffrey and I wanted to watch, the civilians were too blasé; the fight had to be over their noses before they gave it a second glance. Besides, two women playing behind were shouting 'Fore', so we had to go on.

It was dusk on Monday afternoon. Mother and Father had just driven Geoffrey off to town on his way back to camp. 'I can't bear to think what I shall feel when you're both gone again,' Mother said. When they had gone I sat in the lounge and played old gramophone records. 'Two Sleepy People', 'These Foolish Things', 'You Go to my Head' – they were all sodden with nostalgia and significance. Jokes and parties, love affairs and quarrels, came tumbling back to mind; the sentimental trivia of an age that ended while we were sitting on the lawn that Sunday morning in September 1939.[106]

The Sunday morning he was referring to was 3 September, when the family had heard Chamberlain's radio announcement that the country was at war with Germany. Alone in the house, awaiting his parents' return, Anthony's mind conjured up the ghosts of a life which had gone beyond recall. Then the Ack-Ack started up, and he could hear the droning of an enemy aircraft. Shrugging off his reverie, he went to do the blackout.

7

PLATOON COMMANDER, INFANTRY BATTALION

O n 19 October 1940, Anthony, now a 2nd Lieutenant, set off by train for his first officer posting. It was with the 11th Royal Fusiliers at Tenby in South Wales. Typically, Anthony delayed his departure to make the most of his last hours of freedom and caught the afternoon train. As his transport at the other end had been arranged for an earlier train, there would be nobody there to meet him when he arrived.

Sometime after midnight, Anthony reached Tenby and found his way on foot through the small sleeping town. His destination, the requisitioned Coburg Hotel, was dark, silent, and firmly locked up. After knocking hard for a while, he was let in by a half-dressed soldier who showed him into an interior crowded with Victoriana. Some mildly farcical scenes ensued whilst the soldier tried to find Anthony a bed, at one point thunderously knocking on the door of their Commanding Officer, then standing aside for Anthony to make his own arrangements. Anthony instantly recognised that the Major, 'a martial figure even in his pyjamas', wasn't at all pleased at being disturbed. He withdrew hastily before 'the full tide of his displeasure found expression'. A bed was eventually found elsewhere.[107]

A day or so later, Anthony wrote to his parents to tell them of his arrival:

Dear mother and father

I arrived here at 2am. Saturday morning. I had to bang on the windows to get in the hotel ... Finally a batman let me in, but he didn't know where I was to sleep. I had to wake someone up and sleep in his room. He ordered the batman to get me some coffee and sandwiches. The bed was very comfortable. For breakfast I had cornflakes, mackerel (very good) and bacon and eggs. But the coffee is bad. My fellow officers seem very nice but apparently their only interests in life are Rugger and the Army, neither of which entertain me at all. One of the first questions was 'What games do you play?' 'None,' I said. Really at first glance the most agreeable person is the chaplain. Certainly he is the most sophisticated.

I am happy to say there doesn't seem much work to do. I have been given a batman. His name is Barter. He acts like Kenneth Kove. 'I only hope I'll be alright sir,' he said. 'I'm sure you will, Barter,' I said jovially.

This batman business really is stupid. There are about 20 officers living in this hotel so there are 20 men hanging about the place with nothing to do but help the hotel staff. They do everything for you. You don't have to move.[108]

Kenneth Kove was a light comedian, ideal for playing a clueless curate in the famous Aldwych Theatre farces written by Ben Travers. Both Geoffrey and Anthony loved these shows, and Anthony must have derived considerable private amusement from Barter's manner.

Being waited upon hand and foot by Barter was just one part of a new, amazingly civilised way of life. Inured to being harried, bullied and shouted at, Anthony could scarcely believe it when, on his first morning at The Coburg, he was allowed to wake up and get up in his own time. A cup of tea was brought to him, and his roommate's batman then suggested that he might like a bath. It was shattering.

Later Anthony was introduced to his commanding officer, the Major, now out of pyjamas and into an immaculate uniform. The Major was a regular soldier, wedded to military life, and because of this had an entirely different outlook to Anthony. During their three or four months together, their fundamental differences would at times become starkly apparent. On that first day he seemed rather formidable but then Anthony was used to COs being formidable. 'What was so unnerving was his politeness. Within strict limits this bristling Major treated me as a human being – after life in the ranks I couldn't understand it.'

Over the course of the next few days, another pleasant surprise awaited him – his fellow officers were nothing like as dully meritorious as they had appeared at first. When they had asked him what games he played, Anthony's heart sank at the thought of being 'compelled to play games on top of everything else'. But it soon turned out that none of them were at all keen on games either. He completely revised his first impression, writing that the general level of intelligence and amiability in the mess was pleasantly high, 'they seemed to be mostly lawyers or something of the kind'.

Anthony's role at Tenby was Rifle Platoon Commander. Very soon after his arrival, he met his platoon, the men he was supposed to lead into battle if Britain was invaded. They were scrubbing out their billets in a requisitioned boarding house. It was a winter's morning by the seaside and reminded Anthony of 'the more depressing qualities of washing day in an industrial town'.

Anthony was never a man of the people type. In his first weeks in the Army, he had tried hard to accept the democratic nature of a conscription system in which everyone was equal, but by nature he was an elitist who firmly believed in the meritocracy of talent. He was not good with uneducated people and he completely lacked the common touch. Having been forced to muck in with the lower ranks during his first four months in the Army, he did not particularly want to have anything more to do with them. But as Platoon Officer, all of a sudden here were some 25 more of them for whom he bore the primary responsibility.

One of his most important duties was ensure his men's physical well-being. This included inspecting their meals, checking their quarters, and minutely examining their kit to make sure that it would not cause health problems. His very first duty as the new Platoon Officer was to inspect his men's boots to make sure that they were in good repair. One pair was in a terrible state. Anthony asked the boots' owner if he had been drying them in a fire, but the man, not seeing the joke, strongly denied the suggestion. Anthony found it difficult to feel sufficiently indignant with him, or any of the subsequent offenders or malingerers who came to his notice in his first few days as an officer.

Though he would, in time, develop a fine authoritative bark, Anthony would never get used to being a leader of men. He was both too apt to sympathise with rebels against authority, and too impatient with those who were lazy or work-shy because of his own strong self-discipline and driving work ethic.

Soon after his arrival at Tenby he faced a major ordeal, getting his platoon ready for the Brigadier's annual inspection of the Brigade. This required 'a week of scrubbing and nagging'. Each man had to be perfect from top to toe. His boots must be clean but not shone, with the laces tied in the manner laid down by the battalion. His equipment must be clean and blancoed evenly to 'the locally prescribed shade of green'. His tin hat must be worn straight, 'not at an appealing angle'. And so on and so forth, including the way the man stood and the set of his shoulders.

Finally the terrifying day came. Anthony was extremely nervous, desperately hoping that his men were properly turned out and that he knew enough of their personal details, such as who had been on leave recently and who had had their homes bombed, or any other details which the Brigadier might ask for.

In filthy weather, in pouring rain, they all ranged up on the parade ground.

> They were coming nearer now, the Brigadier and his attendants and the CO and the Adjutant, and all the other members of a perfect audience to make a fool of myself in front of. A stray couple of butterflies danced through my stomach.
>
> 'No 3 Platoon – Tchun!' I shouted.
>
> The great man had the assurance of a god, which, locally, he was. He walked slowly along the front rank scrutinising each petrified face as if it was an identity parade.
>
> 'That's not the way to do your bootlaces,' he said, menacingly incisive, pointing with his stick at a ruckled, loosened lace. 'Did you notice that when you inspected your platoon, Platoon Commander?'
>
> 'No, sir.'
>
> 'Well, that's the sort of thing you ought to.'[109]

After picking up another couple of, to the Brigadier's eye, glaring mistakes and leaving Anthony's credibility as an officer in tatters, the great man moved on.

Apart from the trials of being in charge of his men, Anthony thoroughly enjoyed Tenby. It had a picturesque setting and the weather was consistently warm for the time of year. However, as was always the way with delightful postings, this blissful interlude was short-lived. In a letter home, typed by some minion on 11th Battalion Royal Fusiliers notepaper, Anthony told his mother that they were moving to Malvern. He also informed her airily:

> Life as an officer has a lot to commend it under present conditions. There is simply no need to do any work at all on most days. I am well into my novel, using a soldier for secretarial purposes. [...]
>
> We have had rather a lot of rain, and on returning from inspecting breakfast I was blown off my bike (we each have a bike, though I haven't today as it has been stolen). So far I have only heard the sirens once. How are you? Are you all right? It's a pity we are moving, you would have liked this place.[110]

He had been asked to start a battalion magazine, but did not like the idea of working for nothing. He hardly had the spare time. In addition to his novel, he was keeping another very detailed diary, as well as conducting a survey similar to those which he had carried out at the *Daily Express*. There were thirty main questions, including 'How often do you get browned off?' and 'What bores you most about the Army?' Anthony tabulated the answers on two large sheets of squared paper – 'the whole thing was strictly meaningless but it kept me from being bored'. The questionnaire would gradually metamorphose into his second Army book, *Oh, It's Nice to be in the Army!*, a title which Anthony greatly disliked but which was chosen by his publisher, Victor Gollancz. He would write the book extremely quickly, and finish it by March 1941.

Sometime in the previous autumn, Victor Gollancz had accepted *What! No Morning Tea?* for publication. When writing to Mintie to tell her that the book was coming out shortly, Anthony did not express any enthusiasm or hopes about it; his private fear must have been that it would be a nondescript flop like his first book. But once he was at Malvern, something wonderful happened which utterly transformed *What! No Morning Tea?*'s prospects – the *Daily Express* bought it for serialisation. Writing three years later, Anthony quietly laid out what this stupendous piece of good news meant to him:

That was quite a moment. Life seemed to be starting all over again, for of course it automatically guaranteed that the book, which was coming out in a few days' time, wouldn't just lie down and die. I went on leave the same day and never felt happier in my life.[111]

Finally the day came when *What! No Morning Tea?* was published. It was a small book, clad in the standard wartime dust-jacket of dark cream paper with black and cerise type. Priced at 4s 6d, it was a mere 150 pages long but it was about to turn the conventional, flag-waving image of the British Army on its head. Serialised in the *Daily Express*, it became an instant hit. The first edition sold out immediately, as did the two reprints which appeared in the same month. Despite saying many things which were anathema to conventional military types, the book's message – that soldiers were human and that conscripts should be treated as rational, sentient beings – chimed perfectly with the concerns of early 1941. Since the appalling shock of the German conquest of western Europe, morale in the British Army had become a major concern for top soldiers and politicians. Within two months, the book would become recommended reading for Army officers. Within five months it would come to the notice of the big guns in Army welfare and education, who would then arrange for Anthony's transfer to the War Office and radically transform his role in the Army. The book's success would set in train the complex series of events which would, in time, lead Anthony to Brummen.

A copy of it was sent to Anthony's parents, and in an undated letter, written in early January 1941, he asked Mintie what she thought of it. Whilst he was writing the letter, her own letter to him turned up, praising the book. He continued, 'I am glad you liked it. The only thing against it as I see it is that the general atmosphere is a little too peaceful. A pre-broomstick army production.' Anthony's plan to capture a unique moment in time, one which he was uniquely qualified to write about, had succeeded magnificently. [112]

Success was marvellous, but Anthony still felt imprisoned by army life. He struggled on, doing as little as he possibly could whilst spending almost all his spare time – and much of his official time – writing. Undeniably he was a liability as an infantry officer. At times it was only his considerable wit, charm, masterly acting skills and genius for telling lies which kept him out of serious trouble. There were periods when he tried extremely hard to be dutiful and to do his best, but they were more often than not sabotaged by his lifelong tendency to vagueness and inattention when a subject or task did not particularly interest him. His mind focused on the far more fascinating things bubbling inside it, and he lost the faculty to see what lay right under his nose. Clearly he could not keep up with the minutiae of his command, and so he became an unabashed liar whenever necessary. His CO, the bristling Major, might ask him a question like 'How many latrine buckets have you got, Anthony?' and he would reply smartly 'Six, sir,' without having the vaguest idea.

Lying was, of course, one of the essentials of army life, and Anthony was by no means the only one who resorted to it. The difference was that he was quite brazen about it and would admit some of these crimes in his book, *An Apple for the Sergeant*. They appeared in print for all his erstwhile commanding officers to see, but by the autumn of 1944 when the book appeared Anthony had become close to untouchable.

On those occasions when he was caught out, he believed that the best course of action was the immediate confession of full responsibility. 'Say it was your fault even if it wasn't, try not to point to extenuating circumstances, on no account try to pass the buck to someone else.' This was the only way to take rockets, rocket being officer slang for a formal reproof, and this type of rocket being something with which Anthony was to become very well acquainted.

One arraignment – for going on a weekend's leave without the proper permission – took place before the Second-In-Command and the Adjutant, the Major fortunately being away. Anthony wrote:

It is remarkable how effective this kind of telling-off is for, looking at the thing from a completely unscrupulous point of view, you know before you start that there is nothing much they can do to you. They aren't going to cashier you for an offence of this kind. They might make you duty officer for fourteen days running. This would be inconvenient but by no means insufferable. But in point of fact I felt just as anxious as I did on similar occasions at school when there was the immediate probability of being bent over a chair. Officers' discipline in the small offences is based on making a man feel that he has played a pretty poor trick and let down people who trusted him, with the background point that he is making things worse for his brother officers. Then there is the embarrassment of living in the same house with a man who has just told you these things. Altogether it is a very effective system.[113]

Ironically, the very success of *What! No Morning Tea?* was now bringing its own problems. It had awoken the interests and ambitions which he had tried so hard to lull into dormancy because being unable to follow them was so painful. The conflict in his mind and heart became intense, and Anthony began to find army life extremely difficult. He tended to drink far too much – 'drink was the only solution, but a very pleasant solution after all'. Coming back from leave was always a very bad time for him. Once, on returning to Malvern after an extended leave, he wrote of 'the paranoiac gloom', 'the feeling of being sucked back into circumstances quite out of control and almost certainly uncomfortable'. He condensed his view of army life into a short, dark, evocative passage, which showed how hopeless he often felt:

The Army. What a game!
  Always waiting, and thinking about the past. Waiting in the cold dark outside call boxes.
  Extraordinary comfort of primitive beds. Hours spent standing in fields; hours subtracted from any part of the twenty-four, perhaps around dawn, perhaps about midnight, perhaps all the appalling day. Just standing in a field waiting for some unfortunates to advance over a hill. Waiting for the RAF to give a demonstration, in the almost certain knowledge that it would be cancelled at the last minute. Then the long march back, the long way round. Dragging agony of equipment becoming progressively heavier and deader.[114]

The contrast between army life and what he had been doing on the extended leave was acutely painful. People whom he respected were beginning to get very interested in him, and he was once again moving in influential circles. He had been seeing a good deal of American and British newspaper people, who were all full of plans of covering the war in some exciting location. Loss of liberty could not be easily borne when he mixed with other men of his own age group who had not been conscripted.

For part of his leave he had stayed in the same house as Quentin Reynolds, the celebrated American journalist and radio broadcaster with the marvellous gravelly voice, who was then approaching the zenith of his renown. On Anthony's first night back in Malvern as he lay in bed, trying to sleep, he kept thinking about Reynolds: 'No doubt at this moment he would be sitting happily having a quiet drink in some congenial restaurant. Thousands of people were doing that all over the world. Why not me?'[115]

Reynolds and Anthony had almost certainly been staying at Coppins, the Kent farm which belonged to Sidney Bernstein, the Deputy Director of the Film Division of the Ministry of Information. Bernstein, who owned the Granada string of cinemas, was a producer of wartime documentary films such as *London Can Take It*. Reynolds had spoken the commentary for this famous film made in 1940 about the Blitz.

Bernstein was extremely wealthy, tall and elegant with a slightly squashed-in face like a boxer. His wife, Zoe Farmer, was dark-haired, and very chic and attractive. She had been a journalist on the *Daily Express* and was a great friend of Anthony's. A little older than him, she had taught him much about the ways of the world when, some three or four years earlier, they had had an affair. It had not been an intense relationship but more of a casual sexual fling which had nonetheless left them very close. It would almost certainly have been Zoe who had invited Anthony to Coppins.[116]

An invitation to the Bernsteins' house was a splendid treat – they were extraordinarily hospitable hosts and their dinner parties were legendary. Coppins was both a meeting place for highly gifted and influential people and a refuge from the nightly bombing raids on London. On some nights the German bombers flew directly over the farm on their way to the capital, and a few moments later the Bernsteins' guests would see the London searchlights moving like slender attenuated fingers around the sky. On the bombers' return, they would sometimes jettison their bombs in the neighbourhood. One night some fell so close that they shook the farm and annoyed the prize bull, who bellowed angrily in his stall.[117]

Coppins was a reminder of the glittering fashionable world which Anthony had lost. Returning to his bare Malvern billet put him in a very gloomy humour. Before his leave, he had heard rumours that his battalion was locating closer to London, and he had had visions of trips to town and at least an occasional taste of civilised life. When he got back, however, Philip, a fellow officer, disabused him of this happy notion, saying it was going to be hell where they were going – 'company messes, stand tos all day and night' – and that they wouldn't be allowed out of the company lines for more than about an hour at a time. Britain was in the grip of another invasion panic, and the battalion were going to be part of the defensive front line.

Anthony wrote in his diary:

> After lunch I sat around watching the batman pack my things. I walked up to the town and bought some books for the journey and a gramophone record. I went to the Priory tearooms where I have been for tea most days since we have been here, I am sitting there now as I write; I wonder how long it will be before the faces of the people who run it will be unrecognisable again; life nowadays is nothing but reshuffle, one long goodbye.
>
> I walked back to the mess and back up to the town, back to the mess again and back to the town. We had soup, cold meat and tinned pineapple for supper. I went to bed soon after. When they said we were going to the south coast I had visions of Sunday trips to town, but the RASC Captain who is staying with us to superintend the move showed us where we are going on the map; it might as well be BugBug.[118]

This prolonged strain of gloom, bad-tempered moping, and selfish thoughts of his own discomfort was extremely uncharacteristic of Anthony. The disgruntled mood persisted throughout the move, which he wrote up in his diary in a classic piece of griping:

> Reveille was at 2am, breakfast at 2.30am.
>
> We are now on a high ridge with a high wind blowing through the broken windows of the coach. It is 9.20am, on a Sunday morning. We have been on the move five hours and sitting in the coach for six. I managed to doze a bit but very twisted and cramped. Some have been sleeping all through, they could sleep on a clothes line. The others have been swearing at each other, cursing every aspect of the journey, It was like all Army journeys, unexplained delays and apparently endless. It was cold before daylight. I wrapped myself in blankets like a squaw and the driver lent me a bit of sacking as a substitute window pane. [...]
>
> About ten o'clock we stopped for about 40 minutes in the edge of a market town. No one knew what it was called because no one knew where we were, or cared.
>
> The street we stopped in was no Rue de la Paix, aspidistra-ridden Victorian houses and pin-money general shops but of the kind that stay open on Sundays. We couldn't buy any food but I

got a glass of milk at a dairy and a cottager gave me a cup of coffee which was however horrible. I was then cheered up a great deal by buying the Sunday papers and finding my book advertised in them.

We moved on, nearly everyone falling asleep, I read the papers. An hour later we had to get out and push the bus up a hill. We didn't stop for dinner but I didn't feel hungry; one gets very inured to these journeys, the nice thing about them is that you aren't called on to do anything. We drove straight on until 3.40pm, when we arrived in a lane leading past a farm. We were ordered to debus, men are very sluggish after such a long journey, and marched into the farm.

The men were billeted in barns. We were greeted by some RE's who were there as staff to look after the billets which for the current ten days of mass moving were being used by different convoys every night.

'Will there be any food tonight sir?' the RASC driver asked me with the unconcern of one used to the answer being no.

'Everything alright?' I asked the platoon when they were all lying round the hay-carpeted barn floor. One man said 'Well it's a bit rough like sir,' but otherwise the response was not overwhelming.

'One thing I can't stand is blasted farmyards,' said the CSM. 'Always such a bloody mess they are.'

Having attended to the discomfort of the men we went to find our own quarters. [...]

It was still awfully early, when you get up at 2.30am it makes a nice long day. I went to bed at 8.30pm.

The appalling journey continued the following day – another early start, then hours and hours of sitting on the coach. Light-headed with boredom and fatigue, Anthony and his fellow junior officer, John, did something extremely silly.

At 10.20am we stopped; there was a certain amount of comment about the stopping place which was apparently miles from anywhere as usual. John the other subaltern and I walked off down the road and found an admirable olde worlde teashop where we had a boiled egg, read the papers and bought some sandwiches for lunch. We came back in great humour and walked up to the Major. 'We've been doing very well, sir,' I said.

He looked bayonets at us.

'Were you given permission to leave this column?' he demanded in an iced voice.

'No sir.'

'Then will you kindly see that this does not happen again. Whatever are you thinking of, leaving the line of march? I've been over half the countryside where your men have been wandering. Will you kindly control them in future. That is your job, not mine.' And he strode off down the road.

We got back into the coaches feeling rather bedraggled, but Somerset Maugham was right when he said that it you write it all down it soon stops bothering you.[119]

In the late afternoon, they finally arrived at their new posting. Though Anthony does not give the location in his diary, other details suggest that it was between West Itchenor and West Wittering, opposite Thorney and Hayling Islands, very close to Chichester Harbour. Chichester, Portsmouth, Southampton, and the Isle of Wight, were all seeing a huge build-up of defences in anticipation of a German invasion.

The battalion's new quarters were in flat marshy countryside on the coast. It was a holiday area, with numerous bungalows and a holiday camp, but so rural and isolated that when Anthony went into Chichester some weeks later he felt as if he was going to New York. The plus side was that, by Army standards, the accommodation was luxurious. Anthony's platoon were allotted three requisitioned houses and a bungalow. After discovering this, Anthony wrote rather more cheerfully:

> The men can practically have a room each. Although a lot of people are still living in the neighbourhood many of the houses are empty and a high proportion have been left furnished. The billets are extraordinary in that you keep finding things like primus stoves and bicycles, and coal in the cellars and even flour. The troops we took over from just couldn't be bothered to take it away.
>
> This and the empty houses all round make it seem like occupying abandoned enemy territory. We found a wireless set in my bungalow and all sorts of kettles and crockery, not to mention a motor boat in the garage.
>
> As dark fell it started raining. My room is quite pleasant with French windows, though a deplorable outlook onto a grass patch and the back door of another bungalow. Subalterns sleep with their platoons, the Major and the second in command at the Officers' mess which is about 200 yards of mud away. [...]
>
> After dinner I came back and worked in my room, it has a rather pleasant open red-brick fireplace. My bed was made up on the floor but with a mattress, so perfectly comfortable. I rather enjoy the business of making oneself comfortable in new quarters, it's the sort of petty adventure I like, when successful of course.[120]

In telling the story of this posting at the deserted wartime seaside, Anthony would produce some of his very best diary writing. As usual, he did not mind portraying himself in a not particularly admirable light. One of the great characters in the diary is the Major, who was very buoyed up by the move to a critical area of national defence. A professional soldier to his fingertips, at times he must have found Anthony's casual attitude infuriating. Anthony tended to report his contacts with his commanding officer in the manner of a flip, highly intelligent sixth-former. The polar difference between the two men was typified in Anthony's brief account of one particular breakfast time shortly after they arrived.

> I was reading the *Strand Magazine* at breakfast when the Major came in from an early morning tour of inspection. 'What are your platoon doing this morning Anthony?' he asked. He had me there.
>
> 'I didn't know what plans you had for us, sir.'
>
> 'Well in that case you should have asked me. A leg stretcher I think, yes, go for a leg stretcher from ten to half past twelve.'[121]

Anthony had been dawdling over his meal, reading magazine articles and no doubt assessing them with an acute journalistic eye. Meanwhile, the Major had been briskly up and about, ensuring that his particular stretch of the national defences was in tip-top working order. Given the war situation at the time, it is very difficult not to side with the Major against Anthony.

In justice to Anthony, within his own lights he did his best. He was not like a fellow writer and journalist Julian Maclaren-Ross, who simply could not cope with the clash between his own vainglorious self-image and the brutish demands of the Army.[122] Anthony made no attempt to escape by cultivating a nervous breakdown; he played the hand which he had been dealt by fate, and within a few months he would prove to be an enormous asset to the Army.

Saintly forbearance, however, was not something which he ever specialised in. Privately he characterised the Major as being a 'rather naive enquirer' about non-Army subjects. One dinner he became extremely irritated with him when the Major started sounding off about newspaper ethics and methods in writing about Army matters. Though Anthony often felt very critical himself, he resented criticism from outsiders and felt that he knew a great deal more about this particular subject than the Major. His irritation led to a lengthy diatribe in the diary, in which he said all the things he had wanted to say about 'this anti-newspaper nonsense'. He had not turned his intellectual firepower on the Major at dinner – after all, he was his commanding officer.

Yet almost against his own wishes Anthony developed something very close to respect for this man so utterly different from himself. He characterised him as 'very upright, very military, very shy, complete with an Army moustache and a prominent sense of integrity'. The Major did not talk much, and was unsophisticated about much of the world beyond the Army, but he was hard-working, efficient, dedicated, and practical. As Anthony wrote, 'there was nothing ragtime about his approach. He liked everything to be in its proper place and was persistent to have it so.'

The Major stood up as 'the champion of the ten commandments and a glass of port to your dinner as the basis of a sound life'. Anthony thought that there was considerable soundness in another of the Major's views – that professional soldiers were less selfish than civilians. Perhaps referring to some recent infuriating experience in London, Anthony added, 'Most professional soldiers I have met have a pronounced quality of selflessness and integrity on a far more practical plane than a lot of the people who sit around the W.1. grills denouncing blimps – and red tape.'

There is even something close to affectionate amusement in a tiny anecdote about the Major late in their professional relationship: 'At dinner the Major said, "I always say that any fool can make himself uncomfortable but it takes a man of character and vision to make himself comfortable in difficult conditions. Pass the port Anthony."'[123]

In addition to charting his relationship with the Major, Anthony's diary focused on the domestic virtues he was expected to cultivate in looking after the needs of his men. It made him feel 'quite a family man' arranging how the meals were to be done, and making sure that there was enough coal and bath water. The one household problem he did not have was 'What shall we have for dinner today?' because the food always arrived in a truck the night before. His keen eye also noted what others had done unbidden to improve the communal living quarters; for example, the dining room now had table cloths because one of the men had found some old curtains, washed them, and sowed them together.

The problems of living in a war area were sometimes funny, sometimes sad, sometimes just plain macabre. The local Home Guard commander over-zealously brought in a water-logged camera found on the beach because it had been lying 'suspiciously near a bomb crater'. A golfer who wandered into a minefield was blown up and all that came down were his boots (this tale may well have been apocryphal).

One of the platoon's large attachment of stray dogs was run over; the poor animal was in a very bad way and so Anthony's men shot it. Anthony, who loved dogs, would not have enjoyed this incident at all. He was completely unprepared for the reaction of a woman in a nearby house:

[She came out] running, shouting and carrying on.
'Call yourself a man?' she screamed – well, almost screamed – at me. 'You fancy yourself, donchew? Shooting a poor little animal. Great coward, you. You make me sick. Don't half fancy yourself, donchew?'
It always takes me a minute or two to find my tongue on these occasions, but once I have summoned up my little stock of self-assertion I think it pays to be aggressive. 'Back to your kitchen, you silly trollop,' I said firmly; and immediately regretted it, thinking perhaps I had gone too far. But it worked. She stopped in mid-sentence, looked at me uncertainly, and withdrew.[124]

Anthony's men buried the unfortunate dog.

Beyond the human and animal dramas, there were the problems of creating, maintaining and extending the anti-invasion defences. The coast was being eaten up at about a foot a week, and the sea-wall had caved in several months earlier except for one stubbornly resistant section. This blocked a defensive line of fire, and so the men tried to undermine it by digging. They made one small hole and the sea began doing the rest frighteningly fast. The bren gun post they had been building looked like it was going to be pulled in. As Anthony noted, bren gun siting here was an impossible choice – if you put the post far enough inland to allow for a few months' erosion, it was useless for defence as you lost your field of view.

Always observing the tiny vivid details, Anthony recorded two rabbits he saw running along the beach, commenting with his characteristic wit, 'I never thought rabbits were at all maritime'. The rabbits were just a tiny part of the extreme oddity of it all. It was a strange world that the soldiers were living in, halfway between the ghosts of the old holiday resort and the baleful threats of the present. Anthony found it very intriguing:

> Somebody ought to tell John Steinbeck about this place; it has a fascinating atmosphere of decay.[125] I walked down along the front this morning. The beach huts are tumbling to ruin, their doors swing in the wind and inside you find a chaos of old paraffin lamps and broken furniture. I took an inventory of one. There was a smashed-up table, a couple of deckchair frames, a sunshade, a banjo case, faded cotton curtains flapping through the broken windows, and on the floor a record of 'Body and Soul'. I sat on the little railing outside, there was a board nailed to it with the name of the hut 'Wy-Wurry'. Sitting on the railing I couldn't see the sea, the concrete and barbed wire defence works came in the way; all along the beach in either direction there were soldiers sitting with bren guns in little emplacements.[126]

But mostly the practical military view had to prevail over romantic decay. The junior officers – Anthony, Stephen and John – walked the area like demi-gods, deciding which houses they wanted for billets, and which ones had to be knocked down. Stephen and John took the defence situation more seriously than Anthony, but not *that* seriously.

> I spent the afternoon on the beach discussing new wiring and weapon position arrangements. It was a lovely afternoon and the tide was out; it is true that the Army gets you into good scenery as well as bad, including the shot-down German bomber which you can see on the beach at low tide. This business of fixing on how to defend a place can be an interminable business. One difficulty is that you have to be very diffident about knocking down private property in order to get a clear field of view. Stephen and John had an awfully long conversation.
> 'Personally I think the worse thing we have to fear is attack by parachutists from the rear.'
> 'I'd like to get the Vickers on that roof.'
> 'You must curb this itch of yours to get off the ground. It's the sure route to being blown to pieces.'
> 'If we have it there we shall be swamped by the tides, remember the spring tides are coming.'
> And so on until teatime.[127]

8

'PLEASANTLY IRRESPONSIBLE AND RELATIVELY ENTERTAINING'

Whilst he had been at Malvern, Anthony had taken the short preliminary course for training as a Liaison or Motor Contact Officer (MCO). Shortly after he had joined the Royal Fusiliers, he had met a young officer who had chosen this specialisation and Anthony had decided that it would be just the thing for himself. The MCO's job was to liaise with units which had been cut off by battle or other untoward circumstances; he carried orders to the isolated units, found out what was happening there, and reported back to HQ. Anthony wrote:

> Potentially a job of frightening responsibility in battle, it was not at all bad at other times. First of all you were relatively your own master. Secondly [...] you had to spend a lot of time going round units in the pleasantly irresponsible and relatively entertaining capacity of visiting officer from a higher formation.[128]

There would be no men to look after, no boots to inspect, none of the domestic responsibilities of Platoon Officer. There was, however, one major disadvantage – all the travelling had to be done by motorbike. Anthony was not good with things mechanical; following his usual form in the Army, he had only just scraped through the preliminary MCO course. But it was enough. In early March 1941, notification came through that he was to begin on the full MCO course, and so, without much repining he said farewell to his infantry battalion and the men of his platoon.

The MCO course took in map-reading, orienteering, calculating the effects of terrain, and other such esoteric matters. It also meant mastering the motorbike, and just as critically knowing how to maintain it and keep it going in a crisis. Once again, Anthony had no natural aptitude for any of this. He would write of being taught to service his machine:

> The afternoon was spent in the garage, first listening to another lecture from the Scots mechanic. It was about the carburettor, more I did not learn.
> Others seemed to be having the time of their lives, but though I have tried in a mild way I find it almost impossible to be anything but indifferent to the internal combustion engine. From 3–4pm we were ordered to maintenance our bikes, oiling, greasing, blowing up tyres, etc. Someone said I handled the oil can as if I couldn't believe it existed.[129]

The course was held at Oxford, with Anthony's billet being at Brasenose. Soon after arriving he discovered that the Commandant of the School had been at King's School with him, where they had both taken organ lessons. That was about the only bright spot. The course schedule looked appalling – 9.00am to 7.00pm every day, and night work. The long hours were unwelcome, but so were the dangers which were now graphically pointed out to him for the first time.

After breakfast the batman told me that it was a very hard course and there were usually one or two in hospital. He pointed out of the window at two figures hobbling across the quad bent over two sticks. 'Those gentlemen were on the last course,' he said. I could not easily forget this conversation.[130]

It was no idle piece of gossip. Before the end of the course, the Commandant and a former journalist with *The Mirror*, John Irwin, met head-on round a corner and were both seriously injured. The Commandant landed on his jaw; Irwin broke his leg and was looking at a recovery period of six months or more.

Wartime Oxford was a boom town, the hotels crowded and the streets packed. Anthony did not take well to any of it, and wrote one or two ill-humoured diary entries about the locals. After so long in the Army, he could not tolerate the contrast between the students and the armed forces – 'The students look appalling, long hair, stupid clothes.' One evening he and John Irwin (this was before Irwin's accident) went to the Randolph Hotel for a drink.

Standing next to each other at the bar were an RAF DSO and DFC and a young man with velvet trousers, rings on his fingers and a red carnation in his buttonhole.[131] Quite a little contrast in war effort.

We spent the evening with people whose whole life seemed to consist in knowing other people. Never was there such a cavalcade of pretentious nonentity names. Every incident considered in the conversation was preceded by do you know Hugo Earlyman or do you know Brian this or Guy that. All of them taking flats from each other and giving parties at which people threw themselves downstairs or locked themselves in the bathroom or had terrible arguments. There are an enormous circle of these miscellaneous semi-intelligent people. It seems to take an awful lot of mental shams to produce one good mind.[132]

Anthony had never been to university himself, having gone straight from school to medical and dental studies at Guy's Hospital. Being rational and worldly, with an intolerant view of posturing and self-indulgence, he found the students both childish and spoilt. He does not seem to have much liked Oxford either, probably because he was still yearning for London, to him the centre of the universe and his true spiritual home.

At least once on the course, he briefly escaped to London. An evocative diary entry for Friday 25 April, tells much of why he found the capital so entrancing, showcasing as it did an endless variety of things to be seen, of the famous and the infamous in national life.

I had lunch with Godfrey Winn at Simpsons. He has been offered 100,000 dollars for a lecture cum radio tour in America. His pose of not being connected with newspapers, of knowing nothing about money, '100,000 dollars – how much is that?'

'I love your pose of "I may be a bastard but I do stick up for Godfrey Winn".'

I am writing this at teatime in Grosvenor House. There is a pleasant very quiet orchestra and a lot of pleasant though not very quiet girls escorted by sleek, gross, flashy men.[133]

Godfrey Winn was an enormously popular writer of a somewhat sentimental and easily parodied oeuvre. He was a rather strange lunchtime companion for Anthony, but then Anthony was always good at cultivating potentially useful contacts.

The course finished around the end of April. Though Anthony passed, it was yet another instance where he barely scraped through. The final verdict on him would read that he was an officer with a pleasant personality 'who appears to lack the necessary amount of enthusiasm and drive. His written work has been rather disappointing, but he is capable of doing a good job.'

Amazingly, exhilaratingly, his first posting was to London, the answer to all his dreams and prayers. 'Yes, sir, to London. Boy, oh boy!' But this rapturous interlude lasted only a day before he was moved on to the Guards in Surrey, to a very pleasant house next to a fine golf course. Anthony is characteristically vague about dates, but this posting seems to have been in early May, some four months after the publication of *What! No Morning Tea?*

The book's fame was already considerable, and by now it had come to the notice of the higher powers. Anthony wrote:

I sat in the Intelligence Office watching Rosse dealing with the mail. Presently, seeing me doing nothing, he threw me a copy of the last Army Training Memorandum, copies of which are issued periodically to all officers.

I was delighted to find *What! No Morning Tea?* recommended for reading by Army officers. Leaving this casually open at the right page, I retired to my room and worked there for the rest of the day, emerging only for meals and a walk around the golf course.

Anthony's new CO was a Brigadier, a pleasant, generous and amusing man. Soon after Anthony's arrival, he introduced him one teatime to the Commanding Officer of the Irish Guards, a Colonel.

'He probably won't be staying, though,' said the Brigadier. 'He's going off to write a book or some such thing; isn't that it, eh?'

'He ought to stay here and write a book about a Guards Brigade; stay two weeks with each of the battalions.'

'That's what I'm afraid of. That's why I'm trying to get rid of him,' riposted the Brigadier. How we all laughed.[134]

Nothing could be more eloquent of the way that Anthony's star was rising than that Brigadiers and Colonels were beginning to treat him as some sort of pet.

The book the Brigadier mentioned was Anthony's latest project; it was about the women's army, the Auxiliary Territorial Service, or ATS. Though written in his spare time, the research for it would being conducted under semi-official auspices. It was one step nearer to the goal Anthony had set himself, that of becoming an officially sanctioned commentator on army affairs.

On 24 May, only fourteen months after he had been conscripted, Anthony at last got his dream and was posted to London. He would be based in the capital for rest of his time in the Army. Though he was frequently away on assignments and when in London was supposed to sleep in his Army quarters, sometime in late 1941 or early 1942, newly rich from his extra-curricular activities, he took a lease on a tiny flat at 81 South Audley Street. It was a very swish address, near Park Lane and Mayfair, and the other tenants were also very swish and charming. Comfortably appointed, the flat was a single ground-floor room overlooking a street of handsome town-houses. There might have been room for little more than a bed, a table and chairs, but it meant that at last Anthony had won back a degree of independence. He could keep his private things there and take a girlfriend back if he wanted. Being generous-hearted and a very good brother, he would also let Geoffrey use it as his own occasional London base.

Now that he was back in London, Anthony wasted no time in taking full advantage of what the capital could offer him. His life ran along bifurcated lines; in one part he was comparatively free, in the other he belonged to the Army. Thursday 29 May may be taken as fairly representative. In the morning he received a letter from William MacLang of the BBC Ack-Ack Beer-Beer radio programme, asking him to do a script. The programme was dedicated to all the anti-aircraft personnel who manned the guns and searchlights in Britain's defence, and to barrage balloon personnel. For lunch, Anthony met his mother and father at Victor's. The afternoon was 'frenzied' – that is to say, for once Anthony was doing some proper army work. 'There was a significant conference on and I had to organise the distribution of varying numbers of different pamphlets to various colonels and brigadiers, not to mention putting out the pencils. It sounds easy but it was nerve-wracking.'

In the evening he went to the Savoy for a journalists' beano, had a brilliant time, and got very drunk.

The Savoy was the centre of London journalistic nightlife and the beano was just the kind of occasion which Anthony loved. It began with drinks with Quentin Reynolds (who was living at the hotel), Anna MacLanan, and Bib Cooper of *The Times*. Rudolf Hess had recently made his bizarre flight to Scotland, apparently intending to negotiate a peace settlement with the British.[135] The subject had been discussed to pieces, and was now being banned from conversation by various people. But all the journalistic *sang froid* in the world could not quell the excitement about the sinking of Germany's premier warship, the *Bismarck*, two days earlier, on 27 May. On 26 May, the already damaged *Bismarck* had been spotted via her oil slick by an RAF Coastal Command reconnaissance aircraft from 209 Squadron. From that moment, the *Bismark*'s fate was sealed. Whilst Anthony was at the Savoy that evening, the reconnaissance pilot who had spotted the ship came over to Anthony's table full of journalists. The pilot was enjoying his hour of glory, and his bill at the Savoy was being paid by the Ministry of Mines. Anthony noted that the pilot was 24 and had been in the RAF for six years; 'he said there was terrific AA fire from the *Bismarck*.' That the pilot had come to their dinner table was a great honour.

When the band stopped playing, Anthony's party went downstairs to the bar, which was crowded with 'journalists of various kinds in various stages of intoxication'. Anthony finally got back to his billet at 3.00am, had a hot bath and did some exercises, 'my theory being that this reduces the hangover'. The following morning he would curse himself for being so weak-willed when he had to go to Reading as part of the research for his ATS book.[136]

Not long afterwards it happened all over again. The temptations of London were almost impossible to resist now that he was slap-bang in the middle of them.

Saturday May 31

I had dinner at the [Guyon?] House Club and afterwards striding down the street I met Frisco standing in the doorway of his club. He offered me a drink which I kindly accepted. I sat there for an hour.

Just lately I have been having a mental battle trying to make myself work. This morning I was woken at 6.30am but I really felt so pleasantly tired that it seemed short-sighted folly to get up. I stayed in bed until 7am, so I didn't get anything done before breakfast, then I read all the papers so I didn't get anything done after. I still felt sluggish, the result I suppose of reverting to restaurant meals and casual between meal drinking, so I walked across the Park to work. I meant to work in the lunch hour but Keeble rang up. The only triumph of fibre I scored was in not having a drink at dinner. Extraordinary the definite two-sided debate that goes on in one's mind on these occasions. One wouldn't do any harm. Don't be a fool, you know it does you no good. It might just tone me up. Yes and for how long? and so on. After all this I walked straight into Frisco's.[137]

Research for the ATS book was going well. It would be published in 1942 under the punning title *She Walks in Battledress*.[138] A slim volume of less than 100 pages, it told women what to expect when they joined the ATS. Very much centred on the war effort, it is a workman-like and straightforward piece, which shows how deadly serious Anthony was about re-inventing himself as a leading authority on Army affairs. But like a jack-in-the-box his sense of humour was allowed to jump out at times; being the consummate professional, he knew that his audience expected to be entertained as well as instructed.

He began as he meant to go on:

Firstly understand, as many people still don't seem to, that the ATS hasn't been built up for fun, or to insure that young women are inconvenienced as much as young men [...] but because we are urgently short of man-power. In the British Army, as in the German Army, one-third of the men spend their time supplying, repairing and administering the other two-thirds. A lot of this administrative work can't be done by women, but a lot can [...] Already the best part of a hundred thousand men have been released for fighting. And if you think we don't need those men you are living in a dream.

In the nature of things there has been a great deal of criticism of the ATS [...These criticisms] may be classified under the following main headings:

1. The ATS are over-worked drudges.
2. The ATS are under-worked hussies.
3. They spend all their time leading a wild, drunken life with the soldiers.
4. Their uniform is so ugly that no man will look at them.

Now the fact that these criticisms cancel each other out does not necessarily mean that they are groundless [...] But I can only say that from what I have seen [...] this kind of talk is all, substantially speaking, nonsense.[139]

Anthony was able to research the book not only because the Publicity Department at the War Office was keen on the project and had opened doors for him, but also because of the forbearance of his commanding officer. In a diary entry for 1 June, he records asking 'Colonel G's permission to go to see Mrs Mill at the War Office'.

He asked why and I explained that I was writing a book. He was very civil about the other book. I said I ought to tell him that I was going to tell the PR dept that I couldn't write the ATS book unless I had more time. He said there was no need to ask them, that except when he had something special to do I could get on with it. I said thank you very much but that I would like to get this thing absolutely straight; what I did not want was the position of feeling or being made to feel that when I was writing the book I ought to be doing something else. He said I was not to worry about that.[140]

This is surely Anthony at his very best, telling a Colonel – in the politest manner – exactly what he, a very junior officer, wanted and needed. The Colonel, duly tamed, would come in the following lunchtime, a bank holiday Monday when there was nothing much doing, and say in a fatherly sort of way, 'You better go off and write your book'. Anthony would spend the afternoon interviewing Mrs Mill at the War Office on her experiences as a cook in the ATS. It was a very amusing experience. 'Mrs Mill makes me laugh I must say, calling brigadiers darling and I don't know what,' Anthony noted in his diary afterwards.

Despite the latitude extended to him, and the fact that his life was now very much happier, Anthony was still getting into trouble. It was the same old problem – forgetfulness caused by him having his mind on other things.

Saturday June 7

I was day duty officer today and had to relieve the night duty officer, in this case the G2 at 8.30am. The only thing was I forgot. He had been waiting nearly an hour when I arrived. He couldn't have been more pleased to see me. He was furious. 'Just because you're too damned lazy to look at the notice board' he started. I said I had no excuse of any kind and was extremely sorry but of course that didn't help much. Actually it was only by chance that I came in at all, today being my day off but I had come to work on the book.

I was so annoyed I couldn't concentrate. When there are so many things one might get into trouble about I hate to waste apologies and pardons on a thing which it wouldn't have been any trouble to do.

Later on I was summoned to see Colonel G. 'Why were you late this morning?' he said.

'I'm afraid pure negligence, sir,' I said.

'Well, it mustn't happen again. See that you're woken in future. There's another thing. What's this club you've been going to in – Street? What kind of place is it?'

I had only been to one recently so I said, 'It's just a drinking club, sir, run by a man who used to run a night club. He saw me and asked me in for a drink.'

'Well, I shouldn't go there in future.'[141]

There were limits to the Colonel's indulgence. Drinking clubs like Frisco's were rather louche and disreputable, and the Colonel clearly expected better from his officers.

On 17 June, for reasons which he did not explain in his diary, Anthony had an appointment to visit a Prisoner of War cage. The Germans were in a big private house with a lot of wire and military police about. He only saw six prisoners – three naval and three airmen, 'all very young-looking and rather sulky'. They were lethargically filling sandbags. Anthony was told that the naval ones were the sulkiest, and that interrogating them had become easier since their cigarettes had been docked. This was in retaliation for the Germans stopping the cigarette ration to British prisoners. Anthony's escort told him that if you gave cigarettes to the prisoners, they would talk freely.[142]

Anthony did not write the episode up in any great detail in his diary though it must have been an odd experience, the first time apparently that he had encountered the enemy face to face. Probably the last thing on his mind as he made his very short notes was that one day he might be a prisoner of war himself. Possibly he was distracted by excitement about his next military posting, for something of immense significance was about to happen in his life.

Anthony had written of his earlier fortunes in the military:

When you are conscripted you abandon any previous confidence in the smooth running of your affairs. You expect everything to go wrong. After all, when you are a conscript infantry private, sleeping on a wooden floor and queuing with a tin bowl for your meals, the world doesn't exactly seem a conspiracy for your personal advancement. You largely lose the power of self-assertion, though if you manage to retain it you can use it sometimes with remarkable effect in managing your destinies.[143]

Anthony had managed to do just that with *What! No Morning Tea?* and his other writings on military life. Now he was about to reap the very considerable rewards.

9

ABCA-CADABRA

O ne Sunday at the end of June 1941, at very short notice as was typical of the Army, Anthony received a wire telling him that he was required for temporary duty at the War Office. The posting was for fourteen days with a view to a probable, permanent staff appointment.

The telegram was not unexpected but it was a surprise that it had come so soon – Anthony was used to the Army dawdling over what it intended to do with him. This time matters had been expedited at extraordinary speed. Only the week before, he had been interviewed at the War Office by the Director-General of Welfare and Education, Major-General Harry Willans. Willans was looking for two ex-journalists as Staff Captains for a new bulletin that was starting up, and Anthony's name had been put forward by a Major Radcliffe. Radcliffe had read *What! No Morning Tea?* and had suggested Anthony for the job; they had traced him through Radcliffe's brother, who was the chief censor.

Three days after Anthony began at the War Office, the second Staff Captain for the bulletin turned up. To Anthony's delight, it was Stephen Watts whom he used to meet in the lift in the *Express* building in Fleet Street. Although Stephen had been on the *Sunday* rather than the *Daily Express*, their shared background made an instant bond between them. Stephen was a witty and intelligent man with a long, handsome, equine face. Like Anthony, he had held a number of previous roles in the Army. The pair of them hit it off immediately.

The bulletin on which they were to work was part of a new initiative in Army education. Neither Stephen nor Anthony had had any prior connection with education though Anthony had written many a didactic article. In his impressionistic autobiography, *Moonlight on a Lake in Bond Street*, Stephen would write that the role of 'popular educator' was one of the most unlikely with which he could ever be identified, along with such things as Master of Hounds, nuclear physicist, or night club bouncer.[144] As for Anthony, his view on Army education had been given in *What! No Morning Tea?* but he was canny enough never to repeat it once he was at the War Office. He had only been in the Army for six weeks when he wrote the passage in question. It is extraordinarily prescient about some of the problems which were facing the Army educators he was now joining.

Writing in April 1940, Anthony had commented:

> Professor A.L. Rowse, the left-wing pillar whom I met at a Liberal Summer School five years ago, has been staying at [The Antelope] in Dorchester over the weekend [...] He was saying that the Government are likely to embark on a big campaign for giving lectures to the troops. On the theory that the troops must be hungry for enlightenment. Personally I have noticed no evidence of hunger for higher learning.
>
> The idea of these lectures would be to banish boredom. As far as I am concerned, they would definitely produce it. Especially when you think of the bores and charlatans who would inevitably work their way into such a scheme. I don't think people would want to go to lectures, but once they got there, I think that most people would be interested. Just as they don't want to go to church or learn to fold blankets properly, but once they are marched along to it, they take an interest. Which immediately subsides on the command 'Dismiss'.[145]

In his work on the bulletin, Anthony would always bear in mind the harried private and even more harried junior officer he had once been, and would strive to make the bulletin entertaining as well as informative, a combination which he would achieve brilliantly.

Anthony and Stephen ascertained very quickly that they were in at the start of something huge, an extraordinarily radical movement to educate the troops that was powered by a blend of idealism and pragmatism. It was less than two years since most of the personnel of the small Army Education Corps had been transferred to other duties on the grounds that it was all hands to the pump. Education had thereafter been organised chiefly by the Central Advisory Council for Adult Education in HM Forces, formed in the winter of 1939–40, which was supported by the universities, the Workers' Education Association, and other such worthy bodies. They organised lectures and short courses for the troops, but on a very limited scale.

After the fall of France in June 1940, the war situation changed dramatically. With the Germans and their allies controlling Western Europe, it was obvious even to the most obtuse Army blimp that the Army would be stationed in Britain or her overseas territories for years to come. Apart from limited campaigns, or the occasional foray by specialist troops, the only role the bulk of the Army was likely to have in the near future was a defensive one. Considerable anxiety began to brew up that the troops' morale, commitment and effectiveness would be compromised by the lack of any purposeful activity.

In September 1940, a special committee reported that education would be good for, if not indispensable to, the maintenance of soldiers' morale. From this came the idea that every unit should have its own Education Officer. Next came the question of just what that Education Officer was supposed to do. The new bulletin on which Anthony was working was primarily intended to supply raw material for that Education Officer so that he could give a lecture, then chair a discussion and generally get the men motivated by the key issues behind the war. As Willans told Anthony at their interview, the bulletin had the approval of the highest military authorities – 'We want to get rid of this pernicious idea of we can take it. Stop being passive and turn aggressive.'[146]

Willans was just under 50 but so dynamic in manner that Anthony, who was half his age, described him as 'very young and efficient looking'. He had served with extreme distinction during the First World War, winning the Military Cross and the Distinguished Service Order. During the inter-war years he had been with the Territorial Army. An extremely charismatic and energetic man, he was full of charm but his penetratingly intense gaze (Anthony called him 'eagle-eyed') showed that here was a man 'who would like being contradicted up to a point'.

Willans was fond of the expression that something wasn't worth 'two pennyworth of cold gin'. As Stephen wrote, 'Every time he said it, which was at least daily, I had a shuddering thought of how nasty warm gin would be.'[147]

Anthony and Stephen's first office was in the Hotel Victoria in Northumberland Avenue, which had become a War Office annexe. They occupied Room 529, a rather dirty, unfurnished attic bedroom, though – as Anthony flippantly noted – at least it had the benefit of hot and cold running water. Almost at once it was proposed that they should move down to the second floor. Anthony started getting his first story for the bulletin, 'a fairly lengthy affair about tanks, from Captain Barker, who was then just fresh from Libya'. Geoffrey sent in a story about an anti-aircraft crew shooting down a German bomber; it was the bulletin's first outside contribution, 'in fact the first thing written specifically for it'.[148]

Stephen described those early days in his autobiography:

> We were allocated offices with a simple yet alarming brief – to think. Cotterell and I shared a room high up in the hotel, with a private bathroom attached. It had the regulation furniture: two desks, four chairs, table and a filing cabinet, and that was all. We were invited to summon secretarial assistance as required from the typing pool.
>
> Cotterell, a practical man, produced his own portable typewriter and got on with the book he was writing about his experiences as a recruit. He was essentially a writer, and such things as editing and layout were of no interest to him. For myself, I doodled away with coloured pencils and printers' type-specimen books, lists of subject-ideas, and possible authors, to produce a suggested format and contents for our publications.[149]

It took a while for things to get properly organised. In his diary, Anthony told the story of one mildly recalcitrant typist who complained that there was nothing to do and that she was thinking of applying for a transfer. Stephen quipped: 'Some people are incapable of any form of sacrifice for the war effort. Supposing we complained that we had nothing to do.' It was absolutely the sort of witticism that Anthony loved.[150]

Neither Anthony nor Stephen had yet quite understood what was expected of them. Used to being penned in by a rigid Army hierarchy, they had not sensed that the cage door had been opened and that they were free to fly. For this reason, they were in for one or two severe tickings-off by Willans. The diary which Anthony had kept more or less constantly since March 1940 was now coming to an end, but its last pages clearly show the huge contribution of Willans (whom Anthony refers to as the General) in setting the two ex-journalists on the right path.

> Friday
>
> We got to the office [...] to find half the furniture moved from our office but not yet moved into the new office. We hung about for two hours utterly bored and demoralised. Then we had a conference with the General which demoralised us some more. The subject was criticism of our specimen issue.
>
> The criticisms were that the stories we printed didn't give a Platoon Commander material for lectures. In future we were to write the stuff specifically as material for lectures with guidance about giving them.
>
> The General came in to see how we were getting on. He said he thought everything was coming along well, that he didn't want us to get the idea that he was crabbing when he criticised, but he thought we had to do everything we could to anticipate criticisms and meet them where possible, and then take a stand on a certain line of policy and refuse to deviate from it.
>
> 'Remember, nothing people like better than to say something from the War Office stinks,' he said. 'Oh, nothing they like better.' [...]

We had a conference with the General in the morning and another one after lunch, on the question of whether we should have some trial issues or go straight into full circulation. And should we necessarily have a coloured cover; would it be just as good and much cheaper to have a white cover with some kind of coloured band across it? I said I wasn't at all keen on the red cover as it was. 'Then for God's sake why didn't you tell me?' he said. I said I thought it was axiomatic that we should have a coloured cover. He said I was paid to think, not to sit and take things for granted.

Tuesday

There was a conference with the civil servant who looks after War Office publishing, or, anyway, our side of it. It all sounded very smooth except for the clammy-handed phrase 'treasury approval', which crops up all through these discussions.

When the civil servant had gone the General turned on us, and 'turned on us' is the right term to use.

'I am extremely worried, and the more I think about it the more worried I become – about what came out last night. The fact is that you have been keeping your opinions from me.' He raised his voice, he banged the desk. 'Now that is absolutely fatal. What the devil do you think I have you here for? It isn't for your appearance. It's because you're experts and I want to know what you think. I don't care two pennyworth of cold gin what you say, whether I agree with it or not; but for God's sake say it.'

Stephen said: 'Well, in civilian life, sir, I was certainly not afraid to speak up, but since I've been in the Army my whole training has been not to.'

'Well, forget it, man. What's the good of fooling about like toy soldiers? Forget I'm a Major-General or anything else. It doesn't matter a damn. What we're here for is to beat Hitler, and we're not going to do that by place-saving crawling.'[151]

Suitably rebuked, Anthony and Stephen began to expand what they were doing with the bulletin.

The authorities were planning that the bulletin would come out under the aegis of a new organisation – the Army Bureau of Current Affairs, more familiarly known as ABCA. Stephen described how they gave the bulletin its distinctive identity:

Cotterell and I decided on the title WAR, and I drew its glaring red and white cover. Also, while doodling away those warm summer afternoons, I devised the beehive shaped monogram of the letters ABCA which became our trademark. Cotterell was emphatic that our first publication should be called WAR because it afforded the opportunity to answer the telephone with the words 'This is WAR', which are susceptible of a variety of dramatic enunciations.[152]

WAR's first issue appeared on 20 September, by which time the creation of ABCA had been finalised.

The major influence behind ABCA was the Adjutant-General, General Sir Ronald Adam. He had been appointed Adjutant-General at the beginning of June 1941 and thus become ultimately responsible for all personnel matters in the Army, including recruitment, discharge, welfare, and education. A highly influential member of the Army Council, he was one of only two senior officers who were confidantes of Field Marshal Sir Alan Brooke, Chief of the Imperial General Staff, Britain's top soldier and Churchill's principal military advisor. Adam was thus very well placed to protect ABCA from the interference of those, including Churchill, who were strongly against any democratic tendencies in the Army, which they viewed as being subversive to military authority. Churchill never supported ABCA, and at various times tried to remove Adam from his post.[153]

Adam was a deeply thoughtful, practical and compassionate man whose prime concern was for the well-being of the troops. He was particularly mindful of the fact that the Army was taking on hundreds of thousands of conscripts who, like Anthony, had been forced unwillingly into military life. By ensuring that these conscripts became 'citizen-soldiers' rather than disgruntled liabilities, Adam was arguably one of the most influential British generals of the war.

As Anthony had predicted in his semi-serious April 1940 critique of Army education, the only way Army education was going to succeed was if it was compulsory. Adam, having given far more complex and weighty thought to the matter, arrived at the same conclusion and gave three main reasons why this should be so. Firstly, the Army had to make the best of its illiterate or semi-illiterate troops – the manpower situation was such that every man was needed, and no illiterate man could be of much use in a modern war. Secondly, though in 1941 victory seemed an exceedingly long way off, he was already far-sightedly looking forward to mass demobilisation and the soldiers' return to employment after the war. Thirdly (and this was not Anthony's view), he thought that once the soldiers' interest was secured they would continue their education voluntarily, so that they could actively build a new society after the war.[154]

In the early days of ABCA, there had been various problems in deciding how the scheme should be run. Eventually, under Adam's influence, it was decided that a period each week would be given over to compulsory education. The scheme was supposed to operate within training hours and then the troops were very keen on it, but if it was after hours it was thoroughly unpopular and brought down many a curse and execration on ABCA's name. In other words, what Anthony had once with not a great deal of seriousness predicted, was what came to pass.

Part of ABCA's role was to form a bridge between conscripts and regulars, privates and officers. It also aimed to inspire the soldiers with a fervent, almost crusading sense of the justice of the Allied cause. Only soldiers who understood the reasons why they were fighting would – in a stirring phrase – have 'the Will to Victory'. ABCA was to help the regimental officer 'in that most urgent of his tasks, the building up and the sustaining of morale, which will defeat not only the enemy, but that most insidious of possible enemies, the sense of being "browned off."'

> Without morale you will not get the fighting spirit: either the courage never to submit or yield, or the bravery which means initiative in the attack. With it you win the war, without it you lose. Think of Russia – and think of France.[155]

From the outset, Adam made it clear that he did not approve of patronising the soldiers' intelligence by talking down to them. In a 1943 film about ABCA, made by the Army Film Unit for the Ministry of Information, a rather endearingly stilted scene takes place between Adam and William Emrys Williams in which they are acting themselves in 1941 as they plan the formation of ABCA. Williams, a civilian, had been taken on because of his flair and expertise in educational matters; he was one of the most distinguished of a number of educational specialists who had been drafted into the War Office for the duration.[156]

In the scene, Adam is standing before the grand fireplace of his baroque office whilst Williams, in a lounge suit, sits below him in a chair. Willans, a key player, does not appear in the scene because he had been killed in a plane crash in early 1943. Williams' position is deferential but his posture is casual, interested and confident. He is also smoking – an unforgiveable breach of etiquette if not sanctioned by such a senior officer as Adam. The whole set-up of the scene is designed to show informality and human values within the magnificence of the establishment office with its Union Jack hanging from the ceiling. The audience who would be viewing the film were not only the Education Officers who headed the ABCA discussion groups, but the ordinary troops whose counterparts appear in a number of scenes of the film. The intention of the film was to engage and involve both officers and other ranks. It was also to convince them that there was a new weapon against Hitler, 'the weapon of the mind'.

Adam tells Williams about the idea for educating the troops, and Williams suggests its name, saying that ABCA is a nice short word and that it also represents how they will be teaching the Army 'a new sort of alphabet, the alphabet of world affairs, the progress of the war, and all that'. Adam makes his own position clear on the matter: 'There is one thing we must be quite certain about. No propaganda, no long-winded lectures.'[157]

The informality displayed in the film had been a deliberately emphasised characteristic of ABCA since the summer of 1941. Then Willans had delighted Anthony and Stephen by working in his braces, which was unlike anything they had ever expected of the War Office. Adam was also extremely informal for a top soldier. As Stephen wrote:

> The Adjutant-General was no stickler for formalities and he was keenly interested in ABCA's formative days [...] On one occasion he came straight through on the line to our room and asked for me. Cotterell answered, and he was busy.
>
> 'Sorry,' he said, without asking who was speaking, 'you can't. He's in the bath – thinking.' It was a hot afternoon and he was telling the truth. I was in a cool bath and I was supposed to be thinking. The AG fortunately thought it very funny.[158]

In the context of normal army rigidity, this informality was astonishing. Relations between ranks in the Army were still governed by archaic custom, and it took a very enlightened or very senior officer to go against the prevailing mores. By behaving like this, Adam and Willans were giving Anthony and Stephen the clearest indication that freshness of thought, not slavish obedience, was what they valued.

Anthony and Stephen were very different individuals from the standard type of Army Education Corps officer. In a key passage in his memoir, Stephen outlined their essential difference from the 'textbook evangelists, worthy and erudite characters no doubt, [but] as remote from the ordinary soldier as the man in the moon'. Stephen added that unlike these evangelists both he and Anthony had 'served in the ranks and as infantry subalterns and we knew how soldiers ticked'.[159] They were both deeply aware that in order for WAR to succeed, it would have to ring true with the soldiers themselves. Churchill and various other senior figures wanted Army publications to promote traditional patriotic attitudes. Anthony and Stephen were far more realistic. Like other Army publications, such as Eighth Army News, WAR sometimes walked a fine line between what the authorities would countenance and what would retain the interest and respect of the troops, who tended towards great cynicism about official publications and the motives of their leaders.[160]

By September 1941, ABCA's publications had achieved a settled format. Each week a bulletin was published, WAR one week, and a second publication called Current Affairs the next. WAR dealt with military subjects, and was written almost entirely inside the War Office by Anthony and Stephen, although articles by other soldiers were invited and soon began to appear. Current Affairs was written by outside writers, civilians as well as soldiers, who had been individually picked to cover a particular subject such as 'You are Going to Europe' or 'Women after the War'.[161] A beautifully designed Map Review was also printed fortnightly, with photographs and features on one side and a soon-to-be obsolete map on the reverse showing the current military situation in some theatre of war. The map was designed by Abraham Games, one of the best poster designers of the century, which demonstrates once again how great was the importance attached to ABCA.

There is no source which tells us exactly what Anthony thought about the evangelical tone which was early ABCA. Certainly he would work extremely hard to carry its message through, but messianism, however worthy, was incompatible with his mischievous, clear-eyed, elitist intelligence. Ernest Watkins, who would work with Anthony on WAR after Stephen moved on, thought that Anthony had 'an inherent suspicion of vaguely liberal ventures', but whatever Anthony privately thought he had the good sense to keep it to himself.[162]

In *Moonlight on a Lake in Bond Street*, Stephen would give a sketchy but unforgettable portrait of Anthony as he was in 1941–1942. Though the book was written some years after the war, it carries the vivid immediacy of a contemporary account, so perhaps Stephen also kept a diary.

> So long as I was in ABCA I edited Anthony's copy. He professed to be grateful. When I left he did it rather better for himself. That was typical. It was a boring job, especially as his copy was always very messy, full of written-in emendations, balloons of insertions in the margins, and punctuation of a rather impressionistic sort. He loved to dump an article on my desk, the pages unclipped and disordered, the paper crumpled, and watch me wade through it, trying to make the printer's task more tolerable. Secretly, of course, he was laughing at my fussiness. He could do all that was needed with complete efficiency. But if there was somebody else to be got to do the boring job, then the obvious thing was to plead ignorance and let the fool do it.[163]

Stephen greatly admired Anthony's gift for capturing a scene – 'Anthony's eye and ear for the significant line or moment were deadly'. Ernest Watkins also thought very highly of Anthony's work, and would write that what made his writing so distinctive and memorable was 'the occasional unexpected flickers of his own personality. I thought of them as eddies on the surface of a swift flowing river, indications of its depth, its third dimension.'[164]

One of Stephen's best stories about Anthony has already been given, that of the innocent-looking cadet outwitting the fearsome Colonel Bingham. But Stephen makes it quite clear that even in his privileged role at ABCA, Anthony was as quietly determined as ever to follow his own path.

> If I was ignorant and graceless in matters of protocol and precedence Cotterell was much worse. He did what he wanted to do the way he wanted to do it and apologised afterwards if necessary. The trouble was that his apologies were so overdone, so studded with 'sirs' and self-abasement, that I was always sure the recipient was going to realise that the whole thing was an act and that in fact he was being ridiculed by this pale, straight-faced young man with the quiet voice.[165]

Though the size and basic appearance of *WAR* would remain the same throughout its existence, the content and presentation would change markedly as Anthony gained more and more influence. The first issues were published with the subtitle 'News-Facts for Fighting Men'. All the articles in the first two issues were anonymous, and the overall style of the publication was brisk, soldierly, and no-nonsense. Gradually, all this changed. Soon illustrious contributors like Eric Linklater would be named, though it would not be until Issue 23, ten months after *WAR* began, that Anthony's name first appeared above a piece. From then on, all his most characteristic work was signed, and the clear identification of him with the publication had begun.

Other changes also served to personalise the bulletin. In February 1942, the gung-ho subtitle 'News-Facts for Fighting Men' had its last outing, and from then on all the issues would have their attention-grabbing individual subtitle, such as Issue 15's 'The Mind of a Nazi'. Blocks of texts in the articles were broken up with ingenious sub-headings, both for emphasis and to make reading easier on the eye. In other words, *WAR* increasingly used the tricks of popular journalism which both Anthony and Stephen knew inside out.

Over the course of three years, Anthony would take his brief far beyond what Willans had originally envisaged. He would become far more of a war correspondent than a compiler of material for Education Officers, and he would use *WAR* to further his own career as a journalist and a reporter. He would act shamelessly in his own interests, but at the same time he did a most excellent job for *WAR*. The Adjutant-General Sir Ronald Adam would entirely approve of what he achieved, and when *WAR* came to an end he would specifically single out Anthony for high praise.

As Watkins would later write, Willans' appointment of Anthony had been 'a stroke of genius'.[166] As for Anthony, the joy of *WAR* was that he was increasingly left to his own devices. Stephen would write that after he himself left *WAR* in January 1943, Anthony 'went his own way, even more independently, he was too valuable to be interfered with and a difficult man to gainsay'.[167] With Stephen out of the picture, Willans dead, and William Emrys Williams seemingly very uninterested, Anthony would achieve a degree of autonomy which was extremely unusual for the Army. The man who has once been a most unhappy conscript had at last found the perfect Army niche.

10

EXPANDING THE BRIEF

In early 1943, quite unexpectedly and in very mysterious circumstances, Stephen was offered the post of Intelligence Officer. The collaboration between him and Anthony had worked perfectly but Stephen was beginning to get itchy feet. He did not mind being the dogsbody whilst Anthony became more and more 'the star writer' – it was other issues which were causing him to think that he ought to move elsewhere. Not entirely sure whether he was doing the right thing or not, he accepted the Intelligence Officer post.

Ever practical, Anthony began to make arrangements for replacing him with Richard Bennett, a soldier-journalist whom Anthony knew and liked. It is this Richard Bennett whose contribution is acknowledged in the front of *An Apple for the Sergeant*. Anthony writes, 'I should [...] like to thank Major Richard Bennett, RA, for his work in compiling the index'. The index appears underneath. There is only one entry: 'COTTERELL, ANTHONY, Pages 1–185', that is to say, the entire length of the book.

But there were problems with getting Bennett's appointment made permanent by the authorities. Bennett contributed to *WAR* for some months, as did a Captain Lionel Birch who appears in the only known photograph of Anthony in the *WAR* office. Dates are difficult to pin down as articles were not always signed, but Birch appears to have overlapped with Stephen, whilst Bennett's first signed article appeared around the time that Stephen left in January 1943. By June, however, Bennett's posting had been vetoed, and Ernest Watkins had won the job.

Watkins was in his early forties, a pleasant sociable man who had practised as a lawyer pre-war. He was notably pale, with the pallor of someone working in an office who did not get much exercise. Warlike he was not, being of a cautious and rather nervous disposition where physical danger was concerned, as he freely admitted in his autobiographical writings. He had been very keen to work on *WAR* even in the face of some discouragement by Anthony. External factors had swung it for him. The Army Council had recently decreed that officers below a certain age who were already serving in an operational unit should not be appointed to a non-operational staff job. Bennett fell on one side of the age demarker, and Watkins on the other. The decision was, in a sense, forced upon Anthony. Watkins was well aware of this, writing in his autobiography, 'I think he would have preferred the devil he knew to the one he did not, but time ran out on him. I was an alternative. I was free to come at once. He really had not much choice.'[168] In the event they would work together very happily for sixteen months. Harmony was ensured because Watkins completely deferred to Anthony, not only because he was of lower rank but also because he acknowledged without the slightest resentment that Anthony far outshone him as a writer and an editor.

Watkins had been London-based before the war. Unlike Anthony, he was community-spirited, serving as a member of Stepney Borough Council from 1932 to 1935 and of the Council of the University Settlement Association for most of the 1930s (the latter was part of a movement for adult education). After the war he would become a politician in Canada.

Watkins wrote for *The Economist* and for *Punch*. His *Punch* column 'Your Loving Son, Harold' had formed part of the material of his two slim wartime books: a compendium called *Iceland Presents* which included other contributors; and his semi-autobiographical *No Depression in Iceland*. His *WAR* articles would be solid, careful, and meritorious, but would lack the sparkling life which characterised Anthony's best work.

No Depression in Iceland describes Watkins' two year posting on the island. Most of the book is slightly ponderous stuff, but occasionally it is very funny, such as in the story of the storm when an extremely fierce wind hung Watkins up very painfully on a barbed wire fence. His companion was also sadistically mauled by the wind. When they finally staggered back to their army car, they discovered that their driver was in no mood to set off again. 'He said he had been chased down the road by a large section of Nissen hut. It had finally overtaken him in the straight, and, fortunately, passed at a good rate of knots.'[169]

Iceland had been a hugely important experience for Watkins, but he was very glad to be out of it. Since then he had had a couple of unsatisfactory postings, the last being in the War Office at the Directory of Army Kinematography, 'in which position I was not a success'. Working on *WAR* was his dream job, 'I had found what I wanted to do. I had found that I could do it [...] I thought I was very fortunate.'[170]

Watkins had first met Anthony when *WAR* (which had long since left the Hotel Victoria) was based in Curzon Street House. This was a large office building at the eastern end of Curzon Street, in a cul-de-sac close to Berkeley Square. Part of it was Blitz-damaged, and the remainder had been requisitioned by the War Office. Watkins was also working at Curzon Street House, but with Army Kinematography on a different floor to Anthony. A mutual acquaintance introduced them during coffee break.

By the time that Watkins officially became part of *WAR*, various War Office departments had played musical chairs and swopped their premises, and *WAR* was now at 47 Eaton Square. This was in the heart of Belgravia and therefore a location which suited Anthony perfectly. Number 47 was a handsome townhouse with a pillared front door, and far more spacious than it appeared from the street. A row of requisitioned houses had been converted into a single inter-connected building by knocking holes for doorways in all but the top floor. Anthony and Watkins shared an attic room, conveniently isolated because, unlike the other floors, it was only accessible by a single staircase. There they lived a life far removed from the usual military obsessions with order and smartness. Of one visitor, Major Denzil Batchelor, Watkins wrote that 'his service dress was too immaculate to have been brought up any higher than the first floor'.[171]

In his autobiography, Watkins would paint an evocative picture of the attic, which remained *WAR*'s office for the rest of the war. A former servant's bedroom at the rear of the house, it had only one window which looked out towards Victoria Station over a patchwork of back gardens and roofs, singularly undamaged by the Blitz. On either side of the window, Anthony and Watkins faced one another across their two desks and two typewriters.

Watkins appears to have rather liked the office, despite – or perhaps because of – its improvised nature:

> In the winter we were allowed a fire and a ration of coal. The room was carpetless, its wallpaper which was faded had once been proper for a servant's room, and electric lighting hastily installed was adorned with plain white office shades. But it was by no means a cheerless room when we came in it.[172]

The working arrangements were very loose. Watkins wrote that there were no set meetings, routines or agendas, only a deadline to meet every other week. 'Each issue grew into its final shape by fits and starts, but we never failed to produce one on time.' No one interfered with them, and they did not see their nominal head, the Director of ABCA, William Emrys Williams, from one week to the next.

> Occasionally someone suggested something we should look into and write about. If the suggestion came from a sufficiently high level – as for instance when the Director of the Home Guard wanted the Army to be told what the Home Guard was doing in 1944 – we listened and tried to oblige.[173]

Anthony's answer to that particular one was to get Geoffrey to write an article about the Home Guard on the Ack-Ack site which he now commanded.[174]

Anthony and Watkins did their own typing and proofreading of the galleys, and exercised their wits in 'devising cross-heads to break up the solid pages into more digestible sections'. Occasionally they included a map, drawn by Pip Bares, 'the best popular cartographer of the day', and more occasionally black and white sketches.[175] Every two weeks either Anthony or Watkins – usually Anthony, if he was around – spent an afternoon at the printers, Newnes & Pearson, in Shepherds Bush. There the final touches to the bulletin were made, cutting, pasting or editing copy until it all fitted perfectly. Then the thing was done, for another fortnight.

Watkins gives a very clear picture of how Anthony had made *WAR* his personal fiefdom.

> By 1943 Anthony was in complete control of *WAR*. Nominally the two sections of ABCA responsible for publications were in charge of a lieutenant-colonel answerable to Williams and through him upwards to the Director of Army Education and on to the Adjutant-General himself. In this respect, the Adjutant-General resembled a Fleet Street press baron [...] He had the power of instant dismissal. But he did not interfere with *WAR*. Nobody did. There was no editorial board, not even an advisory committee. Anthony decided what went into each issue, how it was handled and what lessons were to be learnt from it. For a military publication in wartime, it had a most unusual degree of independence.[176]

Anthony had worked immensely hard to achieve this independence. He was both the editor and the star writer, but did not let this corrupt him – he had a clear vision of what *WAR* should be and he never lost sight of it. Watkins thought one of his strengths as an editor was 'his firm hold on principle. He was not producing an entertaining news magazine. He was producing a magazine that supplied instructional material to the Army.' Anthony kept to this brief, and within its strict limits sometimes produced material which was first-class in its own right.

Watkins obviously admired Anthony greatly, although he did not romanticise him. In one place in his autobiography he called him 'hard and shrewd', and in another, when Anthony sorted out a problem with an ATS driver, wrote – perhaps not entirely approvingly – 'I was constantly surprised at the charm he could conjure up when he really wanted something from a woman'.[177] But there were gentler passages, in one of which he described Anthony as 'unobtrusive, boyish looking, a born listener, someone you hardly noticed when he was around until you read with pleasure, or shock, how much he had seen and understood'.[178]

In his autobiography Watkins made several attempts to capture the essence of the young man whom, despite the fifteen year age gap, he thought of as a friend. A more extended passage reads:

> Anthony was of average height, slight in build, dark-haired, and cultivated what we would now call a low profile. Life in Fleet Street had eliminated illusions but increased his awareness of all that was happening around him, and his understanding of its significance. He was self-contained; in fact he had not quite lost a youthful determination not to appear impressed by

events. He could be an entertaining companion, and he was a good listener, but I don't think he liked serious conversation for its own sake. One could only understand him at all well by keeping always in mind that he was a writer.

He was that more than anyone I ever met.[179]

WAR was a hugely demanding job now that Anthony had shouldered the major responsibility for it. But it was simply not enough for him. Side by side with his work for ABCA, he continued a relentless program of writing for publication. Two more of his books appeared. Both were very short. *She Walks in Battle Dress* came out in 1942, and *Roof Over Britain: The Official Story of the A.A. Defences, 1939–42*, was published in the following year. The latter was produced by the Ministry of Information; it had anonymous contributors from the Air Ministry (which was in charge of barrage balloons) and only one named contributor – Anthony – which says something of his growing fame. The preface acknowledged that he had been 'kindly lent' by the Army Bureau of Current Affairs to write the Army part of the story.[180]

Anthony's contribution to *Roof over Britain* was written in the brisk, authoritative, slightly clipped military style which he had by now perfected, and which he would use for his next book *RAMC*. His old style – witty, vivid, cinematic, closely observed – was reserved for the long evocative pieces which sometimes appeared, much cut down, in *WAR*. The full version of them was retained for his next book, and they would eventually appear in *An Apple for the Sergeant*, published in late 1944.

At the same time as writing his books, Anthony was turning out a number of articles for newspapers and magazines. Some, suitably tailored, appeared in more than one place, such as his article on flying in an American Flying Fortress on a bombing raid. This appeared in *WAR*, *An Apple for the Sergeant*, and in Cyril Connolly's *Horizon*.[181] Anthony wrote for everyone, including service newspapers like *The Cadet Journal* and *Off Parade*, the latter printing his short story *The Sergeant's High Jump* in January 1944. Not content with such huge productivity, he also wrote plays with his brother Geoffrey. He began planning his own magazine with Ernest Watkins and his old *Daily Express* friend, Harold Keeble. Anthony was working as if Death was snapping at his heels.

The esteem in which he was held continued to rise, and new doors were continually opened up for him. *RAMC*, which was published in late 1943 or early 1944, was an authoritative account prepared with the assistance of the Army Medical Department of the War Office and the RAMC, the Royal Army Medical Corps. So convincing was Anthony's writing on medical matters, utilising his knowledge of anatomy and his medical studies at Guy's, that readers who did not know who he was would assume that the book had been written by a medical officer.[182]

During his research for *RAMC*, Anthony would form such extremely good relations with the Army Medical Department of the War Office that they would connive in getting him across the Channel on D-Day when he had found it impossible to get permission from the authorities. His charm, wit, amiability, and knack of making useful friends seem to have been as indefatigable as his energy.

Not surprisingly, he could not always keep up with everything and everyone, and some old friends fell through the cracks. One such was George Edinger, an enormously witty, flamboyant, and erudite man who had been a mentor to him some eight years earlier when Anthony, then a medical student at Guy's Hospital, was dreaming of becoming a journalist. Edinger had co-founded the famous Oxford student newspaper *Cherwell* when he was a Balliol student. After graduating, he had practised as a barrister, before returning to his first love, journalism, and becoming a feature writer and political correspondent for the *Daily Express*. After meeting this extraordinary character who was living exactly the sort of life he wanted, Anthony took Edinger's advice and followed his dream of becoming a journalist. Now the mentor had, to a very large extent, been outgrown by the pupil. There is one scribbled note written from the Eaton

Square office in April 1944, which speaks volumes about how busy Anthony was. Returning some letters, he writes very hurriedly to Edinger and ends in a rather perfunctory way, 'When are we going to have dinner?' The note was returned to him, neatly typed on by Edinger.

My dear Anthony
I have not moved and the even tenor of my existence has been unbroken but for sundry efforts to get into touch with you, at every one of which I have been informed

a. That there was no answer at the switchboard

b. That there was no answer from your connection

or

c. That you were not available.

ever yours
George Edinger[183]

The signature was inscribed with a great flourish, and Edinger's address and telephone number were written beneath.

By the time his book *RAMC* came out, Anthony had been promoted to Major. There is a rather odd and deeply unflattering photograph of him on the fly leaf of *RAMC*, which does indeed make him look like a Major and one who was rather portly. His face is looking down as if evading the camera; it is set and serious with no trace of sparkle or frivolity. In every way this is an image which is almost irreconcilable with other photographs of Anthony. Perhaps its only truly recognisable characteristic is the impression it gives that he is shying away from being photographed.

Anthony was always evasive about photographs except on very rare occasions. In a group shot, he would usually be at the back, half-hidden; if the photo was of him on his own, he tended to look away. It was as if he was either shy, or preserving his physical anonymity, an anonymity which was essential in his line of work which so frequently rested on people scarcely noticing that he was there. The only surviving photographs which feature Anthony plainly are the glorious picture of him as a cub reporter, taken after he joined the staff of the *Daily Express* in 1936, and a series of professional portraits taken by Howard Coster, some months after Anthony became Major Cotterell.

Coster was a well-known photographer of famous men. Hundreds of his images are held in the National Portrait Gallery in London, amongst them such well-known names as Evelyn Waugh, G.K. Chesterton, A.A. Milne, and Anthony's old boss Lord Beaverbrook. The reasons for this particular Coster photoshoot are lost in the mists of time; perhaps Coster simply wanted to capture Anthony, a rising star, for his collection.

The photographs show Anthony in a most resplendently brushed and pressed uniform, with all his emblems of rank and regiment shining. On his sleeve is a badge with an emblem of a parachute, which dates the photographs as having been taken after October 1943. Anthony is just 27 and in his prime. The Howard Coster images show both his good looks and the elfin quality which could sometimes flicker over them, turning him from matinée idol into something more mischievous, puck-like and elemental. But gentleness is also a quality which can be seen in his intelligent and sensitive face. He is clearly not robust, and, despite the very strong force of his personality, there is something fragile and vulnerable about him. Perhaps one of his girlfriends was right when she compared him, not entirely flatteringly, to a Disney faun.[184]

Though he was not physically strong, and had always been utterly hopeless at anything which demanded muscles, brawn or athleticism, Anthony had a vein of inner toughness which gave him immense courage when facing danger. At WAR, he could easily have continued as a desk-bound editor and writer, but at around the time that Watkins joined him he began to actively seek out more dangerous assignments. He expanded his brief from someone who merely interviewed returning soldiers, airmen or sailors, to someone who actually went to war with them – albeit for a short period – and faced exactly the same dangers that they were facing.

In Issue 3 of WAR, the Editorial had sternly declared 'WAR is not competing with the newspapers', and there was little topicality about Anthony's accounts which always appeared with a time-lag due to the publishing schedule. Nonetheless, Anthony created a unique and vivid form of war reporting, whose outstanding quality – recognised by all who read it – was that he made you feel that you were actually there yourself.

In choosing to cover the war more actively, he was gambling with his life. Why had he chosen to walk this dangerous path? Watkins thought that Anthony chose it 'because of his sense of responsibility. He enjoyed the post he held and all it enabled him to do, but he did not wish to avoid risks that others of his age were compelled to take.' This does not really tally with the Anthony whom we get to know in the diaries, even the one written around D-Day at the period when Watkins knew him best. The tone in the D-Day diary is different from the earlier diaries only in that Anthony was hugely more self-confident, with a very clear sense of purpose and of his own worth. The basic attitudes, however, are not very different from those of the rebellious and unsuccessful soldier he had been in his first fifteen months in the Army. He had by now accepted that he was in the Army for the duration, but he had no intention of cultivating heroic self-sacrifice. Watkins was more accurate when he wrote that Anthony regarded the war and his role in it as the cards which he had been dealt by fate, and that 'he intended to derive the maximum advantage from all the cards in his hand'.[185] Anthony had always been hugely ambitious, and the Army was currently his best means of achieving fame, wealth, and professional standing.

Anthony had a number of reasons for reinventing himself as a war correspondent. There was his rejection of the boredom of a virtuous desk job; his delight in deceiving authority; his huge ambition to make a name for himself; and a mesmerised fascination with testing his willpower to see whether it would carry him through all the trials which he set it. It is also apparent that he found cheating death exhilarating. Then there was the camaraderie of the men he faced danger with. His brother, Geoffrey, who knew him better than anyone, wrote that for Anthony mixing with top-class soldiers and airmen in action and being accepted by them was an intoxicant; he became 'addicted to nobility'.[186] All these things were sufficient to see him returning, again and again, of his own free will, to the experience of front-line warfare.

Anthony had invented an official reason for this course of action, perfectly genuine and valid, but also highly convenient in that it allowed him to do exactly what he wanted. This was that he needed to experience war at first hand in order to do his job at WAR properly. When WAR eventually reached the end of its run in June 1945, no less a person that the Adjutant-General, Adam himself, summed up the extent of Anthony's contribution to it and gave that self-same official reason: 'He believed that you could best describe a thing only after you had done it yourself, and it was to give you that best account that he flew with the USAAF, landed in Normandy at D-Day and qualified as a parachutist.'[187]

Watkins is interesting on the subject of why Anthony courted danger when he himself prudently avoided it. In his autobiography, Watkins makes it clear that he himself kept clear of dangerous situations during his work for WAR, and was appalled when he inadvertently strayed into them. He wrote that Anthony 'had far more courage than I had', but he was also at pains to stress that there was no element of idiotic showing off in what Anthony did:

There was never any touch of 'Look, Ma, no hands!' or 'You can do this if you try' in anything he wrote. No moralising, nothing exhortatory. He described ordinary men with ordinary fears using their skills and experience to succeed in some dangerous duty. It was their confidence in each other that held them together.[188]

Watkins admired Anthony's courage but very much wished to avoid emulating him. On one occasion, however, he felt that he absolutely had to. He wrote of his attempt to fly operationally with the USAAF: 'I was driven to it by the example of Anthony. The decision to make the attempt brought me no joy of any kind.' When he was barred from the flight at the last moment due to a hitch in regulations, he felt the most intense relief. A sense of guilt always remained, but he knew that he could never have showed Anthony's insouciance. 'While I had been away, Anthony had slipped down one afternoon to the RAF station at Gatwick and taken an evening bombing mission over the same set of targets. He said he got back to London in time for a late supper at the Savoy. I believed him.'[189]

In another passage in his autobiography, Watkins tried more carefully to define what he meant about Anthony's sense of responsibility to the men for whom he was writing:

I am not putting this very well. He was ambitious, of course. He wanted to write well, and be recognised as a good writer. But with it there was this sense of responsibility, not to humanity in general, for him an abstraction, but for all the people he met, what they were doing, and why [...] He was driven by something, call it curiosity, call it concern, call it response to a task he had chosen for himself and could not shirk – it does not matter. What a man writes has a life and purpose of its own.[190]

The first time Anthony came under fire during his reporting for *WAR* was almost certainly when he was on a North Sea convoy some time at the end of 1942. When describing this incident, he wrote 'to my horror, we were attacked', but the 'horror' part of the sentence looks fairly formulaic because in fact he seemed rather exhilarated by the experience. His ship was machine-gunned and bombed by a Heinkel III, then a second enemy aircraft. The convoy's naval escorts opened up with everything, and Anthony's ship was 'suddenly like a fountain of red tracer and explosions'. The engagement ended with little damage to the ship and the first aircraft being hit. For a moment everyone thought that they had downed it. '"We've got her, by God, I think we got her," said the captain, but we hadn't. All the same it was very satisfying.'[191]

It was in the following year that Anthony began to put himself in far more serious danger by flying with the USAAF and the RAF. He began his account of flying a handful of daylight sorties in an American Flying Fortress by employing the same term as in his account of the convoy attack: 'In a horrified kind of way I had always wanted to go on a bombing raid'. Then followed a vivid account of various flights at the end of August and beginning of September 1943. One of the most memorable of these saw him and the crew crossing over to France, skirting Paris, catching a glimpse of the Eiffel Tower, and then coming home again, trying to dodge the flak barrage. Probably no one else, looking out on the scene near Paris, would have seen the macabre absurdity of war in quite the same way that Anthony did.

Dotted all over the sky were groups of aircraft, bombers, fighters, American, British, and some German. They all plunged purposefully about their different business. It was like a sort of market day or a lot of people hurrying to work ... It seemed absurd to think of all the work and organization that had gone to bring each of those groups to fly there that sunny afternoon.[192]

In that same year, he made some trips with the RAF, none of them long-distance. Then on 20 December, the day after his 27th birthday, he took part in a major raid on Frankfurt, flying with a Lancaster crew of 619 Squadron. His account of this operation is one of the very best pieces of contemporary writing about Bomber Command.[193] It was a raid in which 650 aircraft took part, forty-three of which were lost. The winter of 1943–44 saw appalling losses in Bomber Command, and Anthony could quite easily have been killed. With stark realism, some of his crew mates did not expect to survive their tour. They could see with their own eyes how many other crews were disappearing off their station, Woodhall Spa. In addition, the authorities published losses very accurately. After they got back, Anthony was given the figure of forty-two aircraft lost on the Frankfurt raid. No one was covering up the appalling death toll.

But his account is not particularly sombre. He was fascinated by the surreal experience of seeing Occupied Europe from the Lancaster's operational height of around 20,000ft, whilst the crew occasionally argued whether some flak-infested area was Aachen or Brussels or Antwerp. He found the situation both ridiculous and utterly bizarre, hearing his crew mates talk of the cities of Western Europe 'in terms of where they were last Friday [...] They knew them not by their cultural monuments, their political significance or hotels, but simply by their flak and searchlight barrages.'

Going over enemy-controlled territory was a thrill in itself even if other British aircraft were being shot down around them.

> Presently the rear-gunner said, 'There's one going down in flames. Right behind us.'
>
> I looked back and couldn't see anything until the engineer pointed it out. I could distinguish a faint, shapeless glow of flames. It served to emphasise that admission to these quarters was not free. The gate was shut behind. The house was haunted. Europe was all around us and we were all alone. Looking down on the ground, you could see odd, inexplicable, unaggressive-looking lights from time to time. They had no apparent operational significance, and may even have been black-out infringements of the grosser kind. But they served to emphasise our sense of being cut off. I need hardly say, because it has been said so often already, that this gives one a tremendous sense of comradeship with the other members of the crew. Your companionship with each other knows no inhibitions of temperament or prejudice. Friendship is perfect and complete. The idea of carrying an irritation or a resentment against one of them into the air seems quite out of the question.
>
> 'Fighter flares in front,' said Knights, the pilot. 'Keep a good lookout, gunner.'

Close to Frankfurt, their Lancaster was very nearly involved in a collision with another Lancaster, an occupational hazard in a campaign where hundreds of aircraft would arrive to bomb the target at the same time. Their aircraft was still rocking from the other aircraft's slipstream when they arrived at Frankfurt. The flak barrage, awesome in its strength and ferocity, opened up around them. With the flares dropped by the Pathfinders and enemy fighters, the moving searchlights, the bead-like pattern of incendiary fires on the ground, and the flashes of gunfire, 'there was a sense of supreme experience and excitement'. The crew were not satisfied with their target-aiming, and with cast-iron nerves went round once and came back again. Anthony wrote:

> Coming back on to the target it was like bright daylight. It is very difficult to describe. Nothing that I have ever read on the subject of bombing gave me anything like the impression which I actually had on the spot. I expected something of the atmosphere of a fire-blitz on the ground. I hadn't allowed for the sense of detachment produced by being so high. You knew that down there was a town of half a million people undergoing the most horrible ordeal. By staring round

the engineer's shoulder I could see the bomb-aimer preparing to press the button which would release another 4000lbs contribution to this ordeal. But it seemed quite unreal [...] The engineer pointed out the burning streets of Frankfurt. I could just make them out from an orange streak in the carpet of fairy-like lights produced by the incendiaries. I tried to think of the spectacle in terms of what was going on below, but it was just impossible to worry about. Mostly, I suppose, because we had plenty to worry about above.

The amount of fun and fury and fighter-flares was extraordinary. The sky was simply full of trouble. Yet oddly enough it was difficult to think of us in this particular aircraft as actively threatened by sudden death. I don't mean that, speaking for myself, I wasn't afraid. Certainly I was in a state of great alarm. But I didn't really expect that we in this aircraft would buy it.

There seemed to be plenty to buy.

When they eventually arrived back safely at the airfield, Anthony was utterly exhausted, too tired even to feel the sense of achievement which he had expected.

11

SHUBBS' WAR, JENNY NICHOLSON, AND ANNE

I t is now time to see what Shubbs – Anthony's beloved brother, Geoffrey – had been up to since conscript camp. At around the time that Anthony had joined ABCA in 1941, Geoffrey had also become an officer, having completed his OCTU training at Shrivenham, a Sandhurst-like artillery establishment near Swindon. His speciality was the Bofors Light Ack-Ack gun, though as an Ack-Ack officer his main duty would be giving orders from the control room, together with a great deal of man-management.

Eyesight problems had kept him out of the infantry, together with disabling hayfever, bouts of sneezing which would be followed by violent and difficult-to-staunch nosebleeds. Not being particularly war-like, he was grateful for the respite, but at the same time he could not help feeling sidelined. In the Ack-Ack you felt out of things. You might be scared stiff of being put in the poor bloody infantry, but you still felt out of things. The party – even if it was a nightmarishly violent one – was always going on elsewhere.[194]

Apart from a stint at Dover (or Hellfire Corner as it was then known), things were quiet and frequently extremely tedious for him. Even at Dover, his main amusement was observing his fellow officers:

Dear Momma,

I hope you didn't imagine we were being invaded last night when I abruptly rang off. There was a nice display of fireworks on. Right at this moment, from my window, I am watching a Spitfire making mock dive bombing attacks on our site. It all passes the time.

Gough has gone on leave and comparative peace now reigns in the mess. Hysterical rows went on right to the moment of departure, between a lunatic on one hand and a megalomaniac on the other. It becomes a bit of a strain.[195]

Despite the demands of Army service, Geoffrey and Anthony were still working together on various literary projects, just as they had done since boyhood. In fact, Geoffrey's account of the shooting down by the Ack-Ack of a German bomber had been the first outsider contribution to *WAR*, printed in November 1941 under the title 'We Bag Our First'.

'We Bag Our First' was not the typical *WAR* article but a camouflaged piece of fiction, evoking the stifling boredom and stagnation experienced by the Ack-Ack crews waiting on their lonely sites for enemy aircraft which never appeared. Geoffrey would not actually shoot down an aircraft until 1944, and 'We Bag Our First' was based on his relentless interviewing of a 2nd Lieutenant Nunn who had actually accomplished the feat:

The story follows one sleepy Sunday afternoon, Visitors Day, when the site has not seen an enemy plane for months. And then suddenly one appears and, amidst immense excitement, they shoot it down.

'My God, we've got it!' the GPO said. 'My God, we've got it. We've got it.' He was flushed and breathing quickly, and all he could do was repeat dreamily, 'We've got it!'

Then he said 'Rest,' and I shouted it out. The Dornier was still fluttering down, though there was no trail of smoke behind it, and then suddenly it fell quickly and crashed on the other side of the river. There was a burst of flame that died out at once. All the boys on the site burst out cheering. It was too good to be true.

The GPO rang up Gun Operations Room and put in the official claim for the plane. Then he put the phone down and looked at me. He was a young man of my own age. 'It was worth it,' he said quietly. I knew he was thinking of the five months that had gone, the monotony and the dreariness and the boredom.

'Yes, sir,' I said. 'It certainly was worth it.'

I looked out at the marsh from the command post. It seemed a new and fascinating place, as though I had never seen it before. Sometime later I remembered it was Visitors' Day and I went back to the football field.[196]

After publication, the story generated a great many complaints about its various inaccuracies. Anthony's reaction was, characteristically, amusement. It was one of the very rare instances when he took an interest in the discussions that were supposed to follow every issue of WAR. The editorial 'Lines of Thought', which both he and Watkins found very tedious to write, were intended to be the starting point for these discussions. Watkins thought that Anthony regarded the discussions as part of the Education Officers' job, and that it was the unit commanders' duty, not his, to make sure that the discussions were effective. Once WAR had gone to the printers, Anthony felt that his responsibility for it ended. The exceptions to this rule were the rare occasions when something sparked his particular interest, as in the storm over Geoffrey's work.

Geoffrey also contributed a chapter to Anthony's 1941 book, Oh, It's Nice to be in the Army!, under the title 'Factory Guard'. At one point in this piece he remembered the searchlights at Wanstead in the summer of 1939, installed once it had become obvious that war was approaching. He would watch them from his bedroom window in Ham Frith, 'moving like straight snakes across the dark night sky [...] They looked splendidly ominous and used to make me think, not too eagerly, of the shape of things to come.'[197] In one of those farcical flukes of chance which characterised his military career, he would be back near Wanstead in 1943 with searchlights of his own. He became senior officer at a battery in Leytonstone, next to Wanstead, as part of the move to establish a large battery on Wanstead Flats. His camp was only a mile or two from Ham Frith, and his batman, Gunner Williams, virtually became part of the Ham Frith establishment, constantly journeying there with his officer's laundry. Williams was rather effeminate and not particularly well suited to being a soldier; however, his temperament was congenial to Geoffrey and he was a very good batman.

By May 1944, Geoffrey was Major Cotterell with a large command. He was in charge of a Mixed 'Z' type anti-aircraft battery, with fifty-two Royal Artillery soldiers, fifty-six women soldiers from the ATS, and about 1,500 Home Guards with fifty-seven Home Guard officers. As the Regular Battery Commander, Geoffrey was responsible for the Home Guard's training and operations, and his chief aim in this respect was to make the Home Guard totally self-dependent and capable of shooting down enemy aircraft by themselves.

The Command Post was well-equipped with plotting teams and telephonists who drew arrows on maps with chinagraph pencils, showing the direction that the enemy aircraft were coming in. When the battery fired, there was 'a noise like the crashing of a tremendous wave upon the seashore' and then the most terrific firework display, the shells bursting in the sky, followed by the tinkling rain of the shrapnel fragments.[198]

After he had been promoted to Major, Geoffrey was told by his colonel that he was one of the six youngest majors in the Royal Artillery. It was certainly a fantastic experience for so young a man, and mainly a political one because of the complications of dealing with the Home Guard. They had their own major, an affluent business man, their own captains and troop commanders. As Geoffrey would later write, dealing with all these people was an incredible political education; 'naturally they were all rowing with each other all the time'.

> My Home Guard major was never a problem, but the captains – oh, my God, I had to deal with so many complaining captains – mostly with each other. I still commanded a nucleus of the so-called regular army, and on Sundays we had a church parade. After that I came back to the mess, in which forty or fifty Home Guard officers were having a drink. When I appeared they all stood up. That is not the thing which is done in normal army messes so far as I know. I was twenty-three when this first happened, and then twenty-four. I let them do it.[199]

Two letters survive from this period, written from Geoffrey to his much-loved aunt Janie who was still touring with ENSA. The first was written from 32 Northumberland Avenue, the Officers' Mess being on the ground floor whilst upstairs was Geoffrey's battery office. Across the road was the well-guarded entrance to his battery which could fire 128 rockets into the air at once, and sometimes did so. Dated 24 August 1943, just after his promotion to Major, hence the reference to wearing the crown which was his new badge of rank, the letter read:

> Darling
> Thank you so much for your letter, I am only sorry I could not share the bar of peppermint cream. Meggs [Janie and Mintie's brother] very luckily was at home when the happy event occurred. I hope I am still wearing the crown when you return. From my point of view the important thing is to have it three months; after that, whatever happens, I am always a captain.
> Meggs was looking very well and had a very good time. Mother had a few days off all meals and they spent a couple of days in town. Only one thing wrong: [Meggs] and father were sent to see 'The Human Comedy' – at which [...] Ma and I and Tone had cried our eyes out – and they came back calling it sentimental tripe. That was not popular.[200]

He told Janie that Anthony had spent some of his leave at Sidney and Zoe Bernstein's Kent farmhouse, Coppins – 'very nice' – and added that nothing was happening on his own literary or dramatic front, but he hoped that she was still 'a raging success'. He ended very affectionately, 'Look after yourself – love and love again, Shubbs'.

The second letter, written on 27 October 1943, wished Janie a very happy birthday and hoped that she was surviving the Shetlands winter which she was encountering as part of the ENSA tour. It continued:

> We have had one or two slight visitations from the Hun, but of no local consequence, and not sufficient to neutralise the growing boredom with which I am regarding Aldersbrook Road. (It has its compensations though.)
> The Regiment is giving a dance for the prisoners of war on Friday night, to which Papa and Mama, the Massons, Townleys, Michael and Nora will be going (quite like the Golf Club!); I cannot help feeling that it ought not to be necessary to give a dance to help the prisoners of war.
> Our dramatic career is as stagnant as ever; so is the literary branch.
> I will now close down as I have to watch some Home Guards.
> ('Trophies later')

Love, XXXX Shubbs[201]

The Massons and Michael and Nora Stark were local doctors and their wives, whilst Mr Townley was Geoffrey's father's usual golfing partner. Clearly the cream of Wanstead society were going to the dance.

When Geoffrey referred to 'our dramatic career', he was referring to the plays which he and Anthony had been writing together for some time. One of these was 'Mixed Battery', the first draft of which they had completed the previous year. Amongst the Cotterell family papers is a contract dated 22 October 1942, between Anthony and Geoffrey and Jack de Leon of the 'Q' Theatre. The Q Theatre was a small playhouse, seating an audience of less than 500, near Kew Bridge in west London. Despite its diminutive size, it was renowned for being one of the best avant-garde theatres in London, its forte being new or experimental plays performed by excellent actors. The contract with the Cotterell brothers was immensely long and detailed, encompassing transfers to West End, film rights, and just about every other permutation of immense success, none of which unfortunately ever happened.

'Mixed Battery' was a comedy about the soldiers and ATS women of an Ack-Ack battery, set in the Officers Mess, which culminated in the shooting down of a plane. Anthony and Geoffrey wrote it together, whenever they could be together, throwing lines at each other and sometimes becoming helpless with laughter. They had a great deal of fun with it, and, as Geoffrey was to say later, it might have been light enough and bad enough to do well if only the Q Theatre had gone ahead with it. Geoffrey would continue to work on the play for another two or three years. On 22 May 1945, he would write to Mintie that he had heard a play was being put on by Jack de Leon about the ATS called 'Temporary Ladies'. Geoffrey thought that this might be 'a competitive factor', adding jokingly 'a nasty cheap title anyway, my dear!'[202]

Anthony and Geoffrey also wrote a comedy about life on the *Daily Express*, inspired by the hit play and movie 'The Front Page'. Again they spent much of their time laughing, and thought that the end result was good, but it never got anywhere.

It was while they working on one of these plays that their collaboration was broken by the interference of another person, a vivacious, talkative, highly intelligent young woman with strong opinions she was not ashamed to voice and a liking for running things her own way. Due to her own, rather limited, experience of theatre and radio, she claimed what Geoffrey thought was spurious professional expertise. He disliked her interference and did not agree with her suggestions. In the end he and Anthony agreed to break off their collaboration. They knew and trusted each other too well to fall out, but for the moment all work on joint dramatic projects ceased.

The young woman in question was the most serious love of Anthony's life. Her name was Jenny Nicholson, and she was the eldest daughter of Nancy Nicholson and the famous writer, Robert Graves.

Since his relationship with Signe had ended, Anthony had had other girlfriends, briefly and anonymously referred to in his writings, but none of them lasting for long. One rather odd little entanglement, which apparently ran its brief course in December 1941, was with Barbara Skelton, who would later marry Cyril Connolly. Barbara was the definitive femme fatale. Extremely pretty in an exotic feline way, she was also highly sexed, volatile, cruel, heartless, and unreliable to an almost pathological degree. She had a string of admirers, which included Feliks Topolski, the artist, and Peter Quennell, a journalist, writer, and editor. Anthony, who was part of the same slightly raffish London scene as Barbara, may perhaps have met her at one of the popular nightspots like Frisco's, the Café Royal or La Cigale.

The only evidence for their love affair is in Barbara's frequently very inaccurate diary, cannibalised in her book *Tears Before Bedtime*, in which she does not even trouble herself to spell his name properly. Nonetheless, it is quite clear that it is Anthony whom she is describing when she writes about a Friday supper of minced chicken and water ices at the Berkeley.

[Afterwards] so as to avoid Feliks who was coming round at ten we went to the pub next door where I had a large brandy and a pork pie as I still felt hungry [...] Peter arrived at the flat at eleven, tipsy as ever but very gay. Cotterill seemed rather put out but took it well. I hope I have not lost a new slave, he is so sweet and reminds me of a Disney faun with his funny sticking-out ears and enormous dimples.[203]

Barbara liked to provoke jealousy amongst her various admirers, and the diary entry above seems to indicate that Anthony had been expecting to sleep with her until the unwelcome appearance of Quennell. Quennell was clearly jealous of Anthony, who was more than ten years younger. In one place in her book, Barbara would describe him as being disparaging about *What! No Morning Tea?* (although, in her usual slapdash way, she gives the name of Anthony's 'little' book as *What No Butter*).

Other very brief entries described Anthony as sharing a stew with her at the flat, and appearing at her office 'looking shamefaced and embarrassed', where after standing in the hall for several minutes 'at a loss for anything to say', he then produced two packets of cigarettes 'as a peace offering'. Barbara concluded that his 'behaviour' of the previous night was worrying him. The 'behaviour' is not explained, but perhaps he had made a pass at Barbara and she had unexpectedly taken the moral high ground.

Anthony had a fairly casual attitude to sexual relations, as can be seen in the occasional remark in his writings, such as in this reaction to a cancelled bombing raid he had gone to report: 'I was surprised to find myself feeling frustrated instead of reprieved; as if I had made an unsuccessful attempt at seduction.'[204] Whatever he was expecting from Barbara, she delighted in refusing it. She led him exactly the same dance that she led her other admirers, stringing him along and not bothering to hide the fact that he was one of several. She wrote of him 'persevering still' in trying to woo her, and of one evening arriving at her flat two hours late without offering any explanation. After placing his hat on the kitchen table he 'stood by the sink and gazed at me'. The meal which she was preparing was then eaten in 'oppressive silence'. Anthony left, but sometime later reappeared 'penitent and forlorn. So we parted friends.'[205]

Anthony was not short of admirers himself, and not the type to persevere in such hopeless devotion. How the relationship ended, Barbara does not tell. Anthony with his usual intense reticence about his private life makes no identifiable mention of her in his surviving writings.

Nor is there any mention there of his relationship with Jenny Nicholson, the most serious love affair of his life. All that remains are a few scattered references to Jenny in his letters to her father, Robert Graves, letters which are preserved in archives around the world because of Graves's iconic status. The dating of these letters suggests that Anthony and Jenny's relationship began sometime in early 1942; it lasted well over two years and faltered to a close sometime after D-Day.

Jenny was an extremely different person to Barbara, and as driven and focused as Anthony himself. Born in 1919 (and thus almost three years younger than Anthony), her childhood had been a difficult one. Graves had deserted his family in the 1920s for the poet Laura Riding, and Jenny had suffered the humiliations of low social status and poverty, whilst knowing that all her father's love and wealth were being lavished upon a usurper. It was not until the mid-1930s that father and daughter met up again after a separation of seven years. Unlike her more amenable siblings, Jenny was unable to forget what her father had made her suffer. Their relationship was tempestuous, not least because Jenny at the time was leading a very rackety life as an actress and dancer. Graves was eager to get to know her again, proud, affectionate and indulgent. He gave her money, and made peace with Winston Churchill when she indiscreetly talked to a journalist about the elopement of her best friend, Sarah Churchill, Winston's daughter. (Jenny and Sarah had been 'hoofers' together.) He also paid for her private medical care when she became seriously ill from gonorrhoea. The disease and an operation, possibly to terminate a pregnancy, may have left her unable to have children.

When her theatrical career went nowhere, Jenny became a journalist based at Bristol. Once the war began, she joined the WAAFs, soon became an officer, then a press officer who specialised in liaising between the WAAF and the BBC. She was enormously successful in this role, and dazzled many people with her vivacity, shining eyes, and tremendous energy and enthusiasm. When recruiting for WAAF cooks became an urgent problem, she found a girl in an RAF cookhouse with a tremendous voice and got her on the radio as 'the Singing Cook', which gave huge impetus to the recruitment drive.[206]

Through her father, Jenny was well-connected and knew many extremely influential people. She was highly ambitious, both for herself and any prospective partner, and Anthony would have been very attractive to her not only because he was handsome but because it was so obvious that he was destined for great things.

Jenny also had great physical courage. After D-Day she would go to Europe as a WAAF war reporter, and travel very close to the front line with a group of top journalists which included Alan Morehead and Alexander Clifford, the man she would later marry. By the time Brussels was liberated, she was right in the vanguard, arriving in the city even before it was cleared of Germans.

Jenny was never short of boyfriends even if she was not a conventional beauty; her animation, intelligence, and determination were very winning. Alan Moorehead, the great friend of Alexander Clifford, described her as having 'a natural vivacity, an unaffected assurance in her own social background, a flair for unusual and optimistic decisions and an astonishing energy in carrying them through: a touch of recklessness and an eagerness for life'.[207] Anthony must have found her attractive for those same reasons, and her lack of physical beauty did not matter so much though generally he was very susceptible to feminine beauty.

Jenny's father took a very kindly interest in the affairs of young writers, and in this capacity gave practical assistance to both the Cotterell brothers. Graves was then living at Vale House at Galmpton in Devon, because he felt that it was his patriotic duty to live in his home country during the war. Both Geoffrey and Anthony visited him there, and Graves made an indelible impression on Geoffrey:

He was very big, very handsome, like a Caesar. You almost thought he should be wearing a toga. He was very witty and enormously well-informed – his talk about the Roman Empire was like gossiping about the Army today – like listening to gossip in a bar in London about the Army.[208]

By November of 1942, Anthony was writing the sort of letter to Graves which showed that he and Jenny were very close:

Dear Robert Graves

Thank you so much for the invitation. Of course I would love to come down with Jenny. At the moment we are precariously shorthanded, but directly I get my leave, I will write and ask you, or ask Jenny to ask you, if it is a convenient time. Assuming that Jenny gets her own leave simultaneously; otherwise perhaps I could come alone.

As you were saying, she lives at far too high a pressure. It is no use reasoning with her. Instead of going home to bed as instructed, she sits up half the night writing some fool script. Where will it end?

Yours sincerely
Anthony Cotterell[209]

In May 1943, another letter to Graves again mentions Jenny, in a way which demonstrates the teasing relationship which she and Anthony had.

> Jenny is sending you the book I have just put together. It really is most kind of you to look through it and I do appreciate it.
> Jenny has been berating me for slovenliness. Something in that I fear.
> Don't be too hard on me. I am only a young chap trying to make a living. [...]
> I am just off to meet the famous orator on her return from quickening Slough.[210]

The only book this can have been is *RAMC*, Anthony's account of the Army's wartime medical services. Perhaps Jenny thought that her father would temper some of Anthony's more slapdash writing habits.

In June, Anthony wrote to Graves thanking him for his suggestions on how to improve the book. The handwritten letter was sent from the *WAR* office at 47 Eaton Square. In it, Anthony explained the reasons behind his apparently careless approach.

> The trouble is that I have been educated to take great care and trouble over newspaper articles, to make each one as good as possible of its kind; and to regard books as mass production work in which broad effects compensated for relatively careless writing. This inverted snobbery was reinforced by sub-editing books for serialisation purposes. They were normally full of duplications [...] When the writers wrote to protest at my butcherings their concern seemed to be much greater than was warranted. They thought the matter more important than it really was; delusions of significance I thought. No doubt I shall learn different.[211]

Anthony could be as strongly opinionated as Jenny. However, when he really wanted a favour from Graves, he was a master of winning flattery and politeness.[212]

Anthony seldom wrote a letter to Graves which did not end with a witticism, such as the one he wrote on 5 November 1943 which told Graves: 'I am feeling rather pleased just now by my inclusion as a member of the War Office Firewatching team for tonight, Guy Fawkes night. All picked men I should think.'[213]

Meanwhile Graves was also helping Geoffrey with his first novel, *Then a Soldier*.[214] He introduced him to a prominent London agent, A.P. Watts, and also made a number of suggestions about the manuscript. Some of these were about the key character Robert Halbrook, Geoffrey's alter-ego, whom he thought was too nebulous, an opinion which Geoffrey shared.

Both Geoffrey and Anthony were very keen to advance their literary careers, and the relationship with Graves was extremely important to them. It would continue independently of Anthony's relationship with Jenny. In 1944, it would become even closer, when Anthony began to plan his own magazine, *The Haymarket*, and Graves agreed to be its most illustrious contributor.

Jenny also used her father for literary favours, and he was always pleased to help her when he could. One desperately scrawled undated letter, written from Adastral House, London WC2, which was part of the Air Ministry, seems to be asking Robert to stop the publication of some article she felt was 'common and inexpert'. She then writes 'Anthony can't advise me'. The letter appears to have been written in 1944, and Anthony might therefore have been away, either on one of his research trips or in Normandy after D-Day.[215]

Jenny was someone who demanded to be treated as an intellectual equal, and she was fiery enough and outspoken enough to make sure that she was. For a while the relationship between her and Anthony was serious enough for there to be talk of marriage. Jenny stayed at Ham Frith at least once, but the impression she made upon Mintie and Graham was not a good one. It is possible that she confided to Mintie that she thought she might be unable to have children, perhaps due to the gonorrhoea or possible abortion. Whether or not such a conversation ever took place, Mintie thought Jenny was not physically good enough for her beautiful son, and was deeply concerned about future grandchildren. Jenny had slightly protruding front teeth, which Mintie held against her on eugenic grounds. Mintie tried to reason her son out of his attachment, but Anthony told his mother 'I can't help it'.[216]

But gradually the relationship petered out. With both of them in the services, it must have been very difficult to arrange times when they could see one another.

Before they parted irrevocably, Anthony began a relationship with someone who could not have been more different than Jenny. She was an extraordinarily pretty and charming young woman of slightly suspect character, whom it may be prudent just to call Anne. Anne lived with her mother in Shepherd's Market, then an extremely louche address, and the contrast between the neighbourhood and this outstandingly beautiful young woman with the superb manners could hardly have been more extreme. When the film, *Gigi*, came out in 1958, fourteen years after he had met her, Geoffrey immediately recognised the similarities between Anne and Gigi, a courtesan being trained by her grandmother to capture a wealthy man.

Signe had been jaw-droppingly beautiful but at heart she was a simple and good-natured girl. Anne was sophisticated, immaculately dressed, poised, elegant, and very probably on the make. The beautiful phrase which may perhaps best describe her is a *poule de luxe*; at least that is the impression she would give to Geoffrey on the one occasion that he met her. Anne had begun grooming Anthony in the manners of the adoring courtier, and that autumn told Geoffrey affectionately about his brother, 'I had to teach him to buy flowers'. Whether this relationship would have endured if events had turned out differently, it is impossible to say.

Jenny was extremely loyal to the men in her life, and she did not abandon Anthony even when things had apparently come to an end between them. After Arnhem, when Anthony was posted as missing but the possibility of his safe return was still in the air, it fell to Geoffrey to tell Jenny about Anne. It may be that Jenny, now in love with Alexander Clifford, had first contacted Geoffrey, wanting his advice about how Anthony would feel about things. Geoffrey was able to reassure her that if she wanted a serious relationship with Alexander Clifford, that would be fine. Geoffrey sensed that Jenny was relieved to have this reassurance: 'It was as if I were giving her a licence to stray, and also that otherwise she might not stray, and I remember feeling the responsibility.'[217]

Jenny would marry Alexander Clifford in the Savoy Chapel in London in early 1945, and Geoffrey would be one of the guests at her wedding. Had it been possible, no doubt Anthony would have been there also. When Jenny and Alexander went on their subsequent travels in liberated Europe, the Cotterell family would ask them to pass back any news which they might hear of Anthony, who was posted as missing. Anne would also ask to be kept up to date with news about Anthony, but after a few months all reference to her fades out of the Cotterell family correspondence.

12

PARACHUTIST

In his last article for *WAR* before D-Day, Anthony reported on the Airborne Forces and the Glider Pilot Regiment. The latter were highly trained soldiers who piloted the seemingly flimsy engineless aircraft carrying not only men but also any equipment which was too heavy to drop by parachute.

The article begins with great cheerfulness:

On the ground gliders don't look so sinister. Their frailty is friendly. The small ones look like drunken bats, the large ones like Disney's elephant Dumbo.

Once, in 1942, I was taken for a flip in a glider. It was referred to locally as 'the glider'. In those days the Airborne Forces had one marked disability; they weren't airborne. Things are rearranged now.

On one airfield at which I landed some weeks ago during a short tour of glider units, we drove up a long archway formed by the wings of gliders parked on either side of a runway of one field.[218]

As he described these superbly equipped airborne units, which were being readied for a massive European invasion, Anthony could not help revealing the acute fascination of someone who was hoping to go into action with them. As the arrangements for D-Day began to firm up, he would apply to join 6th Airborne Division on their drop into Occupied France.

Anthony's interest in the Airborne Forces dated from some time back, possibly even as early as 1941. In December of that year, in the seventh issue of *WAR*, an article had appeared about British parachutists.[219] It was written by Lieutenant-Colonel Flavell, the commanding officer of the 2nd Parachute Battalion. By an extraordinary twist of fate, this would be the battalion with which Anthony was at Arnhem, and Flavell's son, Jim Flavell, would actually be on the truck with Anthony at the time of the Brummen shooting.

Lieutenant-Colonel Flavell's article described the British airborne arm in its infancy. In the following three years it would develop into a highly esteemed, expensively trained and lavishly equipped force which contained some of the best soldiers in the British Army. From the outset, however, the role the airborne forces would play in battle was clearly defined. Flavell described parachute troops as being like cavalry in that they were used for special tasks as a forerunner of a major operation. Their function was to capture key points, personnel or equipment, and (almost invariably) to defend these targets until the main ground forces arrived.

After describing the various technical problems of aircraft and equipment which had to be overcome, Flavell went on to examine the type of man who could become a parachutist:

The delusion still persists in some quarters that in choosing parachutists the selection boards look for men whose hands drag along the ground when they walk.

The medical tests are, of course, very stiff but it isn't so much bulky, muscular development which is wanted as better than average eyesight and hearing. [The] training is very arduous, but the toughness it brings develops great self-confidence.

The worst moment, not unnaturally, is just before you jump. No matter how many jumps you may make, no matter how serenely you approach the process, there is still a tremendously strong instinct not to throw yourself out into the air. It isn't fear, but a strong instinct which has to be overcome by great self-control. [...]

But once you have jumped and the parachute has opened there is a supreme sense of thrill and achievement. One feels utterly alone and completely dependent on oneself, and there is a certain pleasure in that alone.[220]

Anthony must have been particularly struck by the last two paragraphs. When further opportunities to cover the airborne forces came along, he would be the man who researched and wrote the articles for *WAR*. Watkins with his dislike of dangerous situations was doubtless very happy to forego the opportunity.

On 28 November 1942, Anthony wrote a long article which clearly demonstrates why he was so fascinated:

The everyday atmosphere of the airborne forces, like that of any dangerous trade, is essentially matter of fact.

Of course, things aren't exactly easy. It is a hard life, permeated with a tremendous idealism and sense of purpose. Discipline is rigid, smartness is a must [...] It is difficult to get in and difficult to stay in. If they think you are unsuitable in any way, out you go. Tomorrow. Just like that.

One thing that the airborne authorities are most anxious to emphasise is that brains are more important that a tough appearance, and that aggressive behaviour in public-houses constitutes no criterion of anything but unsuitability.

Their platform is that toughness is mainly mental and therefore the first requisite for a recruit is plenty of native common sense.[221]

The article continued with a detailed description of how the parachutists were selected and trained, and how they maintained their physical fitness. It ended with an account of the Bruneval raid, a high-profile attack on a radio-location station in France which had taken place nine months earlier in February 1942. The raid – only the second British airborne assault of the war – was a complete success, not only tactically but from the public relations angle. People loved the derring-do of it, the audacious parachutists catching the Germans by surprise, and then, before the hornet's nest was fully aroused, leaving by boat with parts of the radar and a captured German technician. The commander, Major John Frost, was fêted after his return, and was awarded the Military Cross. He himself was under no illusions about the significance of the raid, referring to it in his autobiography as 'a mere flea-bite', but he knew that it had the most immense effect in lifting British morale. This was at a particularly low ebb due to the catastrophic loss of Singapore and the humiliating escape of German battleships up the Channel. People were doubting that Britain could win the war; now, once again, they were full of hope.

One very beneficial effect of the Bruneval raid, as Frost noted, was that it put the airborne forces on the map. Doubters fell away, and high-level support and increased resources began to come the parachutists' way.

Anthony based his account of the Bruneval raid on the experiences of a Private Freeman. He was not able to interview Frost, who is referred to throughout as 'the Major', and thus he missed the chance to meet the man who would become his commanding officer at Arnhem.

Frost appeared again in *WAR* in March 1943, this time in his own words. The *WAR* editorial, almost certainly written by Anthony, comments: 'We publish this week a detailed, undramatised operational account of 10 days in the life of a parachute battalion in North Africa. It wasn't written for publication, and it hasn't been rewritten for that purpose. Therein lies its value.'[222]

Through his research for *WAR*, Anthony had a reasonable knowledge of the airborne forces when he applied and was accepted for parachute training in October 1943. In an episode rather reminiscent of the way in which he had dealt with his call-up papers, he told no one in his family or at the *WAR* offices about his plans. He arranged the course, went on it, completed it, and then allowed the news to gently disseminate by reappearing with the charismatic parachute emblem sewn upon his sleeve.

When Geoffrey saw the parachute emblem, it gave him a jarring shock, for it was a sign that his brother intended to take a much more active and dangerous part in the war. After the shooting at Brummen, when Anthony was still posted as wounded and missing, Geoffrey would see the parachute emblem on his brother's best uniform and refer to it in a poem about Anthony as 'the quiet sad badge upon your sleeve'.

Anthony wrote an extended piece about his parachute training, beginning with the first day when he discovered that at 26 he was 'the old man' of his group. A cut-down version of the piece appeared in two consecutive issues of *WAR*, and Anthony reserved the long version for *An Apple for the Sergeant*.

The training program was for eight jumps, three from a balloon (two in the daytime and one at night) and five aircraft jumps. The trainees were warned off all sorts of things, including making a nuisance of themselves with the locals, distracting the WAAFs who were packing the parachutes, and in particular from trying to summon up Dutch courage by drinking. Anthony records the particularly vivid homily which they were given by their teacher on the last subject:

> Don't do it. It doesn't make a twopenny curse of difference to how you feel, you will quiver just the same when you have to jump 700 feet in the dark. And it may just make that little bit of difference to how you perform. You know the story of the mouse who came out of his hole and drank drops of whisky, then he went back to his hole, and he came out again and drank some more whisky and then some more, until finally he was shouting 'Bring out your bloody cats!' At which point he was killed. Now, if you go drinking, you will be like the mouse.[223]

The program was very rigorous, tightly controlled and safety-conscious, and there was much talk of 'moral courage'. The afternoon before the first jump Anthony records himself as being 'in a state of constant vibration', but then observed with his usual strict exactitude that self-consciousness played a large part in this physical reaction. If one was alone, it was easier to be composed; it was the anxiety to present 'not too desperate an appearance to other people' that increased the appalling nerves. He felt certain that there was something abnormal in his pre-jump appearance because a WAAF officer sitting next to him at teatime said, 'What are you looking at me like that for?' when in fact he was lost in his 'own little night-mare world'. Others were clearly suffering just as much. When he went to bed that night, he noticed that his room-mate was writing his Will.

The following day, Monday 18 October, Anthony's group took a 40-minute bus ride in the dark to the dropping zone. As day began to break, they became aware of two immense barrage balloons, each with a basket strapped underneath. At 7.15am the jumping started. A balloon would gather up five men and go up to a seemingly impossible height. The five men then jumped through the hole in the basket floor, and the balloon would be laboriously winched down again to repeat the process. You had plenty of time to contemplate the horrors of what you were doing, and Anthony wrote that everyone was 'very composed in a pale kind of way'.

After a very long wait in the rain, it was his turn to get in the balloon basket:

Finally, the moment came to climb in. It was a feeling quite unlike any other feeling I have ever had. You are conscious of the considerable test of will-power [...] There is a feeling of total unreality as the balloon goes up. It isn't exactly like the feeling before the school sports, and I think on the whole it isn't as bad as that [...] Speaking for my own part, this was something which I was actively anxious to accomplish, whereas the one thing I wanted to do before the school sports was to be hidden until it was all over. I kept telling myself [...] 'A lot of people have been through that hole this morning and so are bloody you.'[224]

As he finally jumped, Anthony felt 'some good old primitive fear' and a sense of being utterly and irretrievably out of control. Then everything was accomplished satisfactorily; his parachute opened promptly, he managed the descent well, and with extreme rapidity found himself on the ground. He ran round his parachute to collect it, received praise from his instructor, and went to the YMCA for the traditional celebratory cup of tea.

Buoyed up hugely by their success, his group drove back to the camp complete with the community singing which they been unable to manage in the doom-laden journey to the dropping ground in the darkness. Only one man had refused to jump. Anthony wrote with great sympathy, as if he could all too easily identify with the wretched fellow:

He had been one of the outstanding men in his section. He was young, good-looking, well-built and seemed self-confident, but apparently something snapped. Incidentally, no one felt any sense of contempt; the typical comment was: 'Sorry for that bloke'. This reaction was reinforced, when we got back to the camp, by seeing him standing at ease outside the office, pathetically waiting to be sent back to his unit, and trying to repair his battered self-esteem. When a man refuses, he is sent back to his unit immediately [...] because of the possibly disconcerting effect on the others. When you are jumping, the last thing you want to be reminded of is the case against it.[225]

They made another balloon jump the same day. The following day they began to practise for the aircraft jump. Anthony was given an assessment by their corporal, who, after commending his first jump, said 'I think you were a bit lazy on the ground training'.

I wearily denied the suggestion, because it was one which has pursued me in any course of instruction in any subject which I have ever undertaken [...] I had worked very hard, but it was still the same old reaction. Disappointing.[226]

That afternoon Anthony went down with one of those passing military illnesses to which he was so prone. By the following morning it led to him being carted off in an ambulance to sick-quarters, feeling not only physically appalling but also mentally appalled by the idea of how hard it would be to resume the nerve-racking course.

Sick-quarters was in a requisitioned house. One of the nurses looked strikingly like Veronica Lake, the film star, and this was an enjoyable bonus. Anthony shared a pleasant upstairs room with a young Lieutenant from the South Staffs, who was suffering from light concussion from a balloon jump. Whilst they were recovering, they could contemplate the horrors which still awaited them by letting their eyes track around the frieze on the wallpaper, which, in a cheering way, showed parachutists having all sorts of accidents. It had been contributed by Major Ian Fenwick, the celebrated *Punch* cartoonist, who had recently been in with an injured leg. Some of Fenwick's cartoons of parachuting would appear in Anthony's book *An Apple for the Sergeant*.

After two days of acute illness, in which his temperature rose to 104 degrees, Anthony was finally discharged, feeling very weak and shaky. He was asked if he was fit enough to jump that afternoon, and having directly contradicted advice by drinking 'some strengthening whisky' Anthony said that he was.

Fenwick, who had recovered from his leg injury, was 'attached to our course in a vague way'. Anthony described him as 'an enormous man of slightly horsey mien', adding that his height made it very difficult for him to do the jumping or the landing when one was supposed to roll up into 'a cosy human ball'. Fenwick and Anthony became instant friends, and went on the first aircraft jump together. However, by the second aircraft jump, Fenwick (who had done the first one with 'noteworthy composure') had simply disappeared. Anthony commented rather loftily, given his own propensity for breaking the rules: 'He is a great man for disappearing. You don't really feel that he is involved to the same degree as other people. His air of detachment places him in a little world of his own.'[227] He could have been writing about himself.

The course went on in its inexorable way. Fenwick turned up again, and Anthony and he teamed up for the grand finale, a parachute drop and mock exercise. Anthony played the part of a Bren gunner and Fenwick a rifleman, part of a section whose role was to divert the enemy's attention with gunfire whilst another two sections tried to capture a bridge.

> We came in for a good deal of criticism from the Battle School Instructors who said that we were not properly under cover, and wouldn't accept Major Fenwick's heated rejoinder that neither were the enemy forces which he himself, let alone the rest of us, had already annihilated. The Instructors expressed their displeasure by standing on top of the bank behind which we were crouched, and projecting an extravagant number of thunder-flashes round us. I hadn't taken part in an infantry scheme for some time, but it was all reassuringly familiar. We floundered in the mud and wondered what was happening in just the same old way. Presently we were declared to have captured the bridge and made our way back to the road where the buses were waiting.[228]

Much to his delight, Anthony had passed. Three men had given up during the course, including a man who had won the Military Cross at Dunkirk. The final verdict on Anthony was one with which he was obviously exceedingly pleased given his terrible record on previous Army courses. Written by his section instructor, it read: 'An average jumper, quiet but confident. He is much better in aircraft than on ground training. Good and confident in aircraft. A quiet, intelligent type.'

Fenwick would be killed on special operations in France on 7 August 1944, six weeks before Anthony was shot at Brummen. The news must have come through to the Eaton Square office, because Watkins records that Anthony suffered a 'considerable shock' on hearing of Fenwick's death.[229] It is the one place in any account of Anthony which describes his reaction to the death of a fellow soldier.

13

PRELUDE TO D-DAY

When Anthony had volunteered for the parachuting course, he had evidently been planning to use his new skills in an operational situation, but no such opportunity presented itself for several months. Then, as D-Day approached in the summer of 1944, he optimistically applied to parachute into France with 6th Airborne Division. Another journalist, Bill Richardson, applied with him, but in the event both of them were refused permission.[230]

Watkins' memoirs tell us that, for some time before D-Day, he and Anthony had been studying the possibilities of when, where and how the Second Front would take place. Due to their work for *WAR*, they had a good idea of the numbers involved, from which they estimated the length of coastline which would be required. Their knowledge of the type of training exercises being staged led to them ruling out an assault on cliffs. This left two choices – the beaches east of Calais with much inundated land behind them, or the beaches west of Deauville in Normandy. Correctly, they decided that the latter was the likeliest prospect. Anthony then checked the Channel tidetables and deduced that the landings would take place in the first week in June. Using this extremely accurate guesswork, he and Watkins began to make their own preparations.

Anthony was determined to land in France with the first wave of assault troops; as Watkins observed, 'this would be an event he could not possibly let slip by'. He himself did not covet such reckless glory, but was more than happy to let his own French trip wait until Anthony returned. The time-lag in their arrangements was a relief: 'I made my own plans to go after a suitable interval, when at least the exits from the beaches would have been cleared of mines.'[231]

When the time came, however, Anthony faced a considerable problem in achieving his aim of landing very early in the invasion. But he had made his preparations extremely well and was able to sidestep all the official obstacles. Watkins describes how he did it:

> Montgomery had banned from the invasion force all spectators not specifically authorised by his staff, and, since it is never advisable to ask for a concession which you may be refused, Anthony was evading the ban by crossing with a field ambulance (his connections with Medical Services at the War Office were very good).[232]

Later Watkins crossed out this passage and substituted a more carefully worded version of Anthony's proceedings:

> He was determined to land in Normandy on D-Day in 1944 and his preparations were most carefully planned; as they had to be, for 2 Army HQ, in charge of the British landings, wanted no non-operational bodies on board any of the ships. But, with the connivance of medical authorities (whom he had carefully cultivated for months previously), he crossed with them.[233]

What these slightly different versions show is that Anthony had developed masterly skills in getting his own way. Once his friends in the Royal Army Medical Corps had effectively smuggled him across the Channel, he would be free to do what he wanted. As Watkins added: 'Once Anthony was ashore it would have needed a stiff official prohibition to hold him back from going where he intended to go and doing what he intended to do.'[234] Anthony did not ask for permission to go to France from his ABCA bosses – they were no longer exercising any control over him.

At the same time as making private arrangements, Anthony was trying official channels, including the application to go in with 6th Airborne Division. The final refusal of this request only arrived once he had joined the medical officers with whom he would be travelling. On that same day he was finally offered an officially sanctioned option which would get him into France a few hours after the invasion had started. Anthony rejected this proposal, commenting in his diary: 'Not nearly so satisfactory as where I am now.'

Before Anthony joined the medical officers behind the wall of secrecy which guarded the D-Day assembly camps, he and Watkins were briefly involved in the exercise codenamed *Fabius*. The final dress rehearsal for *Overlord*, the codename for the actual invasion, *Fabius* was part of the massive PR exercise which would generate world-wide publicity once D-Day began. The Ministry of Information had asked the PR people at the War Office to help, and it was thus that Anthony and Watkins became involved.

Watkins wrote:

> We assembled one sunny morning, a motley group, one, Denzil Batchelor smartly turned out as a captain in the Intelligence Corps, the others looking as if they had come from a poorly disciplined Pioneer unit, and we drove off for a four-day tour of Portsmouth, Southampton and the New Forest, the centre of British invasion activity. By then, Exercise FABIUS was in motion.[235]

Pioneer units were the labouring backbone of the Army; they were immensely strong, capable, and as courageous as lions, but not blessed with the usual military smartness. Whether it was the group's motley appearance or not, very soon they ran into trouble. On arriving at 2 Army HQ, which was then stationed in one of the old forts overlooking Portsmouth Harbour, they discovered that their standard War Office passes did not give the special authorisation required. The PR unit at 21st Army Group HQ, which was in charge of both *Fabius* and *Overlord*, had neglected to give them the proper credentials. Their arrival was greeted with the deepest suspicion and they were put under arrest for several hours.[236] Eventually Denzil Batchelor, under escort, was allowed out to get them the proper accreditation, and in the late afternoon they were released.

But then there was more trouble, this time from Mabel, their ATS driver. Mabel, a rather buxom girl of around 28, was deeply upset by her imprisonment. As Other Ranks, not an officer, she had received far less kindly treatment than her passengers, and now she regarded them as highly dubious characters and wanted nothing more to do with them.

> We had intended to pack things up for that day, find a hotel for the four of us for the night, and start afresh the next morning, but that was now out of the question. Mabel would no more have slept under the same roof as us as she would have got into bed with a viper.
>
> It was Anthony who persuaded her to give us one more chance; I was constantly surprised at the charm he could conjure up when he really wanted something from a woman.[237]

Once again, we catch a glimpse of the manipulative side of Anthony's character, of which perhaps Watkins did not entirely approve.

Anthony's pre-D-Day diary runs from 20 May to 5 June 1944, ending at 10.00pm when he was on board the ship taking him to France. The diary begins with him catching the 1.40pm train to Southampton, which ran on the Dorchester line he had known so well in his early months in the Army. He was met at the station by two of the medical officers of the field surgical unit he was to cross with, who took him to Sub-area 2 HQ.

The camp where they were staying was 5 miles out of Winchester, a mixture of huts and square American tents. The place was humming with organised chaos, the phone never stopped ringing, 'each call a catalogue of unforeseen complications'. A pleasant atmosphere of irresponsibility and mildly hysterical hilarity prevailed. At the HQ, they were tearing up and packing.

> Administratively it was a wonderful opportunity to get all sorts of things for nothing, to tear up embarrassing correspondence, to abandon courts of inquiry, to indent for things and, miraculously, get them.
>
> All the things which had never been available were now suddenly available for the asking. And through all these transactions ran a stimulating sense of impunity, summarised in the current tag, 'They can't touch you now.' It didn't matter much what you did, they wouldn't leave you behind.[238]

Summing up the exhilarating pre-holiday atmosphere, Anthony tutted flippantly, 'Really, men's reactions are too much'. He had heard no one discuss the invasion seriously, and what scraps of discussion there were tended to be wildly off-beat. A couple of days after arriving at the camp, he would record one man asking whether there was any scientific possibility of the Germans having electrified all the water. He would also hear demoralising little stories about various training schemes for the invasion which had gone wrong. On one scheme an entire unit had gone to sleep due to a combination of water-sterilising tablets mixed with seasickness pills. Like everyone else over the coming days, Anthony would wonder if the almost inconceivably complex feats of planning involved would actually work when the critical moment came.

His first morning's research was not encouraging. Suffering from an excess of whisky drunk the night before, he went to recce the wiring on a neighbouring camp. Security was paramount and the wire was supposed to keep the troops from leaving now that preparations were approaching their climax and the detailed briefings were about to begin. Anthony noted: 'Of course the effect is purely psychological, nearly all the men in these camps having been trained for years to cope with barbed wire.' He and his small party were taken round by a 'very subalternish subaltern', who pooh-poohed the official estimate that eighty rolls were needed for that particular camp. Apparently the actual requirements were nearer 800, 'so just for one thing there wasn't the slightest hope of getting it done in time,' Anthony commented sarcastically.

After lunch he met the blood transfusion captain with whom he was to travel to France, and they hitch-hiked into Winchester.

> Winchester was not very promising until we found the Royal Hotel where after initial hesitation and some calculations of capacity by the chef, it was decided that we could have dinner, also a bath. The key positions wore all held by grey-haired ladies. The housekeeper was told to conduct us to bathrooms. She gave us a towel and tried to select the right key for the soap cupboard. 'Lock and key, of course,' she whispered. 'Everything's under lock and key.'
>
> She runs the place like fifty years ago. She thinks it is fifty years ago. Locking up the soap. I ask you, who wants soap? [...]
>
> Madman head waiter who took unlimited time to decide which table we were to have. Afterwards we got up to go and asked for our bill at the door. 'Please go back to the table, sir, and

he'll bring your bill. He gets so worried, so many people.' The old fool put his hand to his head and joined in asking us to go back so that he could work out where we were.[239]

Hitch-hiking on the return journey was not quite so successful. Anthony's companion thought that the walk would be useful fitness training, and rather sneered at Anthony's long-cherished maxim that half-prepared was no better than unprepared and that endurance under stress bore no relation to endurance under training. As if to put their competing theories thoroughly to the test, they accidentally went the long way round and had to walk 7 miles back to camp. Due to this and other unaccustomed bouts of physical exercise over the next few days, Anthony developed a troublesome blister which was still being treated the day before D-Day.

He also began to incubate yet another of those myriad infections which were an eternal feature of his military life. On Monday 22 May, he wrote:

> Sooner or sooner still, any diary I keep comes to an illness. I think we are coming to one now. I seem to have caught the same curse (caused, he says, by primitive sanitation and infected water) as one of the doctors in the tent. Identical symptoms – like incipient seasickness – so I took advantage of my present irresponsibility to lie down from 4pm to 7pm when I had been invited to dinner with the Fusiliers.[240] Before that I lay in the sun correcting proofs. [...]
>
> After dinner the officers were censoring letters, complaining of the length, particularly as the writers frequently apologised for brevity, or announced their intention to continue writing long daily letters. 'Christ! he only saw the girl on Friday,' said Lawson, holding up a particularly voluminous one.
>
> 'Marvellous how they find time to do it. How long do you think it would take to write eight pages like that?' asked the Colonel with the naive curiosity of colonels.
>
> Recurring remark in letters: 'I'm sorry I upset your mother.'
>
> The sad thing about having a day off is the acceleration of flying time towards the end. One minute there is a pleasant vista of empty hours in which to read or idle, and then all of a sudden it is nearly time to go to bed.[241]

The following day Anthony caught the train from Winchester to London. He had a slight sense of guilt about going off when others couldn't – 'the excursion is legitimate, but nothing in the Army seems legitimate when it is pleasant'. He was presumably taking copy up to the WAR office, for he was only in the capital for one day.

> 'I thought you'd gone,' people said. 'What, back already?' etc. The usual dissatisfaction of returning immediately after brave farewells.
>
> London very sunny. The prospect of going away keens up the senses.
>
> Letter on my desk reporting final failure of airborne application.[242]

At 7.50pm Anthony caught the train from Waterloo back to Winchester, and walked back to the camp with a padre. 'One never gets over the pathetic, new-boy feeling of returning after leave, even a few hours. The people who stayed behind seem at such an advantage.'

But his schemes were all ripening nicely. He had always intended to abandon the beach group medical unit as soon as they landed in France, and once in the camp he had started looking round for a front-line unit with whom to share the fortunes of war. On the day of the trip to London, 23 May, he found exactly what he was hoping for. He was invited by the 8th Armoured Brigade to join them in Normandy, and he immediately accepted. It was an honour for them to carry him as well as an honour for him to be invited.

The 8th Armoured Brigade was a tank brigade which had borne much of the brunt of the fighting in North Africa. It had played a large part in the final defeat of Rommel, and its emblem of a red fox's mask, stamped on a yellow background, had been much in evidence all along the North African coast to Tunis in the pursuit of Rommel's forces.[243]

The D-Day plan for the Brigade was that they were to support the 50th (Northumberland) Division in the assault on Arromanches, part of the Gold Beach landing. (The landing beaches, from west to east, were: Utah, Omaha, Gold, Juno, Sword.) Sherman tanks with Duplex Drive would be used. DD, which Anthony and no doubt countless others called Donald Duck, allowed the tanks to swim through the sea. The secret of this was so well kept that the Germans had no inkling of the tanks' versatility. When D-Day came, there were severe problems with landing the tanks due to the rough seas. However, the Sherwood Rangers Yeomanry, the unit of the 8th Armoured Brigade with which Anthony would travel, managed to get onto their sector of shore successfully.[244] They would then move inland with great rapidity before encountering extremely tough opposition. Two commanders were lost within a matter of days, Lieutenant-Colonel John Anderson who was badly wounded, and Major Michael Laycock who was killed.[245] Major Stanley Christopherson would then take over, the commander with whom Anthony would spend most of his time in Normandy.[246] Travelling with the Sherwood Rangers through some of the bitterest fighting it had ever endured, Anthony would see sights of extreme horror and cruelty.

But all this was in the future. Back at Winchester, it was agreed that Anthony would join the Sherwood Rangers on the evening of D-Day once everyone was ashore. Whilst matters were being arranged, Anthony met various senior officers, including the Brigadier of 8th Armoured Brigade, Bernard Cracroft, who was very enthusiastic about Anthony's assignment. Anthony wrote that the Brigadier 'wasn't exactly a tower of technical strength on the subject of feature writing, but he was very cordially keen on the idea of his men who had had to keep very quiet about their secret equipment'. He gave Anthony a chit saying that he was free to ride in any of the Brigade's vehicles.

More specifically, it was arranged that Anthony would be attached to one of the Sherwood Rangers' reserve tanks. A normal tank crew compliment was five, but the reserve tanks only carried four, which left a spare seat. Anthony was introduced to his tank crew, but as they would be landing on one sector of Gold Beach whilst he would be landing on another (almost certainly the one codenamed King), there was considerable doubt about whether he would actually be able to find them. 'However, we arranged to look out for each other. I might wear a red carnation.'

The next day, he went to see the crew to ask if they could take his bed roll for him, but they had already left. Anthony contemplated the extra weight of the bed roll philosophically: 'I shall have to carry it. On the other hand, I shall have it with me.'

In his diary Anthony recorded the tiny vivid things which always give his writing so much life. Soon after he had become familiar with the Brigade's emblem of a fox's mask, he came across a man leading a fox around the camp on a chain. The fox was 'huntedly agitated but another younger fox chained up a little way along was quite tame, though very restless'. Presumably these were Brigade mascots.

Another tiny illuminating saga concerned the affair of the sweets. At a lecture by one of Anthony's beach group medicals, Major Clay began the serious business by complaining that there would be a shortage of sweets on the other side. This, he said, could be offset by buying £10's worth in England – did they want them bought out of unit funds or would they like to leave the unit funds at their present level (about £30) and buy as individuals? Needless to say, the vote to deplete unit funds was almost unanimous. Once bought, the sweets needed protecting from the omnipresent rats. The camp administrators were desperately trying to get 400 more rat traps, one trap having caught six rats in a single afternoon.

There is a very funny riff running through the diary about the eccentricities of Anthony's four medical officers, Majors Clay and Dill-Russell, and Captains Parfitt and O'Keeefe. He shared a tent with them and took delight in recording their slightly bonkers conversations. He was particularly fascinated by Parfitt who had been at Guy's Hospital, Anthony's old stamping ground. Parfitt was a highly intelligent crack-pot of the first order, and quite simply not made like other people.

> Back in the tent. Parfitt said 'Now I must cut my mirror in two.'
> 'Cut your mirror in two?'
> 'Too big. You can't cut it with a flint. Make one out of a stone.'
> He went outside and threw a stone on the ground until he had cracked it. Then he pulled to pieces his rather elaborately made mirror, sawed the glass in two and stuck them together back to back.
> 'Every man a substantial pension,' said Major Clay.
> 'It was Christmas Day in the workhouse, the happiest day in the year,' said Major Dill-Russell.
> 'It's tragic that a man like you, of culture and some education, should be reduced to this. They give pensions for shattered limbs, but nothing for your ruined mind,' said Major Clay.
> 'Every man an egg for breakfast,' said Major Dill-Russell.
> Simple humour. I wondered whether the rats had reconnaissance rats out to report that we all had a bag of sweets.
> 'They're briefing now,' said Major Clay.
> 'The rat commander,' said Major Dill-Russell.
> With the other bit of his mirror Captain Parfitt made one for me.[247]

The Parfitt saga continued right up to the D-Day crossing. Anthony would ask him the most ridiculously innocent questions, but Parfitt always came off one better:

> 'Parfitt,' I said, 'if you have a button just coming off is it better to pull it right off and start again, or reinforce the surviving strands?'
> 'When you're just about to invade enemy country pull it off. Unless you can guarantee that all the threads bear an equal strain,' said the sage.[248]

Parfitt had a restless mind, and was always conducting small, slightly lunatic experiments. 'The inactivity was setting his old brain going, he said. It reminded him of a fortnight he spent with nothing to do in Port Sudan. He spent his time drawing everything he could see, including his view of his spectacles.'

During the prolonged waiting period before the move to the ships at Southampton, everyone began to suffer from a mixture of boredom and acute nerves. The strain made people fidgety. 'Colossal problems that beset the mind. Where shall I put my towel? What shall I pack in my mess tin? How many socks shall I put in the dry wrapper? How shall I carry my jerkin? These are matters of great moment.'[249]

For some the tension was too much to deal with. On 31 May Anthony recorded:

> I saw a bedraggled-looking deserter being brought into the barbed wire guardroom enclosure. Waiting outside the Camp Commandant's office were two men standing between escorts, waiting for judgment. What a tangle their emotions might be in. Being had up on an over-hot afternoon while waiting to go on the Second Front and over the public address system a velvety, appealing lady sang 'I couldn't sleep a wink last night'.[250]

Sometimes his descriptions of the camp achieved a kind of poetry, they were so vivid and evocative.

Sat in the sun listening to the amplified radio.

The music echoing in the trees, the men marching about, washing their clothes, and cutting each other's hair in the sun. The patches of bright sunlight in the ground shadow made by the trees. The coolness of the tent. All very stimulating.

The idea that a high proportion of the men will be killed or maimed doesn't really seem likely.[251]

The general expectation amongst the soldiers was that the landing would be ferociously opposed, and that the death rate would be enormous. Anthony thought that the period of waiting was probably easier for the men who had already seen action because as at least they could tell themselves that they had done it before. The only real advantage held by the inexperienced was that in their optimistic moments they could 'visualise a pleasantly film-story immunity from shot and shell'.

There were optimists 'who thought that it wouldn't last for long, that once we got ashore and broke the initial resistance, it would simply be a question of chasing Germans home'. But even these expected a terrific battle in the first few hours, 'and everyone in this camp was going to be landed during the first few hours. Whatever might be in store, was in store for them.'

As indeed it was for Anthony.

Nonetheless, once the camp was sealed and the first top-secret briefings were given on Friday 26 May, the general mood became exhilarated rather than doom-laden.

In the Officers' mess this exhilaration, together with the universal confinement to barracks, produced a more than usually crowded and excited atmosphere. Names were listed for the D-Day plus 365 Reunion Dinner, provisionally at the Adlon in Berlin, alternatively at the Railway Hotel, Dunkirk.

There was a delightful atmosphere of burnt boats and happy-go-luckiness, though there was nothing to drink but stout. But the radio played old dance tunes, and even the puddle of spilled beer and the cigarette ends all over the stone floor didn't seem unpleasant. They were so much in keeping with the barrack-room benches, the rusty stove, the biscuit tins on the elementary bar, the gym-shoed mess waiters, the not very good light.[252]

On the following Tuesday, Anthony and his medical officers moved to a marshalling camp about 2 miles down the road, where they were issued with a great deal of extra kit on top of their own personal equipment. This consisted of the rations for the first two days in France, a tommy cooker with two re-fills, a tin of corned beef, a packet of biscuits, a packet of chewing gum, two packets of chocolate, a waterproofed tin of twenty cigarettes, a water-sterilising outfit, and an emergency ration. As Anthony noted, 'it made an awful lot more to carry'.

And next day we started to carry it. The holiday was over. We formed up after breakfast and travelled the last few miles to the docks.

No one looked very excited. It wasn't much like the Charge of the Light Brigade. But everyone was mighty glad to get started.[253]

14

D-DAY

O n 1 June, Anthony and his medical officers left the camp and moved to Southampton. They travelled by a very circuitous route, 'no doubt to deceive the enemy' Anthony wrote, mocking the elaborate security arrangements, 'possibly embark backwards and they will think we're coming off'. The route was lined with security patrols and warning signs. One sign aimed at civilians read 'It is forbidden to loiter or talk with troops', to which Anthony quipped in a parody of zoo notices, 'It is dangerous to feed the troops with buns'.

At Southampton docks there were further maddening delays. Whilst Anthony was waiting, a colonel, who knew that he would be writing about events, came up and said 'in the slightly laborious way of someone talking for quotation: "I've been round everyone. All got their tails up. Right up. It's really inspiring to listen to them."' Anthony dutifully wrote this down, but commented privately, 'No doubt he had gone round and had really felt emotionally stirred, but he couldn't describe it – few can – without sounding phoney.'[254]

Finally, Anthony and his party embarked. Their new accommodation was a 10,000-ton Victory ship, designed for cargo, but adapted as a troop-landing ship halfway through its construction. There were nearly 1000 passengers and crew on board. When everyone had been accounted for, the ship cast off. But instead of the dramatic voyage to France which most people were expecting, the ship simply made a very brief trip out into Southampton Water. There it stopped, in a formation of ships which stretched far away out of sight beneath a swarm of silvery barrage balloons.

Some of the men who had been deceived into thinking that they were really off had crowded to the sides for a last view of England. Anthony recorded the valedictions:

'I always find it exciting when the journey starts even though it isn't for a holiday,' said a major to me.
'We've had it, chum,' said a second lieutenant to a captain.
'We're fucking off then,' said voices of all ranks.[255]

With the ship anchored and nothing else to do but kill time, men began to relax a little. Previous anxieties about the authorities having made adequate preparations gave way to incredulous amazement at the profligate generosity which was now being shown after five grim years of war and rationing.

From 4.20pm to 5pm the canteen was open to officers. Astonishing scenes ensued. You said 'Chocolate' and they gave you four threepenny bars. There were oodles of everything: tinned peanuts, cheese biscuits, cookies, pepsi-cola, liquorice-all-sorts, bootlaces. I asked if it was advisable to stock up well before the hoarders arrived, but apparently the stocks are built to last the trip.[256]

Parfitt made his last appearance in the diary. Anthony came across him on deck deciphering morse signals passing through the armada. Anthony asked him how long he thought they would stay off the coast of England.

> 'Five days at least. They've made out duty officers for seven,' said the crank. 'If you find yourself with nothing to do, try to find a way of trisecting an angle.'
> 'I'll do that, first thing I do,' I said politely.
> 'Probably the last. It's impossible,' said Parfitt.[257]

The days passed slowly, but in some ways very pleasantly. Amplified dance music echoed across the waters, and regattas of extraordinary vessels were constantly passing. On 2 June, it was 'voluptuously hot'. Anthony and the medical officers lay on the boat deck reading whodunnits and sucking boiled sweets. A tiny adventure the previous night lent savour to these languorous proceedings. A marine captain had taken Anthony and a RASC captain to his cabin and had given them beer in silver metal tumblers. Whenever there was a knock at the door they had to hide everything because drink was strictly forbidden on board.

Anthony continued to be amazed by the lavishness of the arrangements:

> The absurd and immorally attractive feature of this outing is the bandbox spickness of everything. The assault craft slung from the side of the ship look brand new. One's instincts have been so long trained to economy that it seems a great shame for the assault craft to be used only once or twice. Couldn't we fix up some other landings [...]
> It isn't only the assault craft, the soldiers are loaded down with new equipment and most of them are wearing new battledress. The canteen is loaded down with supplies. The food is plentiful. The paintwork is new. Everyone looks splendidly healthy, as who wouldn't when the day is punctuated with bottles of sparkling satisfying Pepsi-Cola, the five cent drink in the big bottle.[258]

Some tried to inject a little more dignity and crusading fervour into the proceedings. One breakfast 'a boyishly intense little subaltern raised the Vansittartist flag'. Robert Gilbert Vansittart was an ex-diplomat who sat in the House of Lords and had become famous – some would say infamous – for his much-argued proposition that the German race was innately evil. In 1940 he had given seven radio broadcasts which were so popular and controversial that they had been turned into a pamphlet, *Black Record: Germans Past and Present*. It had appeared in the same month as *What! No Morning Tea?*, and by September 1941 had sold 400,000 copies. Since then, Vansittart had attracted much publicity by continuing his argument in other publications and by using the House of Lords to expose German war crimes. Anthony was very well aware of his work. In the aftermath of the Brummen shooting, he would summon up the extraordinary courage and presence of mind to make a quip about Vansittart.

As he listened to the boyish young officer rehashing Vansittart's arguments, Anthony observed in the small audience the same indifference he had often seen in soldiers to some momentous event which directly concerned them. No one was interested enough to agree or to differ with the young officer. Summing this up, Anthony wrote: 'There is wonderfully little interest in why, where or when the thing is starting, no doubt largely because of the excellent food and weather.'

The good weather did not last. By Sunday 4 June, it had become windy and cloudy, and the possibility of postponement loomed. The Colonel of the Green Howards was brought into Anthony's cabin after lunch. He had come to see his company on the ship and tell them about the thickened anti-tank defences which faced them when they landed in the first wave of assault troops in Normandy. Now, however, the weather was too rough for the LCA to take the Colonel back. Anthony lent him a book and presently he went to sleep. Anthony was certainly mixing in exalted company.

He was now in such a position of trust that he had been given the full operational orders for his particular sector of Gold Beach. He would produce a readable digest of these orders for an article in WAR which was never published. By now maps had been issued showing real place names instead of the imaginary ones which had been used in the briefings on shore. The reality of the operation was no longer in any doubt, but the weather was so rough that at times it seemed that all the immense preparations would come to nothing.

Never one to be serious for long, Anthony recorded in his diary excerpts from the nightly quiz show given on the ship's radio by the Entertainments Officer. One of the games was to give the correct definition of words. When the Quiz Master asked 'If someone gave you an enema would you bury it in the garden or use it to clear your stomach?', Anthony commented, 'In the near future I won't need one'.

On Monday 5 June, things began to change.

They tell me that this was to have been D-Day morning. But it wasn't. After breakfast I had my blister dressed. The ship was very busy, mostly with loading marking poles, extremity signals and transit signs for marking the beaches. Signs of personal excitement, my own and other people's [...]

The weather was the main preoccupation. It didn't look too good. Then at 1.20pm:

'Attention. All troops all services will pre-load all kit except small kit into LCAs between 4 and 6.

'Canteen will close to all military personnel and Naval Commandos at 8 tonight.

'The purser will change all English money into French at 7.30.

'Library books will be handed in at 8 tonight.'

Recording what was happening moment by moment, Anthony captured the intense rising excitement of those on board.

About 3.30pm the Principal Beach Master, a pale-faced, bemedalled young Lieutenant-Commander, arrived in a lifeboat, together with an Engineer Commander.

Apparently the small stuff has started already, and this is inextricably D minus 1.

At 3.45pm there was a bit of a rumble. 'Those are the engines, I believe,' said the Lieutenant-Commander. He was packing up. 'I always wear gloves. I find you can get a better grip on everything with gloves on,' he said.

While sitting in the canteen two messages were broadcast, one to the Navy, one to the Marines, wishing them good luck in their respective jobs and enlarging slightly on the eve of great events theme. People listened dutifully, but were not, on the face of it, particularly injected with any extra resolve. 'Same old bullshit,' they said, though not in any particular spirit of complaint. Tolerant smiles were more the note.

'Attention. This is the Roman Catholic chaplain speaking. I will be saying the Mass at 6.30 this evening.'

These messages helped to underline the nearness. Singing started down in the troop decks. Very feeble jokes began to seem funny.

At 6.25 the amplified voice said in urgent tones:

'Attention. Men who wish to take their anti-seasickness tablets should take the first one NOW.'

We sailed about 7pm.[259]

If Anthony went to bed at all that night, he cannot have slept for very long. At 10.00pm he was still in the ship's radio cabin, typing up the first part of his report on the back of Naval Message paper. It was a grey night and the English coast was a receding blur. Most people had gone to bed, sleeping in their uniforms which would be rumpled and frowsy by the following morning. They were all being called at 4.00am.

By now Anthony, absolutely focused on arriving as early as possible at the landing beach, had swopped his landing time from H+150 to H+45, that is to say to 45 minutes after the initial assault. 'This should give what is known as a completer picture and will also save humping my unique assault-type valise from LSI to LCT to LCA to shore.' If things went horribly wrong, there was not going to be much leeway for getting out of danger.

Breakfast was at 4.25am. 'Attention. The second seasickness pill should be taken now,' said the ship's amplifier as the liver and bacon was served.'[260]

They were passing up a mine-swept channel marked by red lights, about 8 miles off the French coast. There had been a great many flares and bursts of flak in the distance, but right now there was nothing. As Anthony came out on deck, a solitary fighter flew across the ship.

Over the amplifier the Senior Naval Officer's voice said, 'Telephone operators and winchmen will be required in about five minutes' time.' The critical moment was approaching fast. Anthony prepared himself for the landing:

> I went to put on my Christmas tree-like equipment, and transferred as much stuff as possible from my trouser pockets to my battledress blouse. In the agitated lightheadedness of the moment I decided that the battledress blouse pockets wouldn't take it all and transferred a good deal back again.

The first flight of the assault troops formed up by the two rows of blue and white assault craft. Anthony joined the miscellaneous party with which he was travelling. The crew began wishing them good luck and 'made very depressing comments about the choppiness of the Channel'. The officers and NCOs of the troops were telling their men not to worry, there was miles of time to do everything.

The party with whom Anthony was going ashore consisted of a Beach Company Commander, half his company HQ, seven sappers under an officer, three military policemen, and a party of Royal Navy beach commandos. Various oddments were also going with them, including the Brigadier's jeep and carrier, not to mention (from another ship) the Brigadier.[261]

At 5.28am by Anthony's now rubber-cased watch, he and his party clambered over the rope-laden side of the ship into their landing craft. Gunfire was starting up. The guns of the nearest cruiser looked as if they were firing 'big brown puffs of smoke, which lolloped vanishingly through the air'. Three Naval officers and a Royal Marine major came aboard. Their luggage included two wildly incongruous-looking weekend cases. As the craft was cast off from the side of the ship, it hung suspended over the water from a single derrick, waiting for latecomers. Then, as they were lowered some 10ft towards the sea, a Royal Corps of Signals sergeant appeared, breathless and urgent, shouting to be put on board. He stood there with one leg over the ship's side, undecided whether to jump or not, until someone pointed out a rope down which he slid just as they were finally lowering the craft into the water.

> We weren't being lowered into any mill-pond. Goodness, it was rough, and it went on being rough all the way to the shore.
>
> 'All the way to the shore' – what a simple phrase that is. What a wealth of colourful and seasick events it fails to picture. Before landing at H hour + 45 minutes we were to go to the headquarters ship and exchange the Naval Officers for the Brigadier and staff of the assaulting brigade. We certainly went to the headquarters ship. In fact, we started going through her, and tore a gash in her side.
>
> By sucking boiled sweets I just managed to avoid seasickness. Others had no boiled sweets or found boiled sweets no antidote. We had all been issued with vomit bags, but in the event men leaned over the pitching side. [...]

The barrage had now started all round us. There were ships and landing craft kicking up the devil's own row. A line of assault craft corkscrewed slowly past us, and I thanked my stars I wasn't expected to assault anybody. There was none of the infectiously emboldening qualities of smooth speed. They were being pitched and tossed and soaked, all very slowly.

So were we. The faces of the Brigadier and his staff when we came junketing alongside to take them off were what is known as a study.

With the Brigadier on board, they started on the last run-in to the shore. It was a grey, miserable day and it looked a grey, miserable shore, clouded over with smoke and with only occasional sounds of firing. Most of the noise was being made by the Navy firing over their heads. Anthony could now see the spikes of the beach obstacles above the surface of the water. It was getting on for high tide. The sea was becoming even rougher. Great dollops of surf washed over the sides of the craft, soaking people from head to foot. Anthony had been told that with any luck they would be stepping ashore in water not more than ankle deep, but some 40 yards out the craft stopped, the front door was lowered, and 'we were invited to make for the shore'.

Three men stood hesitating, as well they might. It seemed the moment for encouragement by example and I followed the carrier down the ramp.

The water was quite warm and waist high. We waded towards a narrow strip of shingle into which men and vehicles were beginning to pour. Running parallel to the beach was a track, behind which clouds of smoke were being generated. Through gaps in the smoke you could see English-looking green fields and a narrow road running up hill and inland, to a ridge some 600 yards behind.

To the right of the road on the ridge an ugly-looking house stood against the skyline. There was machine-gun fire away to the left and in the centre. But the main effect on the beach was of some macabre circus coming to town.

A traffic jam of vehicles was already forming. But the minefield between the beach and the parallel tracks was almost cleared, and the outstanding success of the initial assault was obvious to all. Some of the defenders had been killed, but others had surrendered without putting up much of a fight.

In one cleared corner sat about a dozen German prisoners whose attitude was remarkably serene. They sat or lounged there like men whose day's work was done, greeting new arrivals with the wry sympathy of people committed to some boring social function. They weren't under any great constraint. Everyone was too busy trying to get along the beach themselves to waste time with prisoners.

Wounded men were lying on the fringe of the beach, collected together in twos and threes. Beach dressing stations were being established. Anthony came across two sergeants lying together, and asked one of them what he thought of it. He had been hit in the landing craft and again on coming ashore. 'He said it hadn't been as tough as he thought it would be. Apparently he was easy to please.' They were shivering with cold, and Anthony fed them each a little rum.

Further up the beach Anthony came across his first horrific war casualty.

A few yards up the beach [...] a man was dying. His clothes were in ribbons, his helmet was gone. So were his legs. He was terribly disfigured, but still lingeringly alive. His mouth twitched and his arm moved a little. A doctor came and looked at him, but there was nothing he could do except cover him with more blankets. The poor devil stayed alive a few minutes more, and died.

By noon the sun was out, the smoke screens were disappearing, and the beach was remarkably quiet. The tide was going out, and vehicles which had been swamped by the sea could be seen stuck in the sand. Anthony's genius for capturing a scene never missed both the poetry and the mad absurdities:

> Parties of men were drying themselves. A man dressed in a blanket, gym shoes and a tin hat walked along the water's edge looking for his kit. A man came in the opposite direction carrying a primus stove. Two young officers walked along deep in conference, one of them carrying a large penguin doll. About 20 yards out from the shore a man stood marooned on the bonnet of his truck. The fringe of the beach was littered with packs, petrol cans, tins of food, greatcoats and discarded boots which already looked old boots.

He came across a colonel from Combined Operations HQ who was writing a report on the landing, and together they walked the length of the beach. Anthony noted that there were thirteen LCTs beached by the under-water obstacles with varying large holes blown in their sides. Many of these would be floated successfully on the second tide. They met the Colonel commanding the Beach Group, who told them that there were still a lot of snipers about. There was also one substantial enemy party, a platoon or more with anti-tank guns and mortars, who had already destroyed an armoured car.

Anthony and the Colonel walked up the one-way road to the village. An information room had been set up in an amusement arcade called *Les Salles des Fêtes*. There was a good deal of bomb damage, but also many French people moving about, quite unharmed. Anthony and his Colonel peered into one shop which had suffered a little from blast, and were surprised to see the extent of its stock. Such rare things as matches and toothpaste were on display. Everyone had expected the French to be living without basic goods and to be on the verge of starvation.

At the next corner they were warned by a military policeman to keep to the left as some German defensive positions were about to be shelled. They then made their way back to the beach, where the Colonel prevented some sailors from being blown up by booby traps whilst looking for souvenirs. One man was drinking Vichy water in the happy delusion that it was champagne.

D-Day ended with Anthony trying to sleep in a field, 'with a frighteningly noisy but quite ineffectual air raid around midnight'. There had been no possibility of finding his tank crew. He would eventually learn that the Sherwood Rangers had made considerable progress on the first day. They had crossed the river Seulles with the infantry they were supporting, and were currently about 6,000 yards inland. His tank crew was way beyond his reach.[262]

Eight days later, he would go back to the beach. The sight was amazing:

> The under-water obstacles had been cleared away. D-Day debris of drowned and blown-up vehicles had gone, towed into the minefields, now looking like a long strip of junkyard. The beach staff were living in dugouts along the front – the same dugouts they had scratched in the sand on D-Day, but expanded and developed with packing cases and tarpaulins. The beach dressing stations were packing up. Lately their only casualties had been from AA shrapnel.

Anthony could see that it was now a settled organisation, ready to work smoothly for months if necessary. There could be no clearer indication of the great success of the Normandy landings.

15

WITH THE TANK CREW

When he awoke in his field the morning after D-Day, Anthony's immediate concern was how he was going to catch up with his tank crew. As soon as he had had breakfast, he arranged a lift with an RAF lorry going inland. It was carrying men on their way to service the planes which would be arriving as soon as the landing strips were put down. They had come straight from the beach, and were 'still virginally surprised by everything they saw'. One of them, noticing a donkey in a field, expressed surprise that the French had not eaten it; like so many others, he had expected the population to be starving.

The battle situation was still very muddled. Neither Anthony nor his new fellow travellers knew anything about the progress of the beach-head, and everyone was asking everyone else if they had any news. Rumours abounded, most of them wildly inaccurate.

The Germans were recovering from the shock of the invasion, and resistance was beginning to stiffen. Snipers were rumoured to be everywhere, and there was a constant rumble of gunfire ahead. The RAF lorry advanced cautiously and presently stopped. Nearby there were three dead Germans.

> The RAF men were seeing this for the first time and their reactions were mixed. Some got out to look. 'Hope you all come back,' said one non-looker.
>
> The first German was a big lumpy youth who had been killed by something which had blown away part of his face. He lay there with a grenade which he had been about to throw, just fallen out of his hand. A few yards away two more were lying face down. One of them had had the side of his body blown away. Their kit had been looted and the remainder of their belongings lay scattered about them. Buggers are well-clothed, say what you like,' said one of the RAF men.
>
> There were two more lying in the young crops. One had had his head blown in and his face had been crushed into his upturned helmet as though someone had systematically kicked it into pulp. The fifth man had been pepper-potted with bullets and lay with his head in a cluster of wild flowers. Their faces were all a mixture of death-house grey and fruit-juice purple. The RAF men were sickened by the cold and final brutality of what they saw. [...]
>
> 'Photograph there you know. Probably of his mother,' said one man.
>
> 'Well it's the only way to win the war isn't it – killing them,' said another.[263]

They got back on the lorry and it moved on.

After many delays, the party arrived at the small town of Crépon, whose streets were completely jammed with invasion traffic. None of the vehicles bore the sign of the red fox's head against a yellow background, the emblem of 8th Armoured Brigade to which Anthony's tank crew belonged. Anthony decided that his best option was just to carry on with the RAF lorry. But presently they came across a parked squadron of mine-clearing flail tanks, and thinking that they were at least in the same line of business as 8th Armoured Brigade, Anthony took his sleeping roll off the lorry, and introduced himself to the commanding officer.

The CO had been slightly wounded in an unexpected attack by a German infantry gun and was 'trying with much gallantry but not much success to pretend that he hadn't been'. This particular area of countryside had supposedly been cleared, but either the Germans responsible had been missed or they had crept back, as they were so often to do with such murderous effect during the coming days.

A medical aid post had been established in a small copse close by. Two German prisoners came out of the cottage where they had been having their wounds dressed. One was very young and ingratiating. The other was a veteran, around 30, surly and obstinate – 'he didn't look anybody's friend.' They were being guarded by a tall lanky sergeant who was obviously enjoying his baptism of fire and rather overacting the part; '"Why take them to the beach? why not do them in now?" he asked with slightly self-conscious ferocity.' He then went on to talk about what he might well do on the way down to the beach and to make 'blood-thirstily facetious remarks about saving petrol'. Anthony recorded that two minutes later he spoiled the effect by giving each of the prisoners a cigarette and a piece of chocolate.

Snipers were very active in the district, and unknown dangers all around. Anthony prepared to settle down for the night with the flail tanks, which with the approach of darkness came together in a soap-box formation, with their soft-skinned supply vehicles sheltered inside. Anthony was rather tetchy from prolonged lack of sleep:

> It took them hours to settle down for the night. By the time they had manoeuvred their nine tanks into a triangular formation, had picked the guard, held an administrative conference, and settled down for the night, the air-raids started over the beach-head. The noise from there was accentuated by a troop of Bofors sited a hundred yards from us.[264] I had pitched my sleeping bag in the dusk under the tailboard of one of the [two...] lorries in the middle of the blockade. The sergeant-major was sleeping on the tailboard above me. He had a strangely persistent tenor snore. The newly arrived airfield construction group kept shouting at each other all through the night. Of course it was reassuring to hear them so anxious to build their airfield, but I couldn't help feeling that perhaps tomorrow would do. Added to all this the guards kept changing rather argumentatively. So sleep was rather patchy and ended altogether with a stand-to at 5am.[265]

At 6.30am the tanks moved off, with Anthony in the back of one of the supply vehicles. Their progress was marked by a thick cloud of yellow dust, blown off the winding road by the tanks. There were very few signs of battle, except where an occasional group of buildings had been decimated. They passed little knots of dead bodies, sometimes one on its own, but mostly lying in twos and threes. Nearly all of them were German. The advancing British had naturally used what little time they had to bury their own dead comrades.

Though they were not fired upon, the convoy's progress was nonetheless dramatic. One tank got caught on a corner, another knocked over a telegraph pole, and the tank coming along behind Anthony's lorry knocked off part of the corner of a house. Local inhabitants watched the convoy's passage through their narrow lanes with horrified apprehension. 'One lady came out to watch us in her dressing gown. This seemed rather eccentric attire, until I realised that it was only 7am.'

During one of the many hold-ups, a tank appeared which was commanded by a man whom Anthony had met on the boat coming over. As he too was trying to reach 8th Armoured Brigade, Anthony transferred his kit and climbed on board, sitting up behind the turret amongst a miscellany of water-cans, tins, compo-boxes, and a wireless set.

> It was my first ride on a tank. No doubt about it, this form of progress has its compensations, like being King. Everyone stares impressed. Many of them wave. The essential belligerence of a tank makes its every journey a stirring affair. It may only be going to collect the mail, but it always

looks as if it is being thrown in to stem a tide or launch a spear-head. After about two minutes steady progress we were stopped by a line of traffic. Having crushed a hedge, pushed a lorry a little to one side, and ruined a section of the road we marked our way round the obstacle and got moving again. We made our way with many uncertain detours to Brigade Headquarters. This was in a newly ruined field of young crops.[266]

There, parked up in the field, Anthony at last found his tank crew.

Lance Corporal Cook, the tank commander, was only nineteen. Anthony would develop a great respect for this 'dark, vivacious, always smiling young man with a very conspicuous trait of self-reliance'. Other crew members were Hogg, the operator, and Cherry, the driver, a cheerful young man who had earned his nickname because of his flaming red cheeks. Like their commander, Hogg and Cherry were less than 20. The fourth man, Jack Collin, the gunner, was older and had been with the 8th Army in North Africa. He tended to be rather grumpy, doubtless because he had a great deal to put up with from the three youngsters. Veterans were constantly baited and teased because of their tendency to reminisce at great length about their previous glorious campaigns. Anthony recorded a fairly typical exchange which took place some days after he had met up with the crew:

> 'Tell us about the desert, Collin,' said Cook unkindly. 'Tell us what it was like in the 8th Army.'
> The desert warrior maintained a disgusted silence.
> 'Tell him about the time you joined the army, Cherry,' said Hogg. 'Tell the desert warrior.'
> 'You blokes want to watch yourselves and all,' said the desert warrior.
> 'Why?'
> 'The way you're going on you'll have no mucking rations left.'
> 'Liable to get pneumonia,' said Cherry. 'I'll tell you when I first slept like this in a tank in a minute.'
> 'All right, you mark my words,' said the desert warrior.

Their tank was a Sherman, as indeed were almost all the Allied tanks in Normandy. American-built, the Shermans were comparatively agile and manoeuvrable, but neither they nor the other Allied tanks could match the heavy German equivalents – the Panzer, the Panther, and the much-feared Tiger. Though German tanks were clumsy because of the weight of their armour, they were perfectly suited to defence. In a straight contest, the Tigers would win every time, having vastly superior firepower to the Allied tanks and being virtually impregnable unless hit sideways on.

As Anthony and his crew were soon to learn, the Germans had rallied with remarkable swiftness, and the easy gains of the first few hours had now been replaced by a grim, hard slog. There was only one German mobile formation in Normandy on 6 June, the 21st Panzer Division, but this was soon joined by the 12th Panzer Division and others. The country was ideally suited to defence, being hilly and wooded, with small fields with dense hedges which blocked the view. They were intersected by deep lanes similar to those in Devon, which were hidden by banks with thick hedges. The Germans could wait in these lanes completely undetected, and open fire when the moment was perfect. In every way, it was difficult country for an attacking force.

Some days into the campaign, Anthony would write that everything had to be done from hedge to hedge:

> The infantry would look through the first hedge and see if there were any obvious anti-tank positions in the next one. If there weren't, the tanks would poke their noses through and shoot up the next hedge before moving across the intervening field with the infantry, and starting the process all over again. The Germans held successive hedgerows all the way back

and the expenditure of machine-gun ammunition in precautionary hosepiping was something sensational. The Regiments were using more than four times as much .30 calibre ammunition as they had budgeted for. In one spell of five days the Brigade had used nearly a million rounds of it.[267]

The Sherman tank crews with which Anthony was travelling had to use great stealth and caution. If they wanted to engage a Tiger, the only way to do so was to track it stealthily, and come up at its side before it could traverse its massive 88mm gun and blast them into oblivion. The German tanks were supported by tough infantry, adept at using the difficult terrain to their advantage. But far more demoralising were the snipers, who would tie themselves in the leafy branches of trees and wait silently for hours, or even days, until their prey moved into view. Nowhere was safe; even areas which were miles behind the front line and which were supposedly clear had their deadly infestation.

As early as 8 June, the day when Anthony found his tank crew, the snipers were proving an absolute menace. Virtually the first words which Cook spoke to Anthony were to tell him to keep his head down whilst they were moving because so many men had already been decapitated by snipers.

He settled Anthony into the co-driver's seat, next to which there was a browning gun, and they set off.

> 'Have you got one up the spout?' Cook asked. I fed the belt of ammunition, which lay stored in a tin box at my feet, into the browning.
>
> I resolved to borrow at the earliest possible moment some form of goggles, to cope with the cloud of dust thrown up by the vehicles in front. We rumbled along for about half an hour. It was by no means very uncomfortable. The noise quickly faded in one's consciousness, and there was no particular bumping about or vibration.
>
> We turned up into a field, already sign-posted as the Brigade, we were tick-tacked by a Captain into a corner at the far end. We stopped under a tree and a shower of blossom fell into my lap.[268]

They would remain in the same location for some hours, and at around 7.30 in the evening would enjoy a very good supper of stew, sultana pudding, tea and biscuits. The sound of nearby shelling never stopped. After supper, they moved on to join more of the Brigade in another field, which was the stopping place for the night. Kit was unhitched from all the odd crannies in which it was stowed. A big camouflage net was thrown over the tank, and a lean-to shelter was erected along one side, some saplings having been cut to support it. All round the field, men were sitting in little groups, brewing up tea, cooking a meal, or talking. The more hygienically inclined had a rough wash. Anthony noted that the new popular phrase, used when anyone got too full of himself, was 'Garn, he hasn't even seen a dead Jerry yet'.

Anthony's tank crew had been told very little about who Anthony was. It would not be until the following day that their fundamental misunderstanding about his role was cleared up. Cook had been under the impression that Anthony was an Observation Post officer, and 'that I was to jump out of the tank when it couldn't advance any further without being seen by the enemy, and establish an OP for artillery.' Though the crew would carry Anthony amiably enough, they would not be entirely pleased two weeks later when he volunteered them for the battle of Fontenay in order to get some good copy.

The night that he joined them there was a raid over the beach, and 'the crazy fountains of red tracer looked very lovely against a romantically clear blue sky'. At around 11.00pm they all pulled out their sleeping rolls, and retired under the lean-to for the night. The last thing which Anthony wrote in his notebook was that there was a lot of 'alarming talk about moving at 5am.'

In the event they did not move on again until 8.00am. It was pouring with rain, the only advantage of which was to lay the thick dust.

It was now that Anthony began to notice that the sorrows of the poor bloody infantry were everything that they were proverbially said to be. A tank might not be as waterproof as it looked – the rain came pouring in through the most waterproof-looking points – but it was still hugely better than lying in the soaking wet grass. Over the coming days, he would often notice the infantry looking 'pathetically unanxious' to go into battle, and 'certainly the busy and delighted sounding rat-a-tat-tat of the machine guns was not inviting'. Seeing them digging in for the night in some benighted field, or lying in a ditch cooking food, made 'our life in the tank seem unfairly sybaritic'.

Cook, the tank commander, was an active, ingenious, and adventurous young man. Anthony recorded one incident in which Cook was sent for by the captain:

and came back in a dramatic mood, having been told to take two men and reconnoitre an 88 millimetre gun, which had been reported by local inhabitants. Cook was boyishly anxious to go. The rest of the crew maintained a rather more realistic attitude towards such goings on. There was no [...] enthusiasm to go looking for German 88 millimetre guns. But he took two of them, and they went off. While they were gone the fourth man in the crew started brewing up some tea on a petrol cooker, as the crews of the two neighbouring tanks were doing. [...]

After being away about two hours ... Cook and the two men came back having found the 88 millimetre blown up, with only the boots of the Germans left. They were in the usual condition of being half glad, half sorry not to have had more exciting times. However they were flushed with cider, and had mysteriously managed to buy a packet of French cigarettes, without any particular trouble. This seemed much more remarkable afterwards than it did at the time, when we hadn't met enough Frenchmen begging for cigarettes to realise how totally scarce they were.[269]

After lunch, Anthony took a little rapid tuition in how to fire the browning machine gun, noting 'it seemed an idyllically elementary form of gunnery, in its lack of precision admirably suited to my own'. Working the gun was simplicity itself; it was restricted in its movements, and any target would either have to be crossing its path or suicidally advancing head on. It was then simply a question of hose-piping the target with bullets, starting at the feet and working upwards. Anthony would fire on German infantry when the occasion arose, the first combat shots which he had ever fired.

More often than not, however, his tank was the hunted, not the hunter.

We got out to look round and a shot was fired apparently at us. We had no sooner bolted back into the tank than another one came. There were evidently snipers. The order came to stay in the tank all the time keep our eyes skinned for shots.

'We're at 892733. The enemy are in the corner of that wood over there,' said Cook.

'I hope they can't see us,' said someone else.

'Hallo Cooky, good news,' said the operator. 'That wood's clear of the enemy, but there's snipers.'

'Snipers.'

'I say again keep your head down,' said Cook.

'Not arf I won't' said Cherry.[270]

During the morning the infantry had killed or rounded up about forty snipers, but there were still plenty more in the immediate neighbourhood.

In all the mayhem of shooting, shelling, and sniper-fire, the French civilians tried to continue with their lives. Anthony and his crew found one family on a seemingly deserted farm, 'an old man, an even older and much more quavering woman, a little boy, and the little boy's mother who was obviously the administrative brains of the place'. They sat round their kitchen table, listening to the shells pouring overhead in both directions. For four nights they had been without sleep because of the bombardment.

> They were very anxious to know how the battle was going, which of course we didn't know ourselves. I said that the Germans were being forced back quickly, because obviously that was the only thing they could stand hearing at the moment. Meanwhile the Germans busily shelled and mortared the neighbourhood.

Eventually Anthony got tired of trying to talk bad French and went back to the tank, where he ate some more of their endless supplies of sweets and chocolate.

By teatime, a full-scale battle had started up a few hundred yards away. There was terrific machine-gun and mortar fire, and heavy shelling. Shrapnel fragments started showering all over the tank. Cook and Anthony felt it was their duty to do something, and with much crouching and doubling across gaps made their way along a lane in the direction of the firing. They reached a farmhouse, and searched it for a suitable window to shoot from, but none of the windows had any vantage point.

In their search round the house, Anthony unexpectedly came across a mirror and for one brief shocking moment did not recognise the man reflected in it. The stranger was advancing 'pistol in hand and ferocious in mien'. It took him a second or two to realise that the man who he was seeing was himself. The apparition had given him a severe fright. Had his family or friends seen him at this moment, they too might have failed to recognise the Anthony they knew in this sinister prowling figure.

As the farmhouse had been abandoned due to the proximity of the fighting, Anthony curiously looked around it, noting down details of the furnishings and contents in his notebook, and ending with the slightly surrealistic touch that 'the only living occupants were a turkey and young in the scullery'. Then seeing the infantry going down to battle, he followed them through the orchards and meadows until he could clearly see what was happening. The account ends abruptly at this point, possibly because pages are missing, but not before it has become very obvious how actively Anthony was seeking out danger.

16

THE BATTLE OF FONTENAY

In the third week of June, Anthony and his tank crew were involved in a major battle, an action for which he had volunteered the crew without consulting them. After the briefing, Cook, the 19-year-old tank commander, drew Anthony aside:

'Did you ask for us to go on this?' he asked. I made a non-committal answer.

'Just the chance I've been waiting for,' said Corporal Cook who was always ready with the right emotion. This may sound rather unkind, so let me hasten to add that he had also shown himself to be ready with the right action when necessary.[271]

Anthony does not explain why he had taken this rather high-handed action without at least discussing it with Cook first.

In amongst his Normandy papers is 8 Armoured Brigade Group Operation Order No. 26. It is copy number 19, and Anthony has the code letter 'I'. The order contains the battleplan for Saturday 24 to Sunday 25 June, its objective being to clear the enemy from the village of Fontenay and to establish a new frontline running from Vendes to Rauray. This was the battle for which Anthony had volunteered the crew.

Before Cook and the other tank commanders had attended their squadron-level briefing, Anthony had received his own private briefing from the commander of the Sherwood Rangers, Colonel Christopherson. Christopherson was an impressive figure, 'a creditably bemedalled young man with a twinkling personality and an attractive air of unassuming expertness.' Anthony wrote that Christopherson's expertise was not surprising as the Sherwood Rangers had been 'pretty constantly in action for several years, and the atmosphere of professionalism extended through all ranks'.

Christopherson explained the battle plan to Anthony from maps set up on some ammunition boxes in the 3-ton lorry he was using as an office. The current situation was that the wood north of Fontenay, Le Parc du Bois Londes, was held by both German and British forces, and the ground between the wood and the village was a German minefield. In Fontenay itself, there were a number of German machine-gun positions, and behind these lay an artillery battery, heavy mortars, and an unknown number of tanks, including Tigers. It was obvious that Fontenay was heavily defended and would be hard to capture.

Cook's tank, normally attached to Brigade HQ, had been temporarily assigned to B Squadron for the battle.[272] The B Squadron briefing by Major Lawton, the CO, gave them the specific details of the task in front of them, which was to advance at 4.15am under a creeping barrage in support of the infantry battalion who were to capture Fontenay. Because the Germans were using the three church towers in the village for Observation Posts, the essential first move would be to knock the towers to bits. 'It's not a nice thing to have to do,' Lawton informed his men, 'but there you are.'

The order to move towards the battle area came at 8.30pm. There were nineteen tanks in the squadron, besides two medical half-track vehicles and a scout car. The squadron crossed two fields in open order, before moving into single file along the cover of a hedge. Anthony noted that the way was lined with little groups of infantry digging in, standing about, or cooking on 'pathetically little fires'. As usual, Anthony's sympathy was aroused by the foot soldier's tough lot in life, a sympathy probably tinged with a sense of there-but-for-the-grace-of-God-go-I when he remembered his own days as an infantry officer.

Some way along the hedge, Anthony's tank came upon three graves:

'See where that Captain's been buried there, Cook,' said Cherry, 'The little white one next to the hedge.'

'Killed 16.6.44,' said Cook, reading out the dead man's name and Regiment.

The graves vary in condition but usually they all look as if some effort has been made to make them look more attractive, but the workmanship and available materials vary. These three were particularly attractive, small white crosses about eighteen inches high with the dead man's name, rank, unit, and date of death stated in black. There were bowls of roses at the foot of each grave, the bowls being army ration tins.

The isolation and simplicity of graves like these is sometimes more readily suggestive of the horror of it all than the mass mournfulness of a cemetery. It was a lyrically lovely evening, mellow and radiant. We were in a field, and the graves were the only sign that a few hours ago men had lost their lives to take it all to pieces. The grass just went on growing. Nature did not mourn the battle.

They passed on by some ruined shepherds' cottages, and shortly arrived at the field which had been designated as the camp, or harbour, for that night. There they halted across a shallow ditch next to a burnt-out German armoured car. The ditch was littered with bits of British and German uniforms, empty cigarette packets, grenades, rounds of ammunition, and a letter addressed to SS Mann Alfred Arndt, posted in Hirschberg on 19 June.

By now it was 9.30pm. Just ahead of them was the little wood, some 400 yards away, where the German minefields began. Making themselves as comfortable as they could, they and the other tank crews cooked a meal.

Half a dozen British aircraft went over, viciously pursued by barraging enemy flak. The evening sky was now reddening to darkness. 'Look at that sky,' said Cook, 'the life blood of the soldiers, reflected in the sky.'

'When I was in the desert, we had a sky like that every night,' said Cherry. He hadn't been in the desert, but this was the current joke among the non-8th Army men. [...]

We stood there in the gloaming, pondering on the way tea which for minutes has been much too hot suddenly becomes much too cold.

At 11pm a signal came 'All form a tight box in mid-field.' We backed with the others into a closely packed blockade with guns facing outwards in all directions. The two soft-skinned ambulance vehicles were protected inside the blockade.

Night was just about falling and the sky was a colder blue.

There were dangers all around, and even though it was now 11.15pm, Anthony did not feel tired, 'one's whole body was alerted'. At 11.45pm there was a conference of the two commanders. The men stood around Major Lawton in one corner of the blockade:

'Look, gentlemen. Everyone stay in their tank. Keep the usual watch – someone awake in each tank all night. If there's any trouble use the sten-gun, not the browning. Remember in a few hours there will be hundreds of infantry everywhere. They will be forming up in the field just behind. There's already a company out cleaning up as far as the minefields. So for God's sake be careful who you're shooting.'

Someone reported a possible mine, and Lawton and Anthony went to investigate, but there being no touch to shine on the suspicious object in the ground it was decided that it was not a mine after all. Lawton and Anthony returned to the blockade, and Lawton issued a stern warning to his men: '"Now, no one ought to leave camp. Get back in the tanks!" he shouted at some shadowy figures gossiping together in the darkness.'

It was very late and there would be less than four hours sleep. Anthony and his tank crew settled down for what was left of the night. Or at least the tank crew, accustomed to the tank's limited accommodation, settled down. Anthony tried in vain to find a comfortable position.

Our tank wasn't much good as a bedroom. Cook, the gunner, and the operator packed themselves in a sardine formation on the floor of the turret. Cherry and I had to sleep on our seats. The seat is about the same size as the high stool of a cocktail bar. It is built for the driver to sit upright, and therefore is not ideal for trying to recline. There was no support for the head at the back, nor to the left. If lolled to the right it fell among the complications of the wireless. It was impossible to sit facing forward with head in hands because of the guarding machine-guns. I achieved a fair state of equilibrium, with my feet shot in the small space above the tank shaft, and my head nestling against a piece of steel framework. On the other hand, Cherry, whose amenities were no more receptive, dropped off to sleep straight away. Personally I found it difficult. The one thing to be said for the arrangement was that the tank was quite warm.

The British barrage which was the prelude to the battle of Fontenay began at 4.15am. It was still dark and a fine fireworks display could be seen, augmented by the Germans putting up Verey lights, and glowing silvery tracer flying through the trees of the wood.

As the British tanks moved out of their night's defensive position, shells and mortars started exploding close by. Anthony, all his usual cackhandedness forgotten, gave what assistance he could to his tank crew:

'No more H.E. left in the turret,' said the operator.

'OK, could you whip the reserves up, Major?' said Cook to me. Behind my feet there was a rack of 75 mm shells. It was a considerable undertaking to prize them out of their pigeon holes. They were not only clipped in, but stuck fast. [...]

An enemy tank was reported among the trees to the left of the village. Looking hard, I just caught a glimpse of something which might have been it. An indignant voice said over the air: 'Baker, where the hell have you been? There's a bloody Hornet here. Why the hell don't you keep your men on the set?'

Orders were given for the tanks in our troop to attack the enemy tank. We all fired at it.

'Just a bit minus, cock. Up a bit, Jack, up,' said Cook.

I just saw the head of it by drawing in with my browning machine-gun. The hunted enemy bolted, hugging the trees and making for cover. From where we were, unable to appreciate its particular limitations of manoeuvre, it seemed suicidally unresourceful. We were all flaming away at it, and presently it blew up. We all machine-gunned the spot; my browning kept jamming.

The tank burned steadily for a little while, and then its ammunition started exploding, and it sent up a steady column of flame to a tree-top height. I went on handing up more ammunition from the rack just behind me.

Over the air a voice said: 'Our friend (meaning the infantry) don't want any more fire. Our friends are getting into the buildings and they report some white flags waving.'

All this time a running current of shell and mortar and machine-gun fire was being exchanged in and around the village. Sometimes shells would burst overhead, near enough to shake Anthony's tank, and sometimes tracer drifted in their direction, but despite their exposed position they were unharmed.

The battle raged until around 10.00pm, when there was a brief lull; the smoke cleared away, and the battered little village could be clearly seen in the brilliant morning sunlight. Taking advantage of the temporary hiatus, Anthony climbed out of his tank, X-ray twelve, and went to see Major Lawton. But then the shell-bursts started up again, directly overhead, each one producing a belch of blue-black smoke. Knocked over by the blast of a nearby 17-pounder gun, Anthony went back to the safety of his tank, and started listening to the wireless chatter:

'I shall want a running feed,' said one of the tanks.

'Something to eat or drink?' asked the Squadron Commander.

'It's these things we've been flinging about all morning. We've lost plenty of them,' replied the tank.

Coming as a complete stranger to this form of double talk, it didn't take long to realise that they were talking about ammunition and petrol. I shouldn't think it would take any English-speaking Germans long either. This particular conversation continued:-

'I have the soft balls that X-ray would like and I could bring them to his last night's bedroom if that would suit him,' said the man whose business it was to run the forward supply Echelon. Arrangements were then made for individual tanks to return to last night's harbour and replenish their ammunition.

Our next door neighbour asked: 'Can you see those people walking about at figures 50 yards left [sic] to the wood?'

'Not yet.'

'There's two buggers there.'

'I think it's two French people. They're not doing anything active.'

'Yes, I think that's about what it is,' said the Squadron Commander. 'So be very careful not to do anything there.'

Our tank [...] reported having seen a tank left of the burning wreck. The Squadron Commander asked everyone to report if they thought it was a tank. Someone said it wasn't, at which Corporal Cook indignantly maintained that he had seen two men get out of it.

'I believe you're right. All stations train on it,' said the Squadron Commander.

We all started firing again. But no gratifying enemy brew-up resulted.

'Hallo X-ray twelve. If that's the position you mentioned, it looks like a false alarm,' said the Squadron Commander.

'I don't think it is. I bet he'll move in a few minutes,' said Cook.

'OK, give it a few more,' said the Squadron Commander, and we started firing again.

Someone reported some Germans walking about in the foreground and asked if it was worth getting artillery onto them. 'I don't think we dare, without knowing more about the position of our own infantry,' said the Squadron Commander.

'Hallo X-ray one. There's a hell of a scrap going down in the village. Is it theirs or ours?'

'Ours.'

'Going very near our own positions.'

Anthony must have been scribbling like a maniac to get down this wireless chatter; it adds a totally unique intensity to his reportage. His interlinking text is just as effective. Though it is pared down to its simplest details, it never leaves out the tiny embellishments which give his writing so much life. He observed for example, that Cherry, 'who slept very well last night', had fallen asleep again despite the infernal racket of the battle, and he recorded the wildly incongruous remark of Jack, the gunner, that what he would like best now would be 'a nice sultana pudding'.

A terrific machine-gun duel had now started up between guns firing from the village and guns firing a few yards away from the squadron, whilst the squadron's own machine guns were also firing with 'distressing effects on one's ears'. The squadron was being fired on from the woods whilst shells were 'thunder-clapping' overhead. Presently the firing became too hot and they backed away from their exposed position into the shelter of a hedge.

Anthony took stock of the day so far:

> I forgot to mention that a little earlier on we machine-gunned a party of about 50 German infantry who very ill-advisedly started moving across our front in the corn field. The party seemed very unresourceful about avoiding our machine-gun fire. Some went to ground in the corn, others plodded on. I operated my Browning with no real feeling, until they started firing back; at which my feelings underwent a sudden development.

X-ray twelve had unfortunately taken shelter next to a dead cow, one of the thousands whose swollen bodies were strewn about the Normandy fields.

> Like all the others its legs stuck up in a horribly girlish high kick. There was a filthy smell of decay. So outstandingly filthy that presently we moved. We moved some 50 yards, but found that it wasn't enough to get out of range of the unfortunate animal. We found ourselves next to two dead Tommies, from whom we took a Bren gun. It was just a pleasant Sunday morning, shooting at church steeples and replenishing deficiencies from the dead.
>
> To my despondency I found that it was only 1.52pm. The day seemed to have gone on much longer. I started tidying up the heap of cartridge cases in the well of the tank under my feet.

It was 4.30 in the afternoon before they penetrated the outskirts of Fontenay. The village was severely damaged and several houses were on fire. Whenever the noises of battle stopped for a few minutes, Anthony could hear that the place was ghostly still. His acutely observing eye noticed that the desolation was accentuated by a white rabbit which kept running in and out of the houses. The following day he would see another white rabbit rushing round a corner and making off up the road. 'It looked like the same one we saw yesterday. I wonder if it got any sleep.'

Eventually it was judged that this area had been safely secured. Anthony's tank crew got out, made tea, and ate biscuits and jam, their first organised meal of the day. They did not have long before they were ordered to join C Squadron, which was supporting an imminent infantry attack on the German-held parts of the village.

> Down in the village things didn't seem to have changed much. Another house was in flames. The infantry were still digging in. Some of them were manhandling an anti-tank gun into position. They said that enemy tanks were said to be forming up. We let them fill their water bottles from the water cans which we carried roped to our hull. They looked dreadfully tired and grimy, their clothes and features caked with light brown dust. They had been in action for a fortnight. [...]

We now started running through the enemy-held part of the village as I had read the map upside down. Not so much as a single shot was fired at us, although a few hours later a full-scale attack had to be mounted to clear the Germans out of exactly the same area. Perhaps the small groups of enemy scattered about the village thought there was something fishy in this apparently pointless excursion by a solitary Sherman.

Anthony does not record the reaction of the crew to his shamefully inept map-reading. He had perhaps some excuse in that the situation in the village was very confused, with no surety where the front was or who was in front of it. Everything had suddenly fallen very quiet. They proceeded with extreme caution. Then going up a narrow strip of road, they suddenly came upon a small detachment of English infantry with an anti-tank gun.

How they got there and what they were doing there was not particularly obvious. The sight of them was extraordinarily heartening. It made our apprehensive alertness seem rather stupid.

But after all it wasn't so stupid. The infantry men pointed out through a gap in a hedge a German Tiger tank engaged in towing a fellow Tiger which had been knocked out.

The infantry had been trying unsuccessfully to manoeuvre their anti-tank gun into a position from which they could fire at the Tiger. By great good fortune, the Tiger's guns were traversed in the opposite direction, and X-ray twelve backed off a few yards down the hedge to a point where the Tiger was sideways on, the perfect target. X-ray twelve fired a shot and seemed to hit it in the suspension, then hastily fired another and definitely hit it.

With the felicitations of the infantry in our ears we started off up the road at considerable speed. We travelled as far as the end of the village then turned back across and came back by the other road.

Eventually we found 'C' Squadron and attached ourselves to them. We formed up without any particular attempt at concealment on the ground in front of the village. The infantry started working their way up between us. It was raining hard and generally speaking a filthy night. Even with its hatches down, the tank was not as waterproof as it looked. Besides which the rain made it impossible to see through the periscope, so that it was as well to keep the lid open and take the rain.

Of course the unfortunate infantry had no choice but to take it. They were crawling up through the corn or long grass, and digging in. Placed behind the steel walls of our tank, we all felt terrific sympathy and admiration for them. Inside a tank you can at least carry a certain amount of personal kit. You have something to hide behind; a firm base to operate from; reassuringly formidable equipment. The accommodation may be cramped but you get used to that. At least you don't have to carry everything on your back. At least the tank can put you where you have to go. Compared with the infantry, life in a tank seems an unfairly sybaritic existence.

These emotions were intensified when enemy machine guns started opening up from the village. Machine gun bullets simply bounce off a tank. All that happens is a noise like metal rain. But they don't bounce off a human being.

At 10.25pm the tanks advanced slowly into the village, firing at houses and hedges from which tracer was coming. Anthony's tank went across a field, unavoidably squelched over a dead cow, and turned left into a lane which was already crowded with military traffic. It was getting dark and it was difficult to see the long line of infantry who had dropped down in the ditches on either side of the road. Anthony walked through the traffic jam to see what the hold-up was, and met the rather harassed CO of the infantry battalion who said he had, roughly speaking, lost his men.

> 'It's impossible country to fight in,' he said, 'they march up, they lie down, and you've lost them.' As if in illustration of his complaint, a section came up the lane, got into the ditch, and were lost to sight. Indeed, in this country of high lanes and many hedges, corn fields and ill-defined front lines, it was almost impossibly difficult to maintain coherent formation.

Around 1.00am, the tanks withdrew a little from the village into harbour for the night. Anthony was exhausted. He hadn't been able to sleep very satisfactorily the previous night, but found no difficulty now. 'With the wireless set for a pillow, and with most of my body suspended in the air, I went straight off into a dreamless sleep.'

The following day, Monday 26 June, life began again about 5.00am. They had breakfast, then went back into Fontenay to assist with the clear-up operation. By now, Cook had completely got into the spirit of things. Around lunchtime, he called Anthony up to see a Tiger tank. There was a little square yellow box of turret showing just to the right of a pylon. An anti-tank specialist was brought up to see what he could do with the target, and said he thought he could hit it. Then someone remembered that they had a 17-pounder Sherman down at the other end of the orchard. Someone went off to bring it up – very quietly.

> We all moved very quietly. A little group of us stood intensely watching what we could see of the turret of the Tiger. It was about 300 yards away and mostly hidden behind the hedge. Meantime, Corporal Cook, the personality kid, jockied our tank up into position alongside the newly and quietly arrived 17-pounder Sherman. The rest of the crew regarded this as a piece of gratuitous exposure to the Tiger's expected reply. It was all very well to do what you were told, but don't go asking for it, was their point of view.
>
>   'It's either him or us now,' said Cook with his usual gift for the dramatic.
>
>   We moved up the hedge, and then backed a bit, until the gunner was satisfied with the view. The infantry withdrew a few yards to watch the impending duel.
>
>   'Traverse the gun a bit,' said Cook. 'Can you see the target?'
>
>   'Right on that bushy tree isn't it?' said Collin with what seemed deplorable vagueness.
>
>   'Let's see through your periscope,' said Cook. He leant over in front of the gunner. 'No that's not it. Driver come back. No, go forward a bit.'
>
>   'Wouldn't like me to go sideways?' enquired the driver.
>
>   'Now can you see it?' said Cook.
>
>   'There's a twig in the middle but I can see it all right,' said Collin.
>
>   'Wait till that 17-pounder fires first. What do you make the range?'

The excitement mounted to feverish proportions until collapse into dreary anti-climax when they realised they had been attacking an already dead German tank. They had a cup of tea by way of consolation, and then joined a column of tanks who were trying to relieve some pinned-down infantry. This action had not properly begun before X-ray twelve was recalled to Brigade HQ.

There is no doubt that Anthony had thoroughly enjoyed being in action, as had Cook. The rest of the crew seems to have had rather more mixed feelings and may even have been heartily glad to see the back of Anthony with his habit of getting them into trouble. Sadly, the surviving papers do not tell us how he parted from the crew. There is a gap, and then his Normandy account begins again with him covering a completely different aspect of 8th Armoured Brigade's campaign.

The Brigade was a very large organisation, with three Regiments, each with about sixty tanks, and a Brigade Headquarters with about twelve tanks. It also had its own motor battalion, field regiment, signals squadron, Royal Army Medical Corps company, light field ambulance, REME workshop, and Ordnance field park. As Anthony quipped, 'it was like a young Division'.[273]

In addition, each squadron of tanks had its own armoured recovery vehicle (ARV), dedicated to recovering damaged tanks. The man in charge of this vital operation was a Captain Douglas Collins, who had been an agricultural auctioneer in the West Country before the war. On the evening that Anthony joined him to report on his work, there were five Sherman tanks to be reconnoitred and if possible recovered.

Information had come in that inside one of the tanks there were three bodies.

'Want us to dig three graves then sir?' asked the Technical Sergeant Major.

'Yes and get some disinfectant, some of them are very bad. They'll fall to pieces when you get them out.'

Collins and I were travelling in his scout car. He told the ARV crews where to meet us. 'By the monument on the corner where they were digging holes to bury the chaps.'[274]

When they came upon the tank in question, it was a deeply shocking sight; the crew had been burned to death. Other bodies were found at other locations further on. They also came across the aftermath of a firefight. Four German snipers, who had been hiding in the branches of some tall trees, had been killed. Standing beneath one of the trees, Anthony took several minutes to identify the sniper's body, so well had he camouflaged himself. He could just see a boot hanging down and the outline of the helmet. It was a sharp lesson in the obdurate tenacity of German soldiers. It had taken 'a considerable expenditure of time and ammunition to locate and kill them. They sold themselves dearly. They did not give up when they were wounded. They shot it out to the end.'

Anthony and Collins drove back to where they had started. Collins ordered a rum issue for the men who had pulled the burned bodies out of the tank and buried them.

His batman had been particularly upset. It was the first time he had seen anyone he knew in the peculiarly horrible state of death. The boy was sitting apart from the others, and had been crying a little. It was the first time he had seen any of his friends dead. For that matter everyone felt pretty sick.

The last part of Anthony's Normandy account tells the story of a medical operation. Though it is undated, at one point Anthony writes that the operation was 'the 114th which Major Clark had performed in some three weeks'. If Clark had come over on D-Day, the operation would have taken place around 27 June, very shortly after the battle of Fontenay and just before Anthony's return to England.

It was performed on an SS soldier, the 18-year-old SS Panzer Grenadier Thielemann. He had been wounded three days earlier, probably by High Explosive shrapnel, and was now awaiting evacuation. Anthony noted that many men who had been wounded in the morning were operated on two hours later and despatched to England that evening. But Thielemann's wound in the buttocks had become infected with gas gangrene. It was necessary for him to be operated on before leaving for England.

The barn being used as a temporary operating room was high, wide, and musty. Anthony's keen eye noted, amongst other details, the numerous pairs of surgical rubber gloves which were hanging out to dry on a line rigged up across the barn. Along one side of the wall there was a bench on which the anaesthetist had hung up his equipment. There was a hole in the wall just above it, in which a rat presently appeared and briefly watched the proceedings.

Anthony saw that Thielemann's feet were filthy, and that his unconscious face was fevered-looking with many days growth of beard. He looked extremely young, and Anthony wrote that he was 'not a bad-looking boy' who, it was easy to imagine, would not be aggressive in battle.

The prognosis for Thielemann was bad. The surgeon, in the course of his probing, had discovered that the wound went into the bowel.

> The operation changed immediately from a minor to a serious one, and the prospect of Thielemann's survival were greatly reduced. They continued to work on him, and Clark sprinkled the new wonder drug, penicillin, into the wound.
>
> It all seemed so natural, so straight-forward, and so matter-of-fact that I was surprised when the Major told me that Thielemann was in a very poor condition and his prospects of survival were not good. Things were always very difficult once gas gangrene set in. It wasn't so bad in the case of a foot or leg. If you cut them off early enough there was nothing to worry about but you couldn't do that when part of the trunk was involved. Of course the penicillin was capable of wonders in combating gas gangrene. The wound had been powdered with it and he would have injections every few hours for several days, and also an anti-gas gangrene serum on leaving the theatre.[275]

The German youth was being given the very best medical treatment available. Despite the rudimentary nature of the barn, the medical officers were extremely well-equipped. Their caseload was not beyond their capacity to handle, and no one was going to die through lack of care or resources. Things would be very different some eight weeks later when Anthony was shot in the truck in Brummen.

17

INTERLUDE

Shortly after witnessing the operation on Thielemann, Anthony returned to England. Watkins records him as arriving back at the end of June just in time for Watkins' own departure for France.

Anthony had been in Normandy for just over three weeks. He was coming back a changed man, quietly self-confident, happy despite the horrors which he had witnessed, and thoroughly determined to get back to front-line reporting as soon as possible. He told Watkins that his next excursion would be a parachute drop with 1st Airborne Division, wherever and whenever that would be.

Almost at once, he went home to Ham Frith. His mother and father must have been absolutely overjoyed to see him. As for Geoffrey, he was with his battery in Leytonstone when the news came through:

I am in my office at my battery. Telephone.
'Oh, hullo.'
'Oh, my God, is that you? Where are you?'
'At home.'
'Oh, my God, I'll be right round.'
Being the boss I was able instantly to order someone to take over from me and to get transport. So within ten minutes or a quarter of an hour I was at Ham Frith. Imagine how I felt. He was in our kitchen-dining room with mama and papa, looking as if he were back from the holidays.
'Here you are.' He handed me a round carton. A Camembert direct from Normandy.[276]

Once he was back at the *WAR* office in London, Anthony took care of things whilst Watkins was in Normandy.

Although the chronology is slightly confused, it seems that Anthony, who was of course Watkins' superior, had authorised Watkins' Normandy trip just before D-Day. Watkins' plan was to cross over and attach himself to some unit 'in the manner of a lamprey'. Once he had secured such an attachment, he would visit his old friends at 49th Infantry Division with whom he had been in Iceland. Rather hesitantly he had aired this plan with Anthony, and told him of his preferred title for the article, 'The Captain in Search of his Youth'. 'Go ahead,' Anthony said, more encouragingly than I thought likely. 'Follow that line and you may have something. But not too much Iceland.'[277]

Watkins left for France on the first Sunday in July. He was extremely glad to be off because the dangers in London now felt worse than those in Normandy – he had had a couple of lucky escapes from flying bombs.[278] He was in France for about three weeks, rather enjoyed himself, and it was with some reluctance that he returned but it could not be avoided. Though Watkins was well below the level where he might hear anything about a major offensive, there was a vibration in the air which suggested that something huge was imminent. It was bound to involve the elite airborne forces, and if they were to go 'Anthony would be with them, whether I was back in Eaton Square or not. Someone must be there to mind the shop.'[279]

On his return towards the end of July, Watkins and Anthony began to firm up a plan which had been in Anthony's mind for some time. Confident in his skills as a journalist and editor, and financially well off due to his ceaseless hard work, he now wished to found his own publishing house. It was to be called The Whig Press, and was to be formed as a limited company with his old friend at the *Daily Express*, Harold Keeble. Watkins would also be a director and investor; his practical mind would be of great use, and he now put his extensive legal experience into drafting a very long and detailed contract for the company.

The Whig Press's first publication was to be a miscellany called *The Haymarket*, which it was hoped would gradually mutate into a magazine in appearance rather like Cyril Connolly's *Horizon*. In the proofs of *The Haymarket* which he kept long after the idea of the Whig Press had been abandoned, Watkins would give the reasons for *The Haymarket*'s genesis:

> This collection dates back to the summer of 1944, in a back room in Eaton Square occupied
> by Anthony Cotterell and myself for the purpose of producing an ABCA publication known as
> *WAR*. In the short gap between D-Day and Arnhem we were encouraged to think that our task
> there was nearly over. We both felt that we had learnt a good deal in doing it, and that the major
> lesson was that people generally like good writing provided that it is about things in which they
> are interested. *Haymarket*, which we planned then, is just this and no more.[280]

Amongst several contributors solicited for the miscellany were Paul Holt, the famous *Daily Express* journalist, and Jenny Nicholson's father, Robert Graves. Graves would be a major prize, his name guaranteed to attract interest in the publication. Anthony wrote to him in September, shortly after the liberation of Brussels on the 3rd. He addressed Graves by his Christian name instead of the form he usually used of 'Dear Robert Graves'. He asked Graves for advice and help in the launch of a monthly magazine, which now seemed a reasonable prospect with the end of the war approaching. The restriction on wartime publications meant that new periodicals were not allowed, but Anthony hoped to get round this by not actually using the term 'magazine'. Instead the Whig Press would publish issues 'from time to time until such time as we can give each issue a number and a date'.

Anthony's view on the 'magazine situation in this country' was that it was 'pretty barren', mainly because new publications always seemed directed at an intellectual clique or were pallid imitations of some American success. He told Graves that they had already lined up the printer, the paper, and the co-operation of W.H. Smith, so that the production and distribution side of things was 'reasonably in the clear'.[281]

Graves, when he replied, would give a very favourable response.

Anthony meanwhile was continuing on a number of other projects. His book, *An Apple for the Sergeant*, was now close to publication. It covers his Army career after initial training and includes some of his detailed war reports for ABCA. The material is fascinating but the book does not fit together well, as if Anthony had skimped on the editorial work. This was almost certainly because he had far more dramatic, urgent and topical matters to deal with, including his accounts of the run-up to D-Day and the momentous day itself. As for the Normandy campaign, Watkins noted that Anthony much preferred to write about what had happened there than to talk about it, and writing about it was what Anthony was now chiefly occupied in doing. He had a mass of amazing material to work with. By September, he had organised his extensive notes, created a coherent narrative, and had it typed it up, before beginning to correct and redraft it. The first draft has many small gaps where he was temporarily lost for the right word, or needed to check his facts or some arcane piece of military terminology. No doubt, he also occasionally could not read his own shorthand. This must have been particularly true of the operational chatter between tanks, excited dialogue which happened extraordinarily fast.

In several places it is obvious that Anthony was reading his notes out to someone who would later type them up. There are a number of small errors where the wrong word is used but one which sounds extremely like the right one. Anthony would shortly tell an interviewer, John Paddy Carstairs, that he was 'cultivating dictation', and that this helped 'to solve the equation between mental activity and physical translation on to paper'. The method must have helped in getting the text down quickly, but it is clear from the various mistakes that there was no time to check it properly before he went to Arnhem. In particular, whoever was taking down the text often made mistakes with military terminology. For example, 'sometimes tracer would drift in our direction' would become meaningless when the word 'paper' was substituted for 'tracer'. In another place, where Anthony clearly meant 'Tiger', the feared German tank, the typescript reads 'fighter'.

Anthony's account of tank warfare, based on his Normandy notes, appeared in two parts in WAR, the last part appearing on 2 September. His love for punning and for literary allusions was uppermost when he called the article 'Tiger, Tiger, Burning Bright'. For the published text, Anthony cut out anything which might be too revealing of military secrets. He also removed men's actual names and took out the occasional piece of swearing – 'I'm dead sure it was H.E. from the shit all over the place' would become 'muck all over the place' in the WAR article. There were more serious losses. Because of the need to condense and to sound authoritative, much of the vitality, immediacy and originality disappeared, although it would remain in the longer unpublished version.

Anthony was clearly planning another book, one which covered the liberation of Europe. None of his original notes for D-Day and Normandy still exist, and it is possible that some of the material is missing; however, the text as it stands, including the pre-D-Day diary, runs to about 35,000 words. He had found his metier, and the D-Day and Normandy material contains superb writing.

Being in action had suited Anthony. Any natural instinct for self-preservation had frequently been set aside by his compulsion to seek out danger. He had shown immense courage under fire, and considerable resourcefulness in finding his way into dramatic situations, He had been in a major battle, Fontenay, and had fired the tank's browning guns at German infantry, probably killing or seriously injuring some of them. He had seen many wounded and maimed soldiers, death in some of its worst forms and a multitude of corpses. He had come away from it all with a new maturity and confidence, not to mention great kudos. As his brother Geoffrey would later say, mixing with top-class soldiers in action had been an intoxicant and Anthony had become 'addicted to nobility'. He was now about to join the real cream. The officers of 1st Parachute Brigade with whom he would shortly go to Arnhem were, as Geoffrey described them, 'medieval nobles', incredibly impressive men.[282]

According to Watkins, Anthony had arranged the attachment to 1st Parachute Brigade around the time of returning from France, but there is no information as to how he managed this. Once again there was no question of his bosses at ABCA interfering. Watkins would write that by this stage of the war, nobody was giving Anthony any orders at all.

Meanwhile, Anthony remained as mischievous and as much of a tease as ever. Some time in July or August, he was interviewed by John Paddy Carstairs for his new book, Hadn't We the Gaiety? Carstairs, a prolific middle-brow writer who was serving in the Navy, had had a bestseller with a recent novel, and was aiming for a second bestseller with this new book. It was to contain portraits of celebrities whom he had met recently 'in the capacity of film director, novelist, and naval lieutenant'. In the interview, Carstairs comes across as a slightly absurd figure, the prototype of a television Guest Show host, and at times Anthony appears to be quietly ridiculing him. The interview, which was conducted over a glass of beer, began with Carstairs dutifully asking Anthony how he put his books on paper.

He grinned before he replied. I should add perhaps for those that do not know young Mr. Cotterell that he is something of a character. By this I mean that he is very good-looking, has eyelashes that any film star would be pleased to own, and has the sort of face that looks as if he does not have to shave. Don't let this fool you. Major Cotterell is full of surprises.[283]

Anthony told Carstairs that he was trying dictation, and that as for method, he believed 'if I've done it myself I'll know what I'm talking about', his standard official reason for writing about what interested him rather than getting stuck with the boring stuff. Carstairs noted the parachute emblem on his sleeve, and commented that because Anthony wanted to write about parachutists he had qualified for their badge and was thereby qualified to write about them. 'Simple ... if you feel you can do it!' Carstairs concluded.

'I can't work long hours,' Anthony confessed. 'Have had to face this bravely,' he added, peering into his glass of beer. 'Of course, I used to find it much more difficult to concentrate than I do now. Force of habit. But I can't work in the sort of day and night spurts I'm told you do.'
   'I do not,' I said, 'on the contrary–'
   'Nor,' continued Anthony, paying no regard to my denial, 'like many people, do I like working late at night. Late at night I like–'
   'Tell me about your method of writing?' I broke in hurriedly [...]. 'Do you do much re-writing?'
   'Will your readers care?' Anthony asked.
   'There you have me! But I think your readers might!' I countered.
   'Actually, very little.'

The interview ended with Anthony telling Carstairs that he had got his job on the *Daily Express* by writing an article about how to live a full life on the dole. He had been attending the Snow Hill Labour Exchange for a short period having been fired from the *News Chronicle* 'for inefficiency, unintelligence and for asking for more money'. Carstairs did not give the name of the paper – 'I won't embarrass the bloke who fired him'.[284]
   Anthony was on the verge of great success. He did not mention his plans for *The Haymarket* to Carstairs, or that he had been offered a post-war column on *The Observer* by its future owner and editor, David Astor.[285] With *An Apple for the Sergeant* ready for publication and his book on the liberation of Europe in progress, everything seemed to be set for Anthony to become a top-flight author, journalist and editor after the war.
   Everyone was now talking about the end of the war. At last, it really did seem to be in sight. By late August, the campaign in Normandy was coming to an end in an Allied victory. The appallingly savage fighting of the Falaise Pocket saw thousands of German casualties and many more thousands taken prisoner. The trapped German forces had been mercilessly bombarded, and the roads and fields were full of dead men, dead animals, and destroyed equipment. General Eisenhower, touring the scene afterwards, found the scene so horrific that he said it could only have been described by Dante; 'it was literally possible to walk for hundreds of yards at a time, stepping on nothing but dead and decaying flesh'.[286]
   Unknown to the Allies, however, many Germans had managed to escape from that nightmare world of death. Military historians continue to debate how many actually escaped from the Falaise Pocket and how many had never been entrapped in the first place, but those who had endured the bombardment must have been utterly brutalised. The men who had escaped were not just members of the Wehrmacht, the regular army, but also fanatical soldiers of the Waffen-SS. Amongst the units which got out of Normandy was the 9th SS Panzer Division, the Hohenstauffen. On 23 September, it would be a soldier from the Hohenstauffen who would shoot Anthony in the truck in Brummen.

18

'WE ARE JUMPING TO A CONCLUSION'

O n 25 August, Paris was liberated. The road seemed to lie open to Holland and Belgium, and from thence to Germany itself. Everywhere German resistance was crumbling. The usual optimists began predicting that the war would be over by Christmas.

Anthony eagerly awaited his summons to 1st Airborne Division, and before the end of August it arrived. He travelled up to Lincolnshire to join a key part of the Division, 1st Parachute Brigade. The Brigade was under the command of Gerald Lathbury, a personal friend and the acknowledged deputy of the commander of 1st Airborne Division, Major-General Roy Urquhart.

Like all the Division, the Brigade had a very strong corps identity, symbolised by the divisional maroon-red berets and by the maroon and sky-blue flash of the warrior Bellerophon riding Pegasus. Brigade HQ, to which Anthony was attached, was the command centre of the Brigade. It coordinated the activities of its 1st, 2nd and 3rd Battalions, commanded respectively by Lieutenant-Colonels Dobie, Frost and Fitch. It was that same Frost who had been on the Bruneval raid which Anthony had covered in *WAR* in November 1942 and which had quickened his interest in the airborne forces.

Anthony reached Brigade HQ on the evening of 1 September. He at once started work on an article about *Linnet*, the planned airborne operation to assist the liberation of Brussels. Uniquely amongst Anthony's work for *WAR*, there survives a part-pencil, part-typescript draft of this piece, which he entitled 'Jumping to a Conclusion: Part One'. He evidently intended to write the second part once they had landed in Belgium. 'Jumping to a Conclusion' was a typical Anthony play on words, referring to the end of the war which he and the Brigade would reach by parachute jump. Before the end of the month, this mildly hubristic joke would take on a horribly macabre twist. Understandably, Watkins did not use the title in the article which was eventually printed in *WAR*.

'Jumping to a Conclusion' included many operational details about *Linnet*. These would swiftly become irrelevant because less than a day and a half after Anthony arrived at HQ, *Linnet* was cancelled because of the speed of the Allied advance. Nonetheless, Anthony retained much of his initial work because it vividly set the atmosphere at Brigade HQ. The article began:

> I reached the Parachute Brigade HQ on Friday evening, the jump being planned for Sunday morning.
>
> The Brigade staff was in a state of considerable apprehension; not that the operation would take place, but that it wouldn't. This was the third time they had been alerted since D-Day, and they found each stand-down more progressively discouraging.
>
> Typical overheard: the Brigade Major talking on the telephone to someone at Division: 'The only thing that gives us slight sickness is every time we turn on the wireless, hearing the news.'

> No doubt about it the news was depressingly good; the B.B.C. announcers were tediously smug; the arrows on the newspaper maps almost moved nearer Germany as soon as you looked at them.[287]

Anthony was incorrect about the number of stand downs. In fact it had already reached fourteen.

The Brigade Major on the telephone was Tony Hibbert, Lathbury's second-in-command. Courageous, handsome, charismatic and extremely quick-thinking, Hibbert would be a key figure in Anthony's time in Holland. He had only taken up his post with the Brigade on 8 July, and had recorded the details in his diary:

> Arrived 1 Parachute Brigade to take over duties of Brigade Major from Tony Fitch who is going to 3 Parachute Battalion as Commanding Officer. Brigadier [Lathbury] away on leave; Tony Fitch to meet me at Grantham Station. Arrived Brigade HQ at supper time, majority HQ on leave [...] I have to take over duties by Tuesday night, and go on four days leave on Wednesday morning.[288]

Amongst the Brigade personnel whom Hibbert met on that first day were four officers who would soon become well-known to Anthony: Bernard Briggs, the Staff Captain; Douglas Mortlock, the Brigade Royal Army Signal Corps Officer; Bill Marquand, the Signals Officer and David Wright, the Medical Officer.

Hibbert spent his first Sunday reading files and taking voluminous notes. After writing down his official activities, he recorded the war situation, giving the respective locations of the rapidly advancing British, American and Russian forces. His final sentence reflected the brigade's huge impatience to get into action before the war was over – 'there will be nothing left for us except the Japs unless we hurry'.

By the time Anthony joined Brigade HQ some seven weeks later, its officers had endured many cancelled operations and were in an even worse state of impatience to go to Europe. On Anthony's arrival, Hibbert immediately took charge of him. That evening they dined in the mess, and Anthony noted down the conversation of his fellow officers:

> About the operation itself there was not a great deal of evident excitement, no doubt because this was the oldest and most seasoned Parachute Brigade. There was nothing experimental or uncertain in their approach apart from the inevitable personal uncertainties of anyone approaching an operational jump.
> 'What are you going to do – hook up when you take off?'
> 'No, when I pass the coast.'
> 'I'm going to hook up everyone on the ground.'
> 'Oh, I don't know. People want to go and be sick, or move around.'
> The conversation was shot with these technicalities.

The term 'hook up' described the method in which the airborne soldiers used a kind of rigging which would automatically trigger the opening of their parachutes when they jumped from the aircraft in quick succession.

After supper, Anthony read the battle orders for *Linnet*, and then Hibbert explained the plan to him in the briefing hut. The gliders and aircraft had already been loaded for the operation, and many other preparations had been made.

The following day Anthony travelled ten miles to hear the briefing of B Company, 2nd Battalion, whom he was to join after parachuting in. Its CO was Major Douglas Edward Crawley, who had already won the Military Cross and would win a second one at Arnhem. The briefing took place in an oak-panelled drawing-room, with a centre-piece of a large square model of the territory. The drop zone was close to Renaix, a town of about 25,000 people which Crawley helpfully pointed out was about the size of Grantham.

'The general form of the operation is to cut off the German retreat,' Crawley began. It would be idle to pretend that this stirring announcement caused any evident flutter. The riveting fascination of the pre-D-day briefings had flown.

He went on to say that the latest available information was that the 21st Army Group had reached Arras, and the Americans were pushing up into Belgium.

The enemy were thought to be pretty well non-existent about the dropping area, and to be confined to low-grade troops in the neighbouring towns. But there was always the possibility of colliding with a division in transit, apart of course from the people whom we were supposed to cut off.

The platoon leaders then gave their own separate briefings. Anthony had been assigned to No 4 Platoon, headed by Lieutenant Hugh Levien whose name Anthony misspells as Levene. When the battalion finally parachuted into Holland rather than Belgium, Levien's platoon would be ambushed on the way to Arnhem – several would be killed and the remainder taken prisoner. Anthony was not amongst them, either because he had been assigned to another group, or more likely because he had reassigned himself as he had done so often in Normandy.

In his briefing Levien included advice on the pronunciation of Belgian place names, and similar advice would have been given for the even more tricky Dutch names a fortnight later:

'RV at this place, Dergneau, pronounce it as Dern-yo. It's no use saying Derg-no if you ask someone; they probably won't understand you. But you shouldn't need to ask. You can tell it by the church [...] Now you want to memorise this name. What is it?' he pointed to one rather absent-looking member of the audience.

'I've forgotten, sir,' said the man, smartly and in a soldierly fashion.

The briefings ended, and the men went to lunch. Hibbert's diary tersely records that parachutes were drawn and fitted at 2.30 that same afternoon. Anthony's version of this process was that it was accompanied by the invariable ('or so I am told') depressing jokes – 'You've got a blanket in there, not a chute,' or 'Looks like it's full of dirty washing.'

Once drawn, the man's name was chalked upon the package, and the parachutes were piled in the correct sticks, stick being the collective name for a group of parachutists. The parachute was just one of many supplies to be drawn. In his article, Anthony planned to include a standard equipment list, drawn up shortly after D-Day on 9 June 1944 for some cancelled and now long forgotten operation. The list began in very loud type:

YOU SHOULD ALL HAVE THE UNDERMENTIONED ITEMS IN YOUR POSSESSION, HAVE YOU GOT THEM?

From the Company Quartermaster's Stores:
    Lifebelt
    .36 Grenades (2)
    Jumping Jacket
    Whipcord for Respirator
    Ammunition
    Recognition Signal (Yellow Silk)
    Chewing Gum

From Sergeant Johnson
>   24 hr Ration
>   Emergency Ration
>   Tommy Cooker
>   Water Sterilising outfit
>   Tin of Cigarettes (20)

From the Regimental Medical Officer
>   H Hydrobromide (anti air sick)
>   Shell Dressing (2)
>   Benzedrine (Officers only)
>   Morphine Tubes

ALSO YOUR EQUIPMENT AND PERSONAL WEAPONS AND STATICHUTE?

The statichute was the special type of parachute which opened automatically after exit from the aircraft.

Supper was at 5.30pm so that people could get to bed early. The weather had been appalling all day, almost continuous torrential rain and a 50mph gale in the Channel. Anthony wrote:

> And, by way of lending an extra fillip, it was announced that, owing to re-routeing, an earlier start must be made, and reveille would be at 0300 hours. It was therefore in no mood of facile optimism that we retired to bed soon after the stipulated time of 2000 hours. But on the other hand there is nothing like wet weather and the apparent likelihood of frustration to deflate nervous excitement and to induce that, in some ways, advantageous mood of not caring much what happens – not really expecting anything to happen either.

Here the draft article ended. Anthony expected to be writing the second part when they landed in Belgium. Whilst he was typing the last paragraph, Brigadier Lathbury came into his room and confirmed the rumour that Allied tanks were already at the drop zone. Lathbury also said that 'the main remains of the German Army were still back somewhere in the neighbourhood of the Somme'. Anthony added this information as a Postscript.

Three hours after he had gone to bed, he was woken by a knock on the door and the corporal storeman bent down over his sleeping bag and told him that the operation had been postponed for 36 hours. Anthony writes: 'I was not really surprised. I was not really anything.'

His original plan for the article now having been scuppered by events, Anthony crossed out the Postscript, and instead gave some thought to the ordeal which he had been about to undergo. He wrote it as if it flowed on naturally from his retirement to bed.

> None the less, I began to think of to-morrow's jump as an ordeal. Not that I really believed that the parachute wouldn't open or that I should be injured in landing. The apprehension was all connected with the test of will-power involved in jumping out of the aircraft ... And how doubly maddening to break your back or be sniped in the air at this stage of the war.
>
> Such notions made recurrent darts across my mind. The prospect of doing something horribly unnatural in the morning produced a tendency to linger over the normal routine of going to bed, so that the intervening hours would last as long as possible, so that the inevitable despairs of the early morning could be postponed and camouflaged.[289]

The following day there was a plan for a different operation, a different briefing for that plan, then 'a final scrubbing of that particular interlude'. Hibbert meanwhile was noting in his diary 'op cancelled as Americans already through Maastricht'.

During the following three or four days Anthony did not add much to his article but what he did write mainly concerned the awful boredom and frustration of the Brigade, cooling their heels in England whilst all the heroics were going on elsewhere.

> There was no doubt about it. We were doing far too well in France and Belgium. Monday was declared a holiday, or shall we say a half-holiday, because no one was particularly festive. At about 11am the BBC programme was interrupted with an announcement that Brussels had fallen. Brigade prayers for the temporary recovery of the German Army continued. After lunch we went to the movies, came back and listened to records of Frank Sinatra, who enjoyed a considerable following among the Brigade staff. Some went off to town, others fell asleep, with the unhealthy fatigue of Boxing Day.

Amongst those in Brussels when it was liberated was Anthony's girlfriend, Jenny Nicholson. Her article on the joyous welcome given to the British would appear in WAR on 25 November 1944 under the title 'Fair Women and Brave Men'. She and Anthony had doubtless agreed before she left for France that she would write something for WAR about the liberation of Europe. She began her article one week after the liberation of Brussels when she stood on her hotel balcony, looking out over a crowd of cheering, shouting, clapping people, who were lustily singing 'It's a Long Way to Tipperary'. She had thought on the night of the liberation 'that there would never again in the long history of the world be such a pandemonium of welcome', and yet seven days later the festivities were continuing completely unabated.[290] There is a certain irony in the fact that it was Jenny, rather than Anthony, who was witnessing these fantastic scenes of joy.

The liberation of Brussels on Sunday 3 September was followed by the capture of Antwerp on the 4th. However, this great feat of arms was ruined by a failure of intelligence; Montgomery's victorious troops did not know that they also had to secure the Scheldt river because without the river Antwerp was cut off from the sea. As Admiral Cunningham wrote, for the time being 'one of the finest ports in Europe was of no more use to us than an oasis in the Sahara desert'.[291]

The failure to capture Antwerp as a functional port meant that there was no change in the desperate supply problems, and the British and American advances began to grind to a halt. The very success of the campaign had engendered massive problems, with the supply lines stretching back several hundred miles to the Normandy beaches and the port of Cherbourg. The railway system had been badly damaged by Allied bombing, so everything had to be carried by road. The further the armies got from the supply depots, the more petrol was consumed in refuelling them – it had become a vicious circle. The impetus which had carried the Allies so far, so fast, was now beginning to peter out. Meanwhile, the Germans were recovering from the rout. The war situation was about to alter dramatically.

Unaware of how the situation was changing on the ground, shut up in Lincolnshire and still chronicling the frustrated boredom of his companions, Anthony wrote: 'Nothing happened on Tuesday. After lunch we went to the movies again, this constituting the first time the Brigadier had been to the pictures two days running.'

Hibbert records in his diary that the film they all went to see at 2.30pm was Bachelor Mother, to which he gave the terse verdict 'good'. He names the party as Brigadier Lathbury, Bernard Briggs, and Cecil Byng-Maddick. Though Hibbert does not mention Anthony by name (and would not do so for another week), Anthony was clearly already part of the furniture at HQ and the wording of his own passage shows that he too went to see 'Bachelor Mother'. Afterwards, he returned to HQ for tea. Another operation had been confirmed, together with the general area in which it was to take place and who would be involved – 1st Airborne Division with 1st Polish Independent Parachute Brigade. Hibbert recorded: 'Everyone rather gloomy as op already has "faint odour of mortality."' It was an extremely unusual phrase to appear in Hibbert's diary – clearly he was quoting someone else – could the quip have been Anthony's?

Anthony himself wrote:

> Conversation at teatime was depressed. Tomorrow it would be three months since D-day. Self-pity reigned. Most people had seen all the movies. They didn't want to read, get drunk, write letters or play bridge. They had packed and unpacked their kit, cleaned their weapons, and even slept too often to want to do so any more.
>
> However, the six o'clock news did say that the German resistance was stiffening. The firmer resistance of the Germans was repeated at nine o'clock and a wave of enthusiasm swept over the mess. As an expression of rising morale, most of them joined in a thunderflash battle in the garden.[292]

With hindsight this enthusiasm looks stupidly hubristic, but at the time it had a perfect, almost boyishly innocent logic. As Urquhart, 1st Airborne Division's commander, would later write, the Division had for many months been forced to contend with its own phoney war.

> By September 1944 my division was battle-hungry to a degree which only those who have commanded large forces of trained soldiers can fully comprehend [...] We were ready for anything. If there was a tendency to take light-heartedly the less encouraging factors, and even the unknown ones, it was understandable [...] Only the participant can adequately [understand] the effects of the sixteen cancelled operations in a row.[293]

The day after the thunderflash battle, 6 September, planning began for Operation *Comet*. This new plan involved the capture of the road bridge at Arnhem, and without betraying the actual details in his article Anthony described the operation as 'attractively spectacular'. Briefing and preparations took place on Thursday 7 September, with take-off scheduled for 5.15 on Friday morning. Then, at half past 10 on Thursday evening, a postponement came through for 24 hours due to bad weather.

On the Friday, once again it looked as if *Comet* was going ahead. They drew their chutes in the afternoon. It had been an unpromising morning, raining hard, but by teatime the weather had cleared a bit. The operation was still uncertain, but Brigadier Lathbury said that he felt that they were going and others expressed a hunch to the same effect. Practical details were agreed, such as the timetable for the drop – 20 minutes prior warning, four minutes for the red light which indicated that the drop was imminent, then all out on the green light. Anthony reported a fragment of conversation between Bernard Briggs, Lathbury, and a third party, unidentified.

> 'When are you jumping, Bernard?'
>
> 'Number One.'
>
> 'Difficulty with Number One is to know whether to jump or not when you're on the wrong DZ [Dropping Zone].'
>
> 'You jump on the green light,' said the Brigadier firmly.
>
> It began to look as if we were indeed going to jump on the green light. The discontents and frustrations were subtly replaced by the apprehensions of anticipation.

Dinner was at 7.00pm and most people went to bed immediately afterwards. They had been told that in the event of a cancellation they would know by midnight. Anthony wrote that 'the authorities were better than their word', for at 11.30pm he was once again woken to be told that bad weather had caused a 24-hour postponement.

As a writer, he had to make the best of whatever material he could gather as these deadlines came and went without results. Fruitless preparations would be made, such as the field cashier first bringing the men French francs, then Belgian francs, then Dutch guilders and finally German marks – this type of small but telling detail, as always, attracted Anthony's attention. But it was hard to give the article any satisfactory form, and eventually he settled for recording the violent fluctuations in mood of the Brigade during those days of extreme nervous tension and frustration:

> I had now been exactly a week with the Brigade. The seventh day we rested, but feeling progressively more nervy. Towards evening on the eighth day, by one of those odd twists of the human nerve barometer, everyone was unusually gay and almost foolishly confident.
>
> The weather was good and the news gave no signs that advances on the ground would make our landing superfluous. The job itself was attractively spectacular. 'Nothing can save us now,' said the Brigadier, and everyone laughed excitedly.
>
> All the same it wasn't long after dinner when the telephone rang to announce a 24 hour, or perhaps a 48 hour, postponement. For a novel reason, however: not because the ground forces were advancing too fast. This time they were not advancing fast enough.
>
> 'Another day or two, and we'll all be bats,' said the Brigadier, on edge with frustration.

After some further growling and grumbling, the officers settled down to play bridge, only to discover that the mess staff had made the cards filthy. Small annoyances like that increased the pent-up irritability. Due to security, no one had not been able to ring home for days; normal life had completely stopped and time had lost its meaning in this bizarre suspended state. Keen to look on the bright side, Brigadier Lathbury remarked about the postponement, 'Good thing we didn't go last night. With this counter-attack we'd have had it properly.' But the generalised facetious grumbling continued. The Intelligence Officer said that the gliders, which had been loaded for a week, ought to be unloaded or they would fall apart. Byng-Maddick complained that his laundry wouldn't stand much more – like everyone he was down to a short supply of clothing because nearly all kit had been sent overseas in advance. He said that the next intolerable thing would be 6th Division (who had gone to France on D-Day) coming and 'giving us lectures on how to do it'. Having given vent to this appalling idea, he picked up a chair which promptly fell apart, and with it the last shreds of his patience.

> 'Even the bottom falls out of the bloody chair. Next thing'll be route marches again.'
> 'Send them on a route march to-morrow,' said the Brigadier [...] 'Oh no, I suppose we can't.'
> 'Trouble is these 24 hour postponements. Never time to do anything' said Hibbert.

The following day, 9 September, Brigadier Lathbury, clearly at a loose end, took Anthony for a long walk in the grounds. Anthony asked him whether he didn't find the prospect of responsibility for the lives of his brigade in battle a horrifying one. Lathbury told him he was still appalled by the thought of having to make quick decisions in battle, but he wasn't worried when it came to the actual making of them.

He also suffered from a sense of oppression and Oh-my-God when summoned to Division HQ and told to plan an operation in a few hours. I asked just how much of the plan he had to make himself. He said that in this case the General had given him the Brigade role and left the rest to him. Then the General had flown up the next day to ask him what he meant to do. He, in his turn, had given the three battalion commanders their general roles and not bothered them with guidance which they were all too experienced to need.[294]

Once again, the brigade was on tenterhooks about the coming operation, and once again it was cancelled, at 6.00pm, a timing Anthony refers to as 'unique'. The brigade had been on 36 hours' notice for getting on for a month now, and the continued hanging about was purgatory. As Hibbert remarked bitterly, 'You realise that no one's the slightest sympathy with us. You get no marks for mental strain.'

Anthony's article concluded with a fragment of conversation between the extremely fed-up officers.

'You got any aspirins, David?' Hibbert asked the Doctor.
'Hundreds of them, in serried rows.'
'Bloody awful, trying to kill time,' said Hibbert.

The next day, Sunday 10 September, suddenly the spell was broken.

In newly liberated Brussels, Montgomery presented a revised version of Operation *Comet* to Eisenhower, and Eisenhower reluctantly agreed to it. Codenamed Operation *Market Garden*, the new plan involved the capture not only of Arnhem bridge but also of others between Eindhoven and Nijmegen. 1st Parachute Brigade would hear details of the operation that same day, exactly one week before the actual parachute drop took place.

Market Garden was conceived at a time when the bitter rivalry between American and British generals was at its peak. On 1 September, Eisenhower had succeeded Montgomery as supreme head of all Allied ground forces in Europe. Despite the immense honour of being made a Field Marshal on the same day, it was a shattering blow to Montgomery. Some commentators have seen this as the reason for his uncharacteristic misjudgements over *Market Garden*. There were to be many reasons for the failure at Arnhem: the drop being made over three days rather than one; the dropping zones being located too far from the bridge; the breakdown in wireless communication; the dismissal of intelligence reports about Panzer units in the area; and other errors of planning, policy, and supply. But the main reason for the failure was over-confidence, and this can be seen in the mistaken idea that the British ground forces could get to the bridge in 48 hours to reinforce and consolidate the parachutists' positions. They would have to travel more than 60 miles through enemy-held territory, on a road which was frequently single-track, vulnerable to attack, and easily blocked by wrecked or broken-down vehicles. In the event, 30 Corps, who had been given the job, came nowhere near to achieving the timetable.

As soon as he had Eisenhower's go-ahead, Montgomery briefed Lieutenant General Browning, commander of the 1st British Airborne Corps and deputy commander of the 1st Allied Airborne Army. Browning in his turn briefed the senior commanders under him, and thus onwards down the chain of command.

Browning's base was at Moor Park, a very grand mansion situated near Rickmansworth in Hertfordshire. On Sunday 10 September, Hibbert recorded in his diary travelling down with Lathbury to a meeting with Urquhart, the Division Commander:

13.45 – Flew down to Moor Park with Brigade Commander to see Division Commander. Arrived just as plan for which we had been sent to discuss had been cancelled (No 15a) but just in time to hear details of plan 16, which from our point of view differed little from *Comet*. New name *Market*. Warned we would be required again at Moor Park tomorrow, so stayed night at Berkeley.

The airborne part of the plan was *Market*; the ground forces part of the plan was *Garden*.

The Berkeley Hotel in Belgravia was a favoured London base of 1st Parachute Brigade officers, and it was also one of Anthony's haunts. Anthony, who had flown down from Lincolnshire with Hibbert, may also have stayed in the hotel that night, but it seems rather more likely that he returned to his tiny flat in South Audley Street, which was within easy walking distance of the Berkeley.

The following morning Hibbert went to his military tailors. Anthony was also doing a bit of shopping, and spent 17s 8d on a khaki belt at H. Huntsman and Sons, 11 Saville Row. The bill would not be paid until December 1945. Afterwards he and Hibbert met up for lunch at Wheelers. They returned to Moor Park for a further briefing at 5.00pm. The briefing was very short, and at 6.00pm Lathbury, Hibbert and Anthony flew back to Grantham.

From now on everything would gather momentum. Hibbert's diary records the preparations for the operation, including the start of a security drive which began with the arrest of a Private Berry.

All personnel were allowed 24 hours leave on Thursday 14 September. Anthony made use of the time to go to London. He met up briefly with Watkins and gave him the text of his article, which would printed in October in *WAR* under the title 'Airborne Worries: Waiting to be Scrubbed'. Watkins would later recall:

> Anthony and I had dinner together at the Connaught Hotel on the Friday before the Sunday assault. I don't know how much he knew then of the plans for that operation; he would never have broken security by telling me anything, however much he knew. He hadn't escaped the strain of waiting, although he could conceal most of it, and I had no premonition that he was so close to the moment of actual departure. He was a little distrait, which I could understand. We separated about 9.30 and that was the last I saw of him.[295]

It is likely that Anthony did not have time to go up to Wanstead to see his parents, but at some point he spoke to them, probably on the telephone and without divulging where he was going, asked them to keep their fingers crossed for his safe return. After the Arnhem battle, these casually spoken words would come back to haunt his mother. Anthony also scribbled a postcard for his brother which simply read: 'We are jumping to a conclusion.' He knew that Geoffrey would immediately understand the tiny coded message.

It was around this time that Anthony wrote to Robert Graves about *The Haymarket* magazine. He concluded by asking Graves to write to him at 6a Frederick Mews, Kinnerton Street, SW1, which was Watkins' address. Once again he did not say where he was going, but Graves would have drawn the obvious inference from Anthony's closing words: 'I am going away for a few days and hope to see Jenny who seems to be having a marvellous time, which I suppose you have heard about, and wrote to me last from Brussels.'[296]

By the time Anthony returned to Brigade HQ, the packing of the gliders had begun. Containers were being sent to the airfields and the aircraft were being loaded. On Saturday evening Hibbert wrote very hurriedly in his diary, as if scarcely daring to hope that the Brigade would at last go into battle:

Briefing personnel
All HQ flattened by colds and flu
All personnel briefed
Brigade Commanders co-ordinating conference at 1 Parachute Battalion

Weather report good
Hopes for op very high[297]

Anthony would have been in a similar state of excitement, writing his own diary, forming the beginning of a new narrative. But everything he wrote from now on he took with him to Arnhem, and there it would disappear, as would Anthony himself.

The story of what happened to him at Arnhem cannot, therefore, be told in his own words. It is only through other people's accounts that a history can be pieced together. Other voices must tell the story; Anthony's has fallen silent.

PART THREE

ARNHEM: 17–23 SEPTEMBER 1944

Arnhem itself is a quiet Dutch town lying on the northern bank of the river Rhine, there about 150 yards wide, with a fast flowing current. Normally, it has a population of some 94,000. The town itself lies on the flat lands alongside the river, but immediately to the north the ground rises sharply […]. This ridge of high land […] is broken by little valleys and is quite different from the flat, empty fields of southern and western Holland.

Arnhem is something of a spa. Both to the east and the west are suburbs of solid, detached houses and hotels, standing in their own grounds, the countryside around them well wooded. Out to the west it resembles parts of the lowlands of Scotland, with plantations of firs and folds of rough ground covered with a scrub not unlike broom.

On the 16th September it was a quiet and peaceful town, a little excited by the approach of the liberation of Holland in the south but with no presentiment of the events of the following week.

The main road from Utrecht comes in from the west. A little farther north, running south-east, is the road from Ede. Roughly parallel to this road is the main railway line [which crosses] the Rhine on a high steel bridge…

[…1st Airborne Division's] objective was the road bridge carrying the main road from the south across the river into the centre of the town.

'1 Airborne Div at Arnhem', Ernest Watkins, WAR, issue 83, 9 December 1944.

19

SUNDAY, 17 SEPTEMBER 1944

For once there was no knock on the door in the night, no one bending over his sleeping bag to tell him that the operation had been postponed. Sometime in the night, perhaps, Anthony woke with a start, realising that this time there would be no cancellation. Soon there would come that 'horribly unnatural ordeal, the test of nerve involved in jumping out of the aircraft'. But the jump would be the zenith of his career as a soldier-journalist, and he would not have contemplated backing out now.

Even the greatest soldiers in 1st Parachute Brigade were not immune to last minute nerves. On the morning of the 17th, Lieutenant-Colonel John Frost of 2nd Battalion got up with mixed feelings, glad that the day for which his battalion had planned and trained for so long had arrived but also conscious that he and some of his men might not survive it. There was also the natural pull of reluctance to move out of the very pleasant way of life they all enjoyed at Stoke Rochford Hall: 'Like most soldiers, when well dug-in I was inclined to be against moves in any direction, and this promised to be a most decisive one.'[298]

Frost was a tall man, strongly built, with an untidy moustache and sleepy drooping eyelids which belied the fierce intelligence beneath. 1st Airborne Division's commander, Major-General Urquhart, would describe him as having 'an anxious moon face and permanent worry lines across his forehead', but added that he relished a fight and was a highly capable battalion commander despite 'a deceptively slow-motion air'.[299]

Frost had won the Military Cross for his leadership in the Bruneval raid, and had since seen action in Tunisia, Sicily, and Italy. Since the summer of 1943, however, he and his battalion, like the rest of 1st Parachute Brigade, had been kept in reserve. Some of the mixed feelings he felt on the morning of the 17th were due to the fact that *Market Garden* would be his first operational jump since the attack on Sicily some fourteen months before.

Frost went to breakfast. As the battalion would not be leaving until late morning, he ate his bacon and eggs and read the papers without hurry. Afterwards he went to the officers' mess to check morale and found everyone smoking and reading, in the best of spirits. On the surface, it was just like an ordinary day.

> One had the sense of perfect arrangement, the feeling that everything would be so well conducted, that having dined well, slept well and breakfasted well, we would make our leisurely way to the airfield, and from there, having wished each other well, we would fly across the sea undisturbed and gather again some three hundred miles away in Holland and then proceed to do battle for a bridge that Montgomery urgently required.[300]

At Brigade HQ, Anthony would have seen similar instances of sang-froid, only just hiding a dancing excitement. By the time the various units began to arrive at their different airfields, many were infected with what James Simms, a private in Frost's 2nd Battalion, would describe as an atmosphere 'like a school outing or picnic'.

> Someone dished out great mugs of tea and bacon sandwiches, and a camera crew on a truck came along and filmed us. We jumped about and waved our mugs in the air [...] everyone was laughing and shouting.[301]

The camera crew were part of the public relations team which was going to Arnhem with 1st Airborne Division. It included two BBC civilian reporters, Guy Byam and Stanley Maxted, the famous Canadian broadcaster. Heading the team was Major Roy Oliver, a highly capable professional soldier who was also keenly interested in war reporting. Two censors, four signallers, three men of the Army Film and Photographic Unit (the AFPU), and two pressmen completed the team. The latter were Jack Smythe of Reuters, and Alan Wood of Anthony's old paper, the *Daily Express*, both of whom had had their names drawn out of a hat.[302] The presence of these reporters and cameramen indicated the authorities' immense confidence that the operation would be successful. However foolhardy Anthony's action in going to Arnhem may appear in retrospect, he was not actually doing something wildly out of the ordinary.

The AFPU men, as virtually all of the PR team, were going in by glider. The exception was Sergeant Mike Lewis who would parachute in with 1st Parachute Brigade HQ, almost certainly in the same stick as Anthony. Like Anthony he would be laden not only with the parachutist's survival kit such as the 48-hour survival rations, but also with the tools of his trade: in Lewis's case an Eyemo cine camera and many rolls of film; in Anthony's case the punched paper for his tiny pocket notebook, pencils, pens, paperclips, and almost certainly a typewriter.[303]

Dramatic footage of the scenes at the airfields still exists, and the massed aircraft and huge numbers of men were a magnificent spectacle. Few seemed to have any doubts. Stuart Mawson, a Regimental Medical Officer for 11th Parachute Battalion, 4th Brigade, would remember 'the majestic invincibility of the operation':

> To me, and no doubt to nine tenths, at least, of all those waiting for the flight to begin, the outcome was so far from being in doubt that we foresaw only a rather glorified exercise, with the marked probability that [at Arnhem] we would have the chagrin of finding Monty and the liberation army already there with nothing left to be done at all.[304]

At Barkston Heath, which was just one of several airfields being used that day, 1st Parachute Brigade HQ waited with their bulky kit, Mae Wests, and parachutes. Brigadier Lathbury gave a pep talk, and the Women's Voluntary Service went round with tea and buns. With his keenly observant eye, Anthony would have watched the scene, heard the conversations, seen both the excitement and the nerves, and jotted down the details quickly in shorthand.

At last the time came for boarding the Dakota with the officers he had come to know so well in the last seventeen days. He and his party emplaned around 11.00am to take off at around midday, with a scheduled landing of just after two in the afternoon.

Once the aircraft was in the air, Anthony may have silently calculated the gambler's odds on who was going to live and who was going to die. Just as before D-Day, he would have looked at the faces and known that there was a large probability that some of the party would be killed or maimed. But the journey was short and there was not too much time for last-minute introspection. People read newspapers, smoked or ate sandwiches, enjoying the brief interlude before the time they had to jump.

Of that moment fast approaching, Frost, travelling with 2nd Battalion, would write:

> The stick had travelled well, but as usual one could feel the tension among them all. The transparent insincerity of their smiles and the furious last-minute puffing at their cigarettes reminded me that the flight and prospect of jumping far behind the enemy lines was no small test for anyone's nervous system.[305]

Hibbert, travelling like Anthony in Brigade HQ's aircraft, recorded:

> The whole of West Holland seemed to be flooded, and as we passed over the coast, large numbers of C47s which had already dropped their loads flew over us, on their return flight. Approximately ten minutes before the drop we passed over some guns dug in along a hedge; they seemed to be firing energetically, and at us, but it did not worry anyone unduly, and did no harm. Just before this we had seen a glider which had force-landed in a field near a village. Already it was entirely swamped with enthusiastic Dutchmen, and a bean-feast appeared to be in progress.
>
> As we approached the DZ [drop zone] we could see hundreds of parachutes on the ground; the plane throttled down, and plumb over the right place the green light went on and out we went.[306]

As other Dakotas likewise disgorged their loads, the parachutes came gently floating down in their thousands. The jumping height was about 600 feet, and the ground came up in seconds, the parachutes either billowing out to drag their wearer, or coming to a ballooning collapse around them on the earth. Drop Zone X, between Renkum and Wolfheze, was the arrival point, next to Landing Zone Y, an area of land now so covered with gliders that it had taken on the same look as a car park. There was no opposition. The landscape was idyllically peaceful, a large open heath, covered with heather and ringed by pine forests, lying quietly in the sunshine.

As Anthony descended towards earth, he may well have chanted to himself that little parachutist's mantra which he had learnt during his training:

Head well forward;
Shoulders round;
Knees together
And watch the ground.[307]

Just after 2.00am he would have landed, rolled forward in 'a cosy human ball' as he had been taught, then got to his feet and gathered up his parachute. From that point onwards until his arrival at the bridge, nothing is known of what he did or whom he was with, but all the circumstantial evidence points to him remaining with Brigade HQ.[308]

Hibbert noted that everyone was slow getting off the drop zone for the distances were much greater on the ground than they had all imagined from looking at a map. Coloured smoke, which was to have guided everyone to the Rendez-Vous (RV), was 'notable by its absence'. When he first arrived at HQ's RV, ten minutes after the drop, it was to find that no one else was there. At other RVs, men were joining their units in jubilant spirits, delighted to be safe on the ground with no opposition. Simms remembered arriving at 2nd Battalion's RV to the ironic cheers of those already there. Perhaps rather more fancifully, Captain C.A. Harrison, who had jumped with Brigade HQ, compared the cheerful chaos at the landing zone and RV points to 'a social occasion, with slight overtones of Royal Ascot and a big cricket match'.[309]

Soon other men began to join Hibbert at the RV, Brigadier Lathbury being amongst the first. It took a while for everyone to be gathered in, but by 2.45pm 4/5ths of the group were there. Several Dutch people had come out from Heelsum to greet their liberators, and Hibbert had already found two who could speak English. They told him that there were only third-rate troops in Heelsum and the surrounding villages, and that the Germans had very little transport and were probably only armed with rifles. In Arnhem itself, there were more German soldiers, but they were thought to be only Luftwaffe administration, not front-line troops.

Everything was looking very promising. The radio set had been in contact with Frost's 2nd Battalion which had already set off, and also with 3rd Battalion under Tony Fitch which was following a different route into Arnhem. Soon 2nd Battalion reported having taken several prisoners, and these were brought in shortly afterwards. Hibbert described them as 'very nondescript types, some Luftwaffe; no information of importance'. More ominously, he also noted: 'Sound of firing to south. No transport yet arrived. Captain Briggs had gone off at approx 1430 hours to the transport RV with instructions to bring it back immediately, but no sign as yet.'

After further delays for transport and the setting up of radios, which were beginning to prove very troublesome, HQ moved off at a quarter to four, following in 2nd Battalion's footsteps. They were travelling to Arnhem on the southerly *Lion* route which would prove to be relatively unopposed. Other units on the *Tiger* and *Leopard* routes would fare very differently, and very few of their men would succeed in reaching the bridge.

East of Heelsum, HQ came across their first real sight of the opposition, several German lorries and cars strewn about the road with their dead and wounded occupants left in 2nd Battalion's wake. For some young parachutists, this little group of Germans was their first sight of the close-to-mythical enemy who had dominated their teenage lives. This was probably the same group that Simms would later describe. He had never seen a dead body before and, in the hallucinatory strangeness of the moment, a childhood memory suddenly came back to him. His mother had told him that if he traced the cross on the forehead of a corpse, it would not come back to haunt him. In a close to trance-like state, gently he touched the cold forehead of one of the dead Germans. He got a rude awakening from an older and more experienced soldier, who yelled 'What the hell are you doing? ... Get mobile, you'll see plenty more of him before you're much older.'[310]

Simms' extreme youth and inexperience was echoed in many others seeing action for the first time. Simms writes a brief but very touching epitaph on one of these youngsters, Brum Davis, who not long after they had passed the dead Germans was killed by an incendiary bullet – 'at nineteen his great adventure was over before it had scarcely begun'.[311]

The brutal nature of the Arnhem battle was already beginning to reveal itself to the uninitiated. Some three months earlier Anthony had observed, in a group of RAF fitters who had just arrived in Normandy, that same moment of awakening from the romance of war to the true horror of it. Their party had likewise come across a group of dead Germans:

> The [...] men were sickened by the cold and final brutality of what they saw. A few minutes before they had been gaily, adventurously going off to war. The landing which no doubt they had envisaged for months as unlimited carnage had temporarily seemed comfortably romantic and pleasantly safe, though spiced with a satisfying sense of potential danger. The bodies made them realise that they hadn't seen anything yet.[312]

Frost's 2nd Battalion, spearheading the march into Arnhem, continued to run into light opposition. At first, Lathbury travelled with them, but radio communications were so poor that he left to check on the progress of 3rd Battalion. It was the last which would be seen of him by those on *Lion* route, for it was at this point that organisation began to break down under the severe pressure of faulty radio sets and the violent fire-fights taking place on the *Tiger* and *Leopard* routes.

1st Airborne Division's commander, Urquhart, would pass through HQ's column at high speed looking for Lathbury, and then some while later pass back again in a very bad temper, having failed to find him and now very dissatisfied with the way things were going. Again, this was the last time that those on *Lion* route saw Urquhart. Though they did not know it yet, they were now on their own as regards their senior commanders, who would soon be in very serious trouble themselves.

The Germans were recovering extremely quickly from the initial shock of the airborne invasion. The German command structure was so fluid and so brilliantly adapted to improvisation that small units on the ground had begun a ferocious fight-back long before their senior commanders – Field Marshal Model, General Bittrich, and General Student – could take overall command of what was going on.

On *Lion* route, Brigade HQ moved in fits and starts due to the light, patchy opposition. As Hibbert reported:

> In my part of the column, somewhere about the middle, it seemed very like an exercise. We would move about 200 yards in a sort of crocodile, then be held up and go to ground in the ditches, while the junior officers ran to and fro, organising flank protection and so on.[313]

Something other than the enemy was also delaying the soldiers' progress – the Dutch people were immensely pleased to see them. They draped orange paper from the front of their houses, and brought the soldiers milk or water to drink, apples and pears to eat, and orange flowers to wear. Their gratitude to their liberators was boundless. In the small village of Heveadorp, an old gentleman asked Frost if he would like to use his car. 'Knowing well what its fate would be I declined, pointing to the jeep which was moving ten yards behind me.'[314]

Many Germans were still completely unaware of what was happening. Simms gives an unforgettable picture of how, when 2nd Battalion first reached the Rhine, the men were amazed to hear the chug of a small German patrol boat coming up the river. In brief vivid sentences which could have been written by Anthony himself, Simms writes:

> One soldier was leaning over the stern smoking a pipe, at peace with the world. [An] order brought the guns to life. At such short range they pulverised the enemy boat. The pipe-smoker at the stern just toppled over the guard rail into the Rhine. I don't suppose he knew what hit him. The boat heeled over and sank in seconds.[315]

Not far from the Rhine, HQ, tramping along the Lower Road, passed the tiny ancient church at Oosterbeek. The church was almost three miles from Arnhem, but if you stood in its churchyard you could just see the tower of Sint-Eusebiuskerk in the town. St Eusebius was very close to the soldiers' main objective, the road bridge, and its tower would be severely damaged in the bitter fighting of the days to come. On this warm Sunday afternoon, the tower could just be seen through the summery haze, its minute size telling how much further there was to go. If Anthony had known what the tower signified as he passed through Oosterbeek, this is probably the point at which he would have tried to wangle a ride in a jeep.[316]

By now the sporadic opposition on *Lion* route seemed to have died away. But just after HQ passed the church at Oosterbeek, a loud explosion signalled that the Germans had blown the nearby railway bridge. Captain Harrison, who was in the forward unit, saw this happen right in front of his eyes, and noted how, rather than going up in the air as popular belief had it, the bridge merely fell away lazily and slowly into the river. One of the operation's two objectives had thus been destroyed, an immense disappointment to the soldiers who had been so close to capturing it intact. Some of the Sappers had actually set foot upon the bridge when it was detonated, but apparently no one was killed or injured by the blast.[317]

As darkness began to fall, firing became more general. A violent battle could be heard raging to the north and north-west. Very worrying and unexpected news started to come in that German tanks and armoured cars were being encountered, extremely dangerous opposition for the lightly armed airborne soldiers.

Around 7.30pm, when it was dark, Major Freddie Gough, the commanding officer of 1st Airborne Reconnaissance Squadron, turned up with two jeeps mounted with Vickers K machine guns. The original plan for the capture of the road bridge had involved Gough's squadron racing to the bridge in their jeeps in advance of the troops on foot, thus securing the bridge before the Germans could destroy or reinforce it. However, due to serious problems with the transport, this plan had failed.

At quarter to five, the escalating problems with radio communications had caused Gough to leave his Tactical HQ to try to find Divisional HQ.[318] This proved impossible because the situation was rapidly descending into chaos as the Germans mounted an increasingly ferocious defence. By the time Gough wanted to rejoin his squadron, the way back was blocked. Pressing on to the bridge with two of his men, he met up with Brigade HQ. He asked them to pass a radio message back to Division, requesting them to direct all his jeeps along *Lion* route, but once again radio failure made this impossible.

The two men Gough had brought with him were Captain Tony Platt, aged 30, a married man, and Lieutenant Trevor McNabb, an Intelligence Officer, aged 22. Platt would be killed at the scene of the Brummen shooting, and McNabb would die four days afterwards of a lung wound inflicted in the same spray of bullets. Only a series of the unluckiest circumstances had led to them being on the Brummen truck, and this had begun with the transport and radio failures.

Gough was one of 1st Airborne Division's oldest officers; 43 the day before Arnhem, he had served in the Royal Navy in the First World War. Silver-haired and red-faced, he was a giant of a man, possessed of an abundance of natural charisma and authority. Winner of the Military Cross, he was preternaturally calm in battle conditions, and in fact seemed positively to thrive upon them. He was a well-known character throughout the Division, and the sight of him so close to Arnhem would have been hugely cheering.

Perhaps it was because Gough was something of a maverick that he had never made senior rank, but Urquhart and other high-ranking officers, including Lieutenant-General Frederick Browning, commander of 1st Airborne Corps, treated him as an equal.[319] Everything Gough did was always larger than life. On this particular Sunday, Captain Harrison, who greatly admired him, would come across him close to the Arnhem road bridge and offer him a drink out of his flask of precious whisky. Gough replied, 'Thank you very much' and promptly drained the lot, 'for which' as Harrison commented, 'I never quite forgave him'.[320]

Gough would be Anthony's last commanding officer, and he too would be on the truck at Brummen. Unlike his two Recce Squadron men, he would survive the shooting unscathed.

At quarter past eight a halt was called to allow the party advancing on Arnhem to close up. Describing one of the very few light-hearted moments left, Hibbert wrote:

> Major Gough and I went in to the nearest house to have a look at the map with some light, and to find out the gen and the best route from the occupants. These were most helpful, especially the two buxom daughters. Having dragged Freddie away, we resumed the advance.

The party now split up, the medical staff of 16 Field Ambulance going on to St Elisabeth Hospital where they would establish a dressing station and remain throughout the battle. At 8.45pm the remainder of the column once again halted, 500 yards west of the bridge. News had come back that the north end was now in the hands of 2nd Battalion, but it was still necessary to proceed with extreme caution. This proved impossible because the soldiers' presence was constantly being advertised by joyful Dutch civilians, who came 'rushing out of their houses shouting their welcomes at the top of their voices'.[321]

For others who had actually reached the bridge, there was an eerie kind of silence as if before a storm. Captain Harrison enjoyed a victory cigarette by himself whilst sitting in his jeep underneath the bridge ramp. Halfway through the cigarette, he was startled to hear the clatter of speeding vehicles coming from the south, and for one wild moment thought that the Americans had come from Nijmegen. Then:

> a large convoy of horse-drawn transport came across the bridge in the darkness at full gallop. There was only one Army that used horses and it was not ours. I quickly extinguished my cigarette and made myself very scarce.[322]

With Lathbury and Urquhart out of the picture, Frost was now the commanding officer at the bridge. This was a massive structure whose ramp, borne on immense concrete pillars, extended far beyond the river bank and into the town. In the centre of the bridge, over the Rhine, was an immense iron fretwork arch, the shape of which would never be forgotten by those who had fought at Arnhem.

2nd Battalion were holding both sides of the north end of the bridge and the river embankment. A pill-box was still held by the enemy on the north end of the bridge, but shortly it would be destroyed by flame-thrower, a process which accidentally ignited a nearby ammunition dump. The resulting explosions set alight to everything flammable in the vicinity, including the new paintwork of the bridge. The heat generated was so intense that the bridge became impassable for the night. The only chance of capturing the south side before the Germans could reinforce it would be to get some troops across the river. This plan had to be abandoned through lack of boats.

Hibbert now set up Brigade HQ, some 30 yards from Frost's 2nd Battalion HQ, in a large strongly built building which was the headquarters of the Rijkswaterstaat (a government department responsible for the maintenance of waterways and roads). The building overlooked the gardens at the north end of the bridge ramp, and consisted of an impressive frontage flanked by two wings which enclosed an entrance courtyard. There was a charming belvedere on the roof, and other fine architectural details like round-arched windows and decorative stonework. It was in this handsome building that Anthony would spend the battle, and by the end of it all that would be left was a burnt-out, skeletal ruin.

On commandeering the building, the airborne soldiers immediately made it ready for defence. The motor transport was parked in the yard behind the house. In the extensive cellars the two medical officers, David Wright and Jimmy Logan, established an Advanced Dressing Station. Upstairs, the three floors were systematically wrecked. Curtains were ripped down and disposed of, together with any other flammable material. The glass in the windows was smashed out to eliminate the danger of flying splinters. Furniture was piled up at the windows and doorways. All available utensils were filled with water against the time when the Germans followed standard procedure and cut off all the utilities.

Meanwhile the overcrowded attic was full of signals staff under Bill Marquand. There were also orderlies, batmen and clerks, Major Dennis Mumford with the Royal Artillery radio set, and Gough with the 1st Airlanding Squadron set. But despite all this equipment and the protruding aerials, not a single set could pick up the slightest whisper. 'The Brigade 22 set was in touch, loud and clear all the time, with 2nd Battalion HQ – 30 yards away – but that was all.'[323]

The airborne soldiers also fortified other buildings close by, including a schoolhouse on the east side of the ramp where C Company of 3rd Parachute Battalion, under the command of Major Lewis, had succeeded in breaking through from *Tiger* route by taking a side route, the Bredelaan in Oosterbeek. They would play a major part in the defence of the bridge.

There was little left to do now but arrange and re-arrange the guns and defensive positions to the best possible advantage. Major Bill Arnold made the final adjustments to the positions of his four 6-pounder anti-tank guns. Some late stragglers turned up, Hibbert noting that B Company had come in minus one platoon (Hugh Levien's) at 5.00am; it was immediately sent to occupy buildings to the west.

B Company's last minute arrival brought the number of men under Frost's command to about 740.[324] They were almost certainly the last ones to make it to the bridge. From first light the force was completely surrounded and cut off. But a short state of siege had always been anticipated, and the soldiers were confident that they could hold their positions until the ground forces arrived.

At 7.00am a report was received from Major Murray with the highly welcome news that the main bridge had not been prepared by the Germans for demolition. As the British had set up commanding lines of fire, it was very unlikely that the Germans would be able to set demolition charges now. All the defenders had to do was hold out until 30 Corps made their appearance; they were due by the 19th at the latest, 48 hours into the operation.

As Hibbert would say many years later: 'Everyone arrived in bits and pieces at night, and everyone deployed to part of the defensive perimeter. The moment we got organised, light came, and the Germans started attacking immediately.'[325]

20

THE DEFENCE OF THE BRIDGE

When dawn broke, the defenders of the bridge stood to arms, waiting for the attack which would surely come. They had heard a certain amount of movement during the night and knew that enemy scouts had been about, trying to assess the situation. But the first Germans to be move into the area seemed both hesitant and badly informed. Several were killed before they could withdraw to safety. The wounded who had been left behind were carried down to the Medical Officers in the cellars of the Rijkswaterstaat building.

Around 8.30am, the Germans made a much more determined attempt to break through. A group of heavy armoured cars, half-tracks and lorries, carrying around seventy to eighty men, set off across the bridge at high speed from the far bank of the river. A makeshift mine, made up of a daisy chain of Hawkins grenades, had been laid across the road by the defenders during the night. The leading vehicle passed directly over the grenades. Hibbert wrote: 'The first one went slap over the mine belt without damage, and raced up the road. Everyone was so surprised that hardly a shot was fired, and the Germans in the back had the cheek to wave at us.'[326]

The second vehicle also evaded the force of the mines and sped away into the town. But by now, the defenders had found the range and concentrated all their fire-power on the remaining vehicles, wrecking them and setting them on fire. The vehicles at the back ploughed into the vehicles at the front, and the tangled wreckage was strewn all along the bridge from the metal archway down the ramp into the town. The leading vehicles were stopped in their tracks almost opposite Brigade HQ, and as the men inside tried to escape they were shot. Others perished in the explosions and flames. It is thought that about seventy men died, including their commander, Hauptsturmführer Viktor Gräbner, who had apparently been acting contrary to orders.[327]

Simultaneously, German infantry began to pound the defences from the landward side with mortar bombs and shells. Frost wrote that everyone at HQ helped man the defences:

There were no exceptions from the fighting line, all ranks and trades were in it. Staff officers, signallers, batmen, drivers and clerks all lent a hand. We were content. Amid the din of continuous fire and the crash of falling burning buildings, laughter was often heard.

Outside in his jeep, firing one of his twin Vickers machine guns, Gough could just be seen, flushed and beaming and 'grinning like a wicked uncle'.[328]

After what seemed like several hours, but was in reality no more than two, the battle died away and gave the defenders some breathing space. At this stage, morale was still extremely high. Hibbert remembered that 'We were feeling very pleased with ourselves and were rather hoping that we would have the honour of welcoming the army into Arnhem all to ourselves.'

Perhaps the most famous and iconic image of the Arnhem batle is the reconnaissance photograph taken that same day by a Spitfire pilot passing over the town. It clearly shows the burnt-out wreckage of Gräbner's convoy, scattered along the bridge ramp between the as yet unmarked buildings and trees in full leaf. At this point, Arnhem was still easily recognisable, a prosperous town little marked by war. The photograph showed the bridge area well, including the HQs of 1st Parachute Brigade and 2nd Battalion. Beyond them stretched a well-kept, elegant townscape with wide tree-lined streets and leafy gardens. In the photograph, the Grote Markt, a large open-air space, could be seen in front of the just discernible corner of St Eusebius, also known as the Grote Kerk. Within three days, this whole area would be wrecked by mortar bombs, shells, and deliberately started fires.

The foolhardiness of Gräbner's attack would not be repeated. Instead the Germans concentrated on battering the edge of the defensive perimeter. A second, equally ferocious battle was being fought around three miles away at Oosterbeek, just along the river, where most of the rest of 1st Airborne Division were beseiged. The Germans controlled the land between the two British positions and prevented all contact between them.

An intensive stream of mortar bombs and shells now began to arrive in the bridge area. Machine-gunners began to move in, whilst expert snipers picked off anyone who unwisely showed themselves at a window or moved about in the open without cover. Yet the morale of the defending force remained very good; they still believed that the relieving force, 30 Corps, would arrive in high style that day, or at the very latest on the Tuesday.

The fact that the defenders were so lightly armoured had been one of the calculated risks of the operation, as indeed it was of all airborne operations. They were equipped with machine-guns, explosives, flame-throwers, and PIATs, the PIAT being an arm-held gun which fired an armour-piercing shell and was at its most effective against lightly armoured vehicles. There were also Major Arnold's four 6-pounder anti-tank guns. As the fighting increased in violence, the British would try to reuse captured German equipment, but wherever they could the Germans would destroy this, using flame-throwers or incendiary bullets to incinerate vehicles where the crews had fled or been killed.

Close to Brigade HQ, in the carefully chosen defensive positions around the embankment and bridge ramp, the close-quarters fighting became vicious in the extreme. One of the men fighting there was Jim Flavell. A very junior 2nd lieutenant and only nineteen, Arnhem was his first action. Not long before 17 September, he had been placed on the strength of 2nd Battalion and had had very little chance to get to know anyone. Earlier on this Monday he had been sent through heavy fire and an insane din of noise to join B Company under Douglas Crawley. There he was given command of 6 Platoon, whose CO, Peter Cane, had been killed. Almost in his next breath, Crawley told him that an A Company platoon under Lieutenant John McDermont was under heavy pressure and Flavell's platoon must go and reinforce them. 6 Platoon was down from the original 30 men to about 19, including their new and very youthful CO. Flavell did not know any of the men he was now in charge of, and this made his first command even more terrifying than it would have been anyway.[329]

The area was extremely dangerous, with mortar and tank fire ripping through the buildings. Flavell's platoon made their way to the building in which Lieutenant McDermont and his men were holding out. There Flavell found McDermont wounded, as indeed most of his platoon seemed to be. The nightmare scene remained with Flavell for years afterwards: 'There were a number of dead and I vividly recall blood almost flowing down the stairway, which was close to collapse.'[330]

The streets around the bridge had become a violently contested battleground. Buildings, and the control of the small strategic pockets of territory which went with them, were held, lost, regained, lost again. As darkness fell, the Germans set alight to the house which 6 Platoon was defending. By 10.45pm, the flames had taken hold so extensively that it was no longer possible to remain there. The platoon filtered out in small groups and took up defensive positions elsewhere, wherever they could find them. Many buildings near the bridge were now on fire, and night remained as bright as day.

On Tuesday, the battle only increased in ferocity. Little thought could be spared for the civilian population into whose quiet lives war had burst with such hideous ferocity. Any Dutch civilian who had not taken advantage of the cover of night to vanish was now imprisoned in the battle area. Others had already been compelled by the British on the Sunday night to leave for their own good. Writing years later of the Dutch owners of the houses in which B Company were fighting, Douglas Crawley recalled that it had become obvious to him that the civilians remaining in the cellars of those houses must go elsewhere 'as we were obviously in for a protracted battle'.

> About eight of them went out into the dark street under a Red Cross flag, quietly resigned to the possibility of fire being opened upon them. The house owner shook my hand and said 'Thank you for coming. Please use the food we have left in the cellar.' The party went slowly and safely over the street and out of sight to heaven knows where. The next morning, a stretcher party with a wounded man and under a Red Cross flag was shot up crossing the same street. The house was burned out the following night.[331]

On Tuesday morning, the Germans brought up heavy artillery and began to fire at point-blank range into the Rijkswaterstaat building. By now, Frost had also moved into the building so that he could better direct his forces. He wrote:

> Each hit seemed to pulverise the masonry and the appalling crash of these missiles against our walls scared the daylights out of Headquarters. Just as I made up my mind that something drastic would have to be done, our mortars got the range, one direct hit killing the entire crew and apparently disabling the gun. We saw it being towed away round a corner and it troubled us no more.[332]

In the afternoon the HQ attic received three direct hits from another gun, which had been moved up outside under the cover of two Mark IV tanks. This gun 'ventilated' the attic as Hibbert put it, removing large areas of walls and roof. Fortunately, there had been enough warning to move everyone and the radio equipment to safety. When the attic was reoccupied, Hibbert noticed that there was a large crater in the road where the gun had been. The ammunition had been detonated, probably by a mortar bomb.

With the radios still not working and 'feeling that perhaps the situation was a little obscure to the rest of the world', Hibbert arranged for a detailed report to be sent to England by carrier pigeon. It was a distinctly forlorn hope, but worth a try.

Very disturbing information was obtained that afternoon. The latest prisoners had been interrogated and it had been discovered that several were from the 9th SS Panzer Division, the Hohenstauffen. It had been thought by British intelligence that the elite 9th and 10th SS Panzer Divisions had been written off in the Falaise battle. Now the men on the ground knew that this had been wishful thinking. Panzer Divisions meant superb, highly motivated, battle-hardened troops, and tanks which could easily demolish buildings and were almost impervious to most of the defenders' weaponry. Frost understood exactly what this news meant: 'The odds against an outcome in our favour were heavy indeed.'[333]

The defenders had not been equipped to fight such a long and desperate siege. Ammunition was running low, and the medical supplies were completely inadequate for the ever-increasing number of wounded. Food had become a precious rarity. Only a minimum of foraging could be done and little could be found other than apples and pears. Then the water supply failed. This had been expected for some time, and water had been stored in any receptacle available but resources were very limited. The cutting off of the water supply directly affected the treatment of the wounded. Far worse, the defence against the fires raging around HQ was lost. Now the greatest fear of the wounded was that, lying there helplessly, they would be burnt alive.

There was still no sign of 30 Corps and the situation became graver by the hour. Frost wrote:

> Towards evening heavy tanks appeared, incredibly menacing and sinister in the half-light, as their guns swung from target to target. Shells burst through our walls. The dust and settling debris following their explosions filled the passages and rooms. The acrid reek and smell of burning together with the noise bemused us.[334]

The tanks were terrifying even to the bravest; there was something animate about them, as if they were the prowling embodiment of evil. Urquhart, the British general, understood this very well when he wrote of 'the clanking tracks of the Tiger and the weird sighs like a last gasp'.[335]

Away from HQ, the defensive positions round the bridge had become untenable. Most of the streets were on fire or had been demolished by explosives, and, it being an urban area, there was little or no earth in which to dig slit trenches. Wherever they could, the men took up defensive positions in the rubble, in buildings silted with thick soft ash which still retained the heat of the fires.

As hopes began to fade of a successful outcome, outlying groups were recalled to the heart of the defence, the solidly built Rijkswaterstaat building from which the defenders could still dominate access to the bridge. Flavell's 6 Platoon got back there with the greatest difficulty, sometimes going below ground and into the cellars, where by breaking through the walls into the neighbouring buildings they could 'mouse-hole' their way as close to HQ as possible before unavoidably coming out in the open and being exposed to fire. Other outlying forces had no option but to surrender. They took the bolts out of their weapons and threw them away so the Germans would not be able to reuse them.

For some 48 hours, the radio sets had been stubbornly refusing to work. Suddenly, at last, there was radio contact with 30 Corps, but all that they would promise was that they would be there 'soon'.

Another night came, lit by the constant fires. Frost noted that two great churches were burning, St Eusebius and St Walburgis, the latter very close to HQ. Yet it was quieter than on the preceding night. Frost prowled about, occasionally sleeping for a while amongst the litter in one of the rooms. Sometimes a light rain fell. Following the usual principle of shooting anything that moved outside at night, he took a pot shot with a borrowed rifle at two hatless figures. Neither moved. When he looked up after reloading, the figures had gone.

In all this chaos, bloodshed and destruction, where was Anthony?

Little is known of him other than that he was at Brigade HQ, right in the centre of the battle. Few men seem to have remembered much about him afterwards. Anthony had the quiet, self-effacing ways of the born observer, and never deliberately drew attention to himself. He was one amongst many, drawn from a hodge-podge of different units thrown together in desperate circumstances. With such a battle being fought – amidst fire, smoke, explosions, and unrelenting, nerve-shattering noise – it is hardly surprising that he went unnoticed.

For these reasons, little evidence remains of what people thought of him, but what was said was full of praise. Freddie Gough, that epitome of a warrior, would write to Mintie in May 1945: 'He did most awfully well at Arnhem and his bravery and delightful personality were an inspiration to all of us.' In another place, in words which though unattributed clearly came from Gough, Anthony was praised for his courage and cheerfulness, 'he had won all our hearts by the end of the battle'.[336] Hibbert would say of him, years later: 'He was very gentle and very amusing, quiet, with a nice sense of humour, and absolutely unflappable. A very good egg, a super chap.'[337] The brief sentences, or even single words such as 'indomitable', by which people described their experience of Anthony at Arnhem, all stress his bravery and wit, his endurance and unconquerable spirit.[338]

Anthony had never shown any aptitude for the physical side of soldiering. At numerous times in his writing he had mentioned inability to keep up on marches, being a bad shot with a rifle, high blood pressure, flat feet, lack of coordination, and a predisposition to catch every passing illness. But now, in this great crisis, like the signallers, batmen, drivers and clerks whom Frost and Hibbert described as joining the firing line, he must have helped to man the defences; just as in Normandy, he would have had no qualms whatsoever about using a gun.

Like everyone else, Anthony was in dire physical danger throughout his time at Arnhem. Though he was not running the same risks as those who were on active defence or who sat high up in the vulnerable attic trying to get a signal from Urquhart or 30 Corps, his was no sinecure. Over the period of the battle, he filled three books with shorthand notes. That he went about his work with great cheerfulness and thoroughness is obvious from what Gough and Hibbert said about him.

Anthony would not have been the writer he was if he had not, at times, experienced a thrill of intense excitement at the magnificent subject which he had been handed. He must have known that, if he survived, his book about Arnhem would make his name. None of the other reporters and photographers with 1st Airborne Division had reached the bridge. They were all at Oosterbeek, enduring a similar, though as yet slightly less intensive, kind of hell. The only possibility of another journalist being present at the bridge lies in the tantalising possibility of a huge nameless Canadian photographer, mentioned by Simms in his book *Arnhem Spearhead*. But this photographer has never been identified. Simms was seriously wounded, and like all the other wounded was lying in the hideously overcrowded and virtually lightless cellars of HQ. Can the photographer have been a hallucination?[339]

Whether the photograher existed or not, Anthony was the only writer at the bridge. It seems very unlikely that there had been any plans for him to file reports or send information by radio, as the BBC reporters and Alan Wood of the *Daily Express* were doing from Oosterbeek. The difficulties of the operation had never been anticipated, and the expectation would almost certainly have been that Anthony would bring back his journalism in person, as he always had done before.

To safeguard the notebooks against the fires and violence of the battle, Anthony must have carried them with him all the time. In spare moments, conscious of their critical importance, he would have gone over his shorthand notes to make sure that he could decipher them. In previous times of great stress when too much was happening at once, his shorthand had become impossible for him to read back afterwards. During the Lancaster bombing raid in December 1943, he had found it impossible to keep up; he had tried to write down the dialogue between the pilot and bomb-aimer as they approached the target, but it was too fast for his hobbling shorthand. 'I wrote it down, but now I can't transcribe it' he noted ruefully afterwards.[340]

Faced by such dogged resistance and refusal to surrender in the face of overwhelming odds, the Germans had taken to referring to Frost as 'the mad Colonel'. When this was broadcast over enemy radio, the name stuck.[341]

At 10.00am on the Wednesday, one of Hibbert's radio sets, which had been searching fruitlessly for days, suddenly picked up the Division's forward net. He immediately got on the set. 'The first words I heard were Brigadier Hackett remonstrating with Urquhart, "Yes, but you must realise that we have no anti-tank guns" which did not sound too good.'

Frost was called and spoke to Urquhart for the first time since the battle had begun. Urquhart had been missing for two days and there had been various rumours about what had happened to him, so it was very cheering to hear from him at last. Unfortunately he could not tell Frost anything which he did not already know about 30 Corps, and it quickly became obvious that the rest of the Division were in such serious trouble that there was no question of them coming to the rescue of the bridge group.

Urquhart had fared very badly on Sunday, the first day of the drop. In moving between groups of his men, he and Lathbury had found themselves surrounded by the enemy and in serious danger of capture. They had had to go into hiding. When they eventually broke out, Lathbury was severely wounded and suffered a partial paralysis due to a bullet nicking his spine. Urquhart was compelled to leave him behind. After other adventures, he reached Division HQ on the 19th.

The HQ in the Hartenstein Hotel was to be the centre of the increasingly murderous fighting in Oosterbeek. Though he had much greater forces at his command than Frost, Urquhart and his men would also suffer a storm of shelling and mortar fire. So horrific would the situation become at Oosterbeek that the Germans would nickname it the Cauldron because of its resemblance to a constricted mass of boiling, bubbling water.

The situation there, though bad, had not yet become critical, and Urquhart still held hopes that the operation could be salvaged. He asked Frost to pass on his congratulations to all at the bridge for their magnificent feat of arms. Then Frost told him the situation. He said that they could hold out for some while but urgently needed food, ammunition, and medical supplies for the wounded. Urquhart, misunderstanding the dire reality on the ground, suggested that they should organise the local Dutch civilians to bring in supplies from the re-supply containers which had been dropped by parachute the previous day. Frost's reply was recorded by Hibbert:

> He said we were fighting in the middle of a devastated area, that there were no civilians, that we were surrounded by a superior and somewhat aggressive enemy force, and that it was by no means possible for civilians to wander backwards and forwards through the lines carrying containers full of supplies.[342]

The conversation ended with the reassurance from Urquhart that 30 Corps would be with them soon. In reality, though he did not spell it out, Urquhart's forces needed 30 Corps almost as much as Frost's men.

Enemy firepower was now increasing savagely. Amongst those fighting in the positions east of the bridge were Captain Bernard Briggs and Lieutenant John Cairns. Their force, originally sixty men, had by now been reduced to twelve. Under the severest pressure, they withdrew to HQ, as did anybody else from the outlying positions who could make it. The end was in sight, though many could not yet admit that all the superhuman effort had been in vain.

That afternoon, Frost and Doug Crawley were both seriously injured by the same small mortar bomb. Gough assumed command but would constantly refer back to Frost, who though badly wounded in the legs was still mentally alert.

Gough, who was relentlessly cheerful in the heat of battle, told Urquhart on the radio that they could easily hold out for another 24 hours and longer if necessary. Hibbert, with perhaps unconscious irony, wrote:

> This in view of the fact that A and B Companies had been withdrawn almost back to the Brigade HQ building, that there had already been over 50% casualties, that there was no more PIAT ammunition, that the 6 pounders were unable to fire being under direct SA fire, and that ammunition of all types was precariously low, was probably an optimistic statement, but indicated the general feeling at the time.

In the final throws of the battle the Germans completely surrounded the Rijkswaterstaat building, alternating high explosives with smoke bombs which contained phosphorous and set everything alight. There was a constant battle to keep the flames from taking hold. John Killick, a Field Security officer, was sent by Gough to the top floor of HQ, to try to deal with the fires there with a fire extinguisher. It was very lonely up there by himself. He found the whole of the top floor had been shot through, and the decorative belfry on the top of the building was on fire. The wooden ladder which led up to it was so severely damaged that it collapsed under his weight and he dropped the fire extinguisher. Hitting the floor, it 'struck its knob smartly in accordance with instructions and started spraying uselessly all over the place, and from then on we knew we had had it really'.[343]

Thoughts turned to saving the wounded, of whom there were now about 300, so crammed together in the cellar of HQ that it was almost impossible to move between them. A small additional supply of water had been found on Wednesday morning, but there was almost no light and no facilities for anything except the most rudimentary care. Several of the wounded had lost their minds – Frost refers to the 'bomb-happy cases [...] gibbering in the room'.[344] James Logan and David Wright, the Medical Officers, who had been without sleep since Saturday night, were clearly at the limits of their endurance. The time had come to evacuate the wounded, and so at last that most bitter decision was made.

Frost, lying amongst the wounded, sent for Gough and told him to move the able-bodied troops out whilst he could under cover of darkness; he gave him his own belt with revolver and compass, and they wished each other goodbye and good luck.

David Wright, the Medical Officer whom Anthony had got to know well in the lead-up to Arnhem, recalled the evacuation:

> Major Gough [had said] to me if anybody does get out of here, it won't be you. Meaning I had to stay behind with the wounded, which I had already accepted [...] We had a large number of casualties [...] and around fifty German prisoners. I had to give a German prisoner a stick with a white cloth on the end and pushed him out the front door, first I might add, and I followed. A German officer appeared from the embankment area. I explained the situation and he helped organise the evacuation of the basement using some of his own men. We got everybody out by the skin of our teeth and were taken up the embankment to await transportation.[345]

The appalling mental strain that everyone had been under had taken a grievous toll. Simms would remember his Scottish Regimental Sergeant Major lying by the embankment of the Rhine and singing at the top of his voice. A German soldier told the unfortunate man to be quiet and threatened him with his gun, but 'he was completely 'bomb-happy' and thought he was having a sing-song in the mess at home. We mimed his condition to the German, who seemed to understand.'[346]

Frost was devastated by the conclusion of his fight, but through his intense angry bitterness he noted the politeness, sympathy and even admiration of his captors. Before the wounded were evacuated and it was looking inevitable that they were all going to fall into the hands of the SS, he had said to someone 'I don't think that this is going to be much of a pleasure'. Now, despite his acute pain and grief, he recognised professional respect and something like brotherly kindness in these men of such ferocious reputation: 'We had all heard stories of them shooting their prisoners or herding them into burning buildings, but these men were kind, chivalrous, even comforting.'[347]

Other Germans were cock-a-hoop. At the moment of Simms' capture, a tough-looking German sauntered up to him with 'a huge grin on his face', and told him in good English that he had fought in Normandy against Montgomery. When one of the British remarked on the stubborn resistance put up by the German Army at Caen, the man was delighted, and told them beaming that he had had six solid weeks of it, and had then been sent up to Arnhem for a rest – 'Some rest!'

Simms said that the man was as pleased as Punch to be back on the winning side again at that stage of the war. Other Germans, he observed, simply seemed to enjoy the act of fighting. When the wounded were taken away, they passed a number of German tanks, parked nose to tail under the trees of a broad avenue. Simms wrote:

In the dusk it was a truly impressive sight. Seeing my wonder a young enemy soldier remarked, 'Yes, Tommy, these were for you in the morning if you had not surrendered'. Several of the German tank men called out to us 'Well fought, Tommy,' 'Good fight, eh Tommy?' They seemed to regard war in much the same way as the British regarded football.[348]

The wounded were taken to St Elisabeth Hospital, leaving Gough, Hibbert, Anthony, and the remnants of the force in the ruins of Arnhem. Even before the wounded had been evacuated, the fighting had recommenced. That night the German overseas news agency stated: 'Arnhem is in flames and covered with a thick pall of smoke. Small isolated enemy groups have dug themselves in in several parts of the town and are still holding out.'[349]

21

PRISONER OF WAR

What was left of HQ had been abandoned and with it the last faint hope of keeping control of the bridge until 30 Corps arrived. The remaining airborne soldiers slipped away from the ruined building into the shadows, avoiding the bright crackling light cast by the flames. Hibbert had taken Anthony under his wing, recognising how little he had been trained for this type of eventuality. Together, they made their way through back gardens and back yards up the road towards the centre of Arnhem.[350] There they met with others of their party at an abandoned school. The basement of the school had windows at street level and they were able to watch what was happening outside. Presently they saw a large group of British walking wounded being marched past under armed guard, followed by what remained of the British transport being driven by the victors. Not long afterwards, a second batch of airborne soldiers passed by, men who had survived the battle unwounded. For the watchers in the school, these bitter and melancholy sights intensified the blackness of their situation.

The plan now was to try to get to Urquhart at Oosterbeek. But Oosterbeek, through which they had passed a mere three and a half days earlier, might as well have been on the moon for all the chances of getting there. Arnhem was saturated with Germans, of whom more seemed to be arriving by the hour. Hibbert's party had no water, no food, and almost no ammunition. Their best hope was that 30 Corps would at last make their appearance. But no welcome sounds of artillery bombardment or fighting could be heard, and it was very noticeable how casually the Germans were going about their work, not in the adrenaline-fuelled rush which would have meant that the British Army was nearby. The heart-sinking truth had to be acknowledged – 30 Corps was nowhere near Arnhem.

Hibbert decided to split the men into sections, each under an officer; they were to get as far away as possible under cover of darkness, lie up during the day, and then make their way to Oosterbeek the following night. But things did not go well. Several sections had to double back on their tracks, either having run into the enemy or having found their way blocked by fires or debris. A sort of mad congestion developed which took precious minutes to sort out. But eventually everyone got away. Taking personal charge of the last section, Hibbert left the school. Anthony went with him.

It was now approaching dawn, and they needed to hide as quickly as possible. Coming upon the ruins of a burnt-out building, Hibbert told the men to scoop out a trench, bury themselves in the ashes, and remain there until nightfall. Rapidly this proved impossible because the ashes were much too hot. The party moved on to the garden of the next-door house. In his preliminary reconnaissance, Hibbert was nearly shot at point-blank range by Major Dennis Mumford, who had already taken refuge there with his section. Fortunately, at the last second Mumford recognised Hibbert. The two officers joined forces, putting two men in a tool-shed and barricading the rest in a bedroom. Mumford curled himself up inside a wooden crate. Anthony and Hibbert found a very small coal shed, and got in as best as they could, shovelling the coal back over themselves with their hands.

Completely encircled by the enemy, the area in which the remnants of Frost's men had gone to ground was so small and so devastated that almost no one would escape detection. Hiding places were anywhere that could be found in the wrecked houses and gardens, in sheds, stables, or chicken huts, beneath sacks, apple-trays, seed-boxes, bales of hay or straw. A soldier called Trinder with two companions, all that was left of his original group of six, got into a garage and hid beneath a lorry which was jacked up on wooden blocks for repair. The Germans flushed them out with a couple of rounds from a sten gun, and sent them, with their hands up, down the road towards enemy lines.[351]

Others fared just as badly. Jim Flavell wrote:

> Late on the Wednesday night, those still standing were told to try their individual best to 'rejoin the Division'. I was one of the last to leave the garden behind what had been the 2 Para HQ building. As I ventured forth, I came across a large wooden door that had been blown off its hinges. I wormed my way under the door where I immediately fell asleep. During the morning of Thursday I must have been snoring and that is what gave my position away. The SS lifted the door and found me asleep.[352]

Gough, badly scorched from having to lie down in some hot ashes to escape capture the previous night, had by now concealed himself in a woodpile. He was a big man and his left boot remained uncovered. Those hunting him took hold of his foot and dragged him out like a fox from its lair.

> Completely exhausted, he surveyed the faces of the men who had captured him and found that they were little more than boys, which prompted him to burst out laughing. Shortly after, a German Major asked to see Gough, understanding him to be the commander at the bridge. The officer said 'I wish to congratulate you and your men. You are gallant soldiers. I fought at Stalingrad and it is obvious that you British have a great deal of experience in street fighting.' To which Gough simply replied, 'No. This was our first effort. We'll be much better next time.'[353]

The Germans, though still jumpy and trigger-happy, were beginning to realise that the battle was over. One by one the British officers were discovered: Cecil Byng-Maddick, Bernard Briggs, and Douglas Mortlock, all from 1st Parachute Brigade HQ; Trevor McNabb and Tony Platt, who were Gough's men; and many others from a variety of different units, including Dennis Mumford and Digby Tatham-Warter. A key figure in the battle, Tatham-Warter and his second-in-command Tony Franks had both been seriously wounded. They would be taken by the Germans to hospital, from which they would soon escape.

Hibbert and Anthony were not found immediately. Hibbert's diary, written up some days later, related the story.

> Anthony Cotterell and I were sitting hunched up in our coal-shed feeling rather cold and depressed. It was a very small shed, coal-bin would better describe it, with a door eighteen inches square; altogether, we hoped, an unlikely place to look for two bodies. We had heard sounds of German search parties all round us for the past hour, with the usual accompaniment of raucous shouting, and bursts of automatic fire, one of which smacked into the wall a foot above our heads. Several times Germans walked past our shed, and one lent up against it for about ten minutes, while we held our breath. However, the next section went through the garden with a fine comb, and Anthony Cotterell and I, covered in coal dust, and feeling very angry and foolish, were hauled out. They gave us a preliminary search, and unfortunately collared Anthony's three note-books full of shorthand notes of his story of the operation.

Hibbert would later describe this moment as 'the absolute low point of my life', not only the shock and indignity of being taken prisoner but also being besmirched with coal dust.[354] As for Anthony, there can have been no time or inclination for remembering the joke he had made shortly before D-Day: 'I must practice surrendering to myself in the mirror to see if I've got it right.'[355]

The loss of his notebooks must have been a very severe blow to him. They had been written in bad light and at extreme speed, and were probably in places illegible even to Anthony himself. They were notations rather than a full text, an aide-memoir rather than a complete record. They did not give away any military secrets, which is why Anthony had not destroyed them and Hibbert, who clearly knew of their existence, had not asked him to do so. Bringing them out of HQ when all the other records, including Brigade HQ's precious war diary, had been destroyed to stop them falling into enemy hands must have been a calculated risk, based on the assumption that only Anthony could decipher his sprawling shorthand.

As a journalist, Anthony had always relied upon his notebooks. His writing style was built upon the accumulation of small but deeply significant details and the reporting of actual speech. Being a consummate professional, he never worked from unassisted memory and he did not trust it. 'You need a photographic memory and I haven't got one,' he had once commented when asked to memorise a string of facts.[356] For him, the loss of the notebooks was a personal disaster. It would also prove an immense loss to the history of the battle, for in the maelstrom of war the notebooks would vanish, never to be subsequently traced.

Having confiscated the notebooks and satisfied themselves that Anthony and Hibbert were unarmed, the Germans marched them and the other prisoners they had collected to the large market square, the Grote Markt. St Eusebius lay opposite, a huge, plain, redbrick, cathedral-like church which completely dwarfed its surroundings. Although it had suffered a lot of damage, most of the vast edifice was intact and the Germans would shortly utilise it as a makeshift prison.

Though it was only about 9.00am, already the Germans had found almost everyone. The disappointment was crushing. Hibbert would later write in his diary:

> A very depressing sight met our eyes. About twenty officers, and two hundred Other Ranks, which represented nearly all the unwounded survivors of the battle of the bridge, were drawn up into two separate groups, one of officers, and the other of Other Ranks. It was a great shock, one had hoped that a proportion at least would be able to get through.

The humiliations of being a prisoner began almost immediately. Although the guards were lax and allowed the officers and men to mingle, the SS officer in charge of the battalion spent the entire morning showing off in front of his captives; 'He never lowered his voice below a scream, and kept every German within 100 yards hopping with fright.' The captives were having their first real glimpse of the men they had been fighting, many of whom were from the elite SS Panzer units. They were amazed at the extremely young age of the junior NCOs and men; the majority did not seem to be more than sixteen or seventeen, though the least that any of them would admit to was eighteen.

Whilst the prisoners were in the Grote Markt, Killick witnessed the execution of some Dutch patriots who had been helping the British; they were stood up against the wall on the other side of the square and shot in cold blood. Like all the Dutch people who helped the British, those executed would have known that this would be their fate as soon as they fell into the hands of the Germans.[357]

Hibbert wrote of the exultant mood of the enemy:

> All the Jerries were thoroughly pleased with themselves at having put us in the bag and large numbers of them came to look us over. Talking to some of them they said that, though they'd fought on both the Western and Eastern fronts, they'd never had such a hard fight.

The spoils of war belonged to the victors. Hibbert observed sardonically that the Germans found the captured British jeeps 'a never-ending source of delight', and drove them very badly at high speed around the streets, crashing the gears.

Clothing, equipment, arms and ammunition were now taken from the prisoners and methodically stacked in heaps against St Eusebius's walls. Hibbert found it galling to see what 'they had won from us', yet it was very satisfying to see how small the piles of ammunition were. 'It at least made one feel less guilty about being taken prisoner, and made one realise that even if we had sold our lives, it wouldn't have been dearly.'

Because the guards were so lax, a great deal of the captured material was almost immediately pilfered back again, including the water-bottles essential in an escape attempt and the much valued red berets of the airborne soldiers. No matter what threats were made, no one was going to give up on the small defiances.

No roll call was taken and no initial interrogation made. Killick, who was Officer Commanding of 89th Parachute Field Security Section, was not wearing Intelligence Corps badges but those of the Suffolk Regiment which was his original unit.[358] The Germans overlooked him, as they overlooked other valuable prizes. Like Killick, Anthony was not wearing badges which would have given away his particular role; he was simply wearing the insignia of a Royal Fusiliers officer.[359] As will be seen later, Anthony's work was well-known to the German propaganda ministries, but in the chaotic aftermath of the Arnhem battle nobody realised that he was a famous soldier-journalist, one whose capture might be used for propaganda purposes. For the time being, he was safely and anonymously merged in the mass of prisoners, and it was not until two days later that his identity would be revealed. In addition, the Germans' initial carelessness with their prisoners appears to have broken the link between him and his confiscated notebooks. There is no evidence that he was questioned about them even though the little books, full of cryptic code, must surely have been of interest to the enemy.

The prisoners were now moved into the make-shift prison of St Eusebius, and it was here that one of their captors took a photograph of them. A spectacular war trophy, it would be printed in the 1944 Christmas book of the 10th Panzer Division, known as the Frundsberg. *Der Kampf der 10.SS-Division-Frundsberg im Jahre 1944* covered the campaigns of that year in Buczacz, Caen, and Nimwegen (Nijmegen). The photograph taken in St Eusebius shows the British prisoners sitting on wooden church benches in what appears to be a chancel. Their poses are casual, sprawled, and defiant, deliberately expressing their unbroken courage. It is not possible to recognise the faces but it is very likely that these men would have been the officers, the greatest prizes of all. The group of around sixteen men in the foreground (there are other shadowy figures against the walls) was close to the number of officers caught soon after the battle for the bridge ended. Anthony would have been amongst them.[360]

Once they had recovered a little from the shock of their capture, the more reckless and bolshy of the prisoners began to make trouble for the Germans. Killick, who could speak fluent German and who would go on to have a career as a high-flying diplomat after the war, became an unwilling go-between for the two sides:

> [The way we were treated] was, I think, one is bound to say correct in the German sense. They respected us as having given them a hell of a good fight [...] but they weren't kind or benevolent or anything like that [...]. It led to my first experience of diplomacy in a way because the British officers on the one hand [...] kept wanting me to say to the Germans that under the Geneva Convention they must give us food and water and all that, and the SS men on the other side [were] saying, 'Tell those bloody men, if they step off the pavement once again they will be shot,' and you know you had to sort of interpret between the two. And I am bound to say that the SS men themselves didn't have much in the way of food or water.[361]

That night, the prisoners in St Eusebius were moved on. Killick once again acted as interpreter, intermediating between Gough, who was the senior British officer, and the German commander who was issuing orders for the march. These were extremely simple. Strict march discipline must be observed and there must be no talking; anybody breaking ranks would be shot immediately.

Having told his men that they must obey these orders, Gough, to Hibbert's great pleasure, exhorted everyone:

> to pay particular attention to bearing and drill so that we 'could show these bastards what real soldiers look like'. He then put us through five minutes drill for the benefit of our German captors. This increased everyone's morale considerably and gave everyone back that confidence and pride in themselves which had been a bit shaken by the events of the past 24 hours.

Not all the prisoners can have felt as righteously angry and confrontational as Gough and Hibbert. For some, the greatest emotion must have been sheer relief that they were still alive. They were prisoners of the enemy in an apocalyptically wrecked and burning town full of dead bodies, but by some extraordinary miracle they themselves were unharmed.

The next holding-point was a church hall or small concert hall, furnished with hard, comfortless, wooden benches. There was still no food but a nearby pump gave many their first drink of water for 24 hours. The lack of food was not deliberate cruelty but a product of the immense chaos in the aftermath of the battle with so many prisoners and wounded to care for. Some of the Germans went out of their way to be kind. A corporal, taking pity on the famished prisoners, raided a nearby sweetshop, coming back with peppermints and biscuits which were shared out at one each per man. Other Germans handed round their own cigarettes and some evil-smelling cigars.

Despite this fraternisation, the guards were alert to the possibilities of escape, and compelled the prisoners to hand in all their escaping materials with dire threats of mass punishment if anyone held anything back. A large pile was made of maps, files, and compasses, but, in typical covert defiance, the prisoners retained small easily hidden pieces like pen-knives.

The next few hours passed very miserably. The prisoners were desperately hungry, tired, cold, and unwashed. Like their commanding officer, Frost, now in hospital, they must at times have felt very bitter. Frost still could not believe that 30 Corps had failed to come to the rescue. 'It was difficult to feel that there was enough genuine opposition to stop them. It was desperately disappointing that having done everything we had been asked to do we were now prisoners. It was shaming, like being a malefactor, no longer free.'[362]

The future was extremely uncertain for all the British prisoners, both wounded and unwounded. No one knew what would happen when they were moved deep into the heart of the Third Reich. They might be the targets of enemy vengeance; they might be used as hostages; they might be killed in bombing raids or by friendly fire. Only the most obliterating tiredness brought sleep on the hard wooden benches, and only sleep brought temporary relief from the gnawing hunger and anxiety.

About 3.30am they were moved on again. Exhausted and footsore, they marched through the darkness to Velp, a suburbs to the north-east of Arnhem. Velp was like Arnhem had been a few days earlier. A quiet, pleasant, prosperous place, it had many fine houses and villas sited along its wide, tree-lined roads. The new PoW holding cage was a villa called Bena Sita, a large handsome property with its name inscribed on a plaque beneath the three ornate gables. There had been a fashion for such Latinised names when the villa was built around the end of the nineteenth century, and other local houses had similar names such as 'Urbana' and 'Tusculum'.

Bena Sita had a cellar, a ground and first floor with high ceilings, and a very large attic, now occupied by guards armed with machine-guns which covered both the front and back gardens. The small front garden ran alongside the main road from Arnhem to Zutphen, whilst the larger back garden had been used to grow vegetables to alleviate the extreme shortage of food in Holland. There was a monkey-puzzle tree in the front garden, and because of this some of the prisoners dubbed the place 'The Monkey Puzzle House'.

Though Bena Sita was large, Hibbert recorded the situation as being extremely overcrowded with the officers being put into two rooms, twelve foot square, and Other Ranks 'jammed like sardines with not even enough room for them all to lie down at once'. The new set of guards was a mixture of 'extremely unpleasant members of the SS' and 'some very old and quite innocuous Luftwaffe guards'. The prisoners were so exhausted, and there were so many guards around, that all thoughts of escaping were postponed; people simply lay down on the floor, wherever they could, and almost immediately fell into a dead sleep.

When they awoke, it was to thirst and hunger. After numerous complaints, they succeeded in getting an apple each, 'swiped from the neighbouring gardens'. Water was urgently needed for drinking and washing in. One man was allowed out at a time to go to a nearby pump under the supervision of two guards. Hibbert wrote: 'With the water that we collected we managed to wash away the worst of the dirt, and also shave. Anthony Cotterell and I, well bedaubed with ashes and coal-dust, were badly in need of a wash.'

The two-guard principle also applied to going to the latrines. But by keeping up a perpetual queue for water and latrines, the prisoners eventually wore out the old Luftwaffe guards and the escort was reduced from two to one. As Hibbert recalled, some of these old guards were quite kindly and freely admitted that Germany had lost the war and that all they wanted to do was go home. However, their growing laxity with the prisoners was not so promising as it seemed at first – there was an outer ring of armed guards to prevent escape in addition to the machine-guns in the attic.

Nonetheless, escaping was an urgent consideration. Hibbert records everyone as feeling hugely better after they had washed and shaved, and in a rather Boy's Own Paper sort of way 'everyone immediately got busy reconnoitring ways and means to escape'. The incessant trips for water and the toilet had provided good opportunities for checking out the surroundings and dreaming up possible routes to freedom. Some hot-heads were ready to improvise on the spur of the moment; Mumford and Bill Arnold almost made a break for it from the garden, but at the last minute fortunately spotted a sentry with his gun trained upon them.

Indoors there was endless scrutinising of the villa's construction and fittings, looking for a hiding place in which to sit things out. Hibbert tried to wriggle up the chimney but found it to be impassable. With Bill Arnold, he then tried to get access to the space beneath the floorboards and broke several precious penknives on the hard boards before discovering the space beneath them was too narrow to hide a man. It came in useful in another way, however, as a place to conceal objects during the frequent searches by the guards.

During the morning, more prisoners arrived in ones and twos. Then, about midday, Anthony Deane-Drummond arrived 'very damp and bad-tempered', having been captured the previous day. Deane-Drummond, the second in command of Divisional Signals, was one of the most colourful characters in 1st Airborne Division. After a parachute drop on Italy in February 1941, he had become a PoW, and after making two ingenious but ultimately unsuccessful escape attempts, had succeeded on the third try. He got across the heavily guarded Swiss border, travelled back through Occupied France, and reached England in the summer of 1942. His memories of captivity were vivid, 'languishing behind barbed wire with all its mental anguish and petty horrors, which become magnified and distorted in so unnatural a life'.[363] When the Arnhem battle was over, determined not to become a PoW again, he made a typically courageous attempt to get away by swimming the Rhine in the darkness. He could quite easily have drowned or have been shot in the water. However, he reached the far bank safely, only to stumble into a German unit standing-to about an hour before dawn.

A few hours later, he was taken by lorry into Arnhem:

> We crossed the Rhine using the main bridge for which so many lives had been sacrificed. I could see many marks of the bloody fighting which had taken place as we threaded our way in and out of shell holes and burnt-out German tanks. Smoke was still coming from the ruins of the buildings on the north side of the river.[364]

Arriving at Bena Sita the following day, he soon noted that some of the officers were already becoming numbed by the anti-climax of being a prisoner.

> Some of the officers were already saying that they would leave trying to escape till they arrived at the German prison camp ... It is so easy to put off action till to-morrow and all this sort of talk was so reminiscent of my experiences in Italy. I told everybody that I saw their one and only chance of getting away would be before they left Holland.

Completely undeterred by the caution or good-humoured ridicule of his fellow officers, or by the 55 Germans guarding the place, he began to examine critically the entire house and garden, 'There were many smiles cast in my direction. It was not possible to get away they said, they had already been over the place with a fine tooth comb.' But eventually he found a narrow, partially hidden cupboard which he thought would do, removed all his badges of rank, laid in a scanty stock of food and water, got into the cupboard, and prepared to wait things out. He would remain there for thirteen days, and after this incredible feat of endurance he would indeed escape.[365]

The rooms in which the British were imprisoned overlooked the main Arnhem-Zutphen road, Because the front garden of Bena Sita was so narrow, anyone in the window could easily be seen by passers-by. Some of the more high-spirited took advantage of this. Hibbert wrote: 'We found great amusement in chalking up large Vs on the windows, and giving the V sign to any civilians or Germans passing our house. The civilians were delighted and nearly all returned or acknowledged the salute. The Germans were furious.'

The forced exodus of the Dutch inhabitants of Arnhem had already begun. Jac Janssen, a Dutch student in hiding, was amongst those leaving the town. Though it is not certain which day he cycled through Velp, it is possible that it was Hibbert and Anthony's group of prisoners whom he saw, gathered outside Bena Sita prior to their being transported to Germany. Janssen would always retain a vivid memory of a group of airborne soldiers with their highly noticeable red berets standing before a villa and loudly singing 'It's a long, long way to Tipperary'.[366] The tiny glowing picture illustrates both the cheerful defiance of the British and the Dutch people's fascination with them.

By now the villa was seriously overcrowded. To provide extra latrines, deep trenches were dug at the bottom of the garden amongst the vegetable beds, but first the prisoners equally distributed the precious vegetables, receiving half a carrot or onion each. The Germans had been amazingly quick to organise a system and proper food was now arriving even if it was in very small quantities, such as a slice of bread each with a little butter or cheese. That Friday night the meagre ration was augmented by one pleasant old guard who smuggled in a bucketful of apples for his charges.

They still hoped for rescue, and at times could hear heavy barrages, enough to shake the windows and light up the sky at night. Less exhausted now, and with some of their urgent physical needs taken care of, some slept better than the previous night. Others, however, were too restless, cold or uncomfortable to go to sleep immediately, and instead talked quietly amongst themselves. Lieutenant R. Finlay Wilson, a Scot from Troon, was lying on the floor next to Anthony. Nine months later he would write to Mintie:

> I was fortunate enough to have a few cigarettes and we smoked and talked for a short time. I would like to take the liberty of saying that even from the little I knew of your son I was much

impressed by him and I am not easily impressed. He was a really delightful fellow and to use an expression of our Division, 'he was a man with a message'.[367]

Anthony's extraordinarily strong commitment to his work was apparent even in this brief, whispered conversation held amongst the sleeping forms of their brother officers.

Scattered throughout Anthony's writing are clues as to how he might have felt at this point, a prisoner of war, his life insecure and dependent on the mercy of his captors. All were written in comparative safety in England, long before he had seen war at close quarters. Though his flights with the bomber crews had at times been terrifying, it was war at one step removed. Since then he had been through D-Day and Normandy, and had experienced the extreme baptism of fire that was Arnhem. It is possible, therefore, that his outlook had changed but this seems highly unlikely; the soldiers who remembered Anthony's behaviour at Arnhem all described how cheerful, unflappable, dedicated, and amusing he was – in other words, he was the same as he always had been.

In Anthony's earlier writings, any references to his own mortality had always had the same witty self-ridiculing style with which he had described his basic inaptitude for military life. For example, on one daylight bombing mission in 1943 he had beguiled away the nerve-racking experience by writing, 'I found myself wishing we could be shot down in a comfortable way, and have a comfortably exciting escape'. These thoughts naturally led on to what would happen if the shooting down was fatal:

> I have just found myself thinking how sad it would be if I were killed. Sudden pictures of my family opening the little bag with my things in it sent back to them by the Americans. I wonder what they would do with the American cigarettes and the orange I picked off the floor during this morning's lecture [...] Would they eat the orange, or keep it as a souvenir?[368]

This flippant nonsense hid a serious truth. It shows that when in grave danger his uppermost thoughts would have been for his family, for his mother and father, and his much loved brother, Shubbs.

Perhaps as he lay on the bare floor at Bena Sita that night, he remembered how, before leaving England, he had asked his family to keep their fingers crossed for his safe return. Those ordinary, affectionate, formulaic words were now about to take on an almost supernatural resonance. He cannot have realised how deeply his mother would take those words to heart when news of the outcome of the Arnhem battle began to reach home.

On the morning of Saturday 23 September, the prisoners were searched again, a process which Hibbert noted was carried out 'most inefficiently'. The officers were ordered to take everything out of their pockets and place the contents in individual piles. Then an NCO with two guards came round and searched each officer in his turn.

> There was no effort to keep the searched from the unsearched and all the officers were milling about. As soon as we saw what was 'contraband', all the officers who had not yet been searched hid these objects under the carpet or gave them to officers who had already been searched. Unfortunately they found and took one of my watches, but I succeeded in saving three for other people. We were caught on one thing. They took away all chocolate and food we had got, and all cigarettes over twenty per individual. The first two officers were caught badly on that, but most of the remainder managed to hide or eat everything before they were searched.

About midday the prisoners received a meagre lunch, and then two German officer interpreters arrived to take down their details, for they were to begin the journey to Germany that afternoon. Hibbert commented:

This really consisted of splitting us into parties of thirty and taking our name, rank and serial number. Up till this time no effort had been made to take a nominal roll. In fact, this one taken now was very inefficient and I and several other people did not have our names taken.

The roll call was taken so inefficiently that, when the time came to board his truck, Killick managed to evade having his name taken, and the guards checked thirty instead of thirty-one onto the lorry. Killick's subsequent attempt to escape by hiding under the lorry's tarpaulin ended in farce; within less than 24 hours he was back with the other prisoners.[369]

Throughout the afternoon, lorries continued to turn up haphazardly at odd intervals, no attempt being made to organise a convoy. As each lorry arrived, a batch of around twenty-five to thirty prisoners would be loaded into it and taken away. The first load, of other ranks or NCOs, left about half past three in the afternoon. Hibbert noted that the officers were being saved until last. 'This suited our books very well, as it gave us less time before darkness fell.' Meanwhile:

we amused ourselves by baiting the two interpreters. One of them especially rose to every bait dangled in front of him. He had his Nazi creeds and arguments off by heart, and reeled them out like a gramophone [...] We asked him what logical excuse Germany had for invading Poland; his reply was to ask us what excuse we had for invading the Boers in 1899. We were soon back to the Wars of the Austrian Succession, the Seven Years War, the Thirty Years War, and back to Charlemagne.

The other interpreter was 'oldish' and 'quite a sensible chap', and he obligingly told the prisoners that they were to be taken back to the Army HQ prisoner of war cage, and from there by train to a prison camp in Bavaria, not far from Munich. Hibbert thought that the man envied them because they were getting out of the war.

Then another argument started about how could Germany claim to be a civilised country if it had concentration camps. The first interpreter asked how the British could claim that they were fighting for a better civilisation when the Russians, their allies, were 'cruel, uncivilised, and little more than criminals'.

When his most potent arguments were met with howls of laughter by everyone, he grew very angry, but by this time Freddie Gough had lost every trace of temper, and let fly for ten minutes without pausing for breath, saying exactly what he thought of Germany, the Germans, the Nazi Party, and exactly what the Allies would do to Germany when we got there.

Perhaps fortunately at this moment their lorry arrived, and the discussion was at an end.

22

MURDER

This event made a huge impression on us. These British boys have been in our minds forever and all the years long we have remembered them in silence.

Jeanne Slijkoord (née Veldkamp), Dutch eyewitness at Brummen

The truck which had arrived at Bena Sita was a typical army lorry with tailboard and wooden side-boards about three feet high. It being a fine September afternoon, the usual tarpaulin roof had been stacked inside the lorry, making it easier for the guards to keep watch over their prisoners.

The exact number of the German crew is uncertain but it seems to have consisted of five men: a driver and co-driver; two Luftwaffe guards armed with pistols and rifles, who would stand or sit by the tailboard; and an SS soldier with the insignia of an SS Unterscharführer, a rank corresponding to something between a corporal and a sergeant in the British Army. During the journey, the Unterscharführer would stand on the running board next to the driver's door. He was armed with a Schmeisser, a short, stubby, easily handled submachine gun.[370]

Those who now boarded the lorry were a mixed bunch, mostly officers. From 1st Parachute Brigade HQ, there were at least five men, including Anthony, Tony Hibbert, Bernard Briggs, Cecil Byng-Maddick, and Douglas Mortlock. From Frost's 2nd Parachute Battalion, the prisoners included Lieutenants Jim Flavell and Albert Tannenbaum, Captain Duncan McLean who was the Adjutant, and Privates Sydney Allen and George McCracken. McCracken was the batman of Captain S.C. Panter, Officer Commanding of 2nd Parachute Support Company, but it is not known if Panter was also on the truck. 1st Airborne Reconnaissance Squadron was represented by the only three of its men who had got through to the bridge: its commanding officer, Major Freddie Gough, together with Lieutenant Trevor McNabb and Captain Tony Platt. Other officers on the truck included Major Bill Arnold of 1st Airlanding Anti-Tank Battery and Major Dennis Mumford of 1st Airlanding Light Regiment. The remainder of the prisoners came from units as disparate as the Glider Pilot Regiment, the 7th (Galloway) King's Own Scottish Borderers, the Royal Army Service Corps, and the Military Police.

There were about twenty-five to thirty passengers in all. Space was very cramped, and men had to stand, holding onto the metal framework of the tarpaulin roof. Eventually Anthony and another prisoner would find a seat on the metal roof of the cab.[371]

The truck left Velp and began the journey towards Germany, travelling along the main road which led to Zutphen, some fifteen miles away. Zutphen was a small, very old and very beautiful city, almost as untouched by the war as Arnhem had been six days before. Located on the banks of the River IJssel, it had an industrial area known as Bedrijventerrein de Mars where huge warehouses were situated which could be utilised for holding large numbers of prisoners of war. It was almost certainly for one of these warehouses that the lorry was making on the first leg of its journey.

About 25 miles further on, right on the German border, lay the much larger city of Enschede. The first Dutch city to fall in 1940, it had been considerably damaged by Allied bombing because it was known that a German command centre was located there. Zutphen and Enschede were soon to become inextricably associated with the tragedy which was about to unfold.

The prisoners on the lorry were tense and uncomfortable. The lorry travelled at great speed, flinging around corners to deter escape attempts and get the journey done with as soon as possible. Allied aircraft were very active in the district, and would attack moving vehicles which they recognised to be German. The guards would also have been conscious that night would be falling soon and would have wanted to get rid of the responsibility of their charges as quickly as possible.

In Bena Sita the matter of escaping had been urgently debated, and Hibbert and Mumford were amongst those most eager to do so. The truck journey was almost certainly going to be their last chance to escape before they were taken across the border into Germany. Now that they were actually in transit, they prepared themselves for possible action by taking up a position at the tailboard, on the edge of the crowd of passengers. In the built-up areas there were still far too many Germans about, but once the truck entered flat, open farmland all that was needed was a good opportunity and a drop in the speed of the fast-moving lorry.

Meanwhile, they and some of the other passengers contented themselves by making V for Victory signs at the Dutch population they passed along the way, and were delighted when they received a reply. Making the V-Victory sign was strictly forbidden to the civilian population, and the guards began to get increasingly irritated by the prisoners' blatant defiance. In particular, the SS Unterscharführer on the running board took marked exception to it.

Aged around 23–25, with an accent which showed his origin to be central or northern Germany, the Unterscharführer belonged to the elite 9th SS Panzer Division, the Hohenstaufen, and there was an Hohenstaufen arm title on his uniform. Slight in build and not particularly tall, he was not the stereotypical handsome Aryan warrior with blonde hair and blue eyes. Instead, witnesses would describe him as having a sallow complexion, brownish eyes, curly black hair, a pointed chin, and – most chillingly of all – 'Jewish' features.[372]

For an SS soldier to look Jewish was at the very least to invite teasing and bating from his comrades, at the worst could lead him to the fate of nearly all Jews under the Third Reich. Perhaps this led to the Unterscharführer having a short fuse for provocation; perhaps he had been brutalised by his wartime service; but whatever the reason for his reaction, he was soon simmering with rage and resentment. Hibbert would later recall that he came back twice 'to say he would shoot us if we did not stop signing to the Dutch. Well, we just thought they would behave like the Brits' – that is to say, pass it all off as high spirits.[373] The more rebellious and reckless of the prisoners continued to make V-Victory signs and flout the guards' authority. The Unterscharführer's self-control must have rested on a knife edge, needing very little to break it altogether.

Around five or six miles from Velp, still going at great speed, the truck entered the large village of Brummen. Brummen was located between the River IJssel and the canal between Dieren and Apeldoorn. It was a prosperous place with pleasant streets and pretty houses, but like all Holland had been severely affected by the Occupation. In the marketplace one of the houses had become the local headquarters of the 'Organisation Todt' under Albert Speer's Ministry of Armaments and War Production. The Germans often set up local check-points to round up able-bodied men for work on the anti-invasion defences – trenches, tank traps, and other fortifications, which they were building along the River IJssel.

Brummen was already being overrun by refugees from Arnhem. Over the coming days the Germans would forcibly clear the entire town, and a number of those who had lost their homes and nearly all their belongings would end up in Brummen in the most rudimentary lodgings. But even though the British had lost the Arnhem battle, most of the Dutch still saw them as heroes and liberators, and would not blame them for the Germans' reprisals.

On that warm still Saturday, several batches of prisoners had already gone through Brummen, driven past in lorries or marched through under armed guard. Many villagers came out to see them pass. They would never forget the vivid colour of the prisoners' red berets, or their smiling cheerfulness as they whistled or sang the archetypal song of European resistance, 'It's a long, long way to Tipperary'. The villagers gave them what support they could without provoking the Germans' ire. A local dentist named Donkersgoed had already taken things too far by openly laughing with the prisoners and encouraging them; one of the German soldiers had furiously grabbed him by the arm and forced him to join the march.[374]

When the lorry carrying Anthony, Hibbert, Gough, and the others appeared on the outskirts of Brummen in the early evening, its arrival was immediately noticed. People greeted the prisoners with surreptitious smiles and friendliness. Some displayed an item coloured orange, the Dutch national colour, or gave the V-Victory sign.[375]

Travelling into the centre of Brummen, the truck came down the side of Markt Plein, the marketplace, and followed the sharp bend of Zutphensestraat, the road which led to Zutphen. There were many people in the marketplace because it was the time of the weekly distribution of a small loaf of bread and piece of meat for those who had been forced to work on the River IJssel fortifications.[376] Owing to a combination of the bend in the road and the crowd of people, the speeding lorry was forced to slow right down.

Witness reports are contradictory about what happened next. Gough thought that one or two guards got off the lorry in order to deal with some small boys who were openly making the V-Victory sign; these boys then ran off.[377] A Dutch witness said that some Dutch girls, on seeing the paratroopers, gave the V-Victory sign, whereupon one of the guards pointed a revolver at the girls, and a prisoner seized the revolver and shot the guard.[378] Alternative accounts say that it was the escape attempt of Hibbert and Mumford which began the massacre, because one of the British soldiers shot a guard, either to assist the escape attempt or in a bid to take over the lorry. The British witnesses were unanimous, however, in believing that it was the Germans themselves who accidentally shot the guard when they opened fire on Hibbert and Mumford.

Whatever began the chain reaction which led to the mass shooting, the major precipitating factor was undoubtedly Hibbert and Mumford's break for freedom. Mumford was the first to go, jumping off on the left side of the lorry, whilst Hibbert prepared to vault over the high sideboards to the right. As he did so, the Luftwaffe guard next to him began to turn round, shouting, 'Nein, nein'. Hibbert called to his neighbour to keep the guard busy, and jumped. He hit the road hard, fell forward on his face, and cut his eye, hands, and both knees. With lightening reflexes, he jumped up and ran for his life, zig-zagging to escape the bullets which had started flying past him. Good fortune blessed him and he came to a small alleyway, ducked down it, vaulted a fence, broke a hole through another fence, and raced through several gardens before he reached a large road. Not knowing how many Germans were in the neighbourhood, he decided to go to ground even though he had not got very far. He found a small hut filled with logs of wood, got inside, and concealed himself beneath them.

As Hibbert had dropped to the ground, he and Gough had suddenly seen another German lorry, full of SS troops, coming very fast from the opposite direction. The driver of the second lorry, noticing the escape, pulled up and signalled to the first lorry to do the same. SS men jumped off the second lorry, opened fire on the fugitives and gave chase. The firing was wild and indiscriminate, and the Dutch civilians in the marketplace fled in horrified panic.

One of the villagers, Jeanne Veldkamp, a schoolgirl of nearly seven, ran back to her home a few yards away on the corner of Markt Plein and Zutphensestraat. Together with her parents and two older sisters, she watched the scene from behind the curtains of their living room. She saw the first lorry move forward again; it came round the blind bend at the beginning of Zutphensestraat and then braked to a violent stop almost in the middle of the road. It had halted in front of the Post Office, a large, handsome building which stood in a quiet and pleasant street.

The sequence of events at Brummen happened with such lightening speed and such nightmarish consequences that it is not surprising that the eyewitness reports – both Dutch and British – contradict one another on several minor points, including exactly where and how the shooting into the interior of the lorry began. Several of the surviving British witnesses would give statements to the War Crimes Group after the war, but not all of them had had a good view because of the dense crowding in the truck. Cecil Byng-Maddick's post-war statement reflected the situation:

> It was difficult to see, owing to the crowding, exactly what was happening but a few shots were fired, one of which punctured the right-hand back wheel of our truck. Presumably these shots were fired at the escaping officers. The truck pulled up and after it had stopped a burst of light automatic fire opened up. I then realised that the fire was aimed into the truck. I then saw that it was fired by the German on the right-hand running board of the truck, and he had climbed up by the cab. He fired about 30 rounds – the whole magazine. No one was attempting to escape at the time and I could see no reason why he should fire at us.[379]

Byng-Maddick's statement which described the SS Unterscharführer ('the German on the right-hand running board') as firing from up by the cab was not echoed in Douglas Murray's statement. It read:

> We were very tightly packed, being in all about 25 or 30.
> The first thing I knew was that the truck pulled up with a bump and I saw the SS guard get off the running board and run to the back of the truck. He then fired into the truck with a Tommy Gun. As far as I know no one was escaping then. At any rate, as he fired into the middle of the truck, he couldn't have been firing at anyone escaping. He fired the whole magazine – between 20 and 30 rounds – and then tried to put in another magazine which wouldn't fit. He then went to the side of the road, where another SS man joined him. The second SS man pulled out his pistol and took a pot shot into the truck. I don't know if this shot did any damage. As a result of the first SS man's shooting, there were four killed and five or six wounded. The only one I knew was Major Anthony Cotterell, Royal Fusiliers, who was wounded. The Luftwaffe guard was killed.[380]

The second SS soldier would be described by witnesses as fair-haired with a bandage on his head. When the War Crimes Group began the search for the two perpetrators, the composite description taken from the witnesses gave the following portrait of him: '5 8″–5 9″ in height; age 21–23; weight about 11 stone; fair hair; fresh complexion; showed signs of having been in the battle and was wounded.'[381]

Lieutenant Wilfred Morley of the Military Police also saw the second SS man fire into the truck, and he too believed that the main burst of gunfire had come from the back of the lorry.

> The next thing I knew there were bullets whistling past me. They were definitely coming from the rear of the vehicle. I rolled over the cab and took cover by the radiator. I then saw another SS man was standing about 15 yards from the right-hand side of the vehicle firing a pistol into the vehicle.[382]

Captain Trevor Livesey's statement gives a highly plausible explanation of why the first SS soldier, the Unterscharführer, was at the back of the truck.

> The first thing I heard was a shot. The truck started to pull up and the SS Guard on the right-hand running board jumped off, stumbled and got up. As he got up, the truck had passed

him and was pulling up. He was about five yards from the back of the truck when he fired. As he fired, the truck stopped with a bump and I fell forward and I think that that is what saved my life.[383]

Though Livesey does not elaborate, his account raises the immediate suspicion that the SS Unterscharführer, who had become so angry with the prisoners during the journey, had finally lost the last shreds of his self-control. In tripping up, he had made himself look foolish in front of his comrades, his prisoners, and a conquered people. Up on his feet again, his instantaneous reaction was to machine-gun the prisoners at almost point-blank range. He was beside himself with rage and, quite possibly, fear that further prisoners would escape.

The hail of machine-gun bullets hit several prisoners. The two members of Gough's 1st Airborne Reconnaissance Squadron were mortally wounded, Tony Platt dying instantly, Trevor McNabb being shot through the lung. Kenneth Mills, the only member of the Glider Pilot Regiment present, also died instantly. From 2nd Parachute Battalion, Albert Tannenbaum was hit in the thigh and stomach, whilst the two privates were fatally injured, Sydney Allen dying at the scene and George McCracken receiving a mortal wound to the head. The commanding officer, Gough, one of those men who bear a charmed life, did not receive so much as a scratch although two of those killed had been standing close up against him.[384]

The seventh man seriously wounded by the automatic fire was Anthony. But though the injuries which he suffered were severe (they will be described later), his life did not appear to be in immediate danger.

The scene was now absolute confusion: a welter of blood; shouting in English and German; the Germans so highly aroused that a massacre was imminent. Once again there is confusion about the exact sequence of events. Gough remembered 'those of us who were capable of doing so' being ordered off the lorry and placed sitting in a semi-circle on the road with their hands above their heads. Gough had not the slightest doubts of the gravity of the situation:

By this time there were four or five SS men, all of whom were in a highly excited condition, and it is no exaggeration to state that it seemed that it was their intention to shoot the remainder of us as we sat on the ground. We were not allowed to help our wounded, who were left lying on the lorry.[385]

Flavell, who had been splattered with the blood of the wounded, had exactly the same feeling about the SS soldiers:

There was no more shooting but they were all shouting with rage or fear and ordered all of us prisoners to get off the lorry and told to sit in the roadway with our hands behind our heads. To this day, I believe that the Germans were very afraid of us – but believe me, when ordered off the lorry I had a very strong feeling [...] that the SS soldiers were about to shoot and kill me and the other prisoners.[386]

Once seated cross-legged on the ground, Flavell lent against the back of another prisoner whom he did not know and felt some kind of vibrations through the man's back. 'It transpired he was praying. I decided it was also time to pray.'[387]

As if in the heightened colours of a dream, Flavell next observed two things. The first was a Dutch doctor, dressed in a long dark-coloured raincoat and wearing a felt hat, who appeared on the scene to give aid to the wounded and the dying. The Germans violently refused to let him near the British, but ordered him to look at the Luftwaffe soldier who had been shot. The doctor inspected the body, and shook his head from side to side. The second thing Flavell observed took place on the far side of the road. There were two houses opposite him, and the left-hand house had white lace curtains. Suddenly he noticed the curtain was being drawn back slightly, and in the dark interior he could see a fair-haired woman and a fair-haired child. 'My eyes met with those of the woman – we both very quickly and carefully exchanged the V-sign and the curtain closed.' In such a scene of horror, with 'the SS raving about', this tiny glimpse of feminine kindness must have seemed close to a supernatural vision.[388]

The Dutch doctor who had come to treat the wounded was named Anton Korteweg. About 40, built like a bear, and well over six foot tall, Korteweg had a natural air of authority which stopped the Germans from shooting him on the spot for his interference. Nonetheless, they handled him so roughly that Gough thought that they were indeed about to kill him. 'He was most persistent, however, and eventually gained his point.'[389] After the war, Korteweg would be decorated by the British for his immense courage at this critical juncture.[390]

At last the wounded began to receive some form of medical assistance. Meanwhile, Mumford had been brought back, having been knocked unconscious by the butts of his captors' guns. Gough and the others managed to smuggle him amongst themselves, so that he would not be noticed by 'the more hysterical gentlemen, who were brandishing their pistols in front of us'.[391]

The Germans were now arguing violently amongst themselves, and it seemed that they were debating whether to shoot everyone there and then in front of the civilian population, or take them down the road and do it. In this highly charged and volatile situation, anything might have happened. But then suddenly, as if by a miracle, a third German vehicle chanced upon the scene. It was a Volkswagen staff car travelling from the direction of Arnhem. There was an officer in the car, attended by two other men, the driver and an interpreter in the uniform of a Sonderführer, an army specialist who had not been through full military training. All three were Wehrmacht, the regular German Army, and all three were attached to Field Marshal Model's Heeresgruppe B. The Wehrmacht officer, who spoke extremely good English, had been allocated to the interrogation of British prisoners and was on his way to the prisoner of war cage at Zutphen.

He would later be remembered vividly by the British officers. The description of him given by Finlay Wilson was very accurate. He was about 38, 'medium height, fairly broad, clean-shaven, pleasant, rather weather-beaten face, smiled when speaking'.[392] Both Finlay Wilson and Gough would talk to the officer once the situation had calmed down, and then he would freely tell them his name – Gustav Etter.

Etter's car had been following the same route as the prisoners' lorry, and as it rounded the blind bend from the marketplace, it came across an extraordinary scene. In Etter's account (though not in that of the British prisoners), he arrived before the prisoners had been taken off the lorry, seconds after the shooting had temporarily ceased. He saw the lorry, partially blocking the road, and behind it, about six feet away, the SS Unterscharführer, pointing a machine gun at the passengers whom Etter immediately recognised were soldiers from a British airborne unit. They were standing rigid with fear at the back of the truck, and making no movement or attempt to escape.

Etter was an Oberleutnant and as such he outranked the SS guards at the scene. The SS were so lawless, with such a terrifying reputation, that had Etter not been sufficiently high-ranking he might have been too intimidated to interfere. As it was, he immediately took charge of the situation. Shouting to the SS Unterscharführer to cease firing, he jumped from the car and asked what was happening. The Unterscharführer told him that two British officers had escaped, and that a Luftwaffe guard, of the rank of Obergefreiter, had been killed by the British. He pointed out the body which was lying about nine feet behind the truck. Etter recalled:

> The body of this Obergefreiter was lying on its back, with the hands raised and the fingers clenched. I did not go any closer to the body and from where I was standing, which was at a distance of about two and a half metres, I did not observe any wounds nor did I see any

blood on the ground. I did not examine the body of this Obergefreiter, as it was obvious that he was dead.

The SS Unterscharführer gave me the impression of being extremely incensed (*sehr entrüstet*). He did not fire again after I had given him the order to stop firing (*feuer einstellen*). This order is the customary order in the German army which is used to bring the weapons back to the position of at rest and on safe, and therefore is the proper order to give to prevent a repetition of firing or to stop firing in progress. He explained to me that he had had the impression that further prisoners were trying to escape, and for that reason he had fired at the prisoners who were on the truck.[393]

Though Etter's statement portrays him as acting calmly, authoritatively, and in line with the correct procedure, witnesses would recall him shouting in a rage at the SS Unterscharführer, 'What are you doing? These are British soldiers, not Russians.'[394]

Etter would also state that it was he who ordered the prisoners to jump down from the truck, and that he then asked for the senior officer present.

I had these prisoners of war collected in front of the lorry, on the right-hand side of the road; then accompanied by Major Gough, I went to look at the wounded who were lying in the back of the lorry.

With Etter's permission, Dr Korteweg was allowed to help the wounded, who were removed from the lorry to aid their treatment. The dead were also taken off the truck and laid by the side of the road.

Anthony was being cared for by one of the other prisoners, John Cairns. Cairns would later write to Anthony's mother:

He appeared to be fairly badly hurt but never for a moment [did it cross] my mind that he would not recover [...] He was rather in pain but fortunately I had a morphia syringe with me and this appeared to bring relief. A Dutch civilian doctor had appeared and under his direction I bandaged Anthony's wounds.[395]

The exact wounds which Anthony had suffered would later be very difficult for witnesses to recall, but what seems clear is that no one at the scene was expecting him to die. Korteweg would surely have treated him himself if he had considered Anthony's life to be in any danger; instead he treated those who had been critically injured.

One of the Dutch witnesses, Jaap Detmar, who was 22 at the time of the shooting, would remember the wounded stripped of their upper clothing so that they could be medically examined, sitting on their heels in front of the fence of the Post Office. One of these men had a bleeding wound in his right shoulder, exactly the same injury which would later be identified as being the most serious that Anthony had suffered. No other injured man who was fully conscious had a similar wound. The type of wound and the fact that the wounded man was well enough to sit upright by the fence suggests very strongly that the man whom Jaap Detmar saw was Anthony. Detmar's father crossed the road in order to give this prisoner a glass of water. A German soldier forbad Mr Detmar to come any closer and threatened to shoot him, telling him to give the water to the dead Luftwaffe guard instead.

'This German doesn't need water anymore,' Mr Detmar said.

'Get away and hands up,' was the German's reply.

Jaap Detmar remembered his father coming back, trembling, the glass of water still in his hand.[396]

Only Korteweg was allowed close to the wounded; no other Dutch were allowed near them.

One of the Brummen eyewitnesses would later recall that she noticed one of the wounded laughing; she was amazed that he could do so in such horrific circumstances. Geoffrey, who heard this story when in Brummen after the war, clearly thought that this unknown man was Anthony: 'It doesn't seem unlikely to me.'[397] Geoffrey, knowing his brother so well, saw no incongruity in Anthony meeting terrible adversity with his usual irreverent wit. He would have had pity for the other wounded, but none at all for himself. His particular form of courage was always to discover the absurd in his own predicaments.

At this point, Anthony was still effectively incognito. He had not been singled out from the other prisoners during his captivity, and none of the Germans had realised who he was. Had not a final element been added to the drama, the mystery of his subsequent disappearance may perhaps have been more simply answered, or indeed he may not have disappeared at all. But a few minutes after Etter had taken charge, something happened which would later take on the most sinister implications: a Wehrmacht Unteroffizier arrived on the scene, a soldier-journalist who worked for the Propaganda Ministry and collected news for German-controlled Radio Hilversum.

Of medium height and slim build, the man had blonde hair, sharp features, blue eyes, and spectacles. Before the war ended, Etter would meet this soldier-journalist again two or three times at the HQ of Heeresgruppe B. He would characterise him as lively, nervous and intelligent, with a doctorate in economics. Either then or at Brummen, the Unteroffizier told him that he had spent a considerable time in South America, and intended to return there at the end of the war which he regarded as as good as lost.[398]

The Unteroffizier journalist, sniffing out a good story, immediately took an obtrusive interest in what was going on. Somehow or other he found out Anthony's full name – in a later statement he would claim that Gough had particularly pointed out Anthony. The Unteroffizier journalist either recognised Anthony's name or immediately grasped that his fellow journalist's terrible predicament would do to spice up a pedestrian batch of news.

> Hereupon I mounted one of the trucks and looked at the bodies lying there in their blood. I could, of course, not establish which actually were dead or only unconscious, or very nearly dying. I asked the people on the vehicle, who were very excited, where I could find the correspondent. I approached him and he (the correspondent) then murmured in a low voice 'I am dying' or words to that effect. I stayed a few minutes at the place where the incident occurred, to get a clear picture of what actually had happened and met a German officer, who, however, was that terribly excited that he was not able to give me some more particulars.

The excited German officer was clearly Etter. The Unteroffizier journalist's statement added that he got the impression that Etter was 'extremely indignant and that he regretted the incident as much as myself'.[399] Despite this later sanctimonious gloss, the journalist actually wanted to interview Anthony – yet another indication that Anthony was not *in extremis* – but was prevented from doing so by Etter. At some stage, the journalist apparently gave up and went elsewhere. But the damage had been done. Anthony's significance had suddenly been recognised, not only by the journalist but also, due to the journalist's interest, by Etter himself.

The care of the wounded was now taking precedence. Jeanne Veldkamp, the seven year old girl who lived across the way, remembered the scene vividly, how the Germans were in a great state of excitement, and ran about knocking on doors asking for ladders. Butt either people had no ladders or they didn't want to give them to the Germans, so the Germans would run on to the next house.

> The Germans were very agitated [...] My parents saw our position behind the window of our living room was too dangerous, and we went to the loft of our house. From a window we had a

view on the whole scene on the German truck and on the place of execution. We saw how the Germans placed the victims on the gathered ladders. Some of the boys were badly injured, while others were not alive any more. They stacked all the victims on one side of the truck. After that the survivors had to board the truck, and the truck [went on] its way to Zutphen.[400]

There being no stretchers to hand, ladders – often used in battlefield conditions by the Germans – were the best available substitute. The ladders would become part of the general confusion of the story after Anthony disappeared. Gough would recall Anthony being on a ladder rather than a stretcher. This Geoffrey would take to mean that Anthony had not been too badly hurt, otherwise he would have been on a stretcher at the dressing station to which the wounded were subsequently taken. Another witness would see a ladder at the dressing station, and wonder at the incongruous sight and how it got there.[401]

Korteweg would later say that there were many Red Cross vans about. However, no attempt was made to provide a more suitable means of transport than the truck for the gravely wounded.[402] Korteweg also told the Germans that they must urgently take the wounded to the nearest hospital, which was in Zutphen. He would go there to enquire the next day, only to discover that there was no trace of them.[403]

The German care for the wounded was, in fact, of the most perfunctory nature. Once the decision had been taken to move the injured on, they were simply loaded back in the crowded truck, next to – some witnesses say on top of – the bodies of those who had been killed. The Germans showed just as little respect for their own dead comrade. A Dutch witness would remember them swinging the corpse unceremoniously by its arms and legs up into the truck, an action so shocking that it seemed to him to epitomise the heartless nature of the Germans.[404]

At some point, perhaps before the truck left Brummen, one of the airborne soldiers, Finlay Wilson, had the presence of mind to write down Etter's name on a piece of paper. Etter, who either sympathised with the prisoners or was hedging his bets should Germany lose the war, went so far as to give him his home address as well. This piece of paper was confiscated some three or four days later when Finlay Wilson and the others were interrogated at a camp at Oberüsel. All that he or Gough could subsequently remember was that the Wehrmacht officer who had helped them had a name which sounded like Etter, Etting or Ettinger, and that his home was in Stuttgart. They would also recall how he told them that he had once worked in England and had been engaged to an English girl. When an extensive search came to be made for Etter after the war, these were the sole scraps of information to go by.

Anthony as a baby being held by his mother, Mintie. His aunt Janie is front right. At the back (left to right) are Ivor Pool (Janie's husband) and Frank Crews, the brother of Mintie and Janie. The third woman is unknown. (Geoffrey Cotterell)

Geoffrey, Mintie and Anthony. (Geoffrey Cotterell)

The Cotterell family at the seaside *c.*1927. (Geoffrey Cotterell)

The Cotterell family at Ham Frith, used as a publicity shot for an article Anthony was writing. A very young-looking Geoffrey is on the left, with a Royal Artillery badge on his shoulder. (Geoffrey Cotterell)

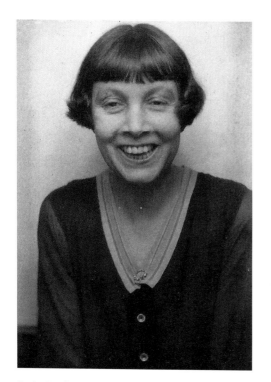

Janie Pool, Antony's aunt, in the late 1930s. (Geoffrey Cotterell)

Anthony at the seaside, probably Brighton, c.1939. (Geoffrey Cotterell)

Anthony the conscript, June 1940.
(Geoffrey Cotterell)

Anthony as a cub reporter. (Geoffrey Cotterell)

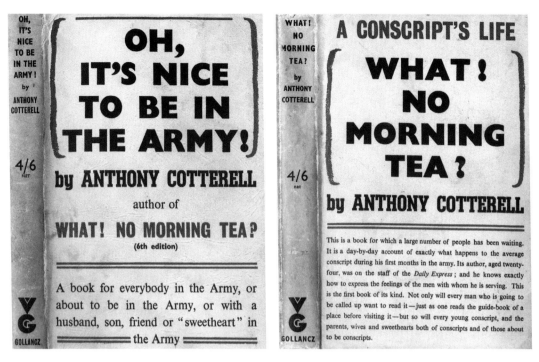

The covers of *What! No Morning Tea* and *Oh, It's Nice to be in the Army!* (Author)

Ernest Watkins in Iceland. (Tim and Nicholas Watkins)

Anthony in the WAR office with Captain Lionel Birch. (Geoffrey Cotterell)

TIGER, TIGER, BURNING BRIGHT

WAR

Issued fortnightly by
THE ARMY BUREAU
OF CURRENT AFFAIRS

RESTRICTED. The information given in this publication is not to be communicated either directly or indirectly, to the Press or to any person not authorised to receive it.

No. 76   August 19th, 1944

Cover of WAR. (Author)

British Reconnaissance Photograph, taken 18 September 1944 – the H-shaped building just to the right of centre is Brigade HQ where Anthony spent the battle. On the bridge are the remains of the ambushed German convoy.

British prisoners being marched through Ellecom under guard. Ellecom is 3 miles from Brummen. Similar scenes would have taken place in Brummen on the day of the shooting. (Kriegsberichter E Seeger, Bundearchiv Koblenz 590/2330/5A)

Before and after: the building with the belvedere is the one in which Anthony, Tony Hibbert, and 1st Parachute Brigade HQ spent the battle. (Gelders Archief, Arnhem)

Sint-Eusebiuskerk seen from across the Grote Markt shortly after the battle. The Markt was where the prisoners were assembled before being taken to the church, and was also the scene of the execution of some Dutch patriots. (de Booys)

The prisoners being held at Sint-Eusebiuskerk from the 1944 Christmas book of 10 SS-Panzer Division: *Buczacz – Caen – Nimwegen: Der Kampf der 10.SS-Division-Frundsberg im Jahre 1944.* (Bob Gerritsen)

Young German soldiers at Arnhem. In the background is seen the Musis Sacrum music hall on the Velperplein. The driver is from the Waffen-SS. (Kriegsberichter E Seeger, Bundesarchiv Koblenz 590/2330/13A)

Bena Sita, the villa in Velp where the prisoners slept the night before the shooting. (Jim Flavell)

Ernst Tigges, the Unteroffizier journalist who arrived at Brummen just after the shooting. (National Archives, WO309-847)

Gustav Etter in 1929, the Wehrmacht officer who prevented further shootings. The photograph was sent to the War Crimes Group by the British Criminal Investigation Department, County Borough of Bolton Police, in a report dated 7 December 1945. (National Archives, WO309-1951)

Tony Hibbert (left) and Cecil Byng-Maddick (centre), with the American pilot of their Dakota. (Tony Hibbert)

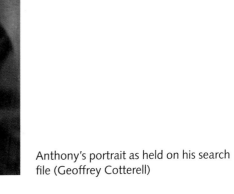

Anthony's portrait as held on his search file (Geoffrey Cotterell)

Geoffrey, Aps Tjeenk Willink, and Sergeant Gerrit Kamp at Aps' house in Brummen (where Tony Hibbert was given shelter in September–October 1944), spring 1946, at the height of the search. (Geoffrey Cotterell)

Geoffrey, Dick Tjeenk Willink, Aps Tjeenk Willink, and Sergeant Gerrit Kamp, spring 1946. (Geoffrey Cotterell)

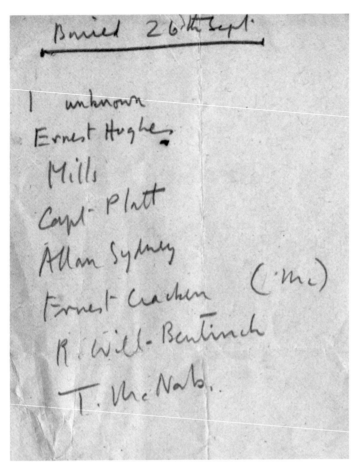

Burial list written by Geoffrey at the time of his first visit to Enschede General Cemetery in October 1945. (Geoffrey Cotterell)

Buried 26th Sept.

1 unknown
Ernest Hughes
Mills
Capt- Platt
Allan Sydney
Ernest Cracken   (.mc)
R. Will- Bentinch
T. McNab,.

St Joseph's Roman Catholic hospital at Enschede, possibly 1930s. (Author)

The 2009 memorial ceremony at the Brummen Post Office. This was where the truck stopped in 1944, and where the wounded were treated and the dead temporarily laid out. (Author)

Memorial tablet on the wall of the Post Office. (Author)

Above: The hallway of the dressing station in Rozenhoflaan, Zutphen, in modern times. Anthony was placed for a while at the foot of the stairs by the window whilst awaiting treatment for his wounds (Author)

Anthony's gravestone in Enschede General Cemetery. (Author)

23

THE DRESSING STATION AT ZUTPHEN

It is not certain what time the lorry left Brummen with its cargo of dead and wounded, with those who were unwounded standing around them. Gough thought that they had been in Brummen for an hour or more, and noted that it was getting dark. It was, therefore, probably after 7.00pm when the prisoners and their escorts left the village.

Gough had given his word that there would be no more escape attempts on the journey, nor were there. He travelled in Etter's Volkswagen car, possibly as some sort of hostage for good behaviour, or perhaps because Etter simply wanted to talk to him. Bill Arnold may also have been in the car – he would later be at the dressing station with Gough – and Etter appears to have taken a strong liking to them both.[405]

The journey was some ten miles, and for the wounded, who were being transported in a basic army lorry, lying upon hard ladders, every jolt must have brought terrible suffering. According to one witness, Anthony had collapsed in great pain after the shooting and now lay on the floor of the truck semi-conscious.[406]

Night would have fallen by the time that the lorry reached Zutphen. The black-out meant that nothing could be seen of the beautiful medieval city, with its tall spires and towers undamaged by the war. The lorry crossed the River IJssel, and entered the more modern outskirts of the city, close to the railway station.

The treatment of the wounded was secondary to making sure that the unwounded prisoners were safely locked up. The lorry's first stop was at a PoW cage, a large warehouse close to the river in the industrial region known as Bedrijventerrein de Mars. There were no facilities for treating the wounded there, so having counted all the able-bodied men off the truck, the lorry carrying the dead and wounded travelled on through the dark streets of Zutphen, Etter escorting it in his car. He would remain with the wounded until the last one of them had been treated because there was nobody else to interpret for them.

Etter must already have been in touch with his superiors, who would have authorised him to stay with the wounded. After questioning the SS guards at the scene, he had already written down a report on what had happened at Brummen and made two copies, one of which he handed in with the unwounded prisoners at the PoW cage. The other would be given to a SS-Hauptsturmführer who was Chief Intelligence Officer of the Second Panzer Corps, under whose command the Hohenstaufen had been placed; it was from this corps that Etter had originally received his orders to carry out the interrogation of prisoners captured by the Hohenstaufen.[407]

Etter would also make – or indeed had already made – a verbal report on the Brummen shooting to Anton Staubwasser, Chief Intelligence Officer of Field Marshal Model's Heeresgruppe B. This verbal report to his commanding officer was almost certainly a phone call. Staubwasser had multiple responsibilities over a very wide area of territory, and it seems extremely unlikely that Etter met him in person to discuss what had happened at Brummen. No documentation appears to have survived about this conversation, so what was said is not known, nor how Staubwasser reacted.[408] After the war, Staubwasser would state categorically that he had no recollection of any conversation with Etter.

The shooting of unarmed prisoners was a very grave matter. Though Etter appears to have believed the SS Unterscharführer's story that he had acted to prevent a mass escape, nonetheless he – and perhaps Staubwasser – would have known that the guard's actions had been grotesquely disproportionate. Field Marshal Model strongly disapproved of any cruel treatment of prisoners, as did General Bittrich, his top commander at Arnhem. However, from an irritated comment which Etter let drop after the war, it is clear that the SS Unterscharführer had not been placed under arrest and was in fact still travelling with the prisoners. He was with the wounded in Zutphen, and Etter's irritation had been aroused by the assumption that the Unterscharführer would not have helped the men that he had shot.[409]

The fact that the Unterscharführer was still with them must have been extraordinarily difficult for the wounded to deal with.

The Zutphen dressing station proved difficult to locate. It appears that Etter and his party were first directed to a dressing station in Oude Wand which had been closed down the previous month. Further delays ensued before the truck drew up at the right place, situated in a short tree-lined street called Rozenhoflaan. Although the darkness prevented much detail being seen, the street was composed of fine terraced houses of large size, most of them being of four floors with airy reception rooms and long elegant windows. The pleasant nature of their accommodation had led to some of them being commandeered by the Germans. The German officers' casino was in one of these houses, and almost directly opposite it was No.12, the dressing station.

In the adjacent street, two minutes walk away, were the offices of the Ortskommandantur (District Command) of Zutphen, whilst in the opposite direction, in Coehoornsingel, also only two minutes walk away, was a large general hospital run by the Dutch. It was to this hospital that Dr Korteweg expected the wounded to be taken, and to which he would go the following day only to discover that there was no trace of them.

Like others in the street, No.12 Rozenhoflaan was large, with handsome rooms with high ceilings. The ground floor was an upper-ground floor, reached by four steps, the exact number of which was deliberately memorised by Gough who after the war would pass this detail on to the Cotterell family. He would also pass on other information, in particular that there were two back rooms and a window to the right of the front door, which most of the houses in the street did not have.[410] One year later, these slender details would help to positively identify No.12 as the dressing station in which Anthony had been treated.

As always during the Occupation, there were eyes watching what was happening in the street. The Dutch neighbours, silently observing, would afterwards report what they had seen, as Geoffrey would tell his mother the following November: 'the truck arriving, the bodies going in, the blood, the Germans shouting, the car (Etter's), the truck at one thirty in the morning, the bodies going out to it. (Yes, of course, they had watched everything <u>and</u> taken the name of the attendant).'[411]

At first there were no doctors and these had to be summoned, meaning yet more delay in the treatment of the wounded. Gough would later testify to the tragic consequences of this. McCracken, who had been shot in the head, was now 'beyond help', and Lieutenant McNabb was 'in a very bad condition which was almost entirely due to the exposure and shock subsequent to receiving his wounds'. When the doctors did finally arrive, however, Gough thought that the medical treatment which they gave was excellent.

There were two doctors, the man who was its usual medical officer and another man who had been brought in specially to deal with the large number of wounded. The first was a fat sleek blonde man who belonged to the Luftwaffe; the second was a naval doctor.

The wounded were treated in the large back room, which was separated from the front room by tall, folding wooden doors which could be opened up to form one beautiful elegant space. A pair of French windows gave onto a garden room, which overlooked the small town garden. In addition, there was a small square back room where Gough and Bill Arnold waited.

The treatment room had a black marble fireplace, high ceilings and beautiful proportions, which gave the sounds made within it a faint vibrato. There was an air raid on, and the doctors worked by the light of lanterns, which cast great shadows on the ornate plaster ceiling. There were the usual medical smells, mingled with that of tobacco smoke, for Etter had ordered one of the medical assistants to give the British some cigarettes.[412]

In addition to the four seriously injured men, there were also some lightly injured prisoners to be treated, and it seems that most of these were also in the back room, or possibly the garden room. As the guards were also present, the ground-floor of the house must have been very crowded. Tannenbaum would later remember that for a while Anthony was placed in the hallway at the foot of the staircase, where narrow steps with ornate banisters ascended steeply into the darkness of the upper floors.[413]

Tannenbaum, who had been seriously but not critically wounded, would later testify that the wounded were at No.12 for half to three-quarters of an hour, but this was almost certainly an underestimate; in his drugged state (he had been given morphine), he may have lost track of time. Gough thought that he himself was there for nearly two hours before being forced to leave by Etter. It was only after Gough left that Tannenbaum would be moved on, and not in the ambulance which Etter had promised Gough but in the same basic army lorry which had transported the wounded from Brummen.

Before being compelled to go, Gough went to see Anthony in the room where he had been treated. Anthony was very cheerful and assured Gough that he was not suffering pain unduly. Gough felt reassured about Anthony's physical condition, 'he was fairly bright and [...] I had no particular qualms about him', but a serious new concern was the interest which Etter was taking in Anthony now that he knew who he was.[414]

Gough's brief final conversation with Anthony would never be forgotten. After the war Gough would tell Geoffrey exactly what Anthony had said to him when they parted. Referring to Lord Vansittart, the diplomat whose writings and broadcasts argued that there was innate propensity to evil in the German people, Anthony quipped to Gough: 'If you get back home before me, tell Vansittart that he has another disciple in me.'

Imbued with his characteristic wit, style and bravery, these are the last known words that Anthony ever spoke or wrote. Once Gough unwillingly left him at the dressing station, obscurity closed over Anthony forever. From now on, nothing is certain about what he did or what was done to him. It is a supreme irony that a life as obsessively and minutely documented as his should now vanish into a welter of mysteries, contradictions, self-serving testimonies, wishful thinking, and anomalies. The one voice which could have made sense of it all was missing – and that was Anthony's.

PART FOUR

THE SEARCH: SEPTEMBER 1944 ONWARDS

A Tribute from the People of Holland

On 27 September 1944, a tribute from the people of Holland by the Dutch writer Johan Fabricius was broadcast on the BBC Home Service.

> For ten cruel days and nights the thoughts of the whole of Holland have been with your men [...] who were fighting in the heart of our little country for an ideal which is ours as well. We know what they must have been going through; we know what we owe them; we think of them as if they were our own boys.
>
> This is what I want to say to you. Your men are no foreigners to us. Maybe they never saw Holland before they floated down over it on a sunny afternoon to liberate her people and the world; maybe they do not speak our language, not one of them, and find it difficult even to pronounce the names of the places where they are fighting, suffering, dying. But they are no foreigners in Holland, and we hope they realise that.
>
> Some of these brave young men will stay behind in our country for ever. They will not rest on cold foreign soil. The soil of Holland, which, in the course of our long and glorious history, received so many heroes for their eternal sleep, will proudly guard your dead as if they were the deeply mourned sons of our own people.

WAR, issue 83, 9 December 1944

24

AFTER THE SHOOTING

After Hibbert had jumped from the lorry on that fateful afternoon of 23 September, he had hidden in a small hut until darkness fell. His subsequent wanderings and adventures did not last for long; extreme good fortune blessed him and he very quickly made contact with the Dutch resistance. On Monday 25 September, only two days after the shooting, a member of the resistance, Dick Tjeenk Willink, smuggled him back to his family house in Brummen, where at the most terrible risk to themselves the family kept him hidden for some three weeks.

The Tjeenk Willinks were one of the most prominent families in Brummen. Aps, the mother, came from a long line of doctors, and her father, who was in his eighties, was still practising. Aps had something rather grand in her manner, but underneath it she was extremely kind and courageous. An implacable opponent of the Germans, she quietly subverted their rule in ways which, if discovered, could easily have led to her being shot or sent to a concentration camp.[415] She lived with her two grown-up sons, Dick and Aat (short for Arendt). Her husband had died some time before, and he too had been a doctor, as was his father, and his father's father before him, and so on, stretching all the way back to Paracelsus probably.[416] Dick, the oldest son, was following in the family tradition and training to be a doctor in Utrecht, although he was often at home in Brummen. He had a faked X-ray of an old tuberculosis infection and a false certificate saying that he had active infectious tuberculosis, which worked very well in keeping German obtrusiveness at a distance.

In looks, manners and intelligence, Dick was rather like Anthony. When the Cotterells got to know the Tjeenk Willinks after the war, Dick's resemblance to Anthony would touch Mintie and Graham's hearts. Aat, the younger brother, was more Germanic-looking. He was very pleasant and very good company, but not of the same intellectual calibre.

During the Occupation, the Tjeenk Willinks brothers were prominent in the local resistance. The Netherlands had no organised resistance along the lines of the French Maquis; the unsuitability of the terrain, the smallness of the country, and the highly centralised nature of government, rendered a semi-military force impossible.[417] However, there were many other ways of sabotaging German rule. Perhaps one of the most dangerous was subverting the German system of food rationing. Food was desperately short as the Germans, contemptuously known as the Moffen, were appropriating huge quantities of it.[418] In a letter of October 1945, Geoffrey told Mintie how the Dutch went about redressing the balance.

> They used to print food coupons in Amsterdam or Rotterdam. The Dutch who did it immediately rang up and gave the underground a code message telling where they were going. Then underground gangs would break in and steal them. Dick was in many of these affairs, including one where the owner of the safe did not want to disclose the way to open it. They held a pistol to his chest, he opened the safe, they took the coupons out and put him in. Apparently he survived, but recognised no one, because 'Of course' said Dick, 'we were masked.' They then distributed the coupons to the hungry.

Dick and Aat also stole back pigs which the Germans had commandeered, and smuggled them over the river IJssel to distribute in Brummen (the penalty if caught was a minimum of four years in a concentration camp). Another trick was to substitute a little pig for a big pig, hoping that the Germans would not realise that the more valuable animal was missing.[419]

After Arnhem, when airborne soldiers who had escaped capture began to seek the help of the resistance, the Tjeenk Willink family became involved in ever more perilous schemes. In the course of one night, Dick, Aat and a farmer's boy dug an immense hole in the woods which became the refuge for ten parachutists. A farm woman cooked some food for them every night, and every night one of the Tjeenk Willinks would call for the food and take it to the woods.[420]

The Tjeenk Willinks' house was in Burgemeester de Wijslaan, a short walk from Brummen's marketplace. Aat had actually been in the marketplace at the time of the shooting. He had immediately run home to fetch Dick and Dr Korteweg, who lived next door. Korteweg seems to have arrived at the shooting independently, but Dick went back to the marketplace with Aat, where the Germans refused to let him near the wounded. It was thus that the family knew at first-hand what had happened that afternoon, and that one British soldier had probably escaped. After Hibbert made contact with the resistance, and it had been established that he was indeed who he said he was, the Tjeenk Willinks gladly gave him shelter.

Hibbert had heard some shooting as he ran for his life from the marketplace, but had no idea of the horrific events which were taking place there. It was only on the Tuesday, the day after the Tjeenk Willinks had taken him in, that Dick gave him the full details of what had happened. The news was absolutely shattering. Hibbert wrote in the diary which he kept throughout his time with the family:

> The account was rather confused but it seems that Dennis Mumford made a break to the left of the road, got into an orchard, and was then recaptured. But the terrible news is that two officers were killed and two wounded. They say that the NCO with the Schmeisser turned the gun on the lorry when I made a break for it, also that one German was killed by one of our own men. Apparently I was the only one to escape [...] I would willingly not have made the attempt had I known that it would have had such consequences.[421]

He also recorded the extremely unwelcome news that 30 Corps was still south of the river and no relief was in sight for the remnants of 1st Airborne Division. As a soldier, Hibbert knew that the end of the battle was in sight for the Division. Writing that same Tuesday of those still holding out at Oosterbeek, he wrote: 'They'd stuck it out for one week and must be getting near the end.'

News outlets in Holland were under rigid German control and no trustworthy information could be gleaned from them. Radios were illegal for Dutch civilians, but clandestine sets gathered information from the free Dutch station, Radio Oranje, which broadcast from London. In Brummen, the news was typed up and circulated on unofficial newsheets, the penalty for compiling and distributing which was death. Usually there were two such newsheets a day, one in the morning and one in the evening.[422] When Hibbert wrote his diary entry about the Division, news had not yet filtered through to these unofficial channels that in fact Oosterbeek had been evacuated the previous night – right under the Germans' noses, the birds had flown the coop.

The beleaguered forces at Oosterbeek had endured days and days of the most vicious shelling and mortaring. The defence centred on the Hartenstein Hotel, which by this stage of the battle was fast becoming a ruin, its garden full of shell craters, debris and fallen trees. The war diary of Freddie Gough's 1st Airborne Reconnaissance Squadron vividly – and with the most staggering and very English poise – recorded the deterioration of the situation.[423]

21st September
[...] 0900 – Capt Allsop reports to Div HQ. The hoped for message – that our friends across the river [30 Corps] have come, is still a ruthless red pencil mark on a map in London – not helpful here.[...]

22nd September
0730 – Fine morning – warm – spoilt by a terrific pounding of mortar bombs. [...]

23rd September
0700 – Rain and cold, lack of food and sleep is beginning to tell. Usual hymn to the morning Sun comes down in the form of mortar fire – heavier today than anything previous. [...]

24th September
0630 – Rain and the mortar bombs. This has no comparison to anything which has come our way previously. The ground shivers like a jelly. Bombs and shells coming into us from all directions.

0930 – A lull. Quite impossible to believe still alive.

1015 – Mortar fire commences mainly from the west. Clearly hear German orders. This is even more fierce than previous plastering. Many near misses. [...]

1930 – [...] Rain very heavy. Lack of food very much felt. Prospects are not at all sweet. Troops still cheerful.

It was on 24 September that the situation – no food, no water, little ammunition, countless dead and wounded – became untenable. Urquhart, who had endured all this with his men, realised that the defenders could not suffer the nightmare any longer. He put in motion a secret evacuation, based on the withdrawal from Gallipoli in 1915 which, as a young officer, he had studied very thoroughly for a promotion exam.[424] Under cover of night, boats would come secretly to ferry the troops across the Rhine. A bombardment would give the Germans something else to think about, whilst those unavoidably left behind – the wounded and those who were caring for them, the medical staff and padres – would maintain the illusion that the main body of the force was still there.

The troops had to go through enemy lines to reach the river, to a frontage reduced to not much more than a third of a mile. The risks of catastrophic failure were immense. Fortuitously, the weather turned out to be perfectly made for a clandestine exit, very dark with a strong wind and persistent heavy rain.

The classic account of the withdrawal was written by Stanley Maxted; it was broadcast on BBC radio after he reached safety and the evacuation was a *fait accompli*. The broadcast was a masterpiece – simple, evocative, and breathtakingly exciting. A transcript of it appeared in *WAR*, from which this extract is taken.[425]

When the various officers were told to transmit [the news of the evacuation] to the thin straggle of hard-pressed men around the pitifully small perimeter, a great silence seemed to come upon them even in the midst of the shelling – you see, day or night the shelling and mortaring never stopped. The ones I saw just drew a deep breath and said: 'Very good, sir.' Then those staring eyes in the middle of black, muddy masks saluted, as they always would, and faded away to crawl out on their stomachs and tell their men. [...]

Well, at two minutes past ten we clambered out of our slit trenches in an absolute din of bombardment – a great deal of it our own – and formed up in a single line [...] We held the tail of the coat of the man in front. We set off like a file of nebulous ghosts from our pock-marked and tree-strewn piece of ground. Obviously, since the enemy was all round us, we had to go through him to get to the River Rhine.

After about 200 yards of moving with extreme caution, they knew that they were amongst the enemy. Sergeant Glider Pilots waited at each turn of the route, stepping silently out of the shadows to point the way and then stepping back into the darkness.

Once we halted because of a boy sitting on the ground with a bullet through his leg. We wanted to pick him up but he whispered; 'Nark it. Gimme another field dressing and I'll be all right. I can walk.' [...]

We waded out into the Rhine up to my hips – it didn't matter, I was soaked through long ago – had been for days. And a voice that was sheer music spoke from the stern of the boat saying: 'Ye'll have to step lively, boys. T'aint healthy here.'

It was a Canadian voice, especially delightful to Maxted's ears because he too was a Canadian. The immensely courageous Canadian Engineers were waiting to take the men across.

Maxted and his party got across the river without incident, followed the guiding white tape up over a dyke, slid down the other side, then made the four and a half mile walk through mud to a barn, and 'a blessed mug of hot tea with rum in it and a blanket over our shoulders'. Then they walked again – all night – and eventually arrived at Nijmegen. Only the last short distance was travelled by truck.

Not only Maxted, but also Guy Byam of the BBC, Alan Wood of the *Daily Express*, and the other members of the PR team reached safety behind the British lines.[426] It seems that Anthony was the only war reporter who did not get out with Urquhart's men.

The evacuation carried on until dawn, when the Germans realised what had happened and opened fire on those still trying to escape. More than 2,000 men had gone, but the success of the evacuation was overshadowed by the immense cost of the Arnhem battle. When the story of the evacuation got through to Hibbert via the secret newsheet, he wrote bitterly in his diary: 'Three-quarters of the world's best fighting Division lost with nothing to show for it. 30 Corps still south of the river.'[427]

25

'MISSING, BELIEVED WOUNDED AND PRISONER OF WAR'

The British newspapers were full of the evacuation. Friends and relatives of the men of 1st Airborne Division were now desperately hoping that their loved one had come out with Urquhart, or that at least some new information about them might be available. Amongst those desperate relatives were the Cotterells. For security reasons, Anthony had not told his family where he was going, but they would have guessed the minute that the news of *Market Garden* broke. The postcard which he had sent Geoffrey before leaving, which contained only the message 'We are jumping to a conclusion', would have made that guess a certainty. Since then, nothing had followed but the most ominous, dreadful, and totally uncharacteristic silence. His family suffered appalling anxiety and grief whilst they waited to find out what had happened to him.

Fairly quickly it became obvious who had escaped with Urquhart and who had not. But what families like the Cotterells did not know for some time was that none of those evacuated from Oosterbeek had any detailed knowledge of what had happened at the bridge – the two forces had been separated by a most determined enemy. It would be another month before information about the bridge force and what had happened at Brummen began to be pieced together.

Whilst Anthony's family waited for news of him, a letter arrived which must have greatly shaken their composure. It was written on 14 October by an Edith Menzies, who lived at South Woodford, London E18, and it was addressed to Anthony himself:

> I trust you will pardon this letter but I feel I should leave no stone unturned, to obtain possible news of my son. I read in the local paper that you landed with the Paratroops at Arnhem. My son, the Reverend Alastair Menzies, C.F., was with the 156 Battalion, Parachute Regiment. The official news is – missing, known to be wounded, believed Prisoner of War on September 26th. Unofficially we have heard he was wounded in the arm, and seen moving about among the wounded, and remained with them to be taken prisoner. If you have any knowledge at all about him, my family and I would be most grateful; the suspense of indefinite waiting is so wearing. We congratulate you on your safe return.[428]

Menzies had been with Urquhart at Oosterbeek. From the absence of his name in the roll of war dead, it appears that Menzies was fortunate and survived the war.

For the time being, Anthony and Menzies were just two of some 8,000–9,000 airborne soldiers whose fate, with very few exceptions, was unknown. The major part of the Netherlands, including Arnhem, Brummen and Zutphen, was effectively sealed off and would remain so for many months. By the end of 1944 only one quarter of the Netherlands territory had been liberated, but less than a quarter of the population. Around 7 million out of a population of just over 9 million were still living under German rule.[429]

The survivors of the Arnhem bridge force – whether in hospital, prisoner of war camp, or on the run – were in no position to pass detailed information through to Britain. Once they had reached permanent camps, prisoners of war were allowed to contact their families, but it was not unusual for the customary first postcard to take two months or more to arrive in Britain. This postcard could contain nothing but the barest details, its purpose being simply to let the families at home know that their loved one was still alive. In the case of the officers who had been with Anthony on the truck (who were the only airborne soldiers other than Hibbert who knew what had happened in Brummen), they were kept moving from camp to camp during the first month of their captivity. Their first postcards home were probably sent around the middle of October from Limburg in the Lahn valley of Germany.[430]

Meanwhile, Bernard Briggs was keeping a record of their wanderings, on a single, easily-hidden sheet of paper that could be folded up to the size of a matchbox.[431] The Germans had a mania for confiscating everything, and at the interrogation centre at Oberürsel took the piece of paper which bore the details of the Wehrmacht officer who had helped the prisoners in Brummen. Bernard Briggs's little record was better concealed. He would manage to keep the precious document safe until his liberation on 29 April 1945, noting in ink on that marvellous day that it was '32 weeks since Drop'. His is the only known record of where the officers on the truck went after Brummen.

It showed that on 25 September the prisoners left the warehouse at Zutphen for another warehouse some 35 miles away, situated in Enschede close to the Dutch-German border. The Germans tightly controlled the local institutions at Enschede, including the Roman Catholic hospital, St Joseph's. Though the prisoners in the lorry did not know it, Trevor McNabb and Albert Tannenbaum, both of whom had been wounded at Brummen, were now being treated at St Joseph's.

From Enschede, the prisoners were taken to Oberürsel in Germany, a journey made partly down the Rhine, arriving there on 26 September. Here they were interrogated, before being moved on to Wetzlar. Bernard Briggs, who clearly did not take well to being a prisoner, spent nine and a half days in solitary there, probably for an escape attempt. On 10 October, they were moved from Wetzlar to Limburg, a permanent camp which was massively overcrowded but which, at this period, was only a temporary stopping point for British and American PoWs. There was a constant turnover of these prisoners, men who had been captured in the west and who were being funnelled through to permanent camps in the east.

Ed Beattie, an American war correspondent who had been captured in France on 12 September, had arrived in Limburg on 7 October. On the 10th he recorded in his diary that there were hundreds of men there from the 'ill-fated British First Airborne Division at Arnhem ... uniformly fed-up at what they consider was a botched job, but they hoot at the trumpeting of the German propagandists that the victory was a supreme result of Nazi cleverness.' Beattie was impressed by the quiet confidence of these men, who had 'the air of soldiers who know they have fought well'. Amongst the stories which Beattie heard tell of the Arnhem battle was that of 'Germans who fired indiscriminately into a truckload of prisoners when one captive jumped off and escaped. Five prisoners were killed.' The only possible source of this story was Bernard Briggs' group.[432]

Bernard Briggs' record shows that he underwent the customary interrogation two miles from the Limburg camp at Diez Castle. Once occupied by the Gestapo, Diez was now under the control of the Wehrmacht. Beattie, who was also interrogated at Diez, noted:

> The army, which prides itself on being *korrekt* in all things, fought clear of the third degree, the water treatment, the electric needle and similar Gestapo refinements. It relied on the forbidding appearance of the castle and the boredom and uncertainty of solitary confinement to make its prisoners talkative.[433]

Bernard Briggs returned to the Limburg camp on 19 October. Here the group briefly lost one of their number, Douglas Mortlock. The following day, the group moved to Hadamar, and here they would stay for three months and Douglas Mortlock would rejoin them.

Hadamar was a mock-Gothic castle which had given its name to the nearby concentration camp with extermination facilities for the mentally ill or handicapped. This was where Freddie Gough reported the shooting at Brummen to the Protecting Power's representative.[434] The Protecting Power at Hadamar was Switzerland, and it was through the Swiss that the first report of the war crime at Brummen reached the War Office in London.

Meanwhile other intelligence had also come in about the shooting from a most unlikely source. On 4 October, at 7.00pm, the BBC had intercepted a broadcast on German-controlled Radio Hilversum. Radio Hilversum was the Netherlands equivalent of the BBC, and 'Hilversum' was a named setting on many British radios. Based at the town of Hilversum, south-east of Amsterdam, the station had been broadcasting since the 1920s, but had been taken over by the Germans immediately after the invasion in May 1940. The information in the broadcast of 4 October was from the Unteroffizier journalist who had wanted to interview Anthony at Brummen, but had been prevented from doing so by Etter.

It was not until 10 April 1945, over six months later, that the War Office would finally acknowledge to the Cotterell family what had been said in the broadcast. In a letter to Anthony's mother, Mintie, an official wrote:

> With reference to your call at Curzon Street House on 9th April, 1945, regarding your son, Major J.A. Cotterell, the Royal Fusiliers, I am directed to inform you that the enemy broadcast on 4th October, 1944, related the capture at Arnhem of a 'British War reporter Anthony (?Cottery)' together with other British paratroopers and there can be little doubt that this referred to your son. The broadcast stated that he was severely wounded during a fight which took place when the British prisoners tried to escape from the lorry in which they were being taken away.[435]

What the War Office did not reveal to Mintie was that other details had also been given in the broadcast, including the name of the SS Unterscharführer who had shot the prisoners. Only on 12 July 1945 would they reveal further information to Geoffrey:

> The enemy broadcast regarding your brother admitted its origin, saying that the information had been furnished by a German war reporter who arrived as Major Cotterell was being put into a lorry with the other wounded; during this operation he lost consciousness. The reporter added that your brother was asked whether he had a last wish and he replied in a low voice, 'I am dying'. In the absence of any definite news of Major Cotterell, this distressing and unofficial information has not been given to your mother.[436]

In fact, Mintie already knew all about the broadcast. She was determined to know everything, however bad it was, and Geoffrey would certainly have given her this particular letter to read.

The broadcast, 'Spotlight on the Invasion', was a pure propaganda piece, made under the byline 'Jerry Calling'. In May 1946, a copy of the section concerning Anthony would be sent by the BBC to the War Crimes Investigation Unit of the BAOR.[437] A transcript of the whole broadcast was also available to the various groups involved in the search.

'Spotlight on the Invasion' began with an interview with an alleged British soldier, who told the world, 'I must say the battle for Arnhem was exceedingly hard', before speaking so indistinctly that his remaining words could not be deciphered. The broadcast then went on to give a flattering account of how generous the Germans were in allowing medical supplies through to the British during the fighting, before progressing to the Brummen shooting. The transmission was not very clear, and the transcript shows this by the use of brackets and question marks. This is the reason for the omission of the name of the SS Corporal who shot the prisoners, although the BBC transcript of May 1946 gave his name as '?Hatska'.

> In the area of Arnhem, the British War Reporter Anthony (?Cottery) was captured and severely wounded, on 26 September. One of our War Reporters was an eyewitness of the event in the course of which Anthony (?Cottery) was wounded. A number of British paratroopers were sent off to a transit prisoner of war camp on a number of lorries. (?Cottery) was on the last but one. Suddenly two British soldiers jumped from that lorry and tried to reach a nearby wood. One of the guards trying to stop them was assailed by the other prisoners and knocked down and before the other one could come to his rescue he was shot with his comrade's pistol. Our War Reporter was too far away himself to join in the struggle, but the incident had been observed from the last lorry of the little convoy. One of its guards, Corporal ( ) of the SS Division Hohenstaufen fired his tommy gun at the escaping prisoners and managed to stop the lot of them. Several dead and severely wounded were the victims of their comrades' foolishness. Our War Reporter arrived on the scene of events when (?Cottery) who was one of the victims was put on one of the lorries with the other wounded men. (?Cottery) lost consciousness at that moment. On the question whether he had a special wish, (?Cottery) only uttered 'I am dying' in a low voice.[438]

The reasons for the Germans broadcasting this particular version of events eleven days after the Brummen shooting would never be satisfactorily established. It may simply have been a workaday news item with no sinister implications, or it may have been intended to give an explanation for Anthony's fate which did not cast a bad light on the Germans. If nothing else, however, the broadcast proved that the Germans knew exactly who Anthony was.

At the time of the Radio Hilversum broadcast, Hibbert was still in hiding with the Tjeenk Willink family. The road in which they lived, Burgemeester de Wijslaan, was a broad, pleasant, tree-lined avenue of prosperous middle-class houses. Number A491 was pretty but not particularly large, and at first sight not well suited to concealing a fugitive. Perhaps this is what made it so successful as a hiding-place. There was a secret trap-door under the sitting room carpet, and an emergency hiding place in Aat's room, a cupboard with a false back. In the attic a more permanent place had been arranged. Here a false roof hid a small room in which there was space for a mattress and rugs. Aat also fixed up a bell so that Hibbert could be warned of approaching danger.

His presence in the house was not a rigidly kept secret. Sometimes the neighbours would scare the family stiff by sidling up with parcels of butter or other items for 'the friend'. The extra rations were welcome, but food was, for the moment, sufficient for them all. It was basic fare – mainly bread, cheese, butter, vegetable soup, porridge, potatoes, apples, pears, greens, ersatz tea or coffee, and very occasionally meat. In the coming winter, food would get very short, but Gelderland would escape the terrible famine of the west of the country, in which thousands died from starvation and the bitter cold.

Hibbert was still hoping that the British Army would arrive. 30 Corps was part of General Miles Dempsey's 2nd Army, and in his diary Hibbert took to referring to the hoped-for relief forces simply as 'Dempsey'. 'A filthy day, cold and wet. No sound of fighting, no news of Dempsey. SA men prowling around in every direction.'[439]

Rather than the SA, the original brownshirts who had brought Hitler to power but who had now been almost totally superseded by the SS, Hibbert almost certainly meant the SD. The SD were the Sicherheitsdienst, who were very prominent in the control of the Dutch civilian population. They were a security and intelligence service, closely allied to the Gestapo. After the war, the organisation would be criminalised and its ex-members put in prison, where several of them would be interrogated about Anthony.

Hibbert found the Tjeenk Willinks very generous and thoughtful, writing of Aps that she was 'very very kind and sweet to me, treating me like one of the family'. Her kindness must have done much to assuage his loneliness. What she could not do was heal his burden of guilt, an unshakeable remorse which would prove to be lifelong.[440] Shut up in his hiding place with little to do, he often brooded on whether he had provoked the murders at Brummen. What he had since learned from the Dutch had given him no comfort. On 3 October, he recorded in his diary:

> Last night introduced to Korteweg, the doctor next door, whose daughter had witnessed the shooting-up of the lorry, and who had himself attended the victims. Dennis Mumford ran into an orchard, but was followed by a German only a few yards behind, so couldn't get away.
>
> Just after we'd jumped, the Luftwaffe guard standing in the back right-hand corner of the lorry was shot dead by one of our chaps according to the doctor. I'm very much afraid it might have been the chap whom I asked to take care of the guard. I certainly didn't mean him to do that. Anyway, this so infuriated the man with the Schmeisser that he let loose, killed two, seriously wounded four, and lightly wounded four others. But for Freddie Gough, I think he might have killed them all.

Gough's natural air of command and authority had been one of the major factors in preventing an escalation of the shooting.

Though Hibbert did not note it in the diary, Korteweg would almost certainly have told him that on the day after the shooting he had gone to the hospitals in Zutphen to check on the progress of Anthony and the other wounded, but could not find them – they had effectively disappeared.[441]

The October days went by with Hibbert frequently noting in his diary the frustrating lack of progress that Dempsey's forces were making. The Dutch were just as eager as Hibbert for Dempsey to arrive; their misfortunes were acute and worsening by the day. The Germans strongly resented the aid which the Dutch had given to *Market Garden*, and had become sullen and vengeful. A railway strike had been part of the Dutch response. Now, as a punitive measure for the continuing strike, the Germans forbad the movement of goods on rivers and canals, something which would lead to dire shortages of food and fuel that winter.[442] They also pilfered everything which they could lay their hands on, including factory machinery and tools, and one of the few modes of transport left – bicycles. As they controlled the police force and had long tried to corrupt it to their own way of thinking, their depredations went uncontrolled. The entire police force was now under suspicion of being a tool of the Nazis. There were loyal policemen who worked with the resistance, but as a body they were deeply mistrusted.

For Hibbert, the monotonous days went slowly on. The only enlivening factor – and that a most welcome one – was the gradual discovery of just how many airborne soldiers had escaped capture and were hiding out in the neighbouring countryside or woods.[443] Sadly for Hibbert, hardly any of them were from the break-out force at the bridge, Digby Tatham-Warter being a notable exception.

Another evader was Anthony Deane-Drummond, whom Hibbert had last seen getting into the tiny cupboard in Bena Sita. After a characteristic series of amazing adventures, Deane-Drummond was now hiding out with four others in Velp. Also hiding out, but at Ede, were Hibbert's senior officer, Lathbury, the commander of 1st Parachute Brigade, and Brigadier John Hackett, the commander of 4th Parachute Brigade. Both Lathbury and Hackett had been badly wounded but had been smuggled out of hospital by the Dutch.

On 16 October, Hibbert at last left the Tjeenk Willinks to join the evaders hiding out at Ede. His diary was taken by the resistance leader Piet van der Kruyff, and hidden in the church at Otterloo, north-east of Ede. The diary and its writer would be reunited after the war.

On 23 October, the famous escape known as Pegasus 1 took place which saw these men, with the aid of the Dutch resistance, smuggled across the Rhine back to the British lines. After the escape, Hibbert broke his leg badly in a freak accident, but by November was safely home.

It was Hibbert who brought the full details of the shooting at Brummen back to England. By 9 December, it was generally known, and Watkins made a very brief statement in *WAR*: 'Major Cotterell was with the troops at Arnhem Bridge, was captured, and subsequently severely wounded in an escape attempt.'[444]

As soon as he was able to, Hibbert got in touch with the Cotterell family. Geoffrey met him twice in London, and heard everything which he had to tell. Regrettably this ended with the Brummen shooting and Dr Korteweg's visit to the Zutphen hospital, only to discover that the wounded had never been taken there.

Hibbert was not welcome at Ham Frith, for Mintie held him personally to blame for what had happened to Anthony. As a soldier himself, Geoffrey had a far more realistic idea of military duty, and understood why Hibbert had made the escape. Meeting Hibbert also gave him a much clearer appreciation of the outstanding calibre of the men with whom Anthony had gone to Arnhem. To Geoffrey's mind, Hibbert, who was so quick-thinking and courageous, was exactly the sort of soldier that one would want to be with in a major battle. For Geoffrey, no blame was attached to Hibbert's actions, nor did he think that Anthony would have held him personally responsible for what had happened in Brummen.

At one point Hibbert took Geoffrey to a place in London which was a sort of club for airborne officers, and there Geoffrey had seen Urquhart sitting on a wooden chair like a throne, surrounded by airborne officers as if they were planning another operation. Though even less of a conventional soldier than Anthony, Geoffrey could not help being overawed by these close-to-legendary figures. Mintie would have no truck with such weakness, and she would never forgive Hibbert to her dying day.

26

WATKINS' PILGRIMAGE

nthony's literary career, which had been fuelled by his restless ambition, brilliant networking skills, and immense capacity for hard work, began to falter within weeks of his disappearance. His new book, *An Apple for the Sergeant*, was published on 5 October, only twelve days after the shooting. It seems to have made little impact despite its modernistic cover which was quite unlike its sober predecessors. Earlier in the war, all Anthony's book covers, in line with other war publications, had been plain to the point of Puritanism. This one, though still simple, was black with jazzy slanting blocks of colour. It seemed to be confidently looking forward to the new world after the war.

The publisher's blurb on the fly-leaf began: 'Cotterell's first Army diary, *What! No Morning Tea?* was an immediate success. *An Apple for the Sergeant* is its direct sequel, taking up Cotterell's highly personal history where the first book ended.'

The publishers must have been hoping for a similar success with this one, but there was no longer an author on hand to promote it.

Had Anthony completed the account of the liberation of Europe which he was so clearly planning when he wrote his D-Day and Normandy reports, it would surely have made his name. *An Apple for the Sergeant* would then have been given great impetus, but instead it sank into obscurity fairly rapidly, as did Anthony's other projects.

The planning for his proposed magazine, *The Haymarket*, was continued out of the loyal hope that he would return. In mid October, Geoffrey wrote to Robert Graves, answering a letter he had sent to Anthony proposing a different contribution to the magazine:

> During Anthony's absence I have to look after his affairs as well as I can, which explains why I have read your letter [...]
>
> We are still going to produce the magazine, although the main spirit is away – it is rather important to get it out before the war ends and nothing would madden Anthony more in his imprisonment than to know it wasn't being published. Your alternative hypothetical contribution based on 'The Roebuck in the Thicket' would, I think, be excellent for us. [...]
>
> Jenny tells me most comfortingly that you can prove you were wounded and dead in the last war. This is most encouraging.[445]

But with Anthony's disappearance, the planned first issue would change tack, and eventually a very considerable part of it would be devoted to Arnhem. A long account was compiled, in three parts written by three different authors. Anthony's last article, 'Airborne Worries: Waiting to be Scrubbed', which he had written at 1st Parachute Brigade HQ, was the opening piece. Then there followed an account by Tony Hibbert of the battle for the bridge, and Watkins' article about his visit to Arnhem in April 1945.

In late 1944 Watkins had interviewed several airborne soldiers who had escaped, either with Urquhart or in Pegasus 1, and he had written a two-part account of the battle of Arnhem for the December 1944 numbers of *WAR*. One of the men he had extensively interviewed for the account was Hibbert, hence Hibbert's connection with *The Haymarket*.

The Haymarket was destined never to appear. The first issue was finally put together in 1946, but the heart had gone out of the project, and a cover and articles in proof are all that remain.[446]

The two-part account of the Arnhem battle published in *WAR* was a piece of work of which Watkins would remain proud, commenting around quarter of a century later, 'it is still a pretty good narrative of the battle'. He also gave his reasons for starting the work: 'I wanted to write an account of the Battle of Arnhem, based on what I could learn from those who had come back. At least I owed Anthony that.'[447]

At the time of writing the two-part account, he had been very much hoping that Anthony would return. The first mention of Anthony's disappearance in *WAR* had appeared on 14 October; it had simply read, 'No news has been received of Major Cotterell since 17 September 1944'. The byline on Watkins' article in the same issue showed that he was still a Captain. But by 9 December, when the first part of his account of the Arnhem battle appeared, he had been promoted to Major and had thus become the senior officer on the *WAR* team. It is difficult not to feel a certain illogical resentment of him for stepping into Anthony's shoes.

Watkins, who had the greatest respect and fondness for Anthony, undoubtedly felt something of the same sort. Many years later in his autobiography he wrote:

A report of 'missing in action' spares those involved the sharp shock that follows an announcement of death. It spreads the emotion over a longer period, and I am not sure which is worse. For me, the practical result was that I succeeded him as the Grade 2 Staff Officer in charge of *WAR*, with promotion to the rank of Major, but the circumstances of that promotion were all too reminiscent of the W.W. Jacobs' story, 'The Monkey's Paw', to bring pleasure.

The monkey's paw in the story was a magical object which could grant its owner three wishes, but these wishes were accursed because the malignant force residing in the paw would always twist them into the owner's worst nightmare.

Newly promoted, Watkins must have deeply felt the significance of his first visit to the liberated areas of Holland in late December 1944. It was a reporting mission that in the normal course of events would inevitably have been taken by Anthony. Watkins did his best to make something of the material he gathered, but it inevitably lacked the sparkling quality of Anthony's best work.

Watkins began his account: 'Brigade HQ were using a barn in which to stage their Christmas dinner. It was a ramshackle affair, of odd corners and irregular beams, rafters and floors [...] in a village in the salient north of Nijmegen.'[448]

The Nijmegen salient was still in the front line after all these months, and being shelled every day.

Watkins visited a number of war-torn locations in Holland, including Eindhoven which had been heavily bombed, had no work, very little light or heating, and 'all the hopelessness of Jarrow in the slump'. Before leaving, the Germans had plundered or destroyed almost everything of value. In Zeeland, Watkins saw extensive damage of a different type. The dykes had been breached by the RAF, and the farmland and water supply were contaminated with salt. The German defensive fortifications, built by slave or press-gang labour, had seemingly been designed to last for millennia. Watkins wrote:

I went out with one Royal Engineers recce party from Middelburg to the western dunes at Zoutelande on New Year's Eve [...] At high water wrecked German strong points became dangerous reefs, and only the upper windows and roofs of the houses showed.

The fortification in the sandhills were immensely solid. It seemed so fantastic that so much work and material should have been poured away just for a defence that lasted four days only.

Three and a half months later, Watkins would be in Holland again under very different circumstances. By then, most of the Netherlands had been liberated. It was mid-April, exactly seven months since the parachute drop, and Watkins had come to see the ruins of the place where Anthony had been under siege with 1st Airborne Division. The article which he wrote on this visit is probably the best he ever wrote for WAR.[449] Simple, direct, evocative, and deeply felt, it remains extremely moving.

So recent was the liberation that signs of it could still be seen everywhere.[450] As Watkins travelled towards Arnhem, he saw celebratory orange flags hanging from all the cottages and men on bicycles wearing orange armbands. His jeep crossed the River IJssel on a Bailey bridge and picked up the main road into the town. They travelled down a broad boulevard where the buildings were structurally intact but bore the marks of a fierce battle, the debris from which still lay in the streets. Arnhem itself was a ghost town. It had not been inhabited since the previous year when all its Dutch occupants had been driven out by the Germans and forbidden to return on pain of instant death. The town had then been divided into four sectors, systematically plundered, and the bulk of the spoils sent to four bomb-damaged towns in Germany. Watkins wrote that the looted goods had been accompanied by the message that it was 'a free-will offering from the Dutch to their less fortunate neighbours'. He added, 'I do not like the German sense of humour'.

The party with which Watkins was travelling did not stop in Arnhem; they drove on to Wolfheze and 1st Airborne Division's drop zones. They then doubled back along one of the Division's routes into Oosterbeek, seeing all the marks of the battle and the burnt-out, shattered houses. Occasionally along the road Watkins would see a wrecked jeep with the maroon and sky-blue flash of Pegasus still on its wing. The woods were said to be full of relics of the battle. Oosterbeek shocked him by the extent of its destruction. The Germans had buried the dead but otherwise left it exactly as it was. The party stopped at the Hartenstein, Urquhart's old HQ, wrecked and empty, with grass growing over the shell and mortar holes in the gardens. Then they continued on into Arnhem.

Here Watkins appears to have left the party and gone off on his own. The town centre was eerily quiet, for the main Canadian Army supply route, 'Victoria Up', ran some distance away from it. Two battles had been fought through these streets, and they remained full of shattered glass and debris of every kind, including a half-demolished barricade built around an overturned tramcar which blocked the main highway.

The bridge over which so much blood had been spilt lay in the Rhine, demolished by the United States Air Force. The remains of Gräbner's convoy were still on the long ramp descending from the bridge into the town. 'They lay at all angles across the road and the verges, a light rusty brown, their wheels gone, the chassis members resting on the tarmac and edged with little ridges of sand and dust blown against them by the wind over the winter months.'

Knowing the topography of the battle so well from his two-part article in WAR, Watkins went to see the main sights: the houses of the defence perimeter; the school held by the Engineers; the substantial building which had once been HQ, where Anthony had spent the battle. All the buildings were burnt-out and some had collapsed. It was a beautiful spring day, very silent in the hot sunshine, and at first 'the clear light seemed to take away all emotion'. But the contrast between 'what had died and what was still growing' began to prey upon his mind:

All that man had made had been destroyed.
    And Nature mocked him with an artifice of which the satire was too pointed, for the trees were undamaged and in full leaf and the grass along the embankment was thick and rank. The candles on the chestnut trees were in bloom and already their petals were falling like a fine, intermittent snow.

Though he does not mention him specifically, his thoughts were clearly dwelling on Anthony. His account of this pilgrimage, on which perhaps he had hoped to find some solace or meaning, ends on a very sombre note. In amongst the immense destruction he suddenly came across a small flowerbed in bloom between the rubble of a house and a recent bomb crater. It was full of red and yellow tulips. Watkins found no comfort in the extraordinary sight:

> They moved gently in the little wind, apart from and indifferent to the wreckage that lay around them.
>
> I should not like to stay in Arnhem now. It is too empty of people and the ghosts have it all their own way.

27

JANIE AND THE SEARCH FOR ANTHONY

On 16 May 1945 a middle-aged English woman, with a sweet, sensitive face and an eager air of enquiry, unexpectedly arrived in Brummen. The European war had been over for eight days, but Brummen had only been liberated in the last month of the conflict. Gelderland was under strict military control and war damage was everywhere. The only reason why the woman, a civilian, had been permitted to go there was because she was on official duty. She was a pianist with the London Ballet Group, which was touring with ENSA H2, attached to 21st Army Group under Montgomery. The programme consisted of pared-down versions of ballets, and, as it was impossible to have a full orchestra, the musical accompaniment was provided by two pianos.[451] The pianist who had come to Brummen was named Janie Pool. She was Anthony's aunt.

It was now eight months since Anthony had left for Arnhem. The only official notification his family had received was that Anthony was thought to be wounded and a prisoner of war. Unofficially, more detailed information had come through, virtually all of it ending with the shooting at Brummen. Some mention had also been made of Zutphen, probably in a letter from a PoW camp. As the prisoners of war were only just beginning to return home, the Cotterells had not been able to talk or write to them in any detail. Little was known about who else had been on the truck, who had been wounded and who had been killed. The family had no knowledge of the injuries which Anthony had suffered, and whether they might have cost him his life. Janie would be the first member of the family able to make first-hand enquiries about the shooting and its aftermath.

Janie was now 60, but so young in looks and attitude that most people thought she was in her late forties. Melancholy, sweet-tempered, and a wanderer by fate rather than inclination, she had separated from her husband Ivor in early 1940 and had spent the last five years on tour with ENSA. An unprecedented stroke of good fortune had led her to Brummen – the London Ballet Group's tour had stopped for a while in the district.

On the evening of 13 May, the Group moved into lodgings a mere seven miles from Arnhem. Their billet was very comfortable, having previously been a rest home for the Hitler Youth and Dutch Navy children. It was in a beautiful spot with a lovely garden in which Janie's fellow performers would spend hours sunbathing. But Janie was unable to rest. On the very evening of her arrival, she managed to find someone who would give her a lift in a military jeep the following morning.

She set off early. Much later that day, she would begin a long letter to Mintie, a letter which would run over the next six days in the form of a daily diary.[452] It began by telling Mintie about Arnhem, which Janie called 'our tragedy town':

One cannot fail to see where all the boys landed, and I should think it had been a very charming place before destruction. The place is full of glass [...]. I still cannot make out quite why things went wrong; at the moment I am imagining we are staying at the place our people were held up.

The first day of the search had not gone particularly well. She had been advised to go to a town 20 miles further on (she does not give its name), but arrived there only to find that the HQ for which she was looking had moved 60 miles away. 'You can guess my disappointment, as I dared not go [that much further on], so I decided to visit the Civilian Hospital there, as the name had once been mentioned by someone who wrote to you as a possibility, but Anthony had not been there.'

Janie, who was demonstrating a resourcefulness which perhaps she had not previously realised she possessed, was lucky with the return transport and arrived back at her lodgings at six in the evening, probably in time for an evening performance. It had been a disappointing start, but she hoped to do much better the following day. As she told Mintie in her characteristic, rather vague and impressionistic style:

I now wish I had gone straight to Zutphen, but I shall be off again the first thing in the morning, which place by the way has only been freed one month. [...]
I shall surely see the exact spot where the thing happened.

By 'the thing', she meant the shooting. The following evening, she wrote again:

Well, I am back from my wanderings. This morning I went straight to Zutphen. There are two hospitals there, the first I went to had treated only two English soldiers, their names were there. At the other one I saw the Directress (whom I had been advised to see), who told me that the Germans had taken over the hospital and she had no records of names of anybody who had been there and she did not know if there had ever been any English. You can imagine how downhearted I felt by this time, so I started back and stopped at the village of tragedy.

The village she stopped at was called Dieren. This village lay a couple of miles before Brummen on the road from Arnhem to Zutphen. The scanty information gathered so far had led the Cotterells to believe that it was at Dieren that the shooting had taken place.

Janie went straight to the British Military Police at Dieren, and asked them if they could take her to any resident who spoke English. The MPs were helpful and English-speakers were found, but these were adamant that the shooting had not happened in their village and advised her to go to the civil police instead. It was only then that Janie learned that the shooting had happened in the village which she had just passed through – Brummen. By that time it was too late to do anything else, and once again she returned to her lodgings.

The following evening she wrote in great excitement to Mintie:

Wednesday

At last I have found the right place, and getting off at the village, I took out my paper with the address of the shop I was to visit. I was hailed by 'Can I help you, I am an Englishwoman'. That was a marvellous piece of luck. She is married to a Dutch Merchant Navy man, and lived at Arnhem, but was evacuated to this village. She had heard about the affair, so she took me to the shop, but the man was not there, his wife could not speak English, so my new friend was very useful and the wife suggested we went to the house where shelter had been given to one of the airborne soldiers. When we arrived, it was to find that it was the home of Major Hibbert's rescuers; apparently he has been there very recently, trying to get news of Anthony and is still persistently trying. They are expecting him back before the weekend.

The home to which she had been taken was that of the Tjeenk Willink family. The Tjeenk Willinks welcomed Janie with the greatest warmth and kindliness, but the tale which Dick had to tell her was not one which could bring any comfort. That evening, after she had returned to her lodgings with the London Ballet Group, Janie wrote to her sister Mintie:

> When the truck was going through the village, the people showed the orange flag and gave the V sign, our boys responded, this went on. This infuriated the Guards, there were two, and finally one of them took up his Tommy Gun to shoot at the civilians, one of our boys took out his pistol (the German's) and shot him. The other German immediately turned his gun on the lorry and shot at the boys. He would not allow a doctor to come near, but by luck a German officer came along and gave the permission.

She also told Mintie that Dick had taken her next door to meet Doctor Korteweg, who had treated the wounded on that fateful day. Korteweg could no longer remember the faces very clearly. He looked for a long time at the photograph which Janie showed him of Anthony, and finally decided that Anthony was the one who had been shot in the head, 'in which case it must prove fatal'. He told her that the two others who were severely wounded had breast wounds, one on the left and one on the right, but though these were severe Korteweg thought that the men would recover. Janie told him that the Cotterell family had heard about the head wound from other soldiers on the truck and that it was not Anthony, but Korteweg was fairly certain that it was.

In her letter to Mintie, Janie had to tell her sister what had happened after the shooting, knowing how unbearably painful Mintie would find it but certain that she would want to know everything, however dreadful:

> Now comes a wicked part. Korteweg told the Germans they must take these boys to the nearest hospital which was Zutphen and he went there to enquire the next day but of course they just had not been taken there. Although there were many Red Cross vans about, our boys were just dumped in the lorry they came up in and were driven off. It seems impossible for such cruelty to be possible. Dick insists that he knows the Hospital to which they were taken. He is going to get information this afternoon and is meeting me there tomorrow morning at 11 o'clock. It is a long way from here, so I hope I shall be very lucky with transport. He will also take me to the Mayor of the town and a clergyman he knows, who are bound to know of any deaths that have taken place. He is going to get the petrol from somewhere and go on his motorbike.
>
> He also took me to the scene of the tragedy.
>
> However Major Hibbert escaped is a mystery, as the village is quite small, but a very charming place. I cannot help feeling grateful to think I have been lucky enough to be sent here and meet these people and to see the exact place. The Doctor has your address, should anything transpire for you to know. I also have several Organisations making enquiries. Now my pen goes away until tomorrow evening.

As Janie, and later Geoffrey, was to discover, the Tjeenk Willink family would do everything in their power to assist the search for Anthony. They would go out of their way to follow every lead, sometimes in their enthusiasm getting madly carried away by some false trail, but always with their intense good-heartedness trying their very best to find out what had happened to him.

The following day Janie left very early for the town to which Dick thought the wounded had been taken for treatment. As happened so often in her letters, she forgot to give the town's name, but it was Enschede, as is confirmed in a later letter.[453]

Janie never reached Enschede. By 10.00am she had only reached Lochem, a little over half-way into the journey from her lodgings. The difficulties of travelling were immense. Lifts had to be begged or scrounged from anyone going in the right direction. The tide of war had scarcely begun to ebb, and there were numerous diversions around fallen buildings or unexploded bombs and mines. The roads were often ruinous, and virtually all the bridges were down.

Dick, who had had better luck on his motorcycle, was waiting for her at Lochem by the time she arrived. He had been 'around the district for miles all to no avail, cemeteries too'. Though Janie did not include the information until a subsequent letter, Dick had also been to St Joseph's, the hospital at Enschede, only to find that it was still under the control of a German staff. He saw a German doctor there and 'demanded to know the names on the records', but could not get any information from him. Enschede had been very much an enemy-controlled town, lying as it did so close to the Dutch-German border, and it seems that the German staff at St Joseph's were determined to be obstructive.

The day was ebbing away much too fast. As Janie was obliged to return to the London Ballet Group by the evening, presumably in time for a performance, the only reasonable option was to go back to Zutphen with Dick. They spent their time finding out the names of the British soldiers who had died there and checking the war graves in the cemeteries. Once again, there was no result for Anthony. Janie had lunch in the town with Dick, and then they parted.

Janie, summoning up yet more ingenuity and daring, went part of the way back to her lodgings with a lorry-load of Poles who were travelling to England. She finished her journey on the back of a motorbike: 'You can imagine I was not very confident, but I safely arrived home.'

As she wrote her letter, the Zutphen search for the Brummen dead was still fresh in Janie's mind. She asked Mintie to get in touch with the relatives of the only two soldiers on the truck who had been confirmed as being killed. Mintie was to try to find out where they were buried, as Dick was anxious to go there and try to establish another lead.

Thinking over the events of the day, it suddenly occurred to Janie that when she next went to Brummen she should take her two highly precious bottles of drink ration whisky, one for the Tjeenk Willinks, and one for Doctor Korteweg. (She would later tell Mintie that they were 'as you can imagine terribly pleased' when they received them on the Saturday.)

Exhausted by the difficult travelling and the intense emotional strain, Janie stayed in bed till lunchtime the following day. It was now almost three weeks since she had heard from Mintie because none of the London Ballet Group's mail had caught up with them. Mintie was 'thirsting for home news' and thought that the mail might have been held up due to 'the festivities', a reference to the celebrations for the end of the war in Europe. Not having heard from her family for so long, she did not know what the latest developments were in the search for Anthony, and must have keenly felt her sole responsibility for the Holland enquiries.

That afternoon, she and some of the ballet company were asked if they would like to be taken for a drive for a few hours in Germany. Janie wrote to Mintie later:

We passed through at least six towns, all of which were absolutely flat, a ghastly sight ... Whilst I was out a new theory came to me. Was Anthony made a victim as a reprisal for the shot German? I think there is a strong possibility of them doing it. I cannot imagine that they would let the crime go unpunished, and they may have chosen the celebrity. What sadness I have felt this week going to all these places and not being able to find any trace. I was so certain if I combed the hospitals I should find something.

On Saturday she returned to Zutphen, but could discover nothing new.

Back at her lodgings, she was delighted to at last find a letter from Mintie, dated 6 May, saying that she had received new confirmation that it was not Anthony who had been shot in the head. The Cotterells were trying to obtain as much information as possible from the returning prisoners of war who had been with Anthony in Brummen, but, as yet, only a very few names were known of the thirty or so officers and men who had been on the truck. Their identities were gradually established as they were repatriated. Some came earlier than others, having escaped from their PoW camps as the Third Reich collapsed. Others were delayed by the need for medical treatment, or by the overwhelming number of ex-PoWs who were waiting for transport home. Other airborne soldiers who might possibly know something had been hiding out in Holland until the very last days of the war, and were only now emerging into daylight.

By 22 April, John Cairns was back in England; by the 30th Tannenbaum, who had been severely wounded; and by 10 May Bernard Briggs, who had kept the little time-chart of the unwounded prisoners' wanderings. Gough, who had escaped from his PoW camp and joined the Americans in Bavaria, got to Brussels on 1 May, where he once again notified the authorities of the Brummen shooting.[454] Fiercely determined to seek justice for his murdered soldiers, once he was back in England he lent his considerable energies and influence to supporting the hunt for the perpetrators.

The process of collecting evidence about the war crime had already begun. Testimonies had been given at Oflag 79 on 11 April by Cecil Byng-Maddick and five others who had been on the truck. Other testimonies were taken as witnesses like Tannenbaum reached England. The due legal processes began to grind slowly into motion. The investigation of the war crime at Brummen would proceed in parallel with the official and unofficial searches for Anthony.

Meanwhile, Mintie was making contact with several of the soldiers who had been on the truck. 1st Parachute Brigade was enormously helpful in passing on addresses and contact details. A letter from a Captain Frank of 2nd Battalion, the Parachute Regiment, was typical.[455] Sending Mintie the address of Tannenbaum in Wembley Park, London, he told her that he had heard a report that Tannenbaum was back in England.

> I may be able to find out the names of some others who were on the truck and their addresses.
> If I can I will send these on to you as soon as I can, for I can well imagine your feelings now.
>   If I can help in any other way please let me know for I will be only too pleased to do so.

This letter was much overwritten in Mintie's handwriting – addresses and names tumbling over one another, perhaps taken down whilst she was on the phone. There was also a phone number for Major Bill Arnold; prior to his return, Mintie had been in touch with his wife Priscilla to ask if her husband had said anything about Brummen in his PoW letters.

Mintie's letter of 6 May, which Janie had just received, contained a transcript of a letter John Cairns had recently sent to Mintie. Mintie had written to his mother whilst he was a prisoner of war, and on his return to England, Cairns had immediately answered her letter. Mintie's transcript read:

> I am sorry to hear that you have no news of Anthony as yet, and sincerely hope that your anxiety will be relieved very shortly. In reply to your query regarding his wounds I will not disguise the fact that he appeared to be fairly badly hurt but I hasten to assure you that never for a moment had it crossed my mind that he would not recover, until I received your letter meaning that I had not heard. Ever since the incident I have been fully confident that he would be alright and for that reason am amazed at your lack of news.
>   As far as I can remember Anthony was hit in two places, in the upper part of the thigh and in the side but I could not be quite sure of these facts now. He was rather in pain but fortunately

I had a morphia syringe with me and this appeared to bring relief. A Dutch civilian doctor had appeared and under his direction I bandaged Anthony's wounds, we were then put on board a lorry and driven to a place called Zutphen about 30 miles east of Arnhem when those of us who were alright were confined in a warehouse, while the wounded were taken to a nearby Hospital as far as I can gather. As I was moved next day I lost all contact with the wounded and have heard no news of them since.

Mintie told Janie that the fact that they had found somebody 'who knew at least something' was a great help. Yet, 'I am doing my very best to keep hoping but I find my spirits very low at times'. She tried to look on the bright side of things – the fact that the war really appeared to be over at last meant that 'many homes will be happier than they have been for many a long day'. She concluded with the news that Meggs, her and Janie's brother, had just taken a cottage and a housekeeper, 'and he likes it very much. He is now out of the Army or just about.' She signed herself 'With love and hope, Mintie'.

Janie took comfort in the fact that Anthony had not been shot in the head as Korteweg had thought. But the mystery of why Anthony had apparently vanished into thin air greatly troubled her mind. She mused in the diary letter: 'Where could he have vanished? He may perhaps have been put in a Concentration Camp, but that I should think improbable, as none of the others were.'

Not long after updating her letter, Janie was having tea with her fellow performers when a colossal explosion went off without warning. Their immediate thought was that it was a mine, of which there were hundreds still around.

A short time afterwards a succession of what sounded like machine-gun fire, then we heard people running and we realised that something had happened at an Ammunition Dump just around the corner from our house which was on the outskirts of the town. We knew there were all sorts of things there, and one colossal bomb. Everything then started, we all went quickly to the cellar, as there was so much glass and plaster falling about, and there was nothing we could do, it was useless trying to run away, as there was so much falling everywhere.

When I was returning in the afternoon, I looked all around me and was struck that this end of the town had survived the ordeal and now it is all just ruined, mainly by fire. As we passed this morning, it was a sorry sight. It is not known yet what caused the disaster, but it was a ghastly couple of hours.

It was a shocking reminder of how much labour and effort would be needed to bring safety and prosperity back to the people of Holland.

There were other letters in the post from Mintie which Janie had not yet received, and vice-versa. The sisters were writing very frequently to one another, often before they had received an answer to the previous letter. The post was highly erratic, with letters sometimes taking weeks and sometimes arriving within three days. The sisters very much needed to be in touch with one another; only Janie could understand the terrible pain which Mintie was suffering, and it was a great relief for Mintie to write to her. The huge disparity in the fortunes of the sisters – Mintie very comfortably off and married to Graham, who had once been Janie's beau, and Janie, without any proper home, separated from her embittered husband, Ivor – had now become utterly irrelevant. With her kindness and passionate interest in the search, Janie was giving something of inestimable value to her sister, who responded with intense gratitude. The ground had levelled between them.

The letters which Janie had not yet received told of the progress of Mintie's own enquiries. On 16 May she wrote to Janie that the previous day she had been to see Tannenbaum at his home in Wembley Park.

He was telling me of his time with Tone – it is heartbreaking he was so well [...] You can imagine my state of mind. I have tried everything but nothing does any good. Each day makes it more awful. I had so hoped he would turn up, it seems now as if the best hope is if he is still in some Hospital.

The following day she wrote again:

Cairns the man who wrote and told me he had dressed Tone's wounds has been out to see me today – and he says that Tone was hit in the left thigh and through the left (under shoulder blade) arm and I suppose body if it went through; he was in great pain, but he said as I told you before that he did not think he would not recover.

I feel in such a state and I try to go on hoping I shall hear from him, but the chances are growing less and less. It seems so cruel; this Cairns says he was well and full of beans. Cairns himself was a very nice young man and I thought it was very kind of him to come out all this way to see me. He said he had made quite a lot of enquiries but never with any success. I don't think there is any chance.

No news from Shubbs much to my sorrow – have not heard from him since Monday eve as he was going out on a Scheme. I think I told you that he [is being posted] to Wales on Saturday. I don't look forward to this weekend or anything at all at the moment. I guess I am a poor specimen, poor old Graham is very good to me and I know his awful despair as you know he worshipped the boys [...].

The garden looks so pretty but it just mocks me. I keep picturing Tone sitting on the lawn with his paper and pencil.

When Janie eventually received this letter with its heart-rending cry of pain, she wrote back with immense tenderness: 'Try not to think of the garden mocking you, try to sit out there quietly and think of the great love he had for you. I think somehow if you can bring yourself to do this, he will somehow manage to be with you and help you.'

Mintie was suffering violent fluctuations of mood between hope and despair as different testimonies came in, often totally contradicting one another. On 21 May, she sent Janie a short note, deeply distressed because she had been told by a Catholic priest that he had heard Anthony 'was taken to Apeldoorn and in a very bad way'. Though she does not give the priest's name, later correspondence would confirm that it was Father Egan, who had been attached to 2nd Parachute Battalion. Father Egan had not been on the truck at Brummen, so had received his information from a third party.

Janie's long diary letter from Holland concluded on Sunday 20 May, at Eindhoven where the London Ballet Company had moved that day. They had been to Eindhoven earlier in the tour; Janie said it was 'rather trying' to be back again, but that she had a good bedroom. Some days later, on receiving Mintie's letter about Father Egan and the Apeldoorn story, she told Mintie that the London Ballet Group would be moving on to Tilburg the following week. Tilburg was 'a little higher up and if it is at all possible I shall visit Apeldoorn again to see if there are any more hospitals but I know I asked before.'[456] Janie had clearly been to Apeldoorn already, looking for Anthony's name in hospital registers, but the letter which described this first visit has been lost.

Lack of time would prevent her from making the second visit. She would write her last letter on 7 June from Antwerp. The London Ballet Group was on the verge of sailing for England after a long tour. Janie's thoughts were turning to home, and how she would have to go to the Woodford Food Office before she could get any rations. She told Mintie various little bits of news: how she had seen Montgomery that day, 'I liked his face very much'; how she and most of the company had been severely bitten by bed-bugs, but she was now hoping for a good night's rest, having managed to buy some citronella. Then there were the last details about the search, including the information that Dick was going round all the cemeteries in Zutphen.

In her long diary letter, Janie had given Mintie the address of the Tjeenk Willinks in Brummen, and had told her to write to Dick; 'He is such a charming man I suppose I must call him, he looks such a boy; I was amazed when he told me he was 26'.

The Tjeenk Willinks were to prove the most invaluable of friends, and it was Janie who had won them to Anthony's cause.

28

WITNESSES, HELPERS AND WAR OFFICE STONEWALLERS

When Janie had concluded her long diary letter on Sunday 20 May, she had written that she hoped the letter would get through quickly as it had been such a long time since Mintie had heard from her. And for once the post proved surprisingly efficient, for Mintie received the letter on the Wednesday, only three days after Janie had posted it. She was touched to the quick: 'What a good soul you have been, and I and Graham both agree as to how strangely wonderful it is that you have been able to make all these enquiries and see the different people.' She gave Janie the latest information she had obtained.

> I have spoken to Tannenbaum this morning – he was taken to St Joseph's Hospital, Enschede, Holland but right on German border. He thinks you probably visited that.
>
> The other man, a Lieutenant Trevor McNabb, went with him and a few days later died of injury to left lung. Also the man who died the same evening [as the Brummen shooting] was shot in head and was a man in the ranks called Mc. Or Mac. Something but he can't remember. [...]
>
> You must have been dog-tired after all your travelling but I know you would not mind that, it was also a great relief to us to know that Hibbert had been trying too. I think they must have taken Anthony into Germany because of his job – since they put out a propaganda story about him on Radio saying that he had been severely wounded trying to escape and that he was now saying 'I am dying' which doesn't ring true especially as the first part of the broadcast was untrue. It is also likely that they would try and keep him to try and get information out of him. We can only still hope and pray that he will be yet found in some hospital.[457]

The information in Janie's letter had stirred up intense emotion. The day after receiving it, Mintie had an errand to run for Janie in the city, and afterwards went and sat in St Paul's Cathedral. 'I haven't been there for many many years. I liked the peace.'[458]

But the calming effect of the Empire Day service which she saw at the cathedral did not last. On 25 May, she told Janie, 'My mind is obsessed from morning till night and every time I wake up ... I am still thinking of the providence that sent you to where you are. There could not have been anybody better and I am extremely thankful.'

In case her previous letter had not reached Janie, she once more repeated the information about the wounds suffered in the shooting.

> Tannenbaum was wounded in thigh, and bullet went through to stomach and out again [...] Tannenbaum said he could guarantee that Trevor McNabb's wound was on the left side and into his lung. Also the man with the head wound died that evening by his side and there is

no doubt of these facts and he was in the ranks of Tannenbaum's company and called Mc or Mac something.'

Mintie was repeating this information because it was absolutely critical to establish the exact nature of injuries suffered by the victims of the shooting. If the injuries could be precisely defined for the other wounded, it narrowed down the possibilities of the wounds which Anthony had suffered.

She also told Janie that Graham had had a very bad cold, but seemed better that day. Like Mintie, Graham was under the most intense emotional strain; 'You can see what he has suffered and is suffering on his face, but don't mention this when you write.'

Mintie now fell ill with a bad throat, aches and pains, which only deepened the feeling of nightmare. A black fear was haunting her that Geoffrey – Shubbs – would be sent out to fight the war with Japan which was expected to last many months.

Nothing to report. Each day drags by. [...]
I am worried to death about Shubbs, as you can imagine it seems as if he will be going to that damnable place.
Excuse this awful letter [...] I was hoping and hoping that Tone would turn up from the eastern prisoners who are being released and then all the time it may be that he never got better. But why didn't we hear?
Forgive dreariness.

Much love – Mintie

The following day cheered her a little when the post brought a letter from Freddie Gough, which gave her fresh hope. Mintie transcribed the letter for Janie. Gough wrote:

I received your letter and am so distressed at its contents. I had hoped that Anthony would be well and back in England now. Anthony was wounded in the stomach, it was a severe wound. He was given morphia, but his general demeanour and condition gave me confidence that he would pull through. I was allowed to escort him and the other seriously wounded cases to a dressing station in Zutphen where they received first-class medical attention. Unfortunately I was forced by my guards to leave them there, but had a final word with Anthony who was very cheerful and assured me that he was not suffering pain unduly.
After that my only information came from Lieutenant Tannenbaum who was sent to a different hospital to your son. I was so hoping to hear something of him on my return and was in fact taking steps to find out your address.
It was a dastardly crime on the part of the Germans and I have already taken every possible step to bring the perpetrators to justice.
I do hope you will hear something of Anthony very soon. I have always had a feeling that he had pulled through. He did most awfully well at Arnhem and his bravery and delightful personality were an inspiration to all of us.

Gough then gave a number of possible explanations why they might not have heard from Anthony. He concluded by saying that he would make further enquiries and would let her know at once if anything came up: 'I do hope that we shall soon have some encouraging news.'[459]

Janie's researches in Holland and the information from the returning prisoners of war like Cairns, Tannenbaum and Gough, fleshed out the scanty information which Cotterell family had gathered in the first months after Anthony went missing. In those early days, the most unhelpful and obfuscated responses to their various enquiries had always come from the War Office, supposedly their first point of contact. The War Office attitude seemed to be that, by asking too many questions, the Cotterells were being impatient and presumptuous, and were interfering in matters which were not their concern. For example, on 9 January 1945, a War Office letter arrived at Ham Frith, answering one which Mintie had sent to their office in Liverpool. She had taken charge of the matter rather than Graham, and was pursuing enquiries with the greatest singlemindedness. But technically Graham, as the male head of the family, was Anthony's next of kin. The War Office official in Liverpool returned her letter with the comment that 'the contents have been noted with interest'. He then continued in the most opaque and unhelpful way:

> No official prisoner of war report has yet been received in respect of your son. You will, it is felt, appreciate that such a report can only originate from enemy sources and pending the receipt of an official prisoner of war report through the recognised channels, or of a card or letter from him confirming that he is a prisoner of war, it will be necessary for him to remain officially recorded as missing, but this should not be regarded as indicating that the Department has any information which throws doubt on the accuracy of the information you have received.

Other tortured sentences followed, telling her that the notification that a man was a prisoner of war varied considerably in its time of arrival in England. The letter concluded:

> It is regretted that it is not possible to state how many personnel who were captured at Arnhem Bridge have communicated with their next-of-kin.
>   I am to assure you that everything possible is being done to obtain news of your son, and that any information which is received will be immediately communicated to your husband.

> I am, Madam,
> Your Obedient Servant
> F.D. Ferris

If F.D. Ferris, whoever he was, was calculating that this close-to-insulting reply would get rid of Mintie, he was sadly mistaken; he did not understand the sort of woman he was dealing with. Like her son, Mintie had a vein of immense tenacity. She would become a thorn in the side of various War Office pen-pushers, especially later that same year when she would frequently call and leave material for them at their offices in London, or would bombard them with telegrams. The War Office was reprehensibly slow and inefficient with regards to missing soldiers, and all too often resorted to stone-walling of the type employed by F.D. Ferris. Mintie, however, was not the type of person that officialdom could brush off like a fly. She persevered regardless of all discouragement.

It became obvious within the early months of the search that very little help could be expected from the War Office, which was always several dozen steps behind the unofficial enquiries. Bypassing its tunnel-visioned bulk, the Cotterells appealed directly to Sir Ronald Adam, the Army's Adjutant-General, who with great kindness and willingness did what he could to help. Later in the search, when Geoffrey was in Germany, he would be very amused to be granted a sight of a dossier which contained the exasperated remarks of several nameless officials: 'The next-of-kin are pressing this case at a very high level.' 'The A.G. is believed to be interested'. If nothing else, at least the Cotterells had succeeded in disturbing the complacency of F.D. Ferris and his ilk.

Adam, in the last issue of *WAR*, published on 14 June 1945, would show how highly he had valued Anthony by writing in his 'farewell message':

I should not like to conclude this message without some reference to Major Anthony Cotterell. Major Cotterell was on the staff of *WAR* from its inception until the time when he dropped with 1 Airborne Division at Arnhem last September – and did not return. He believed that you could best describe a thing only after you had done it yourself, and it was to give you that best account that he flew with the USAAF, landed in Normandy on D-Day and qualified as a parachutist. Many gallant men have lost their lives in this war, and I think that this is the right place to mention this one.[460]

Though he clearly believed that Anthony was dead, Adam did not let this interfere with any help he could give to the Cotterell family.

Leaving no stone unturned in her attempt to trace Anthony, Mintie would try every possible official body, including the Dutch, the German, and the British Red Cross. In addition, the family would utilise every single influential contact they had. They would tap all the famous and infamous journalists they knew, including Paul Holt of the *Daily Express*, and Don Iddon of the *Daily Mail*. Geoffrey would be as pushy – or, indeed, pushier than Mintie – once telling her when she demurred about bothering the Tannenbaums, 'Don't be bashful about ringing up the Tannenbaums. This is no time to spare other people's feelings.'[461]

Driven by their love for Anthony, the family called in favours from all the great men they knew, such as Arthur Christiansen, the editor of the *Daily Express*, and the enormously rich Sydney Bernstein, Anthony's old country-house host. Bernstein, who owned a highly remunerative chain of cinemas, had many business contacts overseas. In August 1945, Geoffrey would write to Janie:

I went to the Bernsteins the other night [...] Sydney has ordered one of his men to search all over the American Zone for clues. He is equipped with full details. They are also writing all over Europe as far as possible. I enclose a cutting from today's *News Chronicle*, which is once again a prop of hope. It is indisputably true that some of the missing are going to turn up. Tom Driberg has also replied to me promising to prod up the War Office at once. Who would have imagined the 'Dragonman' to be doing that for us? I have also written to Tom Driberg and asked him to see the War Minister.[462]

Tom Driberg, in the guise of his alter ego 'William Hickey', had been Anthony's inspiration when he was a cub journalist trying to get onto the *Daily Express*. Now he too was working to find Anthony.

Freddie Gough would also utilise highly placed contacts. In August Geoffrey would write to his mother, telling her:

I spoke to Major Gough this morning. He saw Lord Vansittart, who is seeing the War Minister and also raising the whole incident in the House of Lords within two or three weeks. That at least is a good thing. Major Gough seemed to think that something was really being done, though how much it will help us is another matter.[463]

It is possible that Gough passed on to Vansittart Anthony's last words when they parted, 'If you get back home before me, tell Vansittart he has another disciple in me'.

It would have been around this time that Mintie, Graham, and Geoffrey went to see Gough at his City of London office. This was almost certainly at Fenchurch House, 5 Fenchurch Street, EC3. The office was opulent and very grand, with an immense desk behind which Gough sat and readily answered all their questions. But he could add little to what he had already told them. He had left Anthony alive, cheerful, and apparently doing well; he knew nothing which could explain why he had subsequently disappeared.

Though he had now retired from the Army and was something mysterious in the City, Gough's mind still ran very much on Arnhem. In 1946 he would take part in the extraordinary film, *Theirs Is the Glory*, which was filmed in the still untouched ruins of Arnhem. It told the story of the battle with all the parts played by airborne soldiers who had actually been there in September 1944. Freddie Gough played himself, and Stanley Maxted spoke the commentary. The character of Anthony does not appear.

29

GEOFFREY TAKES OVER THE SEARCH

In addition to their terrible fears and grief for Anthony, Mintie and Graham were enduring the prospect that that they might lose their second son, Geoffrey. Though the war with Germany had ended, the war with Japan was still raging fiercely. The danger that Geoffrey would be sent overseas was considerable, and in a letter to Janie on 16 May Mintie wrote with great bitterness: 'it may be that Shubbs will be swept to the other foul place'.

Geoffrey's anti-aircraft battery near Wanstead had been disbanded around the beginning of the year as there were no longer any German aircraft to be shot down. He had been posted to the School of Artillery at Larkhill, Salisbury Plain, to be trained as a counter-mortar officer.[464] He wrote frequently to his mother, trying to amuse her and keep her spirits up. In a letter of 18 April he told her:

> Exactly five years ago I was wet through, getting to sleep in a rain-sodden tent, with Les and company.
> What's it like here? Like this:
>
> New red brick barracks and old green huts,
> Lots of old soldiers in old soldiers' ruts,
> Occasional gunfire, practice of course,
> A solitary Brigadier riding a horse,
> Garrison, cinema, theatre and church,
> Blue skies, fresh wind, but wherever you search
> New red brick barracks and old green huts.
>
> Which proves I can turn my hand to anything; and is at any rate better than a wet tent.

Knowing how anxious his parents were about his future, his letters kept them up to date with the latest rumours about his next posting. He was hoping to use his fluent knowledge of German to secure himself a job in Western Europe, which would make the search for Anthony very much easier. Unfortunately, it looked as if it was his other skills that the Army wished to utilise, and that it wished to utilise them in China, Burma, India, Japan, or some other similarly far-flung place.

Though he had applied for various Army jobs in Holland and Germany, Geoffrey had not got any of them. His future remained very uncertain. In a letter to his mother of 30 May, he told her that his Colonel had informed him in the middle of an exercise up on a firing range in the Welsh hills, 'Well, Japan for you'.

Later I was returning in a lorry which towed a generator and as we careered over a hill it was suddenly plain to me that after all I might never see Japan: we mounted the left bank at right angles and the generator swivelled noisily behind us, settling lopsidedly over the right bank [...] The front two wheels of the lorry were three inches and two inches respectively from a ditch that was full to the brim with fervently flowing water. And as I stood by the driver and looked the situation over, it began to pour with rain. All this incidentally took place on what is ironically called on the range map the 'Burma Road'.

Though Geoffrey kept up a resolutely cheerful tone in his letters, he was as deeply grieved as his parents about his missing brother. Anthony was constantly in his thoughts. On the anniversary of D-Day, he wrote to Mintie: 'One can't help thinking all today of Anthony on the beachhead a year ago. Only a year ago. And possibly he is now asking a Pole how he likes the camp, and what his job was in Warsaw.'[465]

The little joke about Anthony's interviewing techniques was aimed at raising Mintie's spirits. It also referred to the hope that a possible explanation for Anthony's silence was that he was in Russian-controlled territory. This idea rested entirely on where Anthony had been in the closing months of the war. Had he been of sufficient interest to the Germans to be taken to Berlin, then he might still have been there when the Russians captured the city. Alternatively, like the majority of Allied prisoners, he could have been in a PoW camp in the east; these were the camps which had subsequently been liberated by the advancing Red Army. If Anthony was now with the Russians, he was physically safe and it was only a matter of locating him.[466]

Geoffrey had written to his mother about Janie's investigations that he thought her persistence was 'remarkable and wonderful', and that it would not surprise him to learn that she was now 'on a cattle truck on the way to Eastern Europe'.[467] He too sincerely believed that Anthony might be in the east. Articles were appearing in the British newspapers which stated that British nationals were being held by the Russians and that information about them was exceedingly hard to obtain. The idea that the solution lay in the east was a seductive one, and the Cotterell family, desperate for any hope, took the Russian theory seriously.

The matter of the Russian attitude to American and British personnel would continue to be in the news for months. In October, Geoffrey would write to his father about an article in the *News Chronicle* which had reported that even British and American liaison officers, searching for British and American personnel, had been refused admittance to the Russian-controlled areas of Germany. Geoffrey concluded robustly: 'So that settles that [...] There _are_ British people in Russia.'[468]

Geoffrey saw his role as being to keep his mother cheerful until the worst was confirmed. He hid from her his own black fears about Anthony. He also tried to jolly her along into forgetting about the possible Japanese posting by entertaining her with accounts of his fellow soldiers. The general election in July, which saw the Conservatives thrown out and a Labour government installed, provided much wicked amusement:

Thank God for the election [...] There was consternation in the Mess at the result. Sheer, raving consternation which was maliciously pleasant for me to see [...] The Sergeant Major thought that England was finished [...] Most inconceivable of all, most totally unbelievable, the Major, Bruce and Tim Spencer Cox had a short conversation wondering what the effect on discipline would be. I advised them to go about armed. And the General at Division (where they think the whole country's gone mad) made a joke about our next job not being the Japs but here. SS men are not composed only of Germans. Even so, I notice with interest that the good old instinctive compromise feelings are already settling in.[469]

Geoffrey was now becoming deeply involved in the search for Anthony. Perhaps the family hoped that as a British Army Major he would be taken more seriously by the authorities than Mintie. Yet on 12 July, in answer to his enquiries to the War Office department based at the Blue Coat School, Liverpool, he received a letter worthy of F.D. Ferris in its sly insolence and unrepentant mangling of the English language:

Sir

With reference to your letters dated 5 and 6 July 1945, regarding your brother, Major J.A. Cotterell, The Royal Fusiliers, I am directed to inform you that all available information has been given to the Casualty Section of General Headquarters, 21st Army Group, and they have been requested to make all possible enquiries in an endeavour to ascertain your brother's fate.

Lieutenant Tannenbaum, who was wounded, was recorded and reported in the normal manner by the German authorities, as also were the deaths and burial of those who lost their lives in the incident, the only exception being your brother, of whom no information has been reported officially by the Germans.

Regarding SS records, the reply to your question was that efforts made by officers of this Branch to locate such records were unsuccessful, but it cannot be said that all such matter has been destroyed. Records such as those of Buchenwald captured by our advancing troops have revealed the deaths of British personnel who were, however, employed on very special duties of an entirely different nature to those on which your brother was engaged. It is not considered that Major Cotterell's duties were such as would cause the enemy to single him out for ill-treatment.[...]

In all the circumstances there would appear to be little doubt that your brother must have succumbed to his wounds at Zutphen and, unless the reply to the enquiries at present in progress reveals anything to the contrary, the Department will be constrained to presume his death on this basis.

I am to convey to you an expression of the Department's sympathy in your prolonged anxiety.

I am, Sir,
Your obedient Servant,
E.D. Lloyd [470]

Two important War Office's attitudes were revealed by this letter. Firstly, its minions did not consider Anthony to have been of any particular interest to the Germans, and secondly, the scanty enquiries which they were prepared to make were going to be the definitive answer on whether Anthony had died. Neither of these attitudes was acceptable to the Cotterell family.

Two months later, the momentous news broke that the war was finally at an end. Japan surrendered on 12 September, and after six years of war the British people were at last free to rebuild their lives. The threat of Geoffrey being posted to the Far East vanished overnight. It was now almost certain that he would manage to get a last posting to the Continent before demob, and with any luck this would be in Germany where he would optimally placed to continue the search.

On 22 September Geoffrey wrote to Robert Graves, thanking him for a recent letter, and reassuring him about something which had deeply disturbed Graves. A recent *Sunday Times* article had suggested that Anthony had been killed by the SS. Geoffrey told Graves that the story had been 'a horrible shock', but, when investigated, had turned out to be untrue.

It was just a rumour and we are back where we started. The most embittering thing of all is that the War Office has consistently refused to do anything but search the graves and cemeteries round Zutphen and Arnhem: where he almost certainly was not buried. However we are continuing all our efforts through every kind of MP, peer or general we can get hold of: meanwhile my parents are haunted by thoughts of concentration camps, etc.

I was going to Burma, of course, with this battery but the end of the war has released me, and I am disbanding again (to disband two batteries – my old anti-aircraft one and this – within a year must be quite a record).[471]

Geoffrey told Graves that he had already written to Jenny to tell her that the truth about the *Sunday Times*, 'which has since retracted its story'.

The *Sunday Times* story was seen by other friends of the family, who were as horrified as Graves by its allegations. On 11 September, a Brian Spray, who knew the Cotterells well, wrote from his RAF unit, British Army of the Rhine:

Even after one has been over here and seen and heard evidence of the inhuman bestial behaviour of the SS amongst their own people as well as ours, it is difficult to believe that such a brave, upstanding life as Anthony's should come to an end at the hands of these men.[472]

Spray believed that a duty was owed to Anthony and the other war dead to stop anything of the same sort ever happening again: 'Their sacrifice has placed the opportunity fully in our hands and nothing can excuse us if we fail.' He signed himself 'Most sincerely and sympathetically – Brian Spray'. These very well-meaning, heartfelt words can have brought little comfort to the family, who were desperately trying to preserve their faith that somewhere Anthony was still alive.

Geoffrey was now ardently hoping to get posted to Germany rather than to the Mediterranean, which was being mooted as another possibility.[473] And at last that autumn his wish was granted; he obtained a posting to the British Army of the Rhine, which was desperately short of German speakers to help administer the occupation of Germany. No specific post had yet been identified, but Geoffrey's initial destination was Belgium. He left England around 21 October.

His first few days on the Continent were spent in Ostend, then at Lierre and Antwerp. After six years of being penned-up in severely rationed England, his senses were stunned by what he saw. Writing to his parents, he shared with them his almost hallucinatory sense of wonder.

23 October

We moved from Ostend yesterday morning [...] Shops bright and marvellously lit. We are now at Lierre which is fairly close to Antwerp. I visited Antwerp last night. Marvellous lights, scents, fountain pens, etc: most enjoyable. More British about than Belgians. But the whole impression I found quite unreal; there is also still the same smell of cigar smoke everywhere, though of course not many cigars.

The amazing excess of material goods continued to amaze him with its profligacy. Two days later he wrote again to his parents.

25 October

The food in the officers' clubs is simply superb. My dinner last night was totally pre-war, though perhaps a little less in quantity. All the shops, which have beautiful displays, are lit up at night, and make me realise what a fantastic amount we haven't got. All knick-knacks, of course, scent, grapes in millions, furniture, Frank Harris (in a brown cover), a great many shoe shops with lousy shoes. Not a soul has asked me for a cigarette or offered to exchange something! This is most disappointing. Para 4 of Leave Regulations puts all brothels out of bounds. Everything in the way of drink is vilely expensive once you leave the officers' clubs, which are so good: they are simply hotels taken over by the NAAFI and mainly run by former staff.

But Geoffrey was not content to simply enjoy himself; he wanted to relieve his parents' anxiety about Anthony as soon as possible. The details of where his posting would take him had not yet arrived in Lierre. Taking a mildly reckless chance that they would not do so for three or four days (if he was summoned immediately and failed to turn up, he could get into serious trouble), he left Belgium for Holland on 26 October. The details of his trip he would send to his mother in a long letter concluding on 30 October, using the same diary form which Janie had used to write her letters from Holland.

Since Janie's visit in May, the Cotterell family had been in constant touch with the Tjeenk Willinks in Brummen, and it was for their house that Geoffrey immediately headed. The two families had grown very close in the last five months. There was a constant interchange of letters between Aps and Mintie, and the eldest son, Dick, also wrote frequently. The Tjeenk Willink letters were full of thanks for the parcels which the Cotterells sent to war-ruined Holland, gifts which included clothes, tobacco, and medical books to help with Dick's training as a doctor in Utrecht. Mintie and Aps were fast becoming close friends. They had two sons of roughly the same age, and Dick's resemblance to Anthony could only win Mintie's heart, whilst Aps had the greatest sympathy and understanding for the nightmare of anxiety from which Mintie was suffering.

Because the Dutch family's name was so long (in its most attenuated form it was actually Tjeenk Willink Meinders), Geoffrey usually abbreviated it to Willink in his letters home.

26 October

I hitchhiked my way quite successfully, arriving at Brummen about tea time. Mrs Willink was having tea with a woman who looked like Queen Wilhelmina. I had been driven through Arnhem, over the bridge and then along the road of the fatal journey.

I visited Dr Korteweg next door, an enormous man with wife and small daughter. Both houses, comfortable, the Willinks built rather like the Townleys.[474] Brummen a large and attractive village.

Korteweg took the photograph round all the people who saw the incident but they did not recognise Anthony. Korteweg recognised the face, but couldn't place which it was. He went over the wounds again and gave his opinion that A did not go to Enschede because he was not bad enough. (I am now pretty sure that this is the case.) He had a theory about the dressing station, but the house he had in mind had been bombed since. He rang up a doctor in Zutphen who was inclined to agree with him. Not encouraging. [...]

27 October

During breakfast Dick Willink, the son, arrived. He had at once hitchhiked his way from Utrecht, as soon as he heard I was there.

After breakfast I produced the very generous rations the ration clerk at Lierre had given when he heard I was going to Holland. Mrs Willink was overwhelmed. Their food situation in this district is not at all catastrophic, a not quite so good version of English civilian rations. Plenty of apples, plenty of bread, small amounts of butter and cheese, very thin slices of smoked bacon. Certainly not luxurious. and they certainly like eating. I have just watched Mrs Willink, who is not a fat woman, eat five apples straight off before going to bed.

Willink took me to the scene of the incident and I saw exactly where the wounded were laid. Then we hitchhiked to Zutphen, which had had plenty of damage, especially round the bridge.

I didn't believe Korteweg's theory because it didn't quite fit Major Gough's story. We set off [...] and finally located a small street and a house with three steps, or four including the pavement. This did fit in. It was now the office of the Dutch Political Police, and, yes, they said, it had been a Luftwaffe dressing station. Just inside there was a room and an inner-room exactly as Major Gough described it. So we had found it.

We searched the house for signs of Germans, but there was nothing. There was a paved courtyard at the back, so he couldn't possibly have been buried there. The house was quite large and in the middle of a busy little street.

Geoffrey does not give the address of this house, but it was not No.12 Rozenhoflaan. Through his Dutch helpers, he would find the right house in mid November, but for the moment he and Dick believed that they had been successful.

Afterwards, they went on to the hospital and found the name of a German surgeon who had been there in September 1944 – Richter – but nothing else. Richter would indeed turn out to be the right man, but Geoffrey would not meet him until January 1946.

On their return to Brummen, Aps told Geoffrey that a local woman who had witnessed the shooting had seen one of the wounded laughing and had been amazed that he could do so in such dire circumstances. Geoffrey clearly believed that this might have been Anthony, meeting terrible adversity with his usual gaiety – 'It doesn't seem unlikely to me'. The woman, however, could not be certain if she recognised Anthony from the photograph which he showed her, nor could another man who came to tea that same day who had also seen the shooting. In this man's opinion there were only two gravely wounded men besides the three who had been killed immediately. Geoffrey wrote:

> Since these must have been the two who did die, it does begin to look more and more as if A's was not so severe as we thought.
>
> Mrs Willink's brother-in-law arrived. He had been a doctor at Apeldoorn. Through him and some telephoning we found that Sängerling was the chief doctor there and the Town Major was Von Oldershausen. Then that Döderlein was the Zutphen Town Major, who was under Major Peters, who was at Arnhem and later at Zutphen, and he was under Von Oldershausen. Clues now coming fast.

The search over the coming months would follow this pattern: exhaustive, laborious, time-consuming research, yielding tiny grains of information, some of it useful, some of it false or misleading. It was a colossal task, only made easier because the Dutch were so eager to help and because the events were still within fairly recent memory.

In other ways, circumstances were not at all propitious. Many records had been destroyed, including Dutch civilian records, some accidentally, some deliberately. This included records from the hospitals, some of which had been taken by the Germans when they left. As regards to tracing particular Germans, the military situation at the time of the battle of Arnhem had been very fluid, with many units simply passing through. Afterwards, during the closing months of the war, millions of German soldiers had been captured by the Russians, British or Americans, or had disappeared, committed suicide, or been killed. Whatever fate the individual soldiers had met, the magnificent armies which they had once served had been scattered to the four winds.

Geoffrey, who was very tall and very noticeable in his British Army Major's uniform, was an object of both admiration and curiosity to the Dutch. When he and Dick went out again on the search on 28 October, he soon discovered himself to be a fascinating creature to children.

We cycled very early 16 kilometres to Willink's grandfather, a doctor of 82 who goes round his patients on a cycle. He occasionally cycles the 16 kilos himself. We borrowed his 1928 model Peerless (a firm long since deservedly bankrupt, I hope) and it wouldn't start. Since it hadn't been used since 1942, this did not surprise me, but everyone else was most annoyed. (What had they paid good money in 1928 for?) A garage man was brought in and finally it went. About one and a half miles out of the village it stopped. Then started, did another quarter of a mile and stopped again, this time for good. Willink started walking for the next village. I remained, surrounded by an ever increasing number of small children. I learnt their names, they mine, and then I had the happy idea of suggesting that they pushed me. It was enthusiastically received. Finally about a dozen children arrived and I and Peerless were pushed most comfortably for another three-quarters of a mile, where I found a Canadian who managed to start it again, drove on, and found Willink. The process of stopping every mile or so went on for some time. Finally we got an overhaul at a garage where the proprietor knew Willink. (He knows most people in Holland.)

(Random impressions of Holland. Big beautiful villages, houses built to eat square meals in, everybody fond of eating, habit of letting things go cold, such as soup or tea, habit of sitting round in a circle and staring at each other. Excellent fittings everywhere.)

Geoffrey and Dick stopped for a while at Hengelo to research doctors' names there, and then went on to Enschede, where they saw the hospital register:

I saw the list of names of the Arnhem boys, as written at the time by a nurse. Tannenbaum and McNabb were included. I took a complete copy. There was nothing to be learnt about who had sent them. I went to see Trevor McNabb's grave which was well kept. (Has anyone else seen it? I am sending a note to Gough so that he can tell Mrs McNabb, if no one has.) No sign of a second man who was supposed to have died, Francis Stern – presumably the soldier? Underneath the list of names was written in English handwriting, 'C.E.M. Graham 23/27 Sep 44.'[475]

Then to Almelo. 14 parachutists had been there. Met the son of a baker who had smuggled fruit in to them and just escaped being caught. I saw the letters of gratitude from the boys (all now identified) and also a note smuggled out of the hospital at the time: 'Dear Friend, please try and get us some maches and we shall all be very greatful. Yrs W. Gilchrist.' Very moving. I thanked him for what he had done. Also saw the English graves, but no sign and all named.

We called at Lochem and inspected the complete list of graves there. (Korteweg and Willink have definitely visited every possible hospital and cemetery.) Then returned the car to grandfather, who resembled the Kaiser. We then cycled a longer route back (I don't know how I survived this) via Zutphen, called on the Provost and were told that progress had been made. Returned to Brummen where Sergeant Kemp was waiting for us. He had been investigating the Germans' sex lives.

Geoffrey, reporting what was only his second contact with him, slightly misspelled the name of Sergeant Gerrit Kamp, who would be the greatest of all his helpers in the search for Anthony.[476]

Kamp was about to galvanise the investigation and breathe new life into it. In a letter of 7 February 1946, Geoffrey would pen a portrait of him for Mintie:

You asked what Kamp is like: like an innocent, good-natured young Himmler. People are so busy looking at the innocence of his face that they are unaware that his hands are in their pockets. His address is de Slightestraat 33, Almelo, Holland.

This address appears to have been Kamp's mother's home, and he did not live there full-time. Nonetheless, he had very good contacts with the local police. Police Detective Jan Arend IJspeerd of the Almelo Investigation Department was one of these, and his telephone number appears on a long list of contacts which can only have been compiled by Kamp. IJspeerd would prove of particular help in the search for Anthony, and in January 1946 Geoffrey would write a personal letter of thanks to him.[477]

When Geoffrey knew Kamp, he was a military policeman. He worked for 33 Netherlands War Crimes Commission, which was based at Herford, near Bad Oeynhausen in Germany, Bad Oeynhausen being the location of the British War Crimes Group (NWE) offices. 33 Netherlands War Crimes Commission would make an immeasurable contribution to the search, not least by virtually secunding Kamp for two years. It was Kamp who would unearth myriads of leads to former Dutch Nazis, SS or SD men, who might be implicated in Anthony's disappearance. He would also trace dozens of potential witnesses. His skill at ferreting things out would prove phenomenal.

Kamp had been in the Dutch underground during the war, or at least this is what Geoffrey believed.[478] Kamp almost certainly never told him that before the war he had been in the Nationaal-Socialistische Beweging (NSB), the Dutch Nazi movement. Though he had resigned his membership, he had continued pro-German and during the war was an informant of the SD. It is most unlikely that Kamp's superiors knew of his treasonable behaviour, or that he would ever have held his position had they known. In 1947 he would be accused of collaboration with the Germans and complicity in a war crime. The case went to court, and there was a protracted trial. Ultimately Kamp would be acquitted, but there remained a dark shadow over his reputation.[479] Whether he had actually committed this crime and guilt played some part in what was to be a highly obsessive involvement in Anthony's case, can only be speculation. Geoffrey, however, would always believe that Kamp was innocent. The details of Kamp's trial will be covered in a later chapter.[480]

Kamp was fluent in both English and German. His language skills often allowed him to be highly devious; three months after he had met him, Geoffrey told Mintie of an interview in which Kamp purposefully mislead a Dutch collaborator.

> It was very fascinating interviewing the Dutch collaborationist girl yesterday, as Sergeant Kamp posed as an Englishman and asked a string of leading questions about Zutphen to see if she gave the right answers; unfortunately she did. But it's amusing to reflect that she will never know that the Dutch now know exactly who she is and that she was interviewed by a Dutch man. Moral: you never know where you are.[481]

Kamp was mainly based at Herford, but he also sometimes worked in Zutphen, where there was a Detachment Office.[482] In Kamp's initial report on Anthony's case, he stated that Geoffrey had called into the Zutphen office at 5.00pm on 27 October, asking for their assistance in finding his brother. This was the first time that the two men met. The meeting at the Tjeenk Willinks' the following day took place after Kamp had already done some preliminary research – the 'Germans' sex lives' reference in Geoffrey's letter was to Kamp's investigations amongst Dutch girls suspected of having had relationships with German soldiers.

Kamp may already have known about Anthony's case. Since the end of the war, numerous enquiries about Anthony had already been made in Zutphen, not only by the British and Dutch authorities but also by Tony Hibbert and Freddie Gough. Mintie had written to various organisations, including both the two hospitals. Newspaper appeals had also been made. The War Office summarised some of the enquiries in a letter to British officials in Germany at the end of September 1945.[483] The letter is very pessimistic in tone.

> Since that time [when Gough left Anthony] nothing has been heard of Major Cotterell, and while it now seems certain that he must have died, no reports of his capture, death or burial

have been received from the German authorities, although on the 4 Oct 44 they broadcast their version of the shooting incident and mentioned that Major Cotterell was severely wounded [...] Extensive enquiries have been made of the Burgomaster, Doctors' Association, Hospitals and Political Bureau by the Town Major of Zutphen, without results, and [...] a search of the cemeteries in the Enschede area has also proved fruitless.[484]

It is regrettable that in spite of the information available [...] no firm trace has yet been found of Major Cotterell or any reliable evidence obtained in regard to his ultimate fate.

It is not known whether your 'Searcher' organization has already handled this case, but if not, it is requested that any further steps which may be possible should be taken to clear it up without delay.

The letter concluded that as General Sir Ronald Adam, the Adjutant-General of the British Army, had taken a personal interest in the case, 'an early report would be appreciated'.

Kamp's Dutch bosses gave him *carte blanche* to pursue enquiries about Anthony. His immediate boss, a major whom Geoffrey always referred to as 'Kamp's Major', was consistently friendly and helpful whenever Geoffrey spoke to him. As Geoffrey told Mintie, 'Sergeant Kamp is prepared to stay until the Dutch demand him back'.[485] In another letter to his mother, he wrote: 'Forever be grateful to Sergeant Kamp, a Dutchman possessed of an intense desire to repay the English (as he told Mrs Willink), who had worked on the case almost every day since. His fantastic thoroughness is unbelievable.'[486]

Kamp even devoted much of his own spare time to the case. In Anthony's British case file, there is an undated handwritten note about Kamp, which says that as Kamp had conducted the investigations 'in his own time', he could not be given travel permits by the Dutch War Crimes people, and that as before 'he needs authorities from us', 'us' probably being the British War Crimes Group.[487]

Kamp would become good friends with Aps, whom Geoffrey had chosen as his representative in Holland on all matters concerning Anthony. In early 1946, a letter from Dick to Mintie told her, 'When I came home, in Brummen, a fortnight ago, it was about 12 o'clock in the evening – Mama and Kamp were still sitting near the stove.'[488] These few words conjure up a delightful picture of Aps and Kamp, sitting next to the stove on a cold winter's night around Christmas, bound by their huge common interest – the search for Anthony.

30

HAMBURG

Much though he would have liked to stay on in Holland, Geoffrey had to get back to Belgium before he overstayed his unofficial leave. On 28 October, he left for Lierre, hitchhiking all the way. At Lierre, he received orders to travel to Bünde and at the beginning of November crossed the border into Germany. He was entering an extraordinary world where the British were the all-powerful conquerors and the Germans their subject people. Whilst life in Belgium had seemed normal, even luxurious, in Germany he would see the polar opposite, the desperate struggle for existence of an utterly crushed and demoralised nation.

The victors had divided Germany into four zones: French, American, Russian and British. To the west, the British Zone bordered Holland (and Belgium), which made it easy for Geoffrey to take research trips. To the north were the Baltic and Scandinavia, whilst to the south lay the American Zone and the smaller French Zone. To the east lay the Russian Zone, its territory and secrets ferociously guarded. Berlin lay within this Zone, but was itself divided into four sectors, giving the Allies shared control of the capital.

Each of the four Zones had its own bureaucracy, its own language, its own protocol, and its own agenda. In his search for potential witnesses or guilty men, Geoffrey would gain access to information and people in the British, French and American Zones, but anything under Russian control was effectively off limits. The beginnings of the Cold War lay in this period, and due to the increasingly hostile attitude of the Russians the hope that Anthony might be alive but a Russian prisoner would prove impossible to test.

The British Zone was administered by the British Army of the Rhine, the BAOR, whose Commander-in-Chief was Field Marshal Montgomery. As Military Governor, Montgomery saw the Occupation as 'an act of war', whose aim was to destroy all remnants of the Nazi system in the media, education, the judicial system, and public life.[489] The German people were viewed with the blackest mistrust, and very strict ordinances had been put in place to govern their behaviour and that of the British who were ruling them.

At his new posting with 10 German News Service (British Zone), BAOR, Geoffrey would effectively be a part of the military government. He would be in charge of the German reporters of the News Service, as well as the British reporters who went around with them to keep an eye on what they were doing. His brief was to monitor the news, making sure that it followed approved lines and contained no taint of Nazi thinking.

Initially posted to Bünde, on 2 November Geoffrey dropped a line to his mother saying that in half an hour he was 'accompanying a Colonel, presumably my Colonel, to Hamburg, in a Mercedes Benz'. And it was Hamburg which was to remain his home until he was demobbed eight months later, in June 1946.

Sited on the right bank of the river Elbe, Hamburg had surrendered to the British without a fight at the end of April 1945; its *Gauleiter*, Karl Kaufmann, had no stomach for a pointless last stand – the city had suffered enough.[490] Horribly mauled by Allied bombing raids, the largest port in Germany lay in ruins. You could easily drive for 15 minutes and not see a single standing building, only acre upon acre of dusty rubble. The river Alster wound through the ruined city to feed its two lakes, the Binnen Alster and the Aussen Alster. Geoffrey, who had known Hamburg well during his time in Germany in 1936, soon discovered that the only feature which he recognised was the skyline around the two lakes. A popular saying about the way in which the Zones had been allocated was that the Americans got the scenery, the French got the wine, and the British got the ruins.[491]

Hamburg was a key city of the British Occupation, but, as Geoffrey would soon become aware, much of the most important administrative work was done elsewhere, 'in the mysterious towns of Bad Oeynhausen, Bünde and Herford, where the greatest decisions and most solemn decrees are enacted'.[492] It was from these three German towns that almost all the official work on Anthony's case emanated.

In 1949, Geoffrey would publish a novel called *Randle in Springtime*, which was based upon the diary he had kept during his time in Hamburg with the BAOR. The book was dedicated to Anthony. Howard Randle, the anti-hero of the novel, travels to his first posting in Germany along half-destroyed roads and across Bailey bridges. He sees a sardonic roadside notice which reflects the ruinous state of the highways, its message reading, 'Drive Carefully – Death is so Permanent'. But reckless speed is an impossibility when his Army jeep comes up behind a decrepit German truck, hogging the road at 15 miles per hour.

> A crowd of faces stared out from the back of it. Dressed in the usual variety of semi-uniform, fur coats and dusty rags, they were of every age and the same age, every experience and the same experience. They were defeated, poor, hungry, depressed, pale and helpless. They stared without embarrassment [...Randle] sat up as the jeep came close, conscious that in front of Germans one ought not to slouch [...] They sat, crouched or stood without moving, like a collection of waxworks [...] What lay behind their expressionless eyes was impossible to know.

The driver of Randle's jeep keeps his finger on the hooter button, trying to frighten the lorry out of the way. He and Randle curse the Germans, saying that they would put the whole lot in Belsen, 'a taste of their own medicine'.

> 'It's a pity we can't kill the lot.'
> 'Whoa! Here we go!'
> The lorry swerved into the side to make way for an oncoming staff car. The driver waited for it to flash by, varnished, beflagged, red tabs in the back in sheltered comfort, and then he flung the jeep forward and round the lorry, tearing down the road.[493]

The glamorous staff car with its high-ranking military passengers had swept aside the non-people as if they were gnats. Geoffrey, travelling in the Mercedes-Benz with his Colonel, may well have experienced similar scenes.

Once arrived at Hamburg, he would find life not too bad at all. His new accommodation was 'highly comfortable, my bedroom being the one recently vacated by Mr Sefton Delmer'.[494] Delmer was a highly influential journalist and broadcaster, so Geoffrey had evidently got a very good room. The room had the added bonus of being next door to a very large bathroom. In a letter to his mother of 25 November, he would write that he lived very well:

> A man wakes me up about eight every morning and either supplies a pail of warm water or, if the hot water is running, turns the bath taps on next door. I walk round and breakfast at the mess in the next street. [...]

Wine is suddenly in short supply, which is rather unfortunate for it was extremely cheap, and far healthier than the alternatives – vodka etc, which however I dislike. [...]

I went to the Sadlers Wells Ballet which was here last week; not my cup of tea but they were extremely good.

Excellent music and high culture were features of the occupation, officially considered to be elevating for the human spirit. On a more earthly level, there were good restaurants and clubs to dine out at, such as the Atlantic Hotel and the Officers' Country Club. At Geoffrey's workplace, the offices of 10 German News Service were comfortable. As for the work transport: 'Half the time we drive round in large slinky Mercedes Benzes, the other half in Utility cars as at the gun site.'[495]

10 German News Service was located at 169 Rothenbaum Chaussee. Radio Hamburg lay opposite, where, in April 1946, Geoffrey would begin to make weekly, carefully scripted and rehearsed broadcasts in German. There he would also meet various artistes, including Mrs Max Schmeling, whom he memorably characterised as 'sweet and girlish as a cobra'.[496]

British-controlled Radio Hamburg had begun four days before the war ended. Because Hamburg had surrendered without a fight, the studios and transmitters had been captured virtually intact. Amongst the last transmissions under German control had been the drunken final broadcast of Lord Haw-Haw – William Joyce. He would have been aware that he could expect no mercy from the victors when he made his rambling intoxicated farewell.[497]

By the time that Geoffrey arrived in Hamburg, the station had become North West German Radio, or NWDR, though Geoffrey always referred to it in his letters as Radio Hamburg. BBC engineers and personnel had moved in, including Hugh Carleton-Greene who oversaw the creation of a fine independent service modelled on the BBC. NWDR had the largest audience of any station in post-war Germany.[498] Perhaps Geoffrey's finest hour as a broadcaster was when Kamp told him that he had gone into a German pub and discovered that all the customers were listening to Geoffrey's programme.

That winter would be a hard one, and by January temperatures had fallen so low that both the Alster lakes froze.[499] Geoffrey's billet looked out over a vista of frozen canals, bordered by frost-bitten gardens, but it was warm inside and he did not suffer from the cold. The British had understandably requisitioned the best houses and hotels for their own people, buildings which until very recently had been owned or frequented by Nazi grandees.

The way in the British lived, though not particularly luxurious by pre-war standards, was paradisiacal compared to conditions for the Germans. Most of the population had been reduced to living in one or two rooms, with little fuel for heating and the chills of winter blowing through the dilapidated buildings. On 1 December, Geoffrey would report to Mintie:

We had some snow the other day but it has cleared up and this morning was brilliant sunshine. I went for a walk. Very occasionally you get what appears to be a glance of hate, but only occasionally. They are dressed in slightly pantomimey but warm clothes, on the whole warmer that a similar English crowd I wouldn't be surprised. Nor do they yet – en masse – look hungry, though they are all losing weight. They have plenty to lose. They all complain of the cold in their rooms, as if it is an unjust affliction which certainly no one else has ever experienced. This total lack of perception of other people's worries is fantastic.

Like all the British, Geoffrey had almost no sympathy to spare for the race which had brought such ruination upon the world. There was a deep mutual suspicion, verging at times on paranoia, between the victors and the defeated. The abominations of the concentration camps had utterly poisoned the British attitude to the German people. They had read the papers and seen the news reels, and were now hearing the whole story all over again, in even more horrific detail, in the newspaper coverage of first the Belsen and then the Nuremberg trials.

Geoffrey's novel, *Randle in Springtime*, perfectly evokes the queasy relations between the two nations. To be alone with a mass of Germans, even if you wore the uniform of the victor, was to feel deeply uncomfortable. Yet it was impossible not to form closer relations with individuals. Randle and his fellow Brits kept scraps of their mess breakfast to augment the pitiful rations of their German office staff. The majority of Germans were living in a state of the direst poverty, and cigarettes were common currency. Randle paid two to the man who carried his luggage to the station, two a week to the woman who did his washing. Whenever a cigarette butt was discarded, it was eagerly seized by the Germans as being of great value.

Something like an apartheid system was in operation. There was a curfew for Germans, although they were allowed to go about after hours if accompanied by a British person; the former air-raid siren was used to announce the prohibited hours. Railway stations had platforms reserved for Allied Forces which were often almost empty, whilst those for the Germans swarmed with humanity. There were draconian restrictions on travel, and at the heavily guarded border into Holland armed guards zealously checked the identification numbers and credentials of all vehicles and their occupants.

Observing the Germans was a fascination to a writer like Geoffrey. Soon after arriving in Hamburg, he went to a symphony concert out of curiosity because they were playing Götterdämmerung: 'I thought it would be interesting to watch the Germans at it. They certainly have bought it: passing them in the street they look reasonably all right: but en masse and viewed from the Occupying Officers' Box (!) they look pretty grim.'

In *Randle in Springtime*, he would describe the same concert:

> When you see them pacing up and down in the interval, never speaking, looking ahead, eighty per cent of them are women and half the men minus limbs or eyes. Are they just thinking about their rations and the black market or are they remembering? So short a time ago the place was filled with glamorous uniforms, the women had their men.[500]

Watching the British who were administering the Occupation was equally fascinating. *Randle in Springtime* records their idiosyncratic slang, such as 'fratting', which was short for fraternising, and 'my frat' which meant 'my girlfriend'. Fraternisation had been completely banned during the early months of the occupation, but the decree had proved so unworkable and counterproductive that Montgomery had finally abolished it on 25 September. Another piece of slang was 'Are you black?', meaning 'Are you on the blackmarket?' The blackmarket was a huge problem, but the more upright British would have nothing to do with it because of their moral concern for the good name of the occupation.

For those who were weak-willed, the lure of easy money was hard to resist. The value of ordinary things had become skewed as if in some *Alice Through the Looking Glass* world. Pound notes were supposed to be left in England because of their very high blackmarket value, as were collectors' postage stamps which were a small independent currency of their own.[501] One of the quickest ways of making extra money was to sell one's standard drink ration from the mess. This was two bottles of Schlichte (German juniper-flavoured gin), one bottle of German brandy, and a bottle of whisky, all of which had to be paid for but at minimum cost. Alcohol was hugely in demand, and properly manufactured drink was infinitely preferable to the sometimes lethal bootleg liquor. In Geoffrey's novel, Randle sells three bottles of Schlichte (his own ration and half of someone else's) for 800 marks, a small fortune when a meal at the Atlantic Hotel costs around 20 marks. The bottle is then sold on by a middle man to a waiter for 900 marks, and then is presumably marked up once again when the waiter sells the individual drinks. Meanwhile Randle, whose costs have been less than 100 marks, walks around with the comfortable feeling that he has a month's pay in his pocket.[502]

Despite the benefits – legal or otherwise – of being the ruling elite, many of the British could hardly wait to be demobbed; they had been in uniform and under military governance for years, and only wanted to be set free to get on with their own lives. Only the more thoughtful realised that the extraordinary status which they now enjoyed would instantly evaporate once they returned to England and went back to some tawdry pre-war job on minuscule wages. In Hamburg they were members of a highly privileged ruling caste.

For the time being, being a member of that caste admirably suited Geoffrey's purposes. In the search for information about Anthony, he and his helper, Kamp, the Dutch military policeman, would interfere in the private life of Germans in a manner inconceivable in a normal democratic peacetime society. They had no real licence, warrant or authority except in the uniforms which they were wearing, particularly Geoffrey's as a British Army Major. Germans would read these uniforms as giving Geoffrey and Kamp the power to report them to the authorities for some real or invented misdemeanour if they did not cooperate. But fear, obstinacy, and national group solidarity would, nonetheless, often make them maddeningly incommunicative. Geoffrey frequently complained in his letters home that the invariable German answer to any question was 'I do not know' or 'I do not remember'.[503] Sometimes verbal bullying and threats had to be used to move things forward, something from which Geoffrey shrunk but at which Kamp excelled.

The Germans had another reason for keeping silent. War criminal trials were a completely unexpected development to them despite repeated Allied warnings during the war. They feared incriminating themselves or incriminating others. The speedy hanging in December 1945 of those found guilty in the Belsen trial demonstrated how deeply committed the Allies were to establishing the principle of German war guilt. Ordinary people who had turned into monsters like the Belsen camp guards were almost more shocking to the British than the top leaders of the Nazi state, nearly all of whom were dead with the notable exception of Hermann Göring. The entire nation was tainted by association.

As a perfectly valid part of his work, but also out of a contemptuous curiosity, Geoffrey went to the Belsen trial on 7 November. He told his mother:

> Today I went to the Belsen trial, and had a good gape at the thugs. Fascinating [...] The thugs seemed pretty calm and collected. Professor Smith, an international law expert, made a long speech all day trying to prove that they weren't criminals at all. I was translating this at the end of the day to one of our reporters, who said in bewilderment: 'What a nation!'[504]

Randle in Springtime would describe a concentration camp trial, where one of the horrible fascinations was the calmness and ordinariness of the accused, 'white-faced with prison pallor, with numbers on their chests, as if they were footballers, dull, normal-looking men and women, bored but not depressed, their hair brushed and carefully parted'.[505] The sight of them was nonetheless so terrible that Randle could not bear to look at them.

31

THE WAR CRIMES GROUP AND THE SEARCH BUREAU

On taking up his new post, Geoffrey began the first of a series of highly detailed letters to his mother. It was not possible to telephone home, so he wrote daily, sometimes even twice a day, knowing how desperately anxious she and Graham were for news of Anthony. If, due to some research trip, he could not write for several days, he would give her all the news in one long letter as soon as he was able to. He was not only diligent but also scrupulously accurate in reporting to his mother the details of what he discovered; what he told her can be validated in numerous official documents. He did not hide anything from her, though he often tried to soften its impact by soothing, cheerful words. His letters show an astonishing maturity for a young man who was only 26.

Today it is a one-sided correspondence as Mintie's 71 letters, which were numbered, have nearly all been lost, but what she wrote can often be reconstructed from his replies. Mintie could be rather fiery, and it is obvious that there was the occasional contretemps, as revealed for example in his note of 12 December:

> Post just arrived together with eight uppercuts and a couple of body blows. Numbering is excellent, they are all kept. I am minus approx no. 8 which presumably contained news of RAC. Babers I have replied to. Copy Mrs Willinks I received. Didn't I thank you for the subscription? I can't understand it. I am now in a flaming hurry ... will write from south if I find a post office, otherwise don't expect to hear from me for a few days.[506]

Geoffrey was off on a very important research trip, his first to the American Zone, but he had still made time to answer his mother's admonitions and to tell her that he was going.

From the first days of his arrival in Hamburg, Geoffrey had been on the look-out for anything which might be of assistance in the search. Given the iron curtain which had now descended, even the smallest illumination of what was happening in the Russian Zone was of value.[507] On 7 November, he wrote to Mintie that he had been to a transit camp for German refugees from the Russian Zone, who were going back home to West Germany. Though the camp had been built for 4,000 people, there were only 400 there. He spoke to a good many of them, and observed that none of them were starving, the children were fairly well dressed, 'and I wasn't fed any Russian cruelty stories'. All the same the refugees gave him the impression of 'people just received from a V1 incident – the better ones perhaps more like the tube-dwellers in the Blitz'.

By 10 November, he was telling his mother of meeting the various military government police chiefs – mostly English chief constables. He went to a Polish Displaced Person camp, 'where rape, murder and theft are too common to be discussed. Germans highly scared of them and I'm not at all surprised.' All the same he noted that the 'German capacity for self-pity' was creeping up again: 'They cannot believe that they are not the only people to suffer.'

But they're certainly not having a bright time. We were trying to get our reporters on a higher ration scale because of their irregular hours etc – and we checked over the amounts they get. It didn't seem so bad on the whole – if anything slightly better than the English civilian ration. We pointed this out acidly to the German reporter, who pointed out in his turn that we were looking at the German ration for a <u>month</u>, not a week. (But they have no conception at all that the Dutch are starving as well.)

Work kept him very occupied:

On arriving at the office I check up that all the reporters are busy, ring up anyone necessary to ensure their entrance, arrange for facilities for someone to go down to the Ruhr, go and see someone about is it true two Hamburg councillors have been sacked for being Nazi, read the output of the agency for the day before – about forty pages – the German papers, the English papers which are flown over the same day in good weather [...] so I keep relatively well occupied when not engaged in the search.

The search was the constant preoccupation of himself and his parents. As he once told Mintie, 'Don't think you write too much about it; as you know I think of almost nothing else. In fact, exclude the almost.'[508]

Working alongside Germans was already proving very useful. On 12 November he wrote to Mintie to tell her that there were no new developments to report, but that one thing had been most conclusively proved, 'how right we were and how horribly wrong the casualty department'.

Our chief reporter knew all about Anthony's work. He himself worked in the Goebbels department which watched over English publications and he says that *What No Morning Tea ...* (What something? he said. What something? It was the first one...!) ... was discussed at great length! At any rate it is a comfort to be proved right.

The casualty department of the War Office had insisted that Anthony was of insufficient interest to the Germans to have been singled out for special treatment. But now evidence was beginning to mount up that his name and work had indeed been well-known. The fact that he had been specifically mentioned by name in the Radio Hilversum broadcast of 4 October had always suggested that this was the case. Geoffrey's research in Germany now added further confirmation, even though much of it only related to general Nazi policy as opposed to being specifically about Anthony.

Geoffrey was often very successful in getting such useful background information from the people he met through 10 German News Service. He was in a position of some influence, and, if for no other reason, people wanted to help him because he might do them a favour in return. Towards the end of November, he told his mother that he had had a long conversation with 'a man called Kiowlehn (roughly) who was apparently one of the most famous German journalists' and who very much wanted to work with 10 German News Service. Speaking of how the Nazis would have viewed Anthony, Kiowlehn said that they would have been 'madly interested in him'. Geoffrey therefore advised his mother: 'Don't get too impatient. Am still sure that the solution lies in the east. Incidentally talking of lost memories, what about Hess?'[509]

That Anthony had lost his memory and had therefore not been able to make contact with his home was another hope which the Cotterell family were stubbornly clinging onto.

Hope for Anthony constantly alternated with black fear. Koiwlehn and several others had told Geoffrey that as long as Anthony was with the Wehrmacht forces of Heeresgruppe B under Field Marshal Model, he would have been well-treated. Bittrich, one of Model's two top generals in the defence of Arnhem, also had a reputation for the scrupulous treatment of prisoners.

Albert Speer had met Bittrich at Arnhem, and had found him in a state of fury about the ill-treatment of British prisoners.[510] But this would not have helped Anthony if he had fallen into the hands of the SS or the SD, of whom there were large numbers in the Arnhem district in September 1944.

In his search for information about Anthony, or the situation at Arnhem after the battle, Geoffrey followed every avenue he could think of. On 25 November, he wrote to his mother:

I went down to an internment camp and spoke to several Freiherrs and Grafs of the General Staff [...] I got the name of a man already demobilised in Hamburg. After pursuing a false trail for some miles I found his father. Then finally got hold of the boy himself, a perfect Von Papen who was on the staff in the Arnhem district in September.[511] All he could tell me was the name of another officer who might be useful, and secondly that if a British major who was a war reporter was in Holland in September he himself was bound, through conversation, to know about it.[512] This interview took place in the house of Hamburg's former richest banker, who seems to have saved himself quite a few sticks of furniture.

On 27 November, he tried a different tack:

My spies (now a considerable organisation with fingers in the German Navy and General Staff) report that Staubwasser and Etter must definitely be in the south. Meanwhile Major Vogler, who was the Commander in Chief of Holland's Intelligence Office for prisoners, is being brought to see me on Thursday 29th. I don't think he will be able to help as a matter of fact, but I am seeing him to make sure he isn't a missing link.

To recap, Etter was the Wehrmacht officer who had helped the British prisoners at Brummen, whilst Staubwasser was his superior officer. Kiowlehn had already promised to help find the two men:

He [...] gave me another name to get hold of. He warned me that Model's HQ was severely bombed towards the end of 44. Just a warning. He promised to look for Staubwasser and Etter, in case they dodged the prison cage. As he is fairly keen to work up here, I think he'll try.

With Etter and Staubwasser, the difficulty – as with vast numbers of German ex-military – lay in tracing them. They might well have been killed in the last months of the war, or have disappeared in the chaos at its end. Like their commanding officer, Model, they may perhaps have committed suicide rather than allow themselves be captured. They might be held by the Russians and would thus be totally out of reach. Alternatively, if they were in the British, American or French Zone, somehow they must be found amongst the millions of German soldiers who were being held in prison camps; that process might take months because records were imperfect due to the huge numbers being processed.

Amongst the Germans in the holding camps were thousands of SD men, who in the Netherlands had been prominent in the control of the civilian population. As the SD and the Gestapo had had such a close working relationship, the organisations would be indicted together at Nuremberg, the eventual verdict being that membership of either of them was criminal (with the exception of clerical and stenographic staff). As for the SS, membership of it had always been deemed criminal though this would be formalised at Nuremberg.

Membership of the Wehrmacht, however, was not considered to be criminal, and its soldiers had been granted an amnesty. Though moves were made to define the High Command, the Oberkommando der Wehrmacht, a criminal organisation, Nuremberg would not find it to be such. However, those in the highest rank were castigated as a disgrace to the profession of arms, and it was recommended that where they had been guilty of crimes they should be tried individually.[513]

Both Etter and Staubwasser were Wehrmacht, and very small fry in army terms. Gradually German soldiers of their type were being released and going back into the community, but it was a very long process due to the necessity of checking that they were not members of the SS or SD, going under false names and papers. Archive film footage of German prisoners often shows them being checked under their arms for the tell-tale SS blood group tattoo, but this was not an infallible way of determining who was SS and who was not.

The places where the prisoners of war were held were often former Nazi concentration camps. In those former hell-holes, what was left of the once magnificent German army eked out a wretched half-life in their increasingly ragged uniforms. Staubwasser, when he was eventually traced in August 1946, was found to be in one of the most notorious concentration camps of all – Dachau.

At the same time as the enquiries being made by Geoffrey and Kamp, two parallel British official investigations were going on. These were conducted by the War Crimes Group, looking into the Brummen shooting which by the end of 1945 had officially been registered as a war crime, and the Search Bureau (DP and PW) which was looking for Anthony.

DP and PW stood for displaced persons and prisoners of war, and given the huge number of such unfortunates, the Search Bureau had a massive task on its hands. Its main office was in Bünde, and before he had been posted to Hamburg, Geoffrey had been able to go there and meet the man who was in charge of Anthony's case. This was a Captain Cranford, who allowed Geoffrey to see the 'enormous dossier', which included a photograph of Anthony and letters from the Liverpool department of the War Office with whom Mintie had been in touch. It also contained letters from the Adjutant-General's department. General Sir Ronald Adam, Anthony's old boss at ABCA, who was lending his weight and influence to galvanise the search. Geoffrey would shortly advise Mintie about one particular avenue she was exploring, 'Of course if there is any kind of difficulty with the Yanks, which there won't be, send at once to Sir R. Adam – or right away as you think best'.[514]

Geoffrey shared all the information which the Cotterells had privately gathered with Captain Cranford, and Cranford became extremely interested:

> He is going to ask to go for a fortnight to Russia about it. Permission has occasionally been granted: but of course there is this complete curtain, and there are at least 112 (names, I think unknown) British prisoners in Russia and possibly more unknown [...] he feels strongly that there are possibilities in the east – anyway I am going to have a German general interrogated in Hamburg to see if he has a line on Ettinger. And Cranford is seeing about having Otto Willy questioned in England. They have also got the name of another doctor called Krebs who was believed to be at the dressing station, and are looking for him.

Otto Willy was a lead, momentarily very exciting, which would turn out to be a dead end. As indeed would Dr Krebs, for it would soon be discovered that neither of the men had belonged to the correct dressing station in Zutphen. As for Ettinger, this was another possible name for the Wehrmacht officer who had assisted the prisoners in Brummen. There were three variants of it in circulation: Etter, Etting, and Ettinger.

Geoffrey may perhaps have also seen in Cranford's dossier the letter of 8 October written by the Search Bureau which had been circulated to various offices in the BAOR. It read:

Tracing of Missing Personnel – 153092 Major A.J. Cotterell, Royal Fusiliers

We have received an urgent request from the War Office to investigate the case of the above named officer, who, after being captured at Arnhem, was shot and seriously wounded ... on 23rd September 44. Several other prisoners were killed and wounded at the same time. A Dutch civilian doctor was allowed to render first-aid, and the wounded were eventually taken to a Luftwaffe dressing station at ZUTPHEN, where they were attended by two Luftwaffe NCOs.

Early on 24 Sep 44 all the wounded, with the exception of Major Cotterell, were removed to Germany. Before leaving, Major C.F.H. Gough, who at that time was a prisoner, obtained an assurance from a German Intelligence Officer, believed to be named Etter, that Major Cotterell would be well cared for. Since that time, nothing has been heard of him, despite extensive enquiries by 2nd Echelon.

We should be glad if you would do all that is possible to trace the German Intelligence Officer Etter. It is not known in this Bureau whether the shooting of prisoners at Arnhem has been logged as a war crime; but if such is the case there may be German witnesses who can identify the Intelligence Officer in question.

A reply on 22 October confirmed that Anthony's case was indeed known to JAG (War Crimes Section), JAG standing for the Judge Advocate General in London. The overall responsibility for war crimes investigations involving British nationals lay with JAG, and it was they who had given the Brummen shooting its original case number: MD/JAG/FS/61/4.

By late 1945, the various war crimes units operating with the BAOR had been merged to form the War Crimes Group (North West Europe).[515] There was a JAG (War Crimes Section), attached to the HQ of the BAOR in Bad Oeynhausen, which liaised with the main JAG offices in Spring Gardens, Cockspur St, London. There were also JAG liaison officers in non-British jurisdictions, such as Baden-Baden in the French Zone.

The BAOR had been the initial governing force in the British Zone under its Military Governor, Field Marshal Montgomery. It was based at the spa town of Bad Oeynhausen in Westphalia, because that is where it had been located when the war ended. However, a civilian organisation was now taking over many of the Occupation's functions. Known somewhat long-windedly as the Control Commission for Germany and Austria (British Element), its name was usually abbreviated to CCG (BE) or just CCG. Due to the necessity to liaise with the BAOR, it needed to be as close to Bad Oeynhausen as possible. However, because accommodation there was so limited, the CCG (BE) was based in satellite locations, mainly in Lübbecke, Minden, Herford and Bünde.

The fragmented locations brought administrative problems. The British Occupation would become a byword for a hydra-like bureaucracy, a mad proliferation of reference numbers, rubber stamps and red tape, and incessant duplication of roles and documents. The comparative personnel sizes of the CCG for the British and Americans at the end of 1946 were 24,785 and 5,008 respectively, this being for Zones which were not markedly different in size.[516] In Anthony's case, a blizzard of paperwork travelled between the various JAG and War Crimes Group offices attached to the BAOR, and those of the Search Bureau attached to the CCG (BE). Thus the same document was often copied into multiple dossiers, attesting to the labyrinthine way in which things were organised. Loss of control of the workload was an inevitable consequence. One official noted in ink, almost affectionately, on the brief outline of two war crimes which had just landed on his desk: 'A seems to be new, B seems to be an old friend in which Lieutenant Colonel Gough is interested.' A third party notes on the same document that 'B' obviously refers to Anthony's case.[517]

What appears to be the first surviving document of the JAG case on the Brummen war crime was written on 27 September 1945, a year and four days after the shooting. Addressed to the War Crimes Interrogation Unit (then the PWIS) at 6/7 Kensington Palace Gardens, W2, it gives an extremely brief summary of the war crime. It then describes the content of the Radio

Hilversum broadcast of 4 October 1944 which had named Anthony in person. Despite the poor sound quality of the broadcast, the document gives the name of the German NCO in charge of the prisoners as Corporal Matzke. Matzke was the man who had opened fire with his sub-machine gun, whilst the second perpetrator, still unnamed, was the one who had taken pot shots at the prisoners with a pistol.

Collating the information given by survivors of the shooting, such as Freddie Gough, Bernard Briggs, and Cecil Byng-Maddick, the letter then gave a composite picture of Matzke and his accomplice:

> The two persons concerned in the killing have been described as:
> (1) 5′8″–5′9″ in height; age 21–23; weight about 11 stone; fair hair; fresh complexion; showed signs of having been in the battle and was wounded
>
> 2) 5′9″–5′10″ in height; age 23–25; slim build; black curly hair; brownish eyes; sallow complexion; had a Jewish appearance; dressed in SS uniform and wearing the Hohenstaufen arm title; might have been wearing distinctive colour white indicating infantry; rank SS man.[518]

Someone has noted in pencil in the margin of 2) that this is Matzke.

The letter also noted that Matzke had probably belonged to 'the Provost Section of the SS Division concerned'. The writer of the letter concluded that he appreciated that the task was a difficult one, but could 'you check up to see if members of the SS Division Hohenstaufen have been captured and correspond to these descriptions'. It might also be as well to check for any members of the Provost Section, 'since in all probability the soldier concerned bragged to his comrades of his deeds'. These slender details were all there was to go on. The word 'difficult' was polite British understatement and a very inadequate description for the task of finding the murderers of the British soldiers at Brummen.

32

BACK TO HOLLAND

Whilst Geoffrey and his parents were making extensive enquiries, and the official British bodies were conducting their own investigations, Kamp, on secundment from 33 Netherlands War Crimes Commission, was making very considerable progress on his own. On 30 October, the day after Geoffrey returned to Lierre, Kamp discovered the real dressing station in Zutphen. The fact that it lay in Rozenhoflaan, within a couple of minutes' walk from the General Hospital in Coehoornsingel, would completely change the nature of the investigations. It now became obvious that the British soldiers treated in the dressing station could easily have walked for further treatment at the hospital. There soon followed a discovery of immense significance – two nurses at the hospital described a soldier who was very likely to have been Anthony coming in to be X-rayed on the Monday morning, some 36 hours after Gough had left him. If their testimonies were accurate, Anthony had been alive and still in Zutphen on 25 September 1944.

At the beginning of November 1945 Kamp would make his first report to his superiors.[519] It is incredibly detailed and thorough, and he almost comically concluded the extremely dense and compact document with 'Sir, I have nothing further to report'. He had covered an immense amount of ground in a very short time. Beginning with prominent members of the NSB, the Dutch Nazi movement, who were now in prison, he obtained the names of the Wehrmacht Commandant of Zutphen and his assistant. These names were Major Peters and Hauptman Dödelein, both of which later proved to be incorrect. He also obtained information about the Intelligence Officer in charge of secret papers, who had worked with the Kommandantur. This man was identified as Unteroffizier Form, who had been captured by the Dutch underground near the end of the war and handed over to the Canadian Provost Detachment in June 1945. Form had a girlfriend, now living in Arnhem, who was still keeping in touch with him. Kamp tracked down the girlfriend, Miss Kloet, and got the address of Form at 21 Paprivistrasse in Berlin.

Kamp also saw prominent members of the Dutch underground and members of the local police. He visited 'various girls who were suspected to have been courting with the German soldiers during the occupation'. By dint of these investigations, he managed to prove beyond any doubt that the Krankenstube (infirmary) in Oude Wand, which had been the early suspect for the dressing station in which Anthony was treated, had not been used after August 1944. It was a Miss Duistermaat (who may or may not have been one of the 'various girls') who told Kamp that around 16 September 1944 a Krankenstube had been established in Rozenhoflaan. From then on the pieces began to fall into place.

Miss Duistermaat did not remember the number correctly, thinking it had been No. 16 or 18 rather than 12, but in other respects her information was very accurate:

There are steps in front of the house. A big fat doctor who had been made an Oberstabsarzt just before he came to Zutphen was in charge. In September 1944 a few English soldiers from the battle of Arnhem were treated there at about 14.30 hours. I was working in the Officers' Casino opposite the Krankenstube and there I witnessed the whole incident. After they had been treated at the Krakenstube the English soldiers had to walk from Rozenhoflaan into the direction of the General Hospital.

The following morning, Kamp went to Rozenhoflaan at about 9.00am and soon established that it was No.12 which had been a Krankenstube for a few days in September 1944. Kamp describes it in his report as being the house of 'Dullaert-Bianchi'. The house's owners were Leonardus Dullaert, an iron merchant, and his wife Theodora Joanna, whose maiden name was Bianchi.

In the post-war Dutch records, the Dullaerts are noted as having been paid a substantial amount of reparations for war damages. At 6163.07 guilders, this was considerably more than what was paid to other families living in Rozenhoflaan. What damage the Germans had done to the house is not recorded.[520]

Kamp seems to have found the Dullaerts very willing to help. They clearly gave him the run of the house, for in one of the upstairs bedrooms he found some writing which he thought might include part of the name 'Cotterell'. The words were written where a washbasin was later affixed, so Kamp thought that there might be more writing behind it. Before November was out, Kamp would also find a charlady who had actually worked at the house in September 1944, and she would tell him exactly how the rooms had been used by the Germans. She would also inform him that there had once been a cupboard where the alleged signature was found.[521]

Having established that No.12 was the right house, Kamp then went on to see the next-door neighbour at No. 14, who did not know anything about any English soldiers. However, she could identify a girl named Pfafier who was at No.12, and the German MO, 'a stout blonde fellow with a fresh complexion and a real Hun appearance'.

Kamp next went to No. 7, over the road, where he only gathered the information that a number of English soldiers with red berets had been treated at the Krakenstube in September 1944. He fared much better at No. 5, where a Mrs Beversluis gave him a full statement:

One September night a German lorry pulled up before our house at about 9.30.[522] I heard several noises and looked out of the window to see what was happening. It was very dark and I could not see much but I heard the crackling noise as of straw being handled. A small car was in the street at that time and in the glimpse of the light of the car I saw that a body was removed from No.12 to a truck. A German soldier shouted: Licht aus (Light Out). The next morning we found blood and straw in the street. I remember also somebody asking for water whereupon a German soldier shouted at him: 'Ruhe Mensch' [Be quiet, man]. I got the impression that the Germans were extremely nervous, they shouted all kinds of expressions to the German porter of whom I can give you a rather good description as he always made a queer impression upon me. He was a tall meagre man with a long face and a very white skull. He never wore a hat or cap, he made a very sick impression, had a long white high forehead, practically no hair and a thin face.

At No.10, Mrs Berensen, who had been ill in bed on 23 September and thus had an accurate remembrance of the date, recalled hearing a very unusual noise in the street about 9.00pm. On looking out: 'she saw a German lorry with several injured persons who were handled rather roughly. She thinks that there were about 12 or 13 persons of whom 2 or 3 probably were dead.'

From the various statements he gathered, Kamp concluded that the German lorry carrying the wounded and dead had arrived at about 9.00pm, and that no medical officer had been at the dressing station as none lived on the premises. The MO had to be sent for and arrived by car, perhaps the car which was seen by Mrs Beversluis at 1.30am when he left, having finished his work. As for the small car she saw at 9.30pm, this must have been Etter's, the Volkswagen in which he had brought Gough to Zutphen.

One detail which Kamp would quickly follow up was that of the straw in the lorry. As no one in Brummen had seen straw in the lorry, he reasoned that it must have been requisitioned from a farmer along the road from Brummen to Zutphen. With the meticulous attention to detail which would characterise his work, Kamp went to Zutphen police station the following day to request the help of two detectives in finding out who had given the straw to the Germans. If found, the farmer might be able to identify who was on the truck and in what state the wounded were.

Kamp's team travelled down the road, checking out five farms, with at least another ten to go before they were sidetracked into following a lead on the Vorden shooting. This was a horrible incident in which three Dutch men and two unknown English soldiers had been summarily executed by the SD. The soldiers had not been in uniform as they had hidden themselves in a farmhouse, hoping to pass as civilians. They had jumped off a train transporting PoWs close to the village of Laren in Gelderland. The only description that could be obtained for the moment was that the soldiers were tall, thin men in their twenties. One of them was blonde, and one of them was called something like Lewson. Neither of them seemed likely to have been Anthony, but it was a disturbing precedent.[523]

Kamp would later continue his investigations about the dressing station and add one last testimony, that of a Miss Ooms of Laarstraat 100, who said that a certain Hermann Thomson from Hamburg and Schutte from Berlin, both officers, were working there.[524]

One day in September 1944 at about 14.30 hrs three English soldiers from Arnhem were brought in. One of them was very badly wounded and he was taken inside for treatment. The following morning I heard that he had died. I saw his blanket all covered in blood. I do not know where the Germans buried the dead of the Krankenstube. Certainly not near Zutphen. For the other two, one was a tall man with a pale [face?]; he or his comrade had a wounded shoulder. I presume that these soldiers were removed to Konijnenbelt near Vorde. The Medical Officer of the German [hospital] looked after them, assisted by Hermann Thomson and Schutte. I do not know the name of this doctor but I think he was living at Warnsveld with his wife and children. He was the owner of a very nice big light-grey salon car with a spare wheel with a chromium plated cover.

This car was obviously highly memorable at a time when the Dutch were mostly down to bicycles – unless the Germans had stolen them.

Kamp had followed his Rozenhoflaan investigations by going to the General Hospital in Coehoornsingel, two minutes walk from the dressing station. As has already been mentioned, the information he gathered there suggested the strong possibility that Anthony had been alive and comparatively well on 25 September 1944, two days after the shooting.

Kamp gathered much of this information on 30 October 1945, when he met a Mrs Johanna Sollman at the hospital.[525] She had been a nurse there in 1944, and remembered that around 27 September (she could not give the exact date) at about 11.00am she saw two English soldiers, guarded by three Germans, sitting in the waiting room opposite the porter's cabin. They were taken from there to the X-ray room.

One of them was a tall, dark handsome man with very dark eyes and magnificent teeth. He had a tanned face. The other was ginger-haired. I know that the black one was limping and when I assisted him with his coat, I noticed that his left shoulder was very painful. They left the hospital in the direction of the water-tower.

These two soldiers were treated by an MO named Richter and his Austrian assistant.

In the German Department of the hospital was a charwoman, who spoke German fluently. She was employed not by the hospital but by the Germans. I do not know her name.

The dark English man was a gay fellow.

Mrs Etterman has seen these soldiers also.

Mrs Etterman, duly traced, gave much the same description of the dark-haired soldier. She did not remember any particulars of the ginger-haired one. She confirmed that the date was a Monday because 'Gerrits, the porter, was in his cabin'. Thus the date narrowed down to Monday 25 September. The only troubling anomaly was that Anthony was not 'tall' as Mrs Sollman described the soldier. However, there is a possible reason for the discrepancy. There was still a considerable Dutch hope that the British would manage to liberate Gelderland. The British soldiers seen that Monday at the hospital would have been extremely striking figures, being almost certainly the first British soldiers whom the Dutch at the hospital had seen since the Occupation began. They had come as liberators and they remained imbued with that noble aura even though they were now wounded prisoners. In memory, the height of the dark-haired soldier may well have seemed greater that it really was, given his stature as a hero.

The Dr Richter who had been identified by Mrs Sollman was another promising lead. Kamp discovered that Richter, who had not been fully qualified in September 1944, was a German but known to be 'anti-Nazi'. When Kamp and Geoffrey met Richter the following year, he would be as helpful as he could be.

It was now time for Kamp to share his discoveries with Geoffrey. A telegram was sent to Hamburg, asking Geoffrey to come and see the possible signature written in the upstairs bedroom at No.12 Rozenhoflaan. The hope was that Geoffrey would positively identify this signature as being Anthony's.

Thus, less than two weeks after he had gone to Hamburg, Geoffrey returned to Holland. Having already become acclimatised to the bizarre atmosphere of the British Occupation, it was like going to another world. In *Randle in Springtime*, Randle makes a similar journey, though unlike Geoffrey he arrives as dawn is breaking:

The whole atmosphere was different from the other side of the border. There was friendliness and security in the air. Well-kept gardens could just be discerned reaching down to the pavement on either side of the road. The dust and mustiness which was everywhere in Germany, in rooms, clothes, towns and villages, had disappeared. Here everything was as neat and fresh as if a vacuum cleaner had been passed over the whole place. [...]

The strange clear light of Holland was now dawning quickly. Otto turned the car off the main road, so that they left behind the Rhine Army and Canadian Maple Leaf signs and were in the real country, on a straight narrow cobbled road, with farmland on either side. Now and then they passed an early worker, going placidly on his way. [Randle looked] at the potato fields, orchards, cornfields, and the occasional, still sleeping village, neat, clean and solid, with its easily visible interior scenes.[526]

There could not have been a more striking contrast to the apocalyptic ruins of Hamburg.

As one of the privileges of his position, Geoffrey had managed to get a German car and a British driver, Private Albert Cutts. This made his travelling comparatively quick, comfortable and easy. On his return to Hamburg, he at once wrote his mother to tell her of his trip.

20th November

Darling,

What I am going to tell you is so exciting that I must begin by warning you not to expect too much – and always to be ready for any perhaps saddening anticlimax. (Though not in this letter.)

I returned today from Holland, arriving at Hamburg at three in the morning, after four days intensive and exhausting work.

Briefly the two news items are these.

1. Anthony was seen in Zutphen General Hospital waiting room on 25th September 44 (Monday) at approx 11 o'clock in the morning. He had walked there from the dressing station, accompanied by a fair-haired parachutist who was also wounded, and guarded by three German soldiers. He was limping and his left shoulder was clearly painful, though not very badly. He went into the X-ray room to have an X-ray picture taken, came out again – and they were then last seen going off in the direction of the dressing station.

2. Today I found out the unit and job of Oberleutnant Etter and the hunt for him is on. He was definitely alive at the beginning of April. [...]

We got to Zutphen in the evening and I went at once with Kamp to see the inscription. This was a rough scrawl on a wall, and to my intense disappointment I did not recognise it at all. There was an A at the beginning which was very similar, and the whole word might be construed as Cotterell with a great deal of imagination, but there was no possible recognition. Incidentally we were wrong about the dressing station – they had left it at the beginning of September – and this place, which had <u>four</u> steps, was the real one. Neighbours remembered the truck arriving, the bodies going in, the blood, the Germans shouting, the car (Etter's), the truck at one thirty in the morning, the bodies going out to it (Yes, of course, they had watched everything <u>and</u> taken the name of the attendant) and – so far – nothing more.

Kamp had one other hope. A nurse who had worked at the hospital had seen two British officers on 25 September sitting in the waiting room, and had been immensely impressed by the dark one. He was 'very handsome, had wonderful teeth and he was very gay' (Dutch translation). She was much impressed by his gaiety, but then noticed that his left shoulder was hurting him, so she went over and helped him with his coat. They could not speak as she only knew Dutch.

The next morning we went to see her with all the photographs. As soon as she saw me she thought that I was the officer. Then she said, 'No, he was smaller'. She sat down and looked at the photographs. 'The eyes perhaps. Otherwise no.' Then she saw the picture of him sitting as a 2nd Lieutenant, side-faced. 'That is him,' she said, 'Yes, that is him.'

And so at last some progress has been made. Sergeant Kamp was brought to fever pitch, to say nothing of myself.

During the next three days we travelled all over Holland to Groningen, Almelo, Ede, Utrecht, Rotterdam and Apeldoorn, questioning all the Germans who had been captured in the Arnhem area. I have had happy minutes with several atrocity gentlemen, mass murderers, Gestapo agents, SS men and so on. We built a very comprehensive picture of the situation and it was very fascinating to hear the same names keep cropping up.[527] We learnt the names of the doctors who must have looked after Anthony, of the officers who were present when they were first taken prisoner at Arnhem, and dozens of other details, which I can't possibly put down and were in any case irrelevant. But we were all the time seeking for some kind of clue. And no one had heard of Etter. It is not a German name.

During the questioning we came across a Colonel who had been on the staff at Arnhem, an extremely intelligent man of the General Staff type, with no crimes to his name. I put the case of Anthony's job to him, his accomplishments, etc, and asked him what he thought would have happened to him. Without hesitation he said that the most probable course was that he would be taken to the nearest army group (= for example 21 Army Group under Montgomery) and then straight to Berlin. I felt that this opinion was extremely important, and probably more important than any of the details we had collected.

Meanwhile while we were out, two officers called at the Willinks' house. They had come from the Search Bureau and were dealing purely and simply with Anthony's case. One was an American, Saunders, and the other a Pole, who spoke seven languages. They were the ace team of the Search Bureau. They had woken up again as a result of my visit to their office and the information I had given.[528] They frankly had the old old outlook. 'Frankly old boy, probably some local unnamed grave.' When I gave them the complete details and made them realise the comprehensiveness of the local search that had been made they became doubtful. After they had spent a day by themselves and found that we had been before them everywhere, they became even more doubtful. When I told them about the German Colonel, they were definitely impressed and left yesterday for Germany to continue the search there. And last night, loaded with German names, I returned.

During this second visit to Holland, Geoffrey had once again been a highly welcome visitor at the Tjeenk Willinks' house. Aps, his unofficial representative in Holland in all matters concerning Anthony, had been in a state of extreme excitement about the possible signature. She had written to Mintie about it on 10 November before Geoffrey's arrival:

The Military Police found in Zutphen the house with the four treads where the men from the lorry had been taken. In a room upstairs we found on the wall a signature and we think it is from Anthony.

With very thin paper I passed it over, sent it to Major Cotterell and also to Major Hibbert, and asked them to write me if he thinks it is Anthony's signature but I did not hear anything from him.

It is quite sure that [the wounded] departed from Zutphen at two o'clock in the morning but now it is the great and very difficult question whither.

Geoffrey had clearly hidden from Aps his acute disappointment at the signature's lack of resemblance to Anthony's writing. After his visit, she reported his response, which he had evidently made very tactfully.

I shall tell you about the four days that Geoffrey was here looking for his brother. The signature indeed was on the second floor, but it is certain that Anthony first was admitted into the inner room described by you as the place where Major Gough left him. This room had all the equipment necessary for examining the sick especially very strong lights. From there he must have been taken upstairs. As to the signature itself, the beginning has been identified as being Anthony's writing. For the rest Geoffrey was not sure. He recognised parts of it as being the writing of his brother, but it was different from his usual way of writing, which is not so very strange as Anthony was wounded about the shoulder.

The photographs were very useful, but more useful still was Geoffrey himself who spent a few days with me. When he went to a certain nurse in Zutphen accompanied by Military Police Sergeant Kamp, it was not difficult for her to see the similarity between Geoffrey and Anthony. Without knowing that Geoffrey was Anthony's brother she said straightaway: That is the soldier

I saw in the General Hospital on Monday morning (25 September) who was taken there by German guards to have his X-ray photographs taken.

As to the number of wounded British soldiers who were taken from the Zutphen dressing station, we are not certain. People actually did see a kind of stretcher that was taken from the Field Dressing Station to a waiting lorry, but they did not know whether any person were conveyed on it and how many there were altogether.

Aps also described how they were getting on with finding out about the destination of the lorry. Once again, the search had circled round to Enschede, which Aps' son Dick had visited during Janie's stay in Gelderland in May, seven months earlier.

It is very difficult to find out anything about the Enschede hospital, as this was one of the German hospitals with an entirely German staff. From the underground movement at Almelo we heard that often contact with British and other Allied airmen was obtained via a cunning window-cleaner. A search is now being made for people like window-cleaners ... who might have been able to learn something about what was going on in the Enschede hospital.[529]

What Aps, Kamp, and their helpers were hoping to establish beyond any doubt was that the lorry had gone to Enschede after it left Zutphen in the early hours of 24 September. They also wished to cover the possibility that Anthony might have been removed to Enschede at a later date. As yet, despite Aps' boundless enthusiasm, too many question marks remained for Geoffrey to feel certainty in the pieced-together story of events.

For Geoffrey, now back in Hamburg, the immediate focus of the search had moved elsewhere. His perseverance, patience, and habit of continually asking questions, even in the most unpromising circumstances, had finally paid off, and he was now about to meet the Wehrmacht officer who had helped the prisoners in Brummen.

33

ETTER

The various bodies involved in the War Crimes and Search Bureau enquiries had been on the trail of the Wehrmacht officer ever since Finlay Wilson and Freddie Gough had passed on what they knew about him. After the shooting at Brummen, the officer had given Finlay Wilson his name and address on a piece of paper, but, as has already been described, the note was later confiscated by a German official at Oberürsel. Finlay Wilson and Gough were thus relying on memory for the officer's name, where his family home was, and the details of his stay in Britain in the 1920s. They gave this information not only to the Cotterell family, but also to the Search Bureau and the War Crimes people. By October 1945, the net was drawing in with so many people actively trying to trace the officer, name still uncertain but now settled on as being Etter, Etting, or Ettinger, with the preference being given to Etter.

Shortly after being posted to Hamburg, Geoffrey had written to Finlay Wilson requesting a detailed recap of Etter's details. When he received his reply, he sent the material on to Mintie, telling her, 'Here is something for you take up with the captain at the War Office ... I put first the one that you must follow up.' The letter continued:

1. Etter was an engineer in civil life and worked in England with a firm of cotton machinery manufacturers. Finlay Wilson is not sure but thinks it was in Bradford.
    He spoke English perfectly.
        He was (1944) about 38, medium height, fairly broad, clean shaven, pleasant rather weather-beaten face, smiled when speaking. Was once engaged to an English girl.
        Now it must be possible to get his exact name and possibly his former address from this. The police will almost certainly have records of aliens working in England and in any case the firm itself should not be so difficult to find. There can't be a vast number of cotton machinery manufacturers.

2. The exact name and address was on a note given to him by Etter. This was taken away from Finlay Wilson at a Luftwaffe Interrogation centre at Oberürsel near Frankfurt on Main. It is possible that records may still exist from this place.

3. His home was definitely in Stuttgart. Finlay Wilson still writes Stuggart which is vernacular for Stuttgart and there is definitely no town in Germany spelt Stuggart.

4. Etter said he thought the *Daily Express* would probably make an atrocity story out of the incident.[530]

The last point was worrying in that it showed that Etter, who had acted well towards the British prisoners, had recognised that Anthony had potential nuisance value to the Germans.

Unknown to Geoffrey, moves had already been made which would render superfluous any search for Etter that Mintie could make. The Search Bureau had enlisted the help of the Aliens Department of the Home Office in tracing records of Etter's time in England before the war. This had led to the involvement of the County Borough of Bolton Police Department, where the CID began to look into the matter. On 15 October they reported that the likely candidate for 'Etter or Etting' was one Gustav Etter, a single man born in October 1905 at Rottweil, in Germany. He had reported to their office in June 1929 and had been given an Aliens Registration Certificate. At that time, he had already been in the country for six months, and was living at 173 Chorley New Road, Bolton. His stay had lasted until September 1929, when he returned to Germany.

The CID now went to see the occupants of 173 Chorley New Road. They discovered that it was a house let off in furnished rooms, that the previous owner was dead, and that none of the current residents had been there in 1929. The CID also made enquiries at Bolton Technical College, but found no alien of the name of Etter, Etting, or anything similar.[531] However, on 7 December a more comprehensive report concluded that the only person to have ever registered as an alien in Bolton with a name beginning with the letter 'E' was the same Gustav Etter. The writer of the report had been in touch with the Lancashire Constabulary, the Manchester City Police and the Liverpool City Police Aliens Departments, and had found no possible alternative candidate. A passport-style photograph of Etter was attached to the sheet summarising their conclusions.[532] It showed a good-looking, rather serious 24-year-old man. Fifteen years and a brutal war stood between the handsome young man in the photograph and the weather-beaten, smiling Wehrmacht officer at Brummen. Nonetheless, the photograph might prove highly valuable in locating him.

Now that the War Crimes people had identified their man, they sent out an 'All Points' or 'Haystack' search. Geoffrey, meanwhile, was having his own successes.

This morning I was talking to Lynder, one of the many Germans who are British subjects who work here. His mother was liquidated in 1942 and all their property was sold by auction to the SS. When Lynder returned to Germany after the liberation, he went feverishly round trying to find out who had attended the auction, found them out, and finally arrived at a house in Bremen where, when he gave his name, the housewife turned pale. He sat in the living room looking for what had been their property, but couldn't see anything. Then glancing down at his boots, he noticed the carpet...

Anyway, this gruesome story makes Lynder a firm support. During the war he was an expert on the German army for our Intelligence. This morning we teleprinted London and all over the place with the name Etter, Etting, Ettinger, etc ... but no card index showed him. [...]

This afternoon Lynder said he thought he would go down to the docks to see if there was a story lying about. About an hour later he rang me up. He had been talking to a German friend of his, and the conversation turned to the war. The friend mentioned the time when he was at Army Group B. Lynder asked casually, 'Know an Oberleutnant Etter?'

'Yes,' said the man.

This German had been an officer with him and though he was not intimate with him, his description tallied perfectly with Finlay Wilson's. Oberleutnant Etter was an assistant Intelligence Officer on the staff of Heeresgruppe B, commanded by General Model. [...]

Lynder brought the German up to the office, where we verified beyond doubt that this was the man, that he had been in the Arnhem district, that he spoke English, was an engineer etc.

Then the German mentioned a girl working at Radio Hamburg who had been General Model's secretary even though she had not been present at the time of Arnhem. They got the girl up to the office, Lynder wrote down several names on a piece of paper, and asked if she remembered any of them. She picked out Etter. She had seen him roughly at the beginning of April, just before the end of the war. Geoffrey was now certain that Etter was still alive. He asked Mintie to ring up Anthony's old friend on the *Daily Express*, Harold Keeble, and tell him the good news.

Greatly excited and hopeful, Geoffrey also sent Kamp a telegram on 30 November: 'Have discovered identity of Lieutenant Etter. He was an assistant of and Intelligence Officer to Oberstürmführer Staubwassser of Heeresgruppe B under General Model.'[533] Geoffrey continued to canvas every likely and unlikely source of information. On 26 November he wrote to Mintie:

> My chief reporter's lady friend whom I met last night was one of the secretaries in Hitler's bunker in the last days in Berlin. She escaped with about 8 days to go. She is being asked if by any chance she ever heard etc, but they automatically say no if you ask them yourself.

Reliable information had now come in that Etter and his superior, Staubwasser, must have been captured on 19 April by the Americans. This should mean that they were in the south in the American Zone. Geoffrey began to make the preliminary moves towards getting a permit, exclaiming to Mintie once the process had begun, 'It's more difficult to go to the American Zone than to Holland or Belgium or Denmark! Which must have a moral somewhere I suppose.'[534]

By 8 December he had received permission to go to the American Zone, and on the 12th, wrote his mother one last note before leaving, 'Shall be highly conscious that your thoughts are with me every minute'. It was not until the 23 December that he would write again, an unusually long gap. Immediately he got back, he wrote to Mintie despite the intense rigours of a trip which had covered 1900 miles and had included the Ruhr, Cologne, Frankfurt, Kassel, Rottweil, Tubingen, Munich, and Nuremberg where he had arrived just 'ten minutes late for the bloody trial, and so didn't see it!'

On the first leg of the journey, Geoffrey and his travelling companion, Collins, had arrived at the American HQ in Frankfurt only to discover that all the American prisoner records were in Paris. Geoffrey rang the Paris office up, was connected in a second – astonishingly fast – and was delighted to hear the people at the other end promise to look for Etter and Staubwasser immediately. Excitement bubbled until he rang them back a few hours later, only to be told that neither name was in the book and that he could therefore take it that neither had been captured. It would later transpire that Etter had indeed been captured by the Americans but they had already released him, 'which', as Geoffrey commented, 'shows what records prove'.

Undaunted he travelled on to Stuttgart, where for the first time he met Major David Conroy, a South African with a strong accent, who had been assigned by the Search Bureau to Anthony's case. Conroy would soon prove to be a great ally in the search and would come to take a warm personal interest in Anthony and his family, sometimes speaking directly to Mintie on the telephone from Germany to give her the latest news.[535]

Geoffrey's letter home of 23 December told of this latest development:

> Darling,
>
> I hope you are not prostrate with anxiety. I was warned that writing from the American Zone might take up to a fortnight, and, anyway, I thought it better to complete the mission first. [...]
>
> I got to the Search Bureau at Bünde on 13th December, to find that a South African major was on his way down to the south with the priority job of finding Etter. This seemed of course the usual pattern. The people at the Search Bureau have the case very much on their minds, and all hasten to say that the War Office has been appalling about it – perhaps a touch of guilty conscience. They have a VIP file (=Very Important Person) – for example there was a request from the Duchess of Windsor while I was there – but Anthony is considered above this, and his case is the only one kept directly by the Colonel of the department.[536] They definitely do not give up all chances of survival, which does not mean that they are optimistic; but they

now talk about lost memories, German civilian hospitals (so far unchecked) and of course the hopelessness of dealing with the Russians. Particularly since there is now the parallel case of Ed Beattie, an American war correspondent, who was captured sometime in the past year and sent very speedily to the Propaganda ministry in Berlin, where he was treated as an honoured guest for a week. By the time he made it clear that he wasn't going to play they sent him to a camp, from which he was recovered by the Americans in reasonable health. I am happy to report that the Search Bureau consider this a parallel case – that is, it wasn't my suggestion – and I think that now [...] they will try and start something with the Russians.

Ed Beattie was that same American correspondent, who after being captured in France on 12 September, had ended up at Limburg camp with the unwounded prisoners from the Brummen shooting. He was subsequently removed to Berlin, where amongst others he met Dr Paul Schmidt, chief of the Press Division of Ribbentrop's Foreign Office. Beattie's adventures in Berlin were now being considered highly relevant to Anthony's case.

Whilst in Berlin, Beattie had been kept at a very small camp known as Stalag III-D. From here he was taken to meet various Nazi grandees, who treated him sumptuously to food, drink, and cigars. It seems that far from viciously coercing Beattie into writing propaganda for them, or punishing him for his past frankly expressed views on Nazism, these men simply wanted to talk about the war situation. In particular they were haunted by the inexplicable (to them) grouping of the Allies – why were the British and Americans fighting the Germans when the real enemy was the Russians?

Beattie found Schmidt 'very suave in a bumptious Nazi way', but resisted being in any way influenced by his thinking, his parade of 'all the stock Nazi arguments with a bland assumption that they are as logical to non-Nazis as to himself'. But having put over his world view, possibly hoping to influence anything Beattie might write once he was free again, Schmidt assured Beattie he would be sent on to an officer's camp and exchanged as soon as possible. In the event, Beattie would remain at Stalag III-D until the end of January 1945, by which time his Nazi grandees had long lost all interest in him. It is worth noting that *Kommando 806*, the compound at Stalag-III where Beattie and the other special prisoners lived, was so small that he knew everyone there, and Anthony definitely was not amongst them.[537]

Beattie's last PoW camp was liberated by the Russians and he experienced no problems in leaving their custody. However, the idea that the Russians might still be holding Anthony had not yet been abandoned. Geoffrey's letter of 23 December, in which he told Mintie about Beattie, continued:

The question of being a DP in the Russian Zone may be illustrated by the American. I was talking to a Yank DP officer in Stuttgart who said they were still coming across British and American DPs. What happens, I asked him, if you meet an American DP without papers? 'No papers he stays a DP,' said the Yank. 'Lots of people want to be Americans these days. We got to be careful. If he's got no papers, he's got to see the American consul in the normal way. But there ain't no American consul see? So he stays a DP.' If that can happen with the Americans, you can imagine the Russians. All this is wishful thinking, but it's also the Search Bureau's, which is a pleasant change.

The letter went on to describe Geoffrey's meeting in Stuttgart with Major Conroy of the Search Bureau. On the quest to locate Etter, Conroy had with him the 1942 addresses of fourteen Etters, but had had no results with the first three or four. Geoffrey and Conroy at once joined forces.

The next morning we set out to look them all up in turn. We went to Adolf Etter, Gottlieb Etter, Felix Etter, mostly in workmen's flats and then we arrived at Maria Etter's. This was in a better district. No. 9 was completely demolished, but on the front gate was the brass plate with Etter printed on it. I spoke to the neighbours. Maria had been evacuated, a deaf old widow. Had she a family? Yes, a daughter. No son? Oh yes, a son. Had he been in the army? I think so. Possibly – but try Frau somebody over the way; she used to know them. At last we located the Frau, who said yes there was a son, between thirty and forty, and yes, he had been a lieutenant, and yes, he had lived abroad ... frankly my heart was thumping.

The old lady had been sent to Rottweil about seventy miles away. So we went at once to Rottweil, which was in the French Zone. After some time a nun found us the address and took us along. The daughter opened the door and, like everyone else, was scared stiff. Was her brother living there? Yes. Jesus. But, she added, he was not there now – was anything wrong? No, no, Fräulein, nothing to worry about, can we come in and ask you a few questions. The Fräulein shivered. Inside two minutes we knew that this was the man. Heeresgruppe B, Model, engineer, perfect English, the whole works. He had gone to Augsburg, but would be returning. It was just possible that he would be seeing some friends in Stuttgart. We got two addresses.

We went to the first address in Stuttgart when we returned at night. (We is Conroy and I.) Etter had been there at four o'clock. The next morning we went to the second address. Etter had left an hour ago...

We returned to the first address. Etter was coming to lunch...

We came again, ten minutes early, and waited. You can imagine my feelings, accentuated when we heard the door open outside and knew that it was the famous gentleman at last.

He came in, looking precisely as we had imagined him, the perfect charming Hun, somewhat puzzled.

Although mystified by the visit of the two British officers, Etter was pleasant and confident. He was very much officer-class and a typical Aryan blond, though the blond had lost its yellowness. Geoffrey and Conroy questioned him for about two hours, and, as Geoffrey told Mintie in the letter, 'I don't think there was any question that he was not speaking the truth'.

Etter said that he left Anthony in the dressing station before anyone was taken to Enschede. He merely requested the doctors to see that everyone was looked after. He did not speak to Anthony, simply because he was wounded.

BUT a warrant officer of the Propaganda Ministry arrived at the scene of the incident, while all the fuss was on. He wanted an interview, but Etter refused him. The warrant officer was acting as a reporter for Hilversum Radio station – hence the broadcast. Etter stated in a sworn affidavit that he thinks the Propaganda Ministry will have the answer to Anthony. Tomorrow morning we are sending a teleprint to London concerning an appropriate captured gentleman who may know.

Geoffrey did not hide from his mother how bitterly disappointed he was by his meeting with Etter. It had taken so much effort and ingenuity to find Etter, only to discover that he could not, after all, provide the answer to the mystery of Anthony's disappearance.

Although the propaganda warrant officer was of course a very important piece of information, it was of course the most bitter anticlimax. Etter remembered Anthony from the photograph, that he was 'not too depressed' and his morale was high. He did not see how anything else could have happened to him except the Propaganda people.

By the Propaganda people, Geoffrey meant those who would have been interested in Anthony for his publicity and propaganda value as a captured journalist, in the same way that they had been interested in the American war correspondent, Ed Beattie.

Etter's affidavit, taken down on 18 December 1945 and almost certainly drawn up by Conroy after this meeting, consisted of paragraphs numbered 1-14.[538] The document described the role Etter had had in Heeresgruppe B, how he had chanced upon the shooting in Brummen, and what had happened afterwards.

6. I then took all the prisoners to the camp in Zutphen close to the railway station. The wounded were attended to after some delay by two Doctors, whom I do not know. One, however, I am sure was a Luftwaffe doctor.

7. I saw a private die there and I requested the Doctors to send the wounded to Enschede.

Why had Etter requested that the wounded be sent on to Enschede? There was a perfectly good civilian hospital in Zutphen just around the corner from the dressing station. Etter must have received orders from his superior officer that this is what should be done. Very late in the search, in May 1947, an Obersturmführer Schlueter would state that he was the one who had given the order to take the wounded from Zutphen to Enschede, but it is not known why he did this. It was almost certainly because the Germans' first priority had been to keep a tight control over their prisoners, and the care of the wounded came second to that. Enschede was a German-controlled town, located close to the border with Germany, with a hospital which had a largely German staff. Once the wounded were there, there would have been little chance of them escaping, or details of the Brummen shooting becoming more widely known.

Etter's testimony continued:

8. From the photograph shown me, I recognise Major Cotterell, but I do not remember how badly he was wounded. I recollect, however, that Major Gough told me that Major Cotterell was a pressman of international reputation. [...]

10. After I had left the wounded about 2300 hours on September 22 [sic] with Major Gough I have not set eyes on Major Cotterell, and do not know what happened to this officer.

11. I recollect prior to leaving, Major Gough speaking to Major Cotterell, who did not appear to be too depressed, I do not recollect how he was wounded, but I remember his morale was high (in German the word is 'Haltung' and in English slang 'guts').[539]

Etter gave a description of one of the Doctors who had attended the wounded. He was from the Luftwaffe, and was about 40, stout, with a fencing scar on his face. This was the same man described by one of Kamp's Dutch witnesses as 'a stout blonde fellow with a fresh complexion and a real Hun appearance'. In addition, Etter gave a detailed description of the Unteroffizier from the Propaganda ministry who had supplied the news of the shooting to Radio Hilversum. It turned out that Etter knew him well, though he declared that he could not remember his name:

He is a Doctor in Economics, who used to send news to Hilversum. This Doctor was in South America for about ten years. He is thin, small and fair and very lively, and I last saw him in Brohl on the Rhine near Coblentz in February 45.

When they at last left Etter, Geoffrey and Conroy conferred on what each of them had thought about the meeting, and, 'after meditation', decided that Etter was to be trusted. As Geoffrey wrote to his mother:

He certainly gave us the true facts without help from us. The point is, he thought Anthony was sent to Enschede. That is his explanation for not pursuing the matter himself; he assumed he would come through the normal channels with the others if his wounds were better. He had no opinion to give concerning the probability of him dying, but said that he wasn't taking it too badly and 'hatte Haltung', which is difficult to translate exactly – 'had bearing' – but in any event in view of the nurse's evidence this doesn't come into it.[540] The whole thing becomes more of a mystery than ever.

The questioning which Etter had undergone with Geoffrey and Conroy had been comparatively mild and informal. His further interrogation on 15 January 1946 by a War Crimes Liaison Officer was extremely tough and intimidating. Designed to break down false testimony, it lasted around six hours, during which hot bright lights (in a technique known as the Third Degree) were constantly directed in Etter's face.[541] As Etter had been discovered living in the French Zone, and was therefore under French jurisdiction, he was interviewed by Major Thomas Davies, a British officer in the Grenadier Guards, who was based at the Liaison Office in Baden-Baden. The interview itself took place at Gaggenau, not far from Baden-Baden. When it was over, it was transcribed, and each page was signed by Etter to show that his words had been accurately translated and that he agreed with the contents of the document.

In the statement Etter gave a detailed description of the Brummen shooting. He also gave a clear description of his Army duties and why he had come to be in Brummen.

> I was an Oberleutnant in the German Wehrmacht, and in the autumn of 1944 was employed as an interpreter on the staff of the HQ, Army Group B. Part of my duties consisted of the interrogation of prisoners.
>
> On the 22nd of September [sic] late in the afternoon, in the course of my duties I had to travel from the Command Post of the Hohenstaufen SS Division which at the time was situated at Arnhem, to a prisoner of war collecting point at Zutphen. I travelled in a Volkswagen, accompanied by Sonderführer (G) Dr Braden, who was working with me as an interpreter, and whom I believe now to be living in Freiburg iBr, and by the driver of the vehicle, which came from the Army Group pool, and whose name I do not remember.
>
> Approximately 10 kilometres east of Arnhem, in a village of which I have subsequently heard the name is Brummen, we came to a curve in the road. There were houses on both sides. As the vehicle began to round the curve (see attached sketch map) I heard two burst of fire which sounded as though they came from a machine pistol.
>
> Further around the corner I suddenly saw a German army type lorry standing stopped slightly to the right of the middle of the road. An NCO of the Waffen SS, whose rank corresponded to that of Unteroffizier in the Wehrmacht, was standing about two metres behind this lorry, and was holding a machine pistol in a firing position directed against the occupants of the lorry whom I immediately recognised as English prisoners of war from an airborne unit.

There followed a detailed description of Etter's subsequent actions and the report he had given to his superior, Staubwasser.

The deposition document now recorded a further question and answer session:

> Q: Will you give a description of this SS Unteroffizier? [the one who had shot the prisoners]
> A: Medium height, dark hair, pale face, unshaven, age in twenties. I cannot remember that he spoke with a South German accent, and I therefore assume that he came rather from central or northern Germany. I assume that he came from the Hohenstaufen SS Division as he came from Arnhem. [...]

Q: Did the SS man at any time, in any way, threaten you?

A: No.

Q: Did the Unteroffizier assist you in caring for the wounded?

A: Yes, of course he did, especially at Zutphen.

Etter's language, 'yes, of course he did', seems to breathe exasperation.

When the deposition was sent on to the War Crimes Group, Major Davies included a covering letter. He wrote that at the beginning of the interrogation it had seemed to him that 'this man Etter was lying, and not only knew the name of the SS Unteroffizier, but had also taken part in the shooting himself'. However, he finally came to the conclusion that this apparent lack of good faith was due to the fact that Etter had been frightened of the SS Unteroffizier, and was ashamed to admit to a British officer that he was afraid, hence his shifty manner. Davies therefore decided that the statement had been given in good faith, and a Major Barkworth, who had also been present at the interrogation, was of the same opinion.

Major Davies continued.

I am carrying on the investigation in view of finding Obersturmführer iG Staubwasser IC Army Group B and Dr Braden. However, it would be advisable to put through an all stations call for these German officers.

Do you know anything about a Major Cotterell or Major Conroy, both of whom appeared to have previously interrogated Etter? I have heard nothing of these interrogations until now. Major Conroy it appears is in possession of the name of the SS Unteroffizier concerned.[542]

Major Davies seems to have disliked the involvement of Geoffrey and Conroy. When a few weeks later, he became aware that Etter was actually working for Geoffrey in the search, he would become even more dubious about the set-up, writing to his superiors, 'Etter disappears periodically it seems with Major Cotterell. I imagine you are aware that this officer seems to be investigating this case on his own.'[543] Eventually, after a third letter (which he also circulated to Major A.E.E. Reade, the officer in charge of JAG War Crimes Section at Bad Oeynhausen), he would receive a distinctly frosty reply from a Lieutenant-Colonel Harris at HQ, BAOR. Referring to the letters Davies had sent on the subject in January, March and April, Harris wrote:

1. Major Conroy of the Central Commission Search Bureau and Major Cotterell of 10 German News Service, BAOR, have no connection with BAOR War Crimes Investigation Unit and are NOT under command of this HQ. There is no reason why they should report to you except for assistance if required and this HQ is NOT in a position to issue instructions to them.

2. There does not appear to be any objection to their employment of Etter in view of the fact that the evidence of a number of British witnesses proves that his intervention saved the lives of a number of British PW in Holland in 44.[544]

In the hall of whispers which was the Occupation of Germany, anything unusual had a tendency to create the most intense mistrust which could easily spiral out of control. The best remedy was for an exasperated senior officer to lose his patience, as it appears Lieutenant-Colonel Harris had done. Davies also received a rebuff from Major Reade: 'These independent enquiries are perfectly normal and proper, and if Etter [...] can help, so much the better.'[545] Faced with such strong discouragement, it seems that Davies pursued the matter no further.

Geoffrey's meeting with Etter, though so disappointingly inconclusive, had created a contact which it suited both men to exploit. Etter could be useful to Geoffrey because, as a German, he might get information which would not be volunteered to a British Army Major, whilst because Etter had saved the lives of British officers Geoffrey had offered to help him with his denazification. The process of denazification was a prerequisite of Germans being allowed many types of employment and freedom of travel, and was a complex process which took an enormous amount of time, much of it spent upon a form known as the *Fragebogen*. A current German joke about Hitler's Thousand-Year Reich was that it meant twelve years of Nazi rule followed by 988 years of denazification.[546] In Etter's case, he needed an official certificate from the Americans to show that he had been cleared. He would, in fact, still be waiting for this certificate in September 1946, as is evident from correspondence on the War Crimes Group files.[547] It is not entirely certain what Geoffrey hoped to accomplish in this matter apart from pulling a few British Zone strings, but nonetheless Etter recognised that Geoffrey could be useful to him in this or other respects. In pursuit of this, he wrote to him in January 1946:

Dear Major Cotterell

I really wonder if you succeeded in finding out some more about your brother. I should feel very sorry for you and your family if his life could not have been spared in spite of all I did to save the wounded.

   Could you get in touch with one of the doctors who treated your brother at Zutphen, especially the one I mentioned to you. I am certain that he could give you some very valuable information about your brother. You surely tried to locate him which should not to be too difficult, I guess. Did you find out that Unteroffizier of the press?

   You may hear something some day from the fellow officers of your brother. Please give them my best regards, especially Major Gough and Major Arnold. I am glad to know that they could return safely to their happy families. At around January 15th I'll be in Hamburg and hope to see you and – of course – the Major from South Africa [Conroy]. I hope you will not object then to me asking you a little favour.

   With kindest regards to the South African major as well –

Yours very truly
Gustav Etter[548]

Geoffrey commented to his mother, for whom he had transcribed the letter:

Naturally all Mr Etter was worried about was the favour, no doubt a letter of introduction for a job – but it isn't the letter of a man who could have lied to me, unless he is being too subtle for words. And if he is coming to Hamburg of course he may be the ideal man to do some useful searching.

Though Etter and Geoffrey would meet again several times, nothing much further would come of their connection. Etter would give Geoffrey a couple more details of the night of 23 September, but he appeared genuinely to have no knowledge of Anthony's fate. This lack of knowledge only deepened the cloud of unknowing. Geoffrey would tell his mother after one of their meetings: 'Long conversation with Etter last night. Proving nothing but the mystery of it all.'[549]

34

THE ENSCHEDE CONNECTION

After the severe disappointment of his first meeting with Etter, Geoffrey returned to Hamburg for the first Christmas of the peace. Knowing that Anthony would be uppermost in their thoughts, he wrote to his parents on Christmas Day:

> A happy Xmas is impossible but we can still wish ourselves a happy new year. I am sitting in my warm, centrally heated, utility modern furniture bedroom, thinking of you both. [...]
>
> Tomorrow I have to start my new job, which is taking one of the shifts as editor. Unfortunately there is no more pay – although if I were in the civil service I should be getting £1200 a year. I might consider it for £1200 a year.
>
> We have all been issued with 4 cigars, and I am just going to smoke one now.

Once the editorial job had begun, he wrote to tell them of his new responsibilities.

> Since any mistake we make brings personal protests emanating from Marshal Zhukov and General de Gaulle, this is a ticklish business [...] It will certainly improve my world geography. And I am confident, relying on the above Zhukov and de Gaulle, of my chances of figuring prominently in some future international incident, thus boosting sales all round.[550]

Marshal Zhukov, who had commanded the final assault on Berlin, was the Military Governor of the Russian Zone.[551]

In his new work, Geoffrey would be working different shifts, but the way that his hours were arranged meant that he would get roughly half the week off. This he planned to dedicate either to pursuing the search or to working on his new novel, *This is the Way*. Like Anthony, Geoffrey was obsessively hard-working.

As the end of 1945 approached, he wrote the last letter of the year, wishing Mintie and Graham a happy New Year:

> By now you will have recovered from your doubtless riotous Xmas. More particularly I hope from your cold, which must have made things seem even more depressing.
>
> Nothing to report today. Am spending my time vetting the world's news. In a about a minute's time I shall be reading about the bread shortage in Hungary, a fascinating subject. Now Italian communists.
>
> Interesting light on German mentality. There was a story about sadistic school children about which an article had to be written. An inspector found a German school where the children's drawing lessons was devoted to illustrating Grimms' fairy tales with gay pictures of a skeleton warming itself in front of a fire, a skull as a waste paper basket – another child on an independent tack was happily drawing Dr Ley committing suicide in his cell.[552] The inspector asked how the hell the teacher could allow it and the teacher in amazement asked what was wrong, these

things were different for children. So the article was written and brought to me: it contained a glowing account of the skeleton, quoted the teacher as if in agreement, and ended by pointing out that Belsen etc had made Grimms' fairy tales a reality in modern Germany. I asked exactly where the impression was given that teachers should not let children draw atrocities in school time, and received the answer that after all the news was rather silly, for these things really didn't mean anything to children, did they?

Geoffrey and Mintie were numbering all their letters, to keep them in sequence and to be certain that none had gone astray. At the beginning of January, he wrote that he had not received 'your 27 (no surprise: they often come in peculiar order)', and asked if she has received his letter which had given the full details of his first meeting with Etter. In fact, due to postal delays, this critical letter had not reached Mintie and Graham until the start of the new year. As Geoffrey had expected, the information which it contained about Etter deeply disappointed and upset his mother. Mintie wrote to her sister on 2 January:

> Isn't it a blow, Janie? After all the search for Etter. Poor Shubbs, it made me feel very sad. I guess I had counted so much on that too. However, it is no use uncrossing our fingers and I still feel bound to hope. As said in your card this morning I too feel certain that Anthony is coming back to us again.

Her reference to keeping their fingers crossed dated back to the last time that Anthony had spoken to his parents, when he has asked them to keep their fingers crossed for his safe return.

Janie was now back on tour with the London Ballet Group. The company was in India, and it was from Calcutta that Janie responded to Mintie's letter:

> I do not think we will ever be able to realise the extent of Shubbs' sufferings since the tragedy, he hid it so well. I feel sure that it must have given you a tremendous amount of content to know he is over there and we must sincerely hope that his work will not finish until all is traced.[553]

By the last phrase Janie was referring to Geoffrey's approaching demob, for once he was out of the Army he would lose his extraordinary freedom of movement and action.

For Geoffrey, something seems to have gone out of the search with the failure with Etter. There is a slight change of tone in his letters from January 1946 onwards which suggests that, for him, hope was beginning to die. Love, a brave heart, and dogged perseverance would keep him as active in the search as before, but the first excited flush of optimism had gone forever. Geoffrey, it seems, was beginning to confront the possibility that the truth about Anthony's fate might never be discovered. If his brother was dead, this meant that his family would never know his final resting place or how he had come to lie in it. If his brother was alive, there was the torture of wondering whether he had lost his memory or mental capacity, or was a prisoner of the Russians. There was no happiness or comfort to be found in any of the various imagined scenarios.

His mother and his aunt Janie kept hoping against hope that Anthony would be found alive. Mintie refused to accept the idea that Anthony was dead, and Janie felt exactly the same. She wrote from Calcutta:

> I went to see Major Owen this morning but he was away. I saw Major Wilkins instead. I asked him if he knew A, he answered 'Anthony Cotterell is dead, he died about 8 months ago', to which spontaneously from me 'Oh no he is not'. So trust I am correct. He said A. was with him on the *News Chronicle*. He was a gruff sort of type, and promised to let me know if he heard anything.[554]

Mintie was evidently very nettled by Major Wilkins' remark because she wrote to Janie in mid-January:

> We had a letter yesterday from the Adjutant-General's deputy, Sir Glover, telling us all that had been done to date, to try and discover Anthony's fate and that enquiries were still going on. So that puts paid to Major Wilkins.[555]

The sisters continued to confide their hopes and fears to one another. Even the tiniest things seemed of huge significance while they were so far apart. Janie was having many dreams about Anthony. One in particular struck an emotional chord with her: 'A. sitting on a long park seat, dressed in suit dark green, tightish trousers, swiss hat, looking very sad.'[556] The dream was still affecting her over a week later, when she arrived in Bombay for a brief holiday:

> My usual trend of thought on the train, when a voice said inside me, 'What is your misery compared to his? Waiting and waiting for release.' I think that must be the result of my dream of the green suit where he was looking so despondent. However I just cannot think anything but that he is alive somewhere. It will take a long time for those records to be perused when found, so we must be patient.[557]

In referring to her usual trend of thought, Janie meant her feeling of sadness and loneliness at the failure of her marriage with Ivor. Though she had made several admirers on tour, none of these brief love affairs lasted. After five years of being on the road with ENSA, at times she deeply longed for some emotional permanency in her life. But her primary concern was always for Anthony and his deeply grieving mother.

The search was now splitting off into three main lines: an attempt to trace the still nameless propaganda officer who had made the Radio Hilversum broadcast; the tracing of the doctors and orderlies at the Zutphen dressing station; and a re-examination of the Enschede connection – both the Roman Catholic hospital, St Joseph's, and the Enschede cemetery in which Trevor McNabb and the other victims of the shooting were buried.

Whilst the first two lines were still being actively explored, for the moment Geoffrey's focus turned to what was the saddest, simplest, and most obvious solution to the mystery – that Anthony had died close to the time of the shooting and had been buried with McNabb and the others at Enschede General Cemetery.

As it seemed certain from the testimony of Etter and Gough that McCracken had died at Rozenhoflaan, the only wounded who had been taken on to St Joseph's that night were McNabb and Tannenbaum, and possibly Anthony. The dead – that is to say, McCracken, together with Kenneth Mills, Horace Platt and Sydney Allen, who had all died at the scene at Brummen – had apparently been taken to Enschede in the same lorry as McNabb and Tannenbaum. They had been buried together at Enschede General Cemetery on 26 September. McNabb, who lingered a little longer, had been buried beside them on 29 September. Only Tannenbaum had come home to England.

The problem with the idea that Anthony might also be buried at the cemetery was that there was no evidence whatsoever that that he had ever been taken to Enschede. On his very first trip to Holland, Geoffrey had gone to St Joseph's with Dick Tjeenk Willink and had seen the hospital register. He had seen 'the list of names of the Arnhem boys, as written at the time by a nurse. Tannenbaum and McNabb were included.' Anthony's name was conspicuous by its absence. There was also no mention of Anthony in the cemetery records. On the same visit as he saw the 'names of the Arnhem boys', Geoffrey had taken down a list of the wooden crosses on the graves. Though he had not apparently seen the cemetery register, which did not entirely tally with the crosses, neither this nor the crosses bore any possible variant of Anthony's names. Geoffrey may have seen an additional register as he mentions the absence of a second man who was supposed to have died, Francis Stern. Once again, however, there was no mention of Anthony.

Tannenbaum had always maintained that Anthony had been left behind at the dressing station. Mintie had spoken to him on the telephone in May 1945, and Tannenbaum had told her that McNabb had gone to Enschede with him and had died a few days later. He also recalled that McCracken had died on the evening of the shooting, saying that he had died by his side.[558] His memory was that McCracken had died in the hospital, not in the dressing station as both Etter and Gough had testified.

There is no reason to think that Tannenbaum had confused Anthony with McCracken, and that it was Anthony who had died next to him that evening. Tannenbaum knew McCracken because they were from the same company, 2nd Parachute Battalion. McCracken was a batman, a private rather than a major, and doubtless a very different sort of person from the highly intelligent and articulate Anthony. Besides this, the poor man had been shot in the head, a very visible wound and not one which could easily be forgotten. Tannenbaum was adamant about who had gone to St Joseph's with him. In his affidavit for the War Crimes people, made in April 1945, he stated, 'Then three of us were taken on to the hospital at Enschede. Major Cotterell was the person who was left behind. That was the last I saw of Major Cotterell.'[559]

Before he had left for his posting in Germany, Geoffrey had met Tannenbaum in London. He had found him quite a serious and sensible person, one who was very unlikely to make things up.

> He was medium-sized, quiet. He told me he was starting a business, I think it was some kind of shop, and he was rather amazed to discover how much money you could borrow to do this, and a bit worried about the responsibility for what he had borrowed. That was probably his character. Quiet, dependable, responsible.[560]

Tannenbaum's adamant statement that Anthony did not go to Enschede with him is backed up by the absence of any information about Anthony in the hospital records. These records might perhaps have had sections missing. But Kamp, who thought of everything, interviewed the Mother Superior of the hospital. Although she had been forced to hand over the administration of the hospital to the Germans, this did not mean that she was unaware of what was going on in her own wards. She knew that, after Arnhem, there were English soldiers at the hospital even if she did not know all their names. What she could confirm was that she had never heard the name Cotterell, and that only two British officers had died in her hospital and their names she did know.[561]

Kamp also managed to get information from a voluntary nurse, Ella Van Brandwijk who had worked at St Joseph's at the relevant time. She told him that there had been one English major there and two captains.[562] She did not know their names, but she was still in contact with a British soldier who had worked at the hospital as a PoW. This was Private James Flynn, now living at 49 Charlton Road, Willesden, London. Geoffrey forwarded his address to Mintie who quickly got in touch with him. The War Crimes people would also contact Flynn and take an affidavit from him. In this affidavit, Flynn stated that there had been a British Army major at St Joseph's, kept in isolation, who had died of his wounds. He had been called to see the dying man in his final moments.

> I tried to get some information from him as to his identity. I tried to get hold of his I-disc but he hadn't them on him and there were no Army clothes about [...] Height about 5-9, hair chestnut with moustache, age about 35 to 4-. Religion RC. Very large black Rosary beads. According to what I recollect, he was calling for someone by the name of Katherine or Margaret. I was informed by the Nuns that he had died, and I take this as the truth, as he was very far gone when I left him, a few minutes before.[563]

On 15 January Geoffrey wrote to his mother twice in one day. The first, handwritten, note told Mintie that enquiries were now being made in Berlin by a journalist (the name is indistinct but it looks like Matthewman) who had worked on the *Daily Express* with Anthony. Geoffrey then picked up on what Mintie had written to him about Flynn. Geoffrey, who did not believe that Flynn's major was Anthony, slightly disputed Mintie's take on the story, but added that Kamp would go to Enschede to check it out.

In the second, typescript, letter he enclosed a telegram from Berlin 'to give you documentary comfort that our representative is trying'. He told Mintie:

> This morning I was down at my billet when a message came that an airman had arrived with a parcel for me. He came down and it turned out to be a parcel of eggs from Mrs Willink, enclosing also your letter about Flynn; she sent it because she knew Kamp was with me and she had stopped a transport on its way through Holland.

As Mintie had now written to Aps about Flynn (the enclosed letter), Geoffrey took up the matter in his second letter of the day. He told his mother that in the light of what Etter had told him, which he was now inclined to believe because 'he was almost certainly telling the truth', he felt that the isolated officer at Enschede was less likely to have been Anthony. If it was, then his isolation was for his own good, 'which doesn't seem likely, as I gather from your report that the Major was not especially better treated than the others, but merely isolated'. Knowing his brother so well, he added:

> Incidentally I don't think Anthony would have grown much of a beard in 5 or 6 days. However, to finish with Enschede, I think it is important that Flynn should be shown the most recent photograph. Secondly do not worry about Enschede because we can definitely get to the bottom of the story on the strength of those details and perhaps solve someone else's worry.

Geoffrey never forgot that other families were suffering the same horrible grief and anxiety as his own family. On 7 February, he would write about one of Mintie's letters:

> Bentinck strikes a familiar chord to me: or Will-Bentinck – wasn't that one of the wives who wrote to you? What was his rank and what was her name? Look it up in your file. Because I may have solved her mystery.[564]

The Flynn story continued to preoccupy Mintie. On 22 January, again clearly responding to something she had written, Geoffrey argued:

> But if Anthony did go to Enschede there is again no reason why he should be anonymous. I am not in the least convinced he was Flynn's major. It is even possible that the moving him on took place from Enschede. However I have sent long questionnaires to Gough and Tannenbaum, covering a variety of small points that have cropped up.[565]

In an undated note around this time, Geoffrey said he had also sent a long questionnaire of 30 questions to Flynn, even though the connection with Anthony seemed very unlikely. Geoffrey was inclined to doubt this part of the trail altogether – 'I don't consider it necessary that Enschede was the answer.'

In another undated letter, he told Mintie of receiving Flynn's reply:

Darling

Whether Anthony was at Enschede or not, he was not Flynn's major. Flynn has replied to my detailed questions most willingly and one of them was: was the officer wearing a crucifix? The answer was, yes, with beads. I feel that so rapid a transformation could not have take place in so short a time.

When the 'Brief for Investigation' was drawn up by the War Crimes people, they would also pour doubt upon the idea that this unknown major had been Anthony:

Private James FLYNN, a prisoner of war who worked as a medical orderly in ENSCHEDE Hospital, testifies to the death there after the ARNHEM operation of an unknown English Major, but his description does not altogether tally with Major COTTERELL's, and FLYNN was unable to say whether Major COTTERELL's photograph was that of the officer in question or not. FLYNN says the Major who died at ENSCHEDE was a Roman Catholic, and had a rosary of very large black beads. Major COTTERELL's religion is not known, but in any case the point would not necessarily be conclusive as ENSCHEDE hospital was a Roman Catholic institution, and one of the nuns who nursed there might possibly, without knowing the officer's religion, have given him a rosary when he was dying – it was only in the last few minutes before his death that FLYNN saw him.[566]

In March 1946 Kamp would find one further St Joseph's witness, a Jewish nurse called Emma Egressy, who also remembered an English major at the hospital after the battle of Arnhem. She did not remember which transport he had arrived in. He was injured about the left shoulder and elbow, and had a scratch above the eye; 'his injuries were not very serious and he was able to walk to his room'. But her description did not really fit Anthony – she said that the man she had seen was dark-blonde, rather tall, possibly with a small moustache. Later, having recovered, he was transferred to Oberürsel, the routine destination for British prisoners after Arnhem.[567]

Emma Egressy also gave information about the one unknown grave in the cemetery at Enschede. She said that the man buried in it had been nursed in the same hospital room as a Captain Seccombe, but had died of his very serious shoulder wound. Emma Egressy was evidently in touch with Seccombe because she gave his full address in Muswell Hill, London, saying that he would know the soldier's name. There is no mention of this particular trail in Geoffrey's letters.

The unknown grave at Enschede was now the focus of the search. There was always the terrible possibility that Anthony had been transported to Enschede but had died on the journey. His injuries may have been far worse than had been thought by Gough or Etter, or he may have died from shock. From Zutphen to Enschede was a nightmare journey for a severely wounded man, particularly one who was not being transported in an ambulance but in an army lorry, in darkness, pain, distress, and terrible fear for the future. Had he been dead by the time that he reached the other end, he would probably have been placed immediately in the hospital morgue with the other dead from the shooting.

Though Geoffrey was always brave about what had happened to Anthony, this particular scenario was acutely painful for him. He had a terrible nightmare vision of Anthony having lost consciousness on the journey and awakening in the morgue to the full horror of his situation; the shock of that realisation then killed him.[568]

Geoffrey had been to Enschede General Cemetery on his first trip to Holland, when he had seen Trevor McNabb's grave. He had written a list of the men who had been buried on 26 September, which included the one unknown body. Enschede had been dismissed at that time. But by now it had been realised that there were two other unknown bodies there, and he had to tell his mother that these graves were also a possibility. On 21 January, Mintie wrote to Janie:

Still no news from Shubbs. Everything they do always ends in disappointment and now they are going to search Enschede again, as there were some unknown people who died there, so you can imagine how deeply anxious I feel, but we have to face up to everything – but I can't help still hoping that it won't be that and that somehow one day Tone will come back. I have always felt it so deeply. I only wish I could write you some good news, but everything is being done, that we do know.

Things now began to shift gear. On 26 January, Geoffrey wrote to Mintie:

I hope this will not seem unduly morbid. As you know there are three unknown graves at Enschede and Sergeant Kamp has just rung me up from Holland to say that an American unit has agreed to dig them up. It is a special unit for the purpose. Obviously measurements are what are required and also a plan of the teeth, size of feet etc. Can these macabre figures be obtained? The teeth are above all important.

Geoffrey advised his mother that 'the Army will have them anyway; if necessary ring up the Adjutant-General's office for advice'. The dental chart would, in fact, come from Graham, who had always taken care of his sons' teeth. One particularly important feature on the chart would be the information that Anthony's two front teeth were jacket-capped; he had broken them when he had crashed the car on the way to Wanstead Golf Club before the war.[569]

The chart and information which Graham prepared would be given to the Town Major of Enschede, who would give it to Kamp, presumably acting as the liaison officer with the American unit. This unit was attached to ETOUSA – European Theatre of Operations, United States Army – and the form which they were using was the standard form for the Grave Registration and Enquiries Division who had doubtless handled many hundreds of identification procedures.

Now followed a period of horrible waiting. Janie, who had moved on to Madras with the London Ballet Company, frequently wrote to Mintie to condole and to share their common anxiety, always reiterating that she felt sure that Anthony was alive somewhere. On 13 February, she mused:

Well, I still cannot think that Anthony was ever taken to Enschede, the other wounded have always affirmed not, nothing but conclusive proof will make me think he is dead after hearing that he walked to and from the [Zutphen] hospital ... Finding so many people, surely please God send us the way to the one who actually removed him.

By the time she sent her letter, Geoffrey had been in touch with Mintie with the news that the exhumation had been carried out.

For reasons it has not been possible to ascertain, two of the three unknown bodies had been ruled out and the only one which still remained in question was the original unknown body buried on 26 September 1944.[570] On 5 February, Geoffrey rang Kamp, and heard that he had received a message about the exhumation findings. The Town Major of Enschede had compared the tooth chart sent by Graham with that produced by the ETOUSA unit.

The answer was that the body was not Anthony's! To make sure I enquired if the Americans knew what a jacket crown was and Sergeant Kamp said yes they knew all about them (it was a specialist unit).
Therefore Enschede graveyard is 'out' and as Sergeant Kamp says 'we begin again'.[571]

The dental chart which had been made of the unknown body in the grave would soon be sent on to Ham Frith, because Graham understandably wished to check it for himself.[572] Geoffrey wrote in the covering letter of 5 March:

[...] attached is the dental chart of the body for papa to inspect. The inspection was carried out carefully by an American dentist so I don't think there is any possibility of having missed the crowns (you will see that these are mentioned on the form so he would have looked for them). Unless the fillings bear a marked resemblance, that should be that.[573]

As no more is heard in Geoffrey's letters about the dental chart, it appears that Graham was satisfied with what he saw. Thus, for the second time, Enschede was ruled out. Enquiries would continue to make sure that nothing had been overlooked, but as no evidence had been found that Anthony had ever been there, the search now turned to other channels.

35

DR SANITER AND THOMSON THE ORDERLY

Towards the end of January, Geoffrey met Dr Willi Richter, the doctor at the Zutphen General Hospital who had taken X-rays of the soldier identified as Anthony by the nurse, Johanna Sollman. Richter was very willing to help, answered Geoffrey's extensive questions, and looked carefully at the photographs which he had brought of Anthony:

> He could not say yes or no to the photographs, pointing out that he had dealt with hundreds of English wounded. But he remembered the two coming on the Monday morning and the dark one of middle height and darkish hair, limping and shoulder wound; the shoulder wound was the worst one but it could not possibly have been fatal. Richter then gave me the names of the two doctors in the dressing station.
>
> So now we have to find Dr Lathe and Dr Gruther, two entirely fresh names. After the succession of failures we have had, this morning was a riotous success.
>
> Richter did not know where the British soldiers came from or went to. He also said where the X-ray pictures were put, but did not know if they had been destroyed or taken away later.
>
> So – a little progress.
> Love love love love – Shubbs.[574]

The soldiers that Richter had seen on the Monday would have been particularly memorable to him as they would have been amongst the first British soldiers from the Arnhem battle that he treated.

With regards to the names Dr Lathe and Dr Gruther, it had been known for some time that there had been two doctors at Rozenhoflaan on the night of 23 September 1944 – the man who was its usual medical officer and another man who had been brought in specially to deal with the large number of wounded. The names of the two medical orderlies who belonged to the dressing station had also been discovered early in Kamp's search – a Miss Ooms had told him that both men were officers, and that Hermann Thomson came from Hamburg whilst Schutte came from Berlin.[575]

Richter, who had been anti-Nazi, appears to have wished to help Geoffrey as much as he could and to have pondered over the various ways in which he could do so. A few days after their conversation, he rang Geoffrey, met him, and took him to meet a German contact at Oberürsel. Here Geoffrey acquired the name of the former chief interrogation officer at Oberürsel. This was to cover the possibility that Anthony had been taken to Oberürsel if it had become obvious to his captors that he was well enough to be processed down the normal channels.[576]

In the letter describing his first meeting with Richter, Geoffrey added a postscript, saying that Dr Lathe (whose Christian name was Heinrich) had been interviewed in Essen by Kamp: 'he does not remember Anthony and thinks all went to Enschede: but the doctor Etter spoke to is another one. We have his name.'[577] Lathe would also be interviewed by Etter, and later, in April, by Geoffrey and Kamp together.[578] As for the doctor whom Etter had spoken to on the night of 23 September, this would prove not to be Dr Gruther but Erich Saniter, a Marine Stabsarzt or naval doctor, who was the assisting doctor at the dressing station. Lathe, from the Luftwaffe, was its usual medical officer.

Lathe's deposition of 6 February shed fresh light on the set-up at the dressing station.[579] He described it as normally being open only between the hours of 8.00am and 4.00pm. A dentist, Dr Jacobi, had his rooms on the first floor of the house, and another dentist, Dr Lange, was also based there. It was now obvious that No.12 Rozenhoflaan, far from being a first-aid post with the proper facilities for the injured, had simply been a daily treatment centre. Yet the Germans had elected to take the prisoners there rather to the local hospital two minutes walk away.

Whilst acknowledging that he had worked at No.12 Rozenhoflaan in 1944, Lathe was extremely anxious to establish that he had had no authority over the other medical staff there, and generally to insist that he had played only a very minor role on 23 September. He endowed Dr Saniter with the major part because he 'was duty doctor for that night for the area of Zutphen'. Any orders about the wounded must therefore have come from Saniter, not himself; 'it would not have been up to me to give any such orders'. The only starring role Lathe gave himself was in rebuking an SS guard:

> I know for certain that I energetically rebuked one of the guards of the wounded Englishmen – he was, I believe, an SS-Obertruppführer, who as far as I remember was in black uniform [...] he started discussing medical questions and considered as perfectly sufficient the treatment of the wounded officers. I pointed out to him that we Doctors would treat alike friends and enemies.

As for the treatments he had carried out:

> I only know that I injected the wounded with anti-tetanus, anodyne and tonics for the heart and looked in an unobjectionable way to the comfort and aid of the wounded until they were taken away.[580]

Other than this, Lathe's deposition was very unhelpful, adding no new information about Anthony or about what happened to the prisoners.

Near to the end of January, Geoffrey tried to calm his mother's fears about the lack of progress in the search:

> Remember that the present situation is: we have not heard from Hilversum, or found the propaganda officer; we have not explained the X-ray patient who was recognised as Anthony, whose wounds and description by the X-ray doctor himself fit perfectly; we have not seen, though we have located the naval doctor who treated him. [...]
>
> Oh, yes, and regarding the X-rays, there appear to be no X-rays filed for a gap of four days including September 25 – again a peculiar if coincidental fact, possibly merely due to the battle conditions.[581]

The X-rays records would be found a couple of months later, but this sort of distraction – was some freshly discovered 'peculiar fact' of vital significance or not? – was a regular feature of the search.

Mintie had been pursuing a peculiar fact of her own, something about a belt, but as her correspondence is missing, it is not possible to establish exactly what she was thinking. Geoffrey had already answered her theory about it a little tersely, remarking 'the belt means nothing, everyone has a belt'.[582] As she was still not happy, he wrote in a further letter, 'Ref the belt, everyone also has a revolver and holster, even me; but I am always frightened to wear it in case it goes off. So that was just an unhappy coincidence.'[583] Geoffrey was as resolutely unmartial as ever.

He also told her that he had information from Aps that Hibbert was now at Cambridge University, learning Russian, with the possible view of going to Moscow. Another Dutch friend would also confirm this story, saying that he had not heard from Hibbert recently 'Does he plan to return to the Netherlands or is he already a spy in Moscow?'[584] Hibbert was apparently hoping to clear up the possibility that Anthony had been taken by the Russians.

Meanwhile, the whereabouts of Saniter was still being sought. Geoffrey began the requisite arduous round of telephone calls, asking for information or favours. Various other people were also pursuing Saniter, including British intelligence agencies which, in various letters, Geoffrey named as Special Branch or Field Security. Saniter was rumoured to be on the island of Sylt, off the coast of North Germany near to the German-Danish border, but no confirmation had been received of this. It had also been discovered that the good doctor was doing a three year prison sentence for looting.

On 21 January, Geoffrey made a trip to Schleswig in North Germany, to see Herman Thomson, who had been one of the orderlies at the Rozenhoflaan dressing station on 23 September 1944. He forwarded the details to Mintie on the same day:

> Thomson added some details such as that the officer (Etter) ordered his friend (orderly's comrade) to give the English cigarettes and that the whole affair was carried out in the light of lanterns – and therefore he could recognise no one. He himself took the wounded to Enschede, and there was no one left behind. In the next room there seemed to be, he thought, some lightly wounded or possibly unwounded Englishmen, who were taken away earlier but he did not know where or how. Presumably this was Gough and, possibly, Anthony.

Once again, the evidence had been inconclusive, but there was consolation in the fact that there were now so many other people engaged in the search. On 7 February he wrote, 'The War Crimes are now thoroughly waking up to the case and Colonel somebody is about to ring me up and wants to see me. In fact official interest has never been stronger.' Geoffrey does not give the name of this Colonel Somebody, and in the next letter referred to him as 'the war crimes king'. A meeting was duly arranged on 14 February, but, as Geoffrey left for a welcome leave in England almost immediately afterwards, he would tell his parents about it in person rather than by letter.

Whilst Geoffrey was in England, JAG produced its first 'Brief for Investigation' on 19 February.[585] Drawn up by Major A.E.E. Reade, the officer in charge of the JAG War Crimes Section at Bad Oeynhausen, it was a summary of all the evidence found so far on the Brummen war crime and Anthony's disappearance. There was an enthusiasm and buoyancy about the report which suggested great hopes of finding the SS guard and his accomplice, whilst also solving the mystery of what had happened to Anthony. The brief began:

RESTRICTED
BAOR/15228/2/c.59/JAG.
19th February 1946

Brief for Investigation

ACCUSED: Unterscharführer MATSKE; and another member of Waffen SS serving in 9 (or 10) SS Panzer Division Hohenstauffen of 11 SS Panzer Corps, Army Group B.

VICTIMS: Major Anthony COTTERELL, Royal Fusiliers or -?- Hants. Regt. (Wounded and missing). Lt H.A. PLATT, Airborne Recce Sqn (murdered). Lt T.V.P. McNabb, Glider Pilot Rgt (murdered). Pte McCRACKEN (Capt PANTER's batman) 1 or 2 Parachute Regt. (murdered). and other PWs of Airborne Divn (wounded).

There were some mistakes in this opening section, for example McNabb was Airborne Recce (Reconnaissance) Squadron like Platt, and two of the victims were completely missing – Kenneth Mills, the only member of the Glider Pilot Regiment on the lorry, and Private Sydney Allen. The report spelt Matzke's name with an 's', but then the spelling is variable throughout the various official documents.

The brief went on to give a summary of the Brummen shooting, and what had happened afterwards. Interestingly, it did not have the up-to-date information about the dressing station which by now Kamp had successfully established was No.12 Rozenhoflaan. Once the narrative reached the point when the wounded were at the dressing station, it continued:

About half an hour's delay ensued, and by the time the Medical Officers arrived Pte McCRACKEN was beyond help and died shortly afterwards. For descriptions and possible identification of medical personnel at ZUTPHEN see list of witnesses below. Major GOUGH left the dressing station after about two hours with assurances from ETTER that the wounded would be removed by ambulance – presumably to ENSCHEDE – where ETTER himself (who remained in the dressing station until 2330 hrs) says he ordered their transportation. Lt McNAB, however, died of his wounds soon after Major GOUGH's departure. Major COTTEREL's fate remains, however, unknown, except that he was still alive and in ZUTPHEN on 25th Sept when he was X-rayed in the Roman Catholic hospital there.

Once again there were errors, the most significant one being that McNabb did not die until several days later.

Having taken two weeks leave, Geoffrey arrived back in a very snowy Hamburg on 5 March. He had returned via Holland, where he seems to have picked up the dental chart of the exhumation at Enschede General Cemetery because he included it in his first letter home to his parents.

He had first gone to Bad Oeynhausen to see the British War Crimes people, but had discovered that the relevant search team were out and so went on to Herford, to the HQ of 33 Netherlands War Crimes Commission. He wanted to find out where Kamp was, but it turned out that Kamp was at the Herford office that day.

So we had a long conversation and I was fortunately able to entertain him to a meal and a bottle of champagne. [...]

He is off to Holland with his new boss (a Major whom I met – and who gave full permission to carry on with the case – delightful man) and they are going to question the Dutch chief of propaganda (possibly most important) who has just been discovered in a jail in Utrecht.[586]

Kamp had a full program ahead of him. He had located the doctor who must have been there when the truck arrived at St Joseph's, and was due to interview him and re-interview the nurse Johanna Sollman, who had recognised Anthony in Zutphen hospital. He was also going to make further enquiries as to the whereabouts of Saniter.

The strain was telling on the Cotterells. Mintie and Janie were turning to dreams and the sixth sense for knowledge of what had happened to Anthony. Geoffrey told his mother on 9 March that he was hoping to go to an astrologer the following afternoon with 'the three dates: can't you possibly find out your own time of birth?'

Leads were still coming and going, including yet another one from Kamp who had interviewed a Dr Mumen at Enschede who had treated an English major. Dr Mumen did not recognise the photograph of Anthony, but thought that he would not remember the actual face anyway. It seemed to him, though, that the man whom he had treated was older. The wounded major had been sent to Apeldoorn in early October 1944. Geoffrey remembered a story Mintie had told him some time back about Anthony being sent to Apeldoorn. It had come from Father Egan, the Roman Catholic padre with 2nd Parachute Battalion. Egan had heard that Anthony had been taken to Apeldoorn 'and in a very bad way'.[587] Whether the two accounts were connected or not, the odd thing, Geoffrey considered, about this new story was that the Major was not only wounded in the shoulder but in the leg, the same pattern of injury which it had been established that Anthony had suffered.[588]

On 14 March, for the first time for over four months, Geoffrey took a trip purely and simply for his own amusement. He went to Denmark with a Major Duncomb for a break. After the bleakness of post-war Hamburg, with its desolate ruined landscape and ill-clad ill-fed Germans, Denmark was a dazzling experience. He told Mintie that the shops were 'bewilderingly full of things. So far I have purchased, rather daringly, a nail file.'

He and Major Duncomb then had lunch:

> This experience has clouded the rest of the day so far. Oysters, incredibly rich soup, incredibly rich goose, and incredible ice. We did it for the novelty; it won't be physically possible to repeat it – though Danes were eating it all in large quantities with great abandon. Coming from Hamburg of course it is singularly revolting. There is very little to drink, which is as well.

At the bottom of the letter, he added a further note: 'I see I have given no account of the size of the lunch. We could finish nothing except the oysters.'

Mintie evidently picked up on the subject of this lavish banquet versus meagre German rations, for he would reply once he had returned to Hamburg:

> It seems to me that you may be imagining that we have to tread our way through Hamburg dodging half bricks and bread riots. This is not the case. Nor have I seen the smallest manifestation of it. Eleven pounds of bread a month does not of course keep the population exactly at a fever pitch of pleasure.[589]

On the way back from the Danish trip, he had called in once again to see the orderly Thomson from the dressing station:

> I called on Hermann Thomson in Schleswig on the way back, fortunately finding him at home and not in bed.
>
> He said he made a mistake in signing that two had died on the way [to Enschede]: he was referring to the two besides Tannenbaum whom he delivered, as good as dead. When he returned from Enschede he saw a ladder in the dressing station and wondered where it had come from. Now Gough said that Tone was on a ladder (instead of a stretcher). Now Thomson said they had plenty of stretchers and if the wounds had been very bad they would definitely have put him on a stretcher.

So I am wondering if a) Saniter took him with him personally or b) sometime between 11 and 2am he felt better and tried to get out by himself – and finally ended up in Zutphen X-ray room? Or something.[590]

The Germans had taken these ladders from the Dutch at Brummen in lieu of stretchers; all the wounded had been put on them and had arrived at Zutphen on them, but Thomson had clearly forgotten this.

The web of enquiries was ever-widening. Kamp, for example, had found the address of the clerical orderly at St Joseph's who 'took all the details of everyone who ever came there'.[591] But for Geoffrey for the time being everything was pushed aside by a momentous meeting. Taking matters into his own hands and bypassing all the official agencies who had singularly failed to trace him, Geoffrey finally located Dr Saniter.

24 March

Well – I am now 99% convinced that the man in Zutphen hospital <u>was</u> Anthony and that the man Dr Mumen of Enschede treated and then probably sent to Apeldoorn was almost certainly Anthony.

I found Dr Saniter.

First of all I went up to Sylt and met a girl that he had known in Belgium. She gave me the address of his fiancée, but this turned out to be unnecessary. At the British headquarters where I stayed the night, I searched the records with an RAF security sergeant, where eventually his name turned up. He had been arrested on 24.9.45 and was thought to have been sent to a camp near Neumunster. I visited this on my return this morning: and within half an hour in walked Dr Saniter. By this time I had fully conditioned myself to hearing the old story: i.e. of not knowing why he was not sent to Enschede. Here is Saniter's story.

He was sent for to help out with some wounded and arrived at the Krankenstube with one orderly. The Luftwaffe doctor was already there and told Saniter which people he wanted treating. There were many English officers mostly unwounded or lightly wounded, and most of whom were in the back room. There were however <u>four</u> more seriously wounded.

One was in an especially bad way with a severe head injury. The Luftwaffe doctor attended to him all the time. Then there was one with a bad lung wound, and he did something to prevent the air getting in. The third had a shot in his backside and did not appear in mortal danger. All these were stretcher cases and were attended first.

The fourth was not a stretcher case. His left arm had been hit between the shoulder and the elbow. There was no possibility of it being fatal. All four were given morphia or other means of easing pain. After the fourth one had been treated (and if there was a leg wound it was not worth treating, as it would have been too light), he walked to a seat in the corner of the room near the door and sat down.

Dr Saniter did not know who he was or what happened to him. Physically he could have walked out by himself. He did not require a stretcher. He was between 25 and 30, had not a particularly strong body, and was not very big.

You may ask did he recognise the photograph? I fear the answer is I hadn't got it with me – however there is no doubt who it was and I may be able to go up again with a photograph to make trebly sure: it is already doubly – in fact, certain.

The immense significance of this meeting (which Kamp is passing on in the morning to the War Crimes Commission) is of course the Zutphen X-ray room, and Dr Mumen from Enschede: the wound is <u>exactly</u> right in both cases and it does not seem improbable that he took a trail round.

Now how did he leave the Krankenstube? (a) he may have walked out and been recaptured. More likely is (b) he was returned to the prisoners cage with the other prisoners, but <u>because</u> he was the worst of the light wounded he possibly travelled in the front of the lorry and was then deposited somewhere separate. Possible?

Dr Saniter does not recall anything about a journalist etc. Whether that is true or not is for the moment by the way: we do now <u>know</u> what the wounds were. [...]

I think you will agree that this, after an aggravating interval, constitutes an <u>advance</u>.

Geoffrey did not see Saniter again, but when Kamp went to see him on 2 June to show him Anthony's photographs, Saniter immediately recognised Anthony. Then he thought hard, and said he thought that the man was the one with the injuries which Tannenbaum had suffered. Saniter did not refer to him as Tannenbaum, but identified him by the treatment and advice he had given him, 'for he said he told him what to eat, which is what he told Tannenbaum: but he was very definite at recognising the photograph'.[592]

Geoffrey's meeting with Saniter was a huge relief, for it seemed to scotch once and for all the idea that Anthony had been mortally wounded. It brought the family no closer to actually finding him, but it renewed their hope that they might do so. Though the evidence – as was so disappointingly frequent – contained contradictions, nonetheless it seemed conclusive enough to establish a new and promising theory, that after Zutphen Anthony had gone to Apeldoorn.

36

SCHMIDT, FRITZSCHE AND OTHER LEADS

At the end of March, Geoffrey, who had for some time been trying to arrange a lightening trip to Holland, managed to arrange to go there for the weekend. Only a couple of days before leaving, he received another parcel of eggs from Aps, who was evidently concerned that he was not getting enough to eat in Hamburg. The eggs were brought to him by a Dutch officer of the Netherlands War Crimes Commission, whom she had co-opted as a delivery man.

Ad hoc delivery arrangements were a speciality of Aps. Though the situation in post-war Europe was dire for millions of people, there is something rather beguiling about the way of life which could be lived by others who were positively enjoying the informality, freedom and excitingly make-shift nature of it all. Aps was clearly one of these free spirits, as can be seen in Geoffrey's letter of 1 April, describing his brief, but action-packed Holland trip.

I met Kamp at Bad Oeynhausen on Friday night. He had a small Opel in which there was already a Dutch ATS officer à la Juliana and an MP Corporal.[593] I got in, Kamp got in. He was driving. The entrance to the station was some 50 yards away at right angles to the busy main road. We passed through the entrance at approx 40 mph and reached Almelo, his home in Holland, at 4am. His mother immediately cooked two fried eggs each for us. This had by now developed into a kind of conditioned reflex action at the sight of us; the whole thing is done in complete silence as she speaks only Dutch.

On Saturday, dropping the ATS at her home in Zutphen, where she was ecstatically greeted by the 63 other members of the family, fighting each other down the stairs, we picked up Mrs Willink and went to Utrecht. We had quite a good dinner at a restaurant and then questioned the Dutch Quisling No 2 and a few others in the prison there.

On the way back, we called in at a Dutch SS camp where we arrived at 3am. We continued questioning suitable gentlemen until 7am. Mrs Willink and the Corporal having a chatty conversation with the sergeant in the guard room during this time, interrupted it seems only by Mrs Willink's uninhibited bursts of merriment at the procedure when the guard changed.

It seems to have been considered perfectly normal to interrogate prisoners associated with war crimes without any warning in the middle of the night.

In writing to Mintie on Sunday, 31 March, Aps would describe this prison camp as being in the neighbourhood of Apeldoorn, and add that it contained 4,500 prisoners – SS, SD, and Polizei – facts which she had no doubt gleaned from the chatty sergeant in the guard room. She also gave Mintie many other details. Before leaving for Hamburg, Geoffrey had asked her to write immediately so that Mintie would know what had transpired as soon as possible. Having covered the exhausting itinerary of Saturday/Sunday night, Aps told Mintie:

The boys were so very tired that they slept all the time in the motorcar! Then we have stopped for a short time so that they could sleep altogether. When we came at home it was very nice weather, and I have, after my house, a platform with all sunshine and no wind. We have there the chairs and a long-chair for Geoffrey. I have covered him with a plaid and after having a cup of coffee he was sleeping in the sun till eleven o'clock, I thought, 'If his mother could see him so'. Kamp ordered his papers and his informations, and my other guest made his toilet. I would make dinner for them but Kamp (he was the leader) said that they have no more time, then they would still go to Nijmegen.

I could not go with them, as each Sunday afternoon my father comes to see me on his cycle (he is 82 years old) and it is about 32 kilometres!! So I gave them a lot of sandwiches and hard-boiled eggs and after about three hours they came back from Nijmegen very very satisfied.

That Sunday at Nijmegen, Geoffrey and Kamp interviewed the Dutch propaganda chief (Geoffrey does not give a name), then a Radio Hilversum employee who gave them quite a bit of information about the set-up when the Germans controlled the station. Afterwards they dropped by at the Zutphen hospital and found an old book with entries for 25 September 1944. There were two English names for X-rays, Atkinson and McLoughlin, with upper arm and ankle wounds respectively. Remembering previous witness testimony about the pair, Geoffrey would theorise that, being Scottish, McLaughlin was probably the one with red hair and that therefore, by default, Atkinson must have been Anthony going under a false name.

Or someone else altogether.

But this last possibility did not trouble Geoffrey much because of Saniter's testimony about the wounds: 'as we now know that Anthony was well enough to be moved anywhere at once or, of course, to escape, this is OK'.[594]

After Zutphen, he and Kamp, and possibly the MP Corporal, went to Lochem, to which it was known that shot wound cases had been sent. They could find no trace of Anthony. But they also discovered that there was a house 'down the road' which the Dutch were not allowed into, which was where 'Germans and English (less serious cases) were treated. This is a distinct possibility, being of course investigated.' Geoffrey would later refer to this place as 'the secret hospital at Lochem'.

In a second letter about the trip he told Mintie that they had visited another Dutch friend of the Cotterells, Albert Deuss, a former Dutch resistance man who lived at Arnhem.

He was digging a rockery in the garden. House at the corner of a row, slightly battered about inside but repaired and very comfortable. Children everywhere and pregnant wife, who put in a fleeting appearance to shake hands and then, I think, went upstairs for half an hour to give birth. On top of the dividing door between the living and dining room there was an 18' high cross.[595]

The thing about giving birth was a comic exaggeration because Mrs Deuss – Louise – was so heavily pregnant.

Geoffrey appears to have been very much in teasing high spirits on this visit, and Albert would probably not have been entirely happy had he known that his rebuilding works would be described in a letter home as a rockery. His house had been wrecked and many of his possessions stolen by the Germans; he would demonstrate these losses indignantly to his visitors.

Mintie would also receive a letter from Albert about this visit. The Cotterells knew Albert well as he had stayed with them in Ham Frith in February of that year. Albert told Mintie:

Yesterday when I was happy rebuilding my front garden a small army car stopped and I saw a few smiling faces. Then I recognised Mrs Tjeenk Willink, Sergeant Kamp, and then I discovered

Geoffrey behind in the car. They were on the way to The Hague. First they would not come out but when I insisted Geoffrey said, 'Well, only three minutes,' and the party came out to see my home. Geoffrey could make a report about it then, he said. In a hurry I showed them the brook [?] in my gardens, the smashed windows, the cutting of the carpets by the Germans, the various empty places, the missing of the curtains, [...] the missing stoves. Then Geoffrey halted because he found it very peculiar that in our home we have two stoves and only one chimney like this [small drawing inserted]. He said, 'Well, that is quite primitive'. I looked sharply at him from aside and I detected a soft smile on his face. I wondered whether he got out to see my home only to make such a 'primitive' remark but I did not ask him.

I told Geoffrey that I am in the Army now as a captain. I belong to a so-called purifying committee, the highest committee existing in the Dutch Army to purify all the Dutch officers if there are quislings and collaborators among them. A quite dull job but the amusing thing is that we are our own masters. As a matter of fact I purify most of the officers away, leaving the trouble to our War Office. No harm upon me, you see. [596]

Albert does not seem to have been completely serious about purifying post-war Holland.

In the letter, he continued that during his military work in Gelderland and OverIJssel he would not neglect to follow up any trace of Anthony. He then added, rather tactlessly: 'The more I think about the question, the more I get convinced that Anthony got into the hands of the SD.' Mintie would write to Geoffrey about this very quickly, and Geoffrey reassured her, 'SD stands for security service, a sort of intelligence, and we have in fact questioned many of them and are still doing so'.[597] They had begun on this tack very early in the search; Kamp's report of November the previous year contained a whole list of these people. He had even discovered the whereabouts of the commander of the Arnhem SD, Obersturmführer Thomson, but when he and Geoffrey went to Groningen jail to interview him, they discovered that Thomson had been moved on to Rotterdam, where he had committed suicide.[598]

Albert concluded his rather over-frank letter to Mintie by telling her he had already done some investigating at Apeldoorn. Geoffrey would later clarify this saying that Albert had 'located two unknown graves, had them dug up and taken all measurements and teeth form, etc. Both quite wrong of course.'

Undiscouraged, Albert would continue to search for Anthony in his own way. In a letter to Aps of 9 May, he wrote about his further investigations:

Is there any more news about the fate of Anthony Cotterell? I am very interested to hear about that. During one of my journeys here I happened to meet a military officer of the Service of Identification and Salvage Operations. This Service is still occupied with the exhumation of the bodies of executed people and also of Allied soldiers. I also met an officer on the airfield nearby Enschede, where the Service is in search for the bodies of executed people. Here in Velp lately, several bodies have been excavated: all of them, but two, could be identified. If it is needed for me to be alert in this matter, I would like to have Anthony Cotterell's data, especially those of his set of teeth. In the meantime in Enschede they are making use of a dowser.[599]

The dowser, using a stick in the same way as a water-diviner, looked for metal objects like uniform buttons buried deep in the soil and thus pinpointed unmarked graves.

The new theory about Apeldoorn, sparked off by Dr Mumen's testimony about a major he had treated, did not survive for long. On returning from a second trip to Holland in April, Geoffrey told his mother that it was a red herring:

We went to Apeldoorn to check on the mysterious major we have had reports of from Enschede to Gronau and then to Apeldoorn, who had this severe left arm and shoulder wound. This was very satisfactory. A German doctor had previously told us where he was in Apeldoorn and we found the Dutch doctor who treated him. He gave us the name and address without any hesitation – I forget it for the moment – but that rounded off that theory very nicely. The mysterious major was not Anthony.[600]

However, this particular trip to Holland had not been made for the purpose of checking the Apeldoorn theory but to follow another possible lead.

A story came through from the Dutch police that a former collaborator knew something and wanted to help. In fact she turned out to be a most unpleasant and evil fraud, but the whole episode was most fascinating.

She lay in bed above a grocer's shop in Zutphen where she was supposed to be ill. (We were fairly certain she was a fraud to start with.) I said I couldn't speak German, Kamp that he couldn't speak Dutch, the lady that she knew no English. Finally it went on in German with myself looking innocently out of the window. First she wanted the photographs. Oh yes! That was him, definitely – she had seen him, there was no doubt at all. He had been lying in the window of a dressing station in Oude Wand and they spoke to each other in a non-language way. Then a doctor came in and there was something fishy about him. But she had to go.

But Kamp said, the dressing station had in fact not been in Oude Wand. He was moved at 6 o'clock that morning, she said promptly. And that was all she had to tell us? Oh, no. If we would go away and come back the next day, she would have remembered more. All she wanted to do was to find this officer, on conditions. Isn't it odd, said Kamp, if you don't speak English that there's an English paper by your bed? He then broke into a tirade in Dutch which upset her, though she was not easily upset.

I forgot to say that she had wanted to be put in touch with relatives of the missing major. In fact she was on a charge of being a Quisling, heard about the case and therefore invented a plausible story to try and get some English support. If we hadn't known so much, we might easily have believed her. Nice person? It has settled her fate with the Dutch police, anyway. A most interesting experience.

We returned to the Willinks for lunch. Dick had taken my drivers for a battlefield tour, where one of the drivers found some trenches he himself had dug in the fighting to relieve Arnhem.

With the Apeldoorn theory disproved and the fraudulent Dutchwoman exposed, Geoffrey once again returned to Germany. He found the people at his office were completely absorbed by the Nuremberg Trials, which by order had to be on the front page of the newspapers every day. And it was now that the investigations into Anthony's disappearance went to the highest level – Conroy, the South African major from the Search Bureau, travelled to Nuremberg to interview Dr Hans Fritzsche, one of the accused.

Fritzsche was the former head of German radio propaganda, in charge of the Radio Division of the Ministry of Propaganda from 1942 until the end of the war. He personally had had no control over propaganda – his work had always been overseen by Goebbels – but he was being tried in lieu of Goebbels who had committed suicide in the Hitler bunker in the last days of the war.

On 26 March, Geoffrey wrote to his mother to tell her of the latest developments:

Major Conroy has now departed to Nuremberg for Anthony to interview Fritzsche the propaganda chief – who is one of the accused – and also Schmidt, Hitler's personal interpreter! Although I have no anticipation of anything coming of this, I do feel that it represents quite a victory in our battle – a very long cry from the 'one in every regiment'. In fact it is the highest possible level of enquiry

By 'one in every regiment' Geoffrey was referring to the original casual and dismissive attitude of officialdom to Anthony's disappearance. As for the Schmidt he mentions, this was Dr Paul Schmidt, the same man who had entertained the American journalist, Ed Beattie, in Berlin. It would turn out, however, that there were two Dr Paul Schmidts, and that the relevant one was not at Nuremberg but in US custody at Kornwestheim in the American Zone. Conroy would take a detour there and interrogate him.

At the beginning of April, Geoffrey wrote to tell Mintie what had come out of Conroy's trip:

> These are the facts. Dr Schmidt, the press chief of the Propaganda Ministry, said that Anthony did NOT go to Berlin: but what is very important is that if Anthony <u>had</u> gone to Berlin, Dr Schmidt would have seen him at once. Dr Schmidt knew all about him, books, newspaper, and everything. Dr Schmidt then heard the circumstances of the incident and said, 'Well, then we wouldn't have seen him.' The SS had their own fiercely jealous propaganda system and under no circumstances, he said, would have handed him over to the Ministry, but kept him to themselves. He then gave the names of the SS boys who would be concerned and London has been teleprinted for their whereabouts. Also information was received from one of the Nuremberg people questioned as to the identity of the reporter at the incident. And blow me if Kamp and I didn't come across this name in Holland (not knowing he was our man) and set the Dutch political boys after him. He was an Unteroffizier but in spite of low rank Chief of Hilversum Radio![601] We'll get him all right. [...]
>
> love love love – everything possible is being done:
> Shubbs[602]

In his affidavit, Schmidt commented upon the SS:

> Since Major Cotterell was captured by the SS, there is a possibility that I may not have heard about it, because there was enmity between the Propaganda Organisation of the Waffen SS and the Propaganda Ministry.
>
> Günther d'Alquen, Chief of the Propaganda Organisation of the Waffen SS, in that case would be the man to interrogate.
>
> I would also suggest interrogating Schwarz Von Berg, who was Chief Editor of *Das Schwarze Korps* [*The Black Corps*].

The possible connection between Günther d'Alquen's organisation and Anthony will be examined in a later chapter.[603]

On 8 April, Geoffrey wrote to his mother again.

> This morning I am lunching with Conroy, whom I saw late last night. I have the Nuremberg affidavits in front of me. Hans Fritzsche suggests all sorts of channels that Anthony could have travelled. He says: 'I think I recognise the photo shown me'. He also says 'an important pressman like Major Cotterell'. The interrogation was carried out by Conroy, an interpreter and by – Etter! Anyway all the names suggested are being sought, so we wait a little now.

The wording of Fritzsche's affidavit suggests that he was most anxiously currying favour with the British, almost over-eager to cooperate as in his suggestion that he might have possibly recognised Anthony. His helpful attitude was hardly surprising; he was virtually on death row. Much to his relief and surprise, and the surprise of many others, he would eventually be acquitted, one of only three of the accused who would escape long-term imprisonment or the death penalty.

Fritzsche, like Schmidt, referred to the rivalry between various propaganda bodies, which added to the confusion about where Anthony might possibly have ended up.

> After capture an important pressman like Major Cotterell being dropped by parachute, would have been sent to Oberüsel, and his presence would have been reported at once to the Liaison Officer to the Foreign Office, and to the Liaison Officer of Dr Goebbels. There used to be a race between these two officers for such men.

Fritzsche could not remember having been informed by Dr Goebbels' officer, Lieutenant Bonninghaus, that Anthony was in custody. He not only gave Bonninghaus's name but also a very detailed description of him, including that he was 'an attractive and elegant man'. In addition, he named other men who might have come into contact with Anthony.[604] This appears to have been the end of the matter, although it was subsequently discovered that Fritzsche had been visiting Radio Hilversum about the time of the October broadcast which mentioned Anthony.[605] There is no record of any further interrogation of Fritzsche on Anthony's case file.

The names supplied by what Geoffrey termed 'Fritzsche and company at Nuremberg' would now all be followed up. There is one tiny coda to the Goebbels-Fritzsche connection, to be found in a letter Geoffrey wrote to his mother on 22 April: 'Ref your 81 South Audley Street, I never heard anything about Dr Goebbels having it in for him; but it's very interesting.' Number 81 South Audley Street was Anthony's Belgravia flat. With Mintie's correspondence lost, there is no further detail about what Geoffrey was referring to. However, an official document of that same period describes Geoffrey passing on a remark which he had learned that Anthony had made to his batman just before leaving for Arnhem. Anthony had apparently said that he would have to watch out as Goebbels was after him. It sounds like a characteristic Anthony joke, but it was taken seriously enough to be referred to in a War Crimes report of May 1946.[606]

Sometime in March, Geoffrey must have seen Dr Lathe of the Zutphen dressing station, though there is no description of their meeting in his letters. On 3 April he told Mintie that at the end of the week he hoped to go to Essen to see Dr Lathe for a second time 'as I am suspicious that he hasn't told all he knows. We will have a happy little interrogation. I will probably take Kamp with me.'

In taking Kamp with him, Geoffrey was taking the human equivalent of a pit bull terrier. The results were even worse than Geoffrey had expected:

> Am now back from the visit to Essen, which was possibly or possibly not unprofitable. We organised a revolting episode to make Dr Lathe talk, which was to produce a warrant for his arrest for having given false information. Poor Dr Lathe who was rather like Dr B down the road immediately trembled, while his wife, advised by Kamp to pack a few things, broke down. It was all very repulsive. After a while we went away for an hour or so to let him think on his previous statement (which had a few inconsistencies with Dr. Saniter's).[607]

During the bogus threat session, Geoffrey had wanted to shrink into the floor in shame, but Kamp was implacable. 'Dr B down the road' was Dr Barker, a harmless soul who lived near to the Cotterells in Wanstead, 'a gentle and very nice man, unassuming'.[608] Lathe's resemblance to him greatly tormented Geoffrey's conscience, as did the tears and sorrow of his wife.

On Geoffrey and Kamp's return to the house, Lathe 'did more or less clear himself'. He also gave them what might be a very important name: the officer who was in charge of the prisoners at Zutphen and of their interrogation.

> We then informed him that we would not take him and of course there scenes of great rejoicing. And he also gave us the name of the doctor in charge of the secret hospital at Lochem.

Leaving a greatly relieved Dr Lathe consoling his wife, Geoffrey and Kamp went away.

Yet more names, yet more clues which always seemed to lead nowhere. Geoffrey did his best to keep cheerful at the lack of progress, but it was not always easy. On 12 April, he wrote:

> The question of survival is a matter of faith, not logic. All that can be said is that it is possible. Any fool can say, like Ferraro, that the opposite is more likely. However, Conroy did not, repeat not, tell Selkirk Panton that survival was impossible. In fact apart from many other conversations Conroy asked me: 'Tell me, does your mother believe he is alive'.
>
> I said, 'I think so. Half way, anyhow.'
>
> 'Good', said Conroy, 'because so do I.'
>
> And so he does: but he has no more reason than you or I. But it is possible.

Selkirk Panton was a famous *Daily Express* journalist. As for Captain Ferraro, his real name was Captain M.A.J. de Ferrare, and he was from the Belgian Army, working with the War Crimes Investigation Unit.[609] His remarks have disappeared along with Mintie's correspondence but the general drift of them can be gathered from Geoffrey's response. Returning to the matter two days later, he asked:

> Did Captain Ferraro really say that?
>
> Of course he is only a Belgian, so there is some excuse – the point is his department is chasing up Anthony in the hope of helping with the war crime, so his prominence does not really affect them a lot: Anthony is Search VIP No 1, anyway.[610]

37

DEMOB AND AFTERWARDS

From April onwards, Geoffrey's thoughts increasingly turned towards his demob. Though delighted with the prospect of being a civilian again, he wanted to make sure that he could easily get back into Germany or Holland despite the restrictions on civilian travel. It was vital that he could continue the search if anything important came up. He began to make various arrangements which would guarantee his passage. As he told his mother, 'it will not be impossible I am happy to say, as I have been slightly worried about it'.[611] But the arrangements, being complicated, would take some time to firm up, and he continued to feel anxious about them.

In Hamburg there was something of a party atmosphere as colleagues and associates who were being demobbed earlier than him were having farewell celebrations before going home. He and Conroy, the South African Major from the Search Bureau, had a celebration of their own, this time for Easter. It took place in Geoffrey's room, and consisted of two bottles of champagne, one bottle of gin and one bottle of brandy – 'shared with colleagues I hasten to add'. It was during this rather pleasant visit that Conroy told Geoffrey that he had discovered that when they had been in the French Zone before Christmas, looking for Etter, 'we were followed every yard of our going about by a French detective'.[612] Once again one catches a glimpse of the paranoid suspicions which were endemic in the Occupation of Germany.

At the end of April, Geoffrey made his debut on Radio Hamburg. He wrote to Mintie:

> In an hour's time my voice will be addressing the German people in German from Radio Hamburg in a question-by-German and answer-by-a-British-officer programme [...] My German radio voice is a great success, and, I think, totally unrecognisable. Perhaps I could have been a spy after all: lucky we didn't find out.

Geoffrey's performance had been rehearsed by a German producer who, like a conductor, had taught him the inflections, the rising and falling of the words, and only when he was satisfied allowed him to speak. Their association on the broadcasts would continue, though not always satisfactorily, and Geoffrey took to calling him 'my comic opera producer'. For himself, he disliked his German radio voice – 'I must say it sounds thoroughly unpleasant to me'.[613] Nonetheless, he made several attempts to make sure that his parents would catch the weekly broadcast, writing, for example, on 29 April:

> I keep wondering if you heard me [speaking on the radio]: it would have been very difficult to recognise me – it was a recording, of course – but they mentioned my name several times, so I hoped you got on to it. [...]
>
> I persuaded the girl at the Foreign Office to call you up, upon which a slightly irate operator interfered and said this could not possibly be allowed. I said I think you are absolutely right, and

he replied, Oh well Derby County are winning, will let it go through. The girl then reported that she had spoken to you.

After the broadcast George suddenly turned up. He was of course funny. We discussed the case at length. He showed me the book he is writing about the last ten years which is dedicated to Anthony, who, George says, will have a very wonderful story to tell when he comes back. With which refreshing thought I close.

George was George Edinger, Anthony's old mentor, who some ten years earlier had inspired him to abandon his medical and dental studies for journalism. Edinger was wildly flamboyant and theatrical, a man of immense intellectual brilliance whose voice was very loud, very educated, and very Oxford. This combination guaranteed that his presence was virtually impossible to ignore. On 30 April Geoffrey wrote home:

Life for the past 24 hours has been a succession of meals with George, drinks with George, complaints from George, missed appointments for George, loud criticism of the Navy from George in the hearing of astounded senior NCOs at the mess where he is staying, where the staff have now developed a fascinated interest in their lodger. Last night he went off alone into Hamburg with his conducting officer, who I need hardly say has come in for his share of criticism and I also need hardly say is a modern poet: 'You are an excellent poet, although I cannot understand a single word that you write, you have been a gallant naval officer, and as a companion you are charming, but as conducting officer–' I think he leaves tomorrow: if he isn't in jail by now.

At the time of Edinger's visit, one of the main preoccupations of the search was the hunt for Dr Eberhard Taubert, whom it was thought might have been the journalist who had tried to speak to Anthony at Brummen after the shooting. Though this would prove not to be the case, Taubert was a very important scalp in other respects. A vicious anti-Semite, he had been involved in the making of the notorious 1940 Nazi propaganda film 'The Eternal Jew', and is sometimes credited with its screenplay. Aged around 40, Taubert had been born near the border with Holland and spoke good Dutch. For the Dutch authorities, he was of prime interest because of his take-over of Radio Hilversum. As Geoffrey told Mintie (who was anxious about the significance of Taubert in relation to Anthony), 'I think the Dutch merely want him in the same way as we would want whoever took over the BBC'.

Not only had Taubert been the head of Radio Hilversum, but he had also founded the Arnhem Broadcasting Station in October 1944 with the help of Helen Sensburg, usually known by her nom-de-guerre of 'Mary of Arnhem'. There had been at least two broadcasters known as 'Mary of Arnhem', women with seductive voices who had tried to instil defeatism in the young British soldiers fighting in Holland. Helen Sensburg, however, was the foremost Mary of Arnhem. She had once been married to an Englishman, and she had a line with which she always ended her broadcasts, 'Good-night, boys. Take care of yourselves', which she always managed to imbue 'with a sort of sinister sex appeal'.[614] Helen Sensburg was captured in May 1945, and Geoffrey would note on 1 June that she was being interrogated by the Dutch police about Anthony's case. Taubert, however, continued to be elusive. He had seemingly disappeared in the confusion of the war's end, and although there had been a number of leads, none of them had led anywhere.

During Edinger's visit, another lead as to Taubert's whereabouts arrived. Geoffrey noted, 'I am now merely waiting for Conroy to report on the Taubert interview, and hoping that it is the right man. I think Conroy will get somewhere as he went off like a bloodhound.'[615]

Once again it was not the right Taubert. According to the statement of the real Taubert, made on 23 June 1946 after he had finally been located, he had been in custody all along. He said that he had surrendered to the 1st Canadian Army in early May 1945, and had subsequently been imprisoned at Scheveningen, then Vilvoorde near Brussels, before being released on 19 June 1946. Almost immediately, he was back in prison. His in-depth statement about his broadcasting activities was translated for the War Crimes people by the ubiquitous Kamp.[616] Taubert could add nothing about Anthony's disappearance.

On 1 May, Geoffrey attended the May Day gathering in Hamburg:

> with approx 60,000 huns, of whom one of them next to me said wittily: these of course are all the half % that voted against Adolf.
>
> Then I had a final lunch with George. Then I met the War Crimes captain who now has Anthony's case in hand: he seemed intelligent and what is perhaps even more important will stay here until October. I am meeting him once again tomorrow, and I think he will do some thorough investigating: he also has a great many more facilities than the Search Bureau, and will cable for me in England after my return when necessary.

The captain he mentions was almost certainly H.P. Kinsleigh from the Cheshire Regiment, who was a chief investigating officer with No 3 Team, Field Investigation Section, War Crimes Group (NWE). Many years later Geoffrey would describe Kinsleigh as 'blonde, slim, and not someone you'd like to be arrested by. Otherwise good company.'[617] Kinsleigh and Geoffrey would not always see eye to eye, and Geoffrey would not agree with Kinsleigh's conclusions on Anthony's disappearance which would be summarised in a report that September.

Kinsleigh would be the man who finally got to interview Etter's old boss, Anton Staubwasser, on 20 September 1946. Once again, it had taken a very long time to find a man who, after an extensive and complex search, proved to have been in custody all along. Staubwasser had fared much worse than his former subordinate, who had been released after only a few months. His pitiful belongings were a sign of his abject condition, being merely a wallet, a pencil and some personal photos. Held by the Americans at Dachau, his transfer to British custody was requested in August 1946. By the time of the Kinsleigh interview, he had been in detention for five weeks at the War Criminals Holding Centre at Minden, which with warped humour had the code name of 'TOMATO'.

On the 19 September, Staubwasser sent a plaintive note to the Chief of the War Crimes Commission at Bad Oeynhausen. This may have been what finally prompted Kinsleigh to interview him the following day. Staubwasser was claiming the international rights for prisoners of war, saying that he had been taken to TOMATO from Dachau without any explanation. In the transcript of the interview, Staubwasser is clearly very harassed and upset, eager to protest both his innocence and his willingness to cooperate.

As Wehrmacht soldiers were not in a proscribed category like the SS, Staubwasser's official status was that of a PoW who had not yet been cleared for release. His note to the Chief of the War Crimes Commission sparked off a minor furore. The British handling the liaison with the Americans had been specifically told by JAG that Staubwasser was not a war criminal, but when Staubwasser arrived at TOMATO his hands were manacled as was customary for that category. Major Reade, the JAG War Crimes officer whose name appears so often in Anthony's casework, wrote a severe rebuke:

> I am requesting the Commandant of TOMATO to apologise to Obersturmführer Staubwasser, and I should be obliged if you see to it that this is not repeated upon his return to the US Zone, and would make some arrangement to ensure that this kind of thing does not occur again in other similar cases.[618]

The message which had been sent with the request for Staubwasser's transfer back would read: 'subject is witness Not rpt NOT war criminal(.) status is P.W (.) ensure he is not manacled (.)'[619]

Staubwasser had suffered his miserable experience pointlessly because he could add nothing whatsoever to the case. He said he had no memory of the Brummen incident. However, to make sure that his interrogators would believe that he was not simply being uncooperative, he added: 'In order to explain why this incident is no longer memorable to me, I would like to give a brief overview of the scope of my work and my method of working at the time of the Arnhem landing.' He then described his very heavy workload with Heeresgruppe B, which ranged over an extremely large area of territory. All affairs that did not concern the enemy's position were delegated to his two main subordinates, Oberleutnant Utermann and Leutnant Mackenroth, and he believed that Utermann was the most likely candidate to know about Brummen.[620]

There seems to be a strong likelihood that Kinsleigh had deliberately kept Staubwasser waiting in TOMATO. Whether this was from a desire to soften him up, from contempt, from inertia, from a conviction that it would not be worth bothering with him, or a combination of all four, it is impossible to say. The idea that Kinsleigh considered Staubwasser a waste of time is certainly a feasible one. In all Kinsleigh's memos, there appears to run a thread of impatience with the investigation into Anthony's disappearance, which was so prolonged and so expensive in terms of man-hours and other resources. Kinsleigh seems to have had a habit of making up his mind fairly rapidly and thereafter being resistant to further investigations. This was not merely in matters which concerned Anthony, but also in those which concerned the hunt for the Brummen war criminals, who were generally referred to as 'Matzke and his accomplice'.

In the summer of 1946, it was thought that Matzke had at last been found, and a war crime trial began to look a serious possibility. A note with an illegible signature requested that Freddie Gough should be informed and gave his office address and telex number in Fenchurch Street. The note added: 'Gough has been expecting this for many months and so will be more than ready to come', the hope being that he would identify Matzke.[621] But unfortunately it soon became clear that the authorities did not have the right man.

By now Matzke had been implicated not only in the Brummen shooting but in a prior incident in Arnhem, in which he and some others were suspected of having thrown a hand-grenade into a cellar where British prisoners were being kept. This second case would never accumulate sufficient evidence, and it is not entirely certain that the incident actually took place.[622]

In the summer of 1946 a huge shadow was cast over the search for Matzke. The authorities finally succeeded in tracking down the Radio Hilversum journalist who had tried to interview Anthony at Brummen and who was behind the 4 October 1944 broadcast which had identified Anthony and Matzke. Although the journalist was at first thought to be Dr Taubert, it was finally established after interviewing Taubert that the man's name was Dr Ernst Tigges.

Kinsleigh's report of September 1946 gives details of Tigges's arrival at the scene of the shooting:

a German NCO of the Propaganda Dept, Dr Ernst TIGGES, appeared at the scene. He enquired what it was all about, got the story, spoke to Major COTTERELL, who said to him something like 'I am dying'. This Dr TIGGES is also responsible for the above quoted wireless transmission. He states, however, that he cannot remember the exact name of the above named SS NCO [Matzke], and is of the opinion that he invented this name, as he often did, to give the report more colour.[623]

Tigges, of course, could not have been acting as a free agent when employed by Radio Hilversum. All such programs would have been vetted, Goebbels' department being very jealous of its prerogative. The broadcast was probably made from Bremen, having first been sent from Holland to Berlin, that being the normal procedure.[624] In this type of complex propaganda set-up, there was no latitude for journalistic independence.

Kinsleigh would still be working on the search for Matzke in early 1947, by which time it had not advanced one iota. Several Matzkes had been found, interrogated, and dismissed as possibilities, or in one case accidentally released before he could be interviewed (those concerned in this appalling error fell over themselves reiterating that he was not the wanted man). But success never came.

Kinsleigh had written in his report of September 1946 that Matzke was quite possibly not the chief suspect's name anyway. The Radio Hilversum broadcast had been rather distorted, but the BBC's transcript of May 1946 had suggested that the name of the SS NCO might be Hatska, and Kinsleigh had become convinced that this was likely.[625] By 17 February 1947, he was writing irritably of a fresh request for him to interrogate another suspect: 'Willi Matzke has not been interrogated as it is believed, as pointed out repeatedly, that the name of the accused might be Hatska.' He added: 'There are not sufficient investigators and/or transports available to this Team as to warrant the interrogation of yet another Matzke.' He had already written earlier, on 28 January, making the same point about the name. On receiving the second note, Major Reade of the Legal Section of War Crimes Group (NWE), who outranked Kinsleigh, wrote a polite but extremely firm reply, quashing the dispute about the name. 'I must ask you to give some priority to the interrogation of Willi MATZKE ... I cannot agree with your contention that "a man with the name of MATZKE has no bearing on the case whatsoever".'

After setting out the legal niceties of the case in some detail, Reade concluded firmly:

> Whatever ultimately happened to COTTERELL, the fact remains that SS-Unterscharführer Rudolf MATZKE of 9 (or 10) SS Panzer Division, Hohenstauffen of II SS Panzer Corps, Army Group B, is still wanted for the murder of Lieutenant H.A. Platt, Lieutenant T.V.P. McNabb, and Private McCracken.[626]

A memo of 3 March from Kinsleigh then announced that he would proceed to Leck near Flemsburg at some time during the following week to interview Willi Matzke. This was closely followed by another memo saying that he would be returning on 11 March, 'having interrogated another Matzke, probably without result'. And then came the final memo of 17 March, that of a man quietly vindicated, saying that Herbert Willi Matzke had turned out 'not to be the wanted man'.

Neither Matzke not his accomplice were ever found. Whether Kinsleigh was right about the name Hatska or not, or whether Dr Tigges had simply invented the name to add colour to his radio report, Matzke continued to be the name on the files and any further enquiries were related to it. In June 1947, Reade began asking for confirmation of Matzke's alleged death 'which it now appears must have occurred at some date in or prior to January 1945 whilst Matzke was in the company of Hauptscharführer Schwegler, CSM, 9 Company SS Panzer Grenadier regiment 19'.[627] This seems to have been the end of the line for the hunt for the Brummen war criminals. No one was ever brought to justice for the murder of the British prisoners on the truck.

On 5 May 1946, Geoffrey wrote to his mother, thanking her for news of Janie's return from her Indian tour with ENSA. Janie had had mixed feelings about the tour, perhaps partly due to a bad accident she had suffered soon after her arrival in India. She had written to Mintie on 19 November:

> We are still at Rangoon; yesterday riots were expected, so we had to be guarded if we went out. I was persuaded to go to a party last evening. We went in a lorry, the roads are simply terrible here, and just as we arrived at our destination the lorry gave the most terrific jolt. I was of course the only one to be thrown. I think I might have come a little unstuck inside, as I feel somewhat sore there this morning, but otherwise I only cut my knee. The food of course at these parties is always wonderful. I have to say I had enjoyed myself, the ride home in jeeps was

wonderful, at certain spots we just shot through so we drew our own conclusions. The breeze was welcome. The more I see of the place, the gladder I am that Shubbs did not come here. He would have hated it.

Janie was still mentioning the fall at the end of March; 'I am a little better internally, but that fall certainly upsets my inners, actually I suppose I should have stayed in bed for a few days. However, the sea trip home will certainly put me right.'[628] She sailed for home around 10 April, telling Mintie before she left, 'if there is any such thing as being reborn, then I hope I shall not be an Indian'.[629] It was probably on this voyage home that all her special friends in the company signed one of their old programmes for her in memory of their happy days together. One of the contributors, Bessie, wrote: 'To Dear Mrs Pool, the lady with fingers like tripping fairies'.

Whether it was due to the fall she had suffered at Rangoon, or to some other factor, Janie was now terminally ill. Nobody appears to have realised this, least of all herself, for she was planning to go on an ENSA tour in Germany for three months, the last one before ENSA closed. With Geoffrey's imminent demob and return to England, the main preoccupation of aunt and nephew was that they were likely to cross in transit and miss one another.

The seriousness of the illness manifested itself very suddenly, seemingly after she reached England. As late as 15 May, Geoffrey was asking his mother if Janie was reading the manuscript of his new book, *This is the Way*, which he clearly would not have done if he had realised how ill she was. Janie was by now staying at Ham Frith instead of her old flat in a rather grim 1930s purpose-built block in North London.[630]

Unaware of the situation at home, Geoffrey continued to write cheerfully about his approaching demob. He had told his mother that 'the individual booze ration is now lousy, so I shall not be able to bring any back. Sorry if this is disillusioning.'[631] He had also given her the latest developments in how the search would proceed once he himself was back in England:

> George [Edinger] has turned up again. I have just had lunch with him. He has gone off to see some politician this afternoon and I am meeting him again tomorrow. The mechanism of my coming over here after demob when something happens has been assisted by him. So far there have been two methods discussed 1) to get accredited to the *Express* or other paper 2) to get War Crimes or Kamp or Search Bureau to wire for me and then argue my way over – quite simply. They all agreed to do this. But now what is the simplest plan is for Kamp to wire for me from the Netherlands War Crimes Commission and George to go to the Dutch Embassy in London, which he knows: then I shall come straight over with diplomatic priority – so that's that.
>
> Nor do I think now that (in view of the above) my going matters, for the thing has now established its importance – which is the most basic thing I did – and they can't help going on with it. Also having all their addresses it is perfectly easy to keep on wiring them and being as much a nuisance from London as from Hamburg. The question of my demob had been a great worry to me, but it is no longer.[632]

At the time of writing the letter, Edinger had just left to talk to the Russians in Berlin, hoping to get information from them where others had failed. The situation with the Russians was continuing to deteriorate. Geoffrey had had to tell his mother in April, 'As regards the Russian Zone and Russia, this is the up to date position. If you have no papers or means of identifying yourself, you have had it. However, you are well treated and fed.'[633] The only consolation was that the occasional British soldier was still being unexpectedly released, such as a South African officer in March, 'recovered from the Russians [...] quite suddenly and out of the blue – and with no explanation whatsoever'.[634]

In early May, an unexpected parcel arrived at Ham Frith, sent by Ernest Watkins, Anthony's old colleague at ABCA. It was a full set of *WAR*, beautifully bound in red leather and cloth, the colour being chosen to compliment its red paper cover. The rough war-time paper had been given a touch of glamour with a gilt top-edge. A note accompanied the four resplendent books, saying that Watkins would like Graham and Mintie to have them 'as some very slight token of the gratitude I have for Anthony and for the time I was working with him which were two of the happiest years of my life'.[635]

Mintie wrote to Geoffrey that same morning:

And now my dream is broken. Just after I had posted my letter to you a parcel came addressed to Mr and Mrs Cotterell – it was the bound volumes of *WAR* from Ernest Watkins – they are beautifully bound and a very appealing note inside [...] My dream you will note was two bulging letters from Anthony packed with writing from him. It's very odd, isn't it. It made me feel very shaky inside [...] but I must keep my fingers crossed and hope and hope.

Mintie bravely tried to continue the letter by discussing the current state of the search, but soon broke off – 'I don't know what it is but I seem to be in an awful state today. I woke up like it.' Then she asked Geoffrey about himself, how was his hayfever, and so on, and ended, 'I am thinking about you all the time. Yr Loving – Mother.'

The search, meanwhile, was wandering into fresh channels. In mid-May Geoffrey wrote:

Today I spoke to the War Crimes captain [Kinsleigh], who has been to Zutphen and seen the nurse from the hospital – and she insisted again that the person in the hospital was Anthony, who was put down in the X-ray book as 'Atkinson'. So he has asked the Airborne Records office for any record of any Atkinson who was in the 1st Airborne Division; and if there is no such person who was wounded in the upper left arm, then Anthony must – most probably – have diddled them. You will note that this is a far more intelligent official approach to the problem than we have so far encountered.

[Kinsleigh] also went south to see Etter, but the latter was away, legitimately, on his textile business [Kinsleigh] has not yet been up to see Saniter, but the latter is safely locked up, so we needn't worry about him. I do not think Saniter has anything to do with it, personally. The guarding of prisoners was in no way his concern, even if he did know who Anthony was.

Perhaps too little credit has been given to Anthony's intelligence and initiative: his capacity for being quite unobtrusive, in view of the fact that he could walk, was as you know immense and it is quite on the cards that as 'Private Atkinson' he swallowed himself up with the men: remember it was dark and there was an air raid on. Other ranks are not documented as carefully as officers. And in that case he could have travelled with any bunch of men quite anonymously.[636]

With regards to Saniter knowing who Anthony was, there is no fuller reference to this in any other family letters.

Geoffrey was now packing for his departure, and his room was full of debris. On 20 May for the first time he heard the news that Janie was ill, though clearly his mother had not given him great cause for alarm. He replied, 'I am so sorry to hear that Janie is not 100% and hope that she will be well by the time I return – or will she be here by that time?' Geoffrey was still expecting that Janie would soon be on tour again, arriving in Germany just as he was leaving it.

Shortly afterwards, however, his expected demob date, was put back.

My demobilisation now may be delayed a week or so. I had to see an 18th Century Foreign Office gentleman this afternoon who made a pathetic little speech about a gap of approx a week or ten days during which there would be no one to do the job. He was a director general and for a few minutes in polite but unrestrained language a colleague and myself informed him of our opinion of his director generalling.[637]

He added a very short note at the end of this letter, addressing Janie by the name which he had always called her:

> Dear Judy
> Herewith my deepest love – are you any better?
> Yr affec neph – Shubbs

He continued to try to tie up all possible loose ends before his demobilisation. Towards the end of May, he went to Husum in Schleswig-Holstein, to try to find a woman announcer connected with Radio Arnhem, possibly Frau Warko-Meents, a former 'Mary of Arnhem'. This mission failed: 'no sign of the radio announcer but transport nice, the former Japanese ambassador's car'.

On the way back, he called for one last time at the house of one of the medical orderlies at the dressing station, Hermann Thomson. Geoffrey had taken great consolation in the way that Saniter had described the wounded at the dressing station; it had meant that Anthony was not seriously wounded, and had been fit enough to walk – or indeed to escape. Believing that Saniter's evidence was rock-solid, Geoffrey told Thomson what 'the real wound' was. Thomson then shook him by declaring that:

> he held it impossible that he did stay behind but left very soon after the Enschede truck. I have therefore been onto the Search Bureau again to hurry them up about the interrogation in Vienna of the other orderly. Otherwise, he said, he must have gone with the lightly wounded or escaped. Ah well, there is not much profit in endlessly speculating. I still don't know what my demob position is, so it is equally useless to speculate about that. [638]

The other orderly was a man called Marcowitz, who had been tracked down in Vienna at the beginning of May.[639]

On 25 May, Geoffrey received a letter from Ed Beattie, the American journalist, who had been 'entertained by Goebbels for a week', as Geoffrey put it rather inaccurately. Beattie was writing from New York to suggest one or two German names which might be helpful. He had been put in touch with Geoffrey by Don Iddon, one of the top journalists whom the Cotterells had enlisted to Anthony's cause.

Geoffrey now had a new date for his possible demob which he told Mintie about on 27 May:

> June 4th now seems a more likely date – in which case I shall arrive back in wonderful time for the London Victory Parade: no doubt you have all got seats.
>
> I had a visitor this morning, sent down to me in connection with his denazification by Conroy: Mr Etter. He said that without any doubt at all Anthony did not go in the lorry with the rest of them to the PW centre, even as a private: as he, Etter, saw them off the lorry at the other end. This means, I am 100% certain, that Anthony escaped from the dressing station. I think he was then picked up and gave a false identity – probably Atkinson: and then if he wasn't seen by Taubert continued to be a private

Etter had accompanied all the lightly wounded officers, together with Gough, back to the warehouse in Bedrijventerrein de Mars after they had been treated at Rozenhoflaan.

On the same day as Geoffrey wrote this letter from Hamburg, Aps was writing to Mintie from Brummen:

What a very bad intelligence you have sent me about your sister. I hope that you are too grumbling and that she soon will be a little better.

I send you with the same post six fresh eggs, and I hope that they arrive in good condition.

Hard-boiled eggs are very good for a seriously ill person. [...]

Geoffrey will be soon at home now. He told me between 1-10 June he was going out of the Army. Then you are together again, and I wish you that this shadow soon will change into sunshine.

I am very very thankful for the cigarettes you send Dick. But I know there are in England also no cigarettes. Please do it no more. Spare them for your husband and Geoffrey as in difficult days they cannot be without smoking![640]

This kindly letter and the parcel of fresh eggs were sent on Monday 27 May. On the Thursday of that week, Janie died.

On the 30th, the same day as Janie's death, Mintie wrote to Geoffrey with her sorrowful news. He received her letter two days later.

Received your 70 with its news about J, just as I was on my way to record my broadcast. So as you can imagine I hardly knew what I was saying. I was upset and still am, but it seems to have been a quite a peaceful release – or I hope so – and in view of the general trend of her life, release is on the whole the right word. [...]

I shall be finally back by about Friday or Saturday: I wish I could come before for you must be feeling very low.

During her last illness, Janie had been treated at Ham Frith by the Cotterells' local friend, Dr Masson, and a specialist, Mr Leech. Their fees, of respectively £17 6d, and 3 guineas, were amongst the debts which Mintie settled from Janie's estate, together with the costs of her funeral. Mintie also arranged the clearing of Janie's effects from her Amhurst Court flat, the cleaning of the flat, and its renting-out to another tenant. Amongst the monies Mintie collected for Janie's estate was £42 from ENSA, The Theatre Royal, Drury Lane. After all the expenses were paid and a kiss-off bequest of £100 was made to Janie's estranged husband, Ivor Pool, the residue amounted to just over £1,000. Janie had stipulated that it was to be divided amongst her closest relatives, including Anthony, his eighth share being reserved for him indefinitely.

Geoffrey was now counting the days to his release. He had had his medical and, as he observed flippantly, 'proved unqualified for a pension'. He continued to make arrangements for how the search would be run in his absence, writing on 1 June that 'Kamp and his Major are coming to see me tomorrow; so future policy can be settled then'.[641] Meanwhile, there was little in the way of search news, though 'Major Conroy has immediately sent out a request for the men Ed Beattie mentioned: Beattie's letter incidentally said that no similar prisoner to himself was ever documented in the normal way at all, he was quite sure.'

On 4 June, Geoffrey wrote his final letter home: 'Just received your 71, which is the last one I shall get, for in a few hours I start the journey home.' He had received a note that morning which gave him the name of the Commander of the SS at Arnhem, 'and I have just been to see him in his prison (which made my last day slightly complicated)'. The SS Commander gave him the name of the Intelligence Officer responsible for prisoners and other interesting details, but, as Geoffrey did not want to arouse his suspicions, he did not press him hard in case it caused him to clam up during future questioning.

There was nothing more which could be done in the time that was left. Telling his mother that there might be a considerable gap before she heard from him again, Geoffrey signed his last letter from Hamburg, 'Looking forward to seeing you, Love love love, Shubbs'. Thus ended a unique correspondence which, on Geoffrey's side alone, had run to over 30,000 words.

Not long after Geoffrey arrived back at Ham Frith, the War Crimes captain, Kinsleigh, sent him the details of all soldiers named Atkinson and McLoughlin who had been with 1st Airborne Division at Arnhem. To recap, Atkinson and McLoughlin were the two names which Geoffrey and Kamp had discovered in an old book at Zutphen hospital, the patients being listed as having upper arm and ankle wounds respectively. Witnesses had remembered that one of these men had red hair.

Geoffrey now got in touch with the five possible witnesses, four Atkinsons and one McLoughlin. Two of the Atkinsons, it soon emerged, had never been at Zutphen, but the other two had both been treated at the hospital on 25 September 1944. One, Private K.D. Atkinson, had little to add apart from the fact that he had been there with Private McLoughlin. McLoughlin for his part remembered two soldiers being treated who were both wounded in the left arm or shoulder, but he did not recognise the photo of Anthony.

It was the last man, E.E.G. Atkinson, a sergeant, who did remember Anthony – and he did so very precisely. On 10 July, writing from a house called Sunny Vale, in Shanklin on the Isle of Wight, he told Geoffrey that he had received his letters of 24 June and 3 July at same time.

> I am the same Sergeant E. Atkinson who was treated for a shoulder wound on September 25th 1944 and I was in the company of a red-haired solder whose name I could not find out and I was also helped on with my battledress jacket by a Dutch nurse when we were ordered to leave the hospital to go to a collecting centre which was about two miles away. This short march took place at about dusk and there were about 200 men who could be marched, that was including officers, a Padre and a couple of MOs. There was a halt after a short distance had been covered and part of the column were halted by a spinney and it was whispered that some of these officers and men were going to make a break for it (escape). We were eventually started on the march again to the collecting centre and on arriving we found out that the escape had been made and there were three officers and seven men gone. We were a rather mixed lot and different men from different branches and regiments started to check up who was gone and I knew of several of the people who did escape who did belong to my own battalion.
>
> I can also remember a Major Cotterell being with us when we started to march because he had wounds in the left thigh and shoulder and a head injury which had been dressed by the Dutch nurse who assisted me with my jacket; but on the check-up I could not find him and I had hopes that he had been lucky enough to make good his escape for I heard no more of him until I received your letters.

The escape, Atkinson thought, had taken place at about 8.30pm to 9.00pm in the evening of 25 September, the same day that Anthony had been identified by the nurse, Johanna Sollman, as being at Zutphen hospital.

Later Atkinson would add more details, which Geoffrey passed on to Kinsleigh and Conroy. He said that he recognised both Anthony's name and photograph, and strongly confirmed that it had been Anthony who had been with him in Zutphen hospital.

> Major Cotterell had high cheekbones, slight build. I first saw him sitting in the hospital corridor. When I came back from an X-ray I saw a Dutch nurse wash his face, bandage his left arm and thigh. He had a wound on the left of his forehead which she bandaged. I spoke to him. He was not worried. On the march he wore battledress trousers, shirt and I think no hat. He possibly carried a jerkin.

He added that the collecting centre which they had marched to was '2–3 miles outside Zutphen, a mile from a level crossing where we got on the train for Germany'.[642]

There is no corroboration for Atkinson's statement, nor does there appear to be any supporting evidence for the escape of the three officers and seven men. As with so much else in the search, Atkinson's evidence was inconclusive, although Kinsleigh chose to take it as such. He used it to close his report on Anthony's disappearance, stating that he had escaped at Zutphen and that thereafter his fate was unknown.

Whether Atkinson's testimony was rock-solid or otherwise, it appears to have been the last significant piece of evidence discovered about what had happened to Anthony. After that, it was just small tantalising fragments, and no comprehensive narrative could be built from them.

Conroy, the South African major from the Search Bureau who had become personally involved in the search, was demobilised on 20 July and returned to South Africa. Before he left, he did everything he could to tie up any loose ends, particularly stressing the various question marks over Dr Taubert's and Dr Tigges's involvement. Tigges had not yet been interrogated because he was in hospital following a road accident. Knowing that he himself would not be able to interrogate Tigges, Conroy wanted to brief whoever would be doing so. He spoke to Major Reade on the telephone, and in a letter marked 'IMMEDIATE', sent that same day to the War Crimes Investigation Unit, Reade described Conroy as being 'extremely anxious to see personally an officer of War Crimes Investigation Unit before such officer interrogates Tigges and Taubert'.[643] After their phone call, Conroy also dashed off an urgent handwritten note to Reade stressing his own views on Taubert, and adding:

S/Major Kamp of the Netherlands War Crimes at Herford – Tel 52 – has come to the conclusion that Taubert is determined to fool us [...] Kamp has posed as Taubert's friend and I would suggest before T is interrogated, S/Major Kamp be first consulted. I am satisfied that T knows a hell of a lot which may be useful to you in your work generally. He lives for Germany only.[644]

With Conroy returned to South Africa and Geoffrey back in England, only Kamp remained on the spot, the last of the original highly dedicated team of three.

Gradually Anthony's family learnt to live with his absence, though they never ceased to think of him and mourn him. In the latter part of 1946, Mintie went to Holland and stayed with Aps, visiting all the scenes which Geoffrey had visited. She sent a postcard home from Zutphen, saying that she had 'been out all days and a bit complicated', so would write a letter. The postcard showed a distant view of Zutphen, with its characteristic towers and steeples seen from across the water-meadows. It is a haunting image in hazy black and white, the beautiful medieval city looking more like a mirage than a real place. For Mintie this was a most meaningful pilgrimage. In the absence of any certainty about what had happened to Anthony, Zutphen would remain the location most deeply associated with him. No.12 Rozenhoflaan was the one true point of focus, the last place where he had been seen alive by men who knew him well. After that, there was nothing but half-light and shadows, a reality infinitely more insubstantial than the fairy-like Zutphen of Mintie's postcard.

In May 1947, Geoffrey went back to Zutphen during one of his perennial visits to the Tjeenk Willinks. He wrote his mother one of his old-style diary letters about the visit:

The journey over was excellent except that I caught a cold [...]
   Arriving at Utrecht I was greeted by the loudspeaker calling out for 'Mr Geoffrey Cotterell'. I then saw Aps, Dick and Kamp. I kissed Aps, which was unfortunate as Kamp had arranged the broadcast with the stationmaster by saying that I was a detective arriving on a job. The kiss, which took place in front of him, added colour but not conviction to this story. [...]
   Kamp has promised to write more regularly. In Germany there are 3-4 people of importance who may be the missing links whom he has to interrogate, so there is still something doing.

Geoffrey would later clarify whom Kamp was going to interrogate – they were: Colonel von Katte who had been in charge of prisoners at Zutphen; a paymaster who was at the PoW Collection Centre (the warehouse at Bedrijventerrein de Mars); an NCO of the interrogation service 'who now appears to have had considerable power in dealing with the prisoners'; and an SS intelligence officer of the nearest Corps HQ, 'who is believed to have a report of the incident'.[645]

It was now more than eighteen months since Geoffrey had first arrived in Holland, and he found that it looked 'slightly more prosperous, more buses, more cars, better clothes, food as before'.[646] He had come over not only to see Kamp and the Tjeenk Willinks, but to follow up on various leads, including a report about a prisoner found hiding on the lorry which had taken the seriously wounded from Rozenhoflaan to Enschede.[647]

He was also following up on information that articles belonging to British soldiers had been found at No.12, but this last proved to be a sad disappointment:

I am afraid Zutphen was nothing. A man had found and destroyed some bits of uniform, a crucifix, and an identity card, name forgotten, in the cellar of the dressing station. These were probably McNabb's, but in any case the thing was of no use.

Four days later he would tell Mintie that he was going again to Zutphen the following morning, to buy a ticket for Strasburg and 'to look at the dressing station again in the hope of getting some inspiration'. His brother was constantly on his mind and he suffered from guilt from neglecting the search, as can be seen in a letter home when, having told of some small advance in getting British officials interested, he would describe himself as 'at last with a very slight feeling of satisfaction at doing something'.[648]

His last letter before leaving Brummen for Strasburg was written on 2 June.

I suppose it is as baking with you as it is here. [...]
Benadryl is having a considerable battle with my hay fever which is persistently boiling up and down inside me. The past two days have been full of inactivity, except for a visit I paid to Zutphen, where I gazed at the dressing station and the hospital and went for a swim in the Waal river last evening, which was preceded and followed by a nice walk of about ten miles. Otherwise I have been working a few notes on my pad and have finished *Vanity Fair*. A horse and cart have just passed down the road. Aps is making me a cup of coffee. By the way I hope you are not staying in Ham Frith all the time, but are having the proposed hour or two on the golf course.

Two months later, a last Progress Report was deposited on Anthony's case file with the War Crimes Group. It read:

This case has been in a passive state in the hands of various teams for nearly two years. No investigations are carried out unless fresh evidence is obtained independently or from the Netherlands War Crimes Commission who are interested in the case for personal reasons. Every possible clue has been followed and no convincing evidence has been obtained as to the fate of Major Cotterell. It does not appear worth while keeping this file open on this basis and it is proposed to close it as far as this Section is concerned.[649]

In this private memorandum, 33 Netherlands War Crime Commission received its rightful due as the organisation which had contributed most to the search. Kamp had been its star investigator, ferreting out witnesses and information with the most extraordinary tenacity. But now, by the strangest twist of fate, Kamp was suddenly removed from the picture. That August he was charged with complicity in German war crimes committed against the Dutch civilian population.

Ironically, Kamp had been spotted by his accuser, Oskar Gerbig, an ex-SD man, when Kamp was visiting Avegoor, a former training school for the Dutch SS and now the prison where Gerbig and others like him were being held. Kamp was there to interrogate a German general, Von Wuelisch, regarding the terrible war crime at Putten in 1944.[650] Ironically it was Kamp's car, with its official British insignia, which first attracted Gerbig's attention.

Gerbig had formerly been Hauptsturmführer of the SD at Almelo, and in that capacity he had known Kamp as an informer. His evidence led to Kamp being put on trial, accused of betraying his fellow countrymen and passing information to the SD, so many of whose ex-members Kamp had interviewed during the search for Anthony.[651]

For his part, Geoffrey was convinced that Kamp's involvement was only 'the unluckiest kind of co-incidence of circumstances'. He would do his best to help him, for example, writing to a Captain Springett at the British Embassy in The Hague to make sure that Kamp had a crucial German witness for his defence, one Willi Nolten. His letter would conclude: 'I should be very grateful indeed if you could help or advise in this matter as we owe this family so much.' As for Aps, 'the embodiment of patriotism' as Geoffrey would later describe her, she also did not give up on her old ally who had done so much to try to find Anthony.[652]

Kamp's lawyer was an influential man who lived in Kamp's home town of Almelo. A member of the Second Chamber of the Dutch Parliament, his name was E.G.M. Roolvink. Roolvink must have done well for his client, for after a long trial Kamp was found not guilty. However, not long afterwards, perhaps unable to stand the slur on his reputation, he moved to Italy, possibly near to Ventimiglia. There he ran a restaurant, mainly for Dutch visitors. Geoffrey did not see or hear from him again.

With Kamp's departure, the official search for Anthony was at an end. The documents in the multiple files of the War Crimes Group ceased to be active. They lay, gathering dust, preserved for many years because they related to a war crime. Eventually they would find a new home in the National Archives.

The Cotterell family archives about the search for Anthony likewise cease in 1947. Only one letter survives from a later date. It is a bizarre and disturbing document which holds a strange fascination. In June 1948 Aps wrote in great excitement to Mintie after she had seen a medium. Some very strong impulse had called her, Aps said, to go and see this man give a public performance in Amsterdam, a considerable distance from Brummen. There, to her amazement, the medium picked her out from 100 other people. He then very accurately described Anthony without seeing any photograph, and even gave the extraordinary information that Anthony had been at Arnhem, then Velp, had been a prisoner and had tried to escape. The man told Aps that he had contact with Anthony, that he was alive and had been taken to the concentration camp at Mauthausen. 'I have contact with him in 1945 and 1946. He is delivered ... and then nothing more, but he is alive.' By 'delivered', Aps meant liberated. Mauthausen was liberated by the Americans in the last days of the war. Conditions there were terrible beyond words.

38

WHAT HAPPENED TO ANTHONY COTTERELL?

A fter Geoffrey's demob, life at Ham Frith resumed its former quiet course. Geoffrey moved back in, and set about the business of becoming a famous and well-paid novelist, something he would accomplish very successfully in the next few years. He would be particularly acclaimed in America and one of his best-sellers, *Tiara Tahiti*, would be made into a Hollywood film. He spent months away travelling and made a host of wonderful friends abroad, but the centre of his life always remained his parents.

At home, the old settled routines of Ham Frith ran as they seemingly always had done. As formerly, Geoffrey would get up and take the dog for a walk on the Green, have his breakfast, and then settle down to work on his latest novel. He worked upstairs in his bedroom all day until the chink of ice cube or mixing spoon against glass signalled that Graham was preparing the evening drinks. Then he would go downstairs and join his parents. Sometimes things, in their quiet orderly clockwork way, could almost seem as they had done pre-war. But the vivid spirit of Anthony was missing and his absence was deeply felt.

Two hopes which the family clung on to for a long while were that Anthony had lost his memory and was an unknown inmate of some hospital, or that he was being held by the Russians. The first could not be proved; the second would be discounted by the passage of time. Even the 30,000 German prisoners of war held by the Soviet Union as war criminals were all home by early 1956.[653]

Even though Anthony had long been assumed by officialdom to be dead, it was only in 1955, eleven years after his disappearance, that the War Department finally confirmed it. They notified the Registrar of Births, Deaths, Marriages and Wills, at Somerset House in London, that Anthony's death was presumed to have taken place on or after 25 September 1944. However, it was not until the end of 1962 that Graham, who had now retired and moved with Mintie and Geoffrey to Bexhill-on-Sea, felt compelled to acknowledge that his oldest son had died. He instructed his solicitors to try to locate a will and to wind up Anthony's estate. No will was found, though enquiries about this matter with the military authorities turned up the odd fact that Anthony was owed £97 10s in back pay and the War Gratuity.[654] Graham, who was beginning to suffer from Parkinson's Disease, must have wished to sort out Anthony's estate so that Mintie as next of kin would not have to deal with it after he himself had gone. He would die, aged 78, in April 1967.

For her own part, Mintie absolutely refused to accept that Anthony was dead. Meanwhile, Geoffrey kept up a small but persistent hope that new information might be discovered about his brother. He made periodical trips to Holland, following up on any tiny leads which cropped up, but finding nothing substantial. When former airborne soldiers began to make annual trips to Holland around the 1970s, he met several of them, including Jim Flavell, but no one could add anything which helped to solve the mystery of Anthony's disappearance.

Mintie lived another fifteen years after Graham, dying in 1982 at the age of 91, still obdurately believing that her beloved son was alive somewhere. Geoffrey helped to nurse her through her final illness, just as he had helped to nurse Graham.

Not long after Mintie's death, some information came in which caused Geoffrey to believe that, all along, it had been Anthony who was buried in the unknown grave at Enschede. Though this evidence was very slender and circumstantial, it seems that Geoffrey, having lost both his parents and having no family of his own, could no longer bear the thought that Anthony had no gravestone.[655] He approached the Commonwealth War Graves Commission, and eventually it was agreed that a gravestone should be erected over the unknown grave at Enschede. It bears Anthony's name, together with the message 'Buried near this spot', reflecting the still unresolved ambiguities about whether this is Anthony's grave. The stone also bears Geoffrey's moving epitaph for his brother:

Writer
Remembered with Love

He would make provision for his ashes to be scattered at this grave when he himself died. Yet in his heart of hearts, Geoffrey remained unconvinced, remarking many years later, 'there is no certainty in any of these things'.[656]

Anthony's fate endures as a mystery precisely because no absolute proof has ever been found. What follows now is a summary of the evidence.

All theories about what happened to Anthony must have their starting place in the dressing station at Zutphen. This is the last, absolutely indisputable, sighting of him, fitting in exactly with what is known of the aftermath of the shooting, and confirmed in detail by the testimonies of Gough and Tannenbaum. If the testimony of Etter is to be believed – and none of the British officers who interrogated him ever succeeded in breaking his story – he also saw Anthony for the last time at No.12 Rozenhoflaan, leaving him there in the care of the doctors before returning Gough and the lightly wounded prisoners to the PoW collecting pen in the warehouse at Bedrijventerrein de Mars.

The question of what happened to Anthony after Etter and Gough left Rozenhoflaan largely hinges upon the seriousness of his injuries. Only four things can have happened to him from this point: he escaped; he was taken somewhere else by the Germans; he was shot by them in cold blood, possibly somewhere between Zutphen and Enschede; or the injuries which he had received at Brummen were so serious that he died within a couple of hours of Gough leaving him. It is the last possibility which needs to be examined first, not only because this is the simplest explanation but also because it is the reason why Anthony is now thought to be buried at Enschede.

Although Anthony's exact wounds were never established with total certainty, the overwhelming balance of evidence suggested that he was hit in the left arm between the elbow and the shoulder, and that he also had superficial leg and head wounds. The gunshot wound to the arm might also have penetrated the chest but apparently not seriously.

There were four seriously wounded men who did not die immediately at the scene of the shooting. These four were then taken on to Rozenhoflaan for treatment, and they were Tannenbaum – who, in the end, was the only survivor – George McCracken, Trevor McNabb, and Anthony. There were a number of lightly wounded soldiers who were also treated at Rozenhoflaan. The bodies of the three men who had died at Brummen were moved to Rozenhoflaan in the same truck as the wounded.

With regards to the seriously wounded men, self-evidently Tannenbaum would have had a very accurate recollection of his own injuries. Eight months after the shooting, he told Mintie what these injuries were. He also described those of McNabb and McCracken, but not Anthony's.

However, when Mintie visited him at his home in Wembley Park, he did not give her any cause to fear: 'He was telling me of his time with Tone – it is heartbreaking, he was so well.'

Tannenbaum was thought by the Cotterells to be a very reliable witness, quiet, dependable and responsible. The details of the injuries which he described to Mintie were recorded in one of her letters to Janie:

> Tannenbaum was wounded in thigh, and bullet went through to stomach and out again ... Tannenbaum said he could guarantee that Trevor McNabb's wound was on the left side and into his lung. Also the man with the head wound died that evening by his side and there is no doubt of these facts and he was in the ranks of Tannenbaum's company and called Mc or Mac something.'[657]

Other returning PoWs gave evidence which suggested that they had confused Tannenbaum's injuries with Anthony's. In writing to Mintie, Freddie Gough stated, 'Anthony was wounded in the stomach, it was a severe wound'. Also writing to Mintie, John Cairns wrote: 'As far as I can remember Anthony was hit in two places, in the upper part of the thigh and in the side but I could not be quite sure of these facts now.' Nonetheless, both Gough and Cairns fully expected Anthony to survive, and were greatly shocked to discover that his family had not heard from him.

Not long after sending his letter, Cairns visited Mintie and slightly modified what he had written in his letter. Mintie, who had already copied his letter to Janie, told her sister of his visit in a further letter:

> Cairns the man who wrote and told me he had dressed Tone's wounds has been out to see me today – and he says that Tone was hit in the left thigh and through the left (under shoulder blade) arm and I suppose body if it went through; he was in great pain, but Cairns said, as I told you before, that he did not think he would not recover [...] It seems so cruel, this Cairns says he was well and full of beans.[658]

Cairns had parted with Anthony in the evening of 23 September, being one of the prisoners who were taken off the lorry at the Zutphen warehouse before the wounded travelled on to Rozenhoflaan. What condition Anthony was in later that evening is covered by the testimonies of Etter, Tannenbaum and Gough, all of whom thought that he was doing well.

Gough was an utterly reliable witness, one who could be counted upon never to exaggerate or add ornamental details. He had been in battle many times and had a soldier's experience of gunshot wounds. He wrote to Mintie in May 1945:

> Anthony's general demeanour and condition gave me confidence that he would pull through. I was allowed to escort him and the other seriously wounded cases to a dressing station in Zutphen where they received first-class medical attention. Unfortunately I was forced by my guards to leave them there, but had a final word with Anthony who was very cheerful and assured me that he was not suffering pain unduly.[659]

Etter remembered the same scene:

> I recollect prior to leaving, Major Gough speaking to Major Cotterell, who did not appear to be too depressed, I do not recollect how he was wounded, but I remember his morale was high (in German the word is 'Haltung' and in English slang 'guts').[660]

Dr Saniter treated a number of the wounded at Rozenhoflaan, and obviously his testimony is the most valuable of all. His memory of events is likely have been fairly accurate, given the drama of the British airborne soldiers appearing suddenly in Zutphen and him being called from another location to treat them. Though the possibility remains that he may have been deliberately hiding something or shielding a guilty party, no one who interrogated him managed to break his story.

Saniter told Geoffrey that there were only four seriously wounded cases. Dr Lathe was very busy attending to the man who was 'in an especially bad way with a severe head injury' – this was evidently McCracken. It seems that Saniter dealt with the other three. The first two were stretcher cases and were given priority. One of these had a bad lung wound, and treatment was given to help him breathe. The other had 'a shot in his backside and did not appear in mortal danger'. These two were clearly McNabb and Tanenbaum. In Tannebaum's case, 'shot in his backside' and 'wounded in thigh, and bullet went through to stomach and out again' are not exactly identical, but they are roughly in the same anatomical region and perhaps Tannenbaum preferred to say 'thigh' rather than 'backside' to Mintie.

And then there was the fourth seriously wounded man:

> The fourth was not a stretcher case. His left arm had been hit between the shoulder and the elbow. There was no possibility of it being fatal. All four were given morphia or other means of easing pain. After the fourth one had been treated (and if there was a leg wound it was not worth treating, as it would have been too light), he walked to a seat in the corner of the room near the door and sat down.
>
>   Dr Saniter did not know who he was or what happened to him. Physically he could have walked out by himself. He did not require a stretcher. He was between 25 and 30, had not a particularly strong body, and was not very big.[661]

There can be very little doubt that this was Anthony.

The JAG 'Brief for Investigation' of 19 February 1946, which was drawn up before Saniter was located and interviewed, gave a summary of what evidence their enquiries had gathered so far as to the nature of Anthony's injuries:

> According to the existing evidence, he had collapsed in great pain from two bullet wounds, and during the drive to Zutphen was semi-conscious, but both Major Gough and Etter describe him as being fairly bright at the dressing station. He had been hit in the arm and in the shoulder or chest, though according to another report both bullets had entered or emerged near the spine, but his condition – though obviously serious – does not seem to have given rise to anxiety.[662]

The origin of the report about the bullets entering the centre of Anthony's body was Bernard Briggs.[663] What he says clearly does not agree with the evidence given by Cairns, Gough, and Tannenbaum, or indeed Saniter, who does not describe that type of injury in any of the patients. The closest equivalent is McNabb's lung wound. It would seem reasonably safe, therefore, to disregard the idea that Anthony had suffered these far more critical injuries, and to conclude that Briggs, in looking back over a year after the shooting, had confused Anthony's wounds with McNabb's.

Another witness, one who did not give an affidavit at the time of the search, was Jess Roberts, a private or sergeant from 2nd Parachute Battalion, who was alleged to also have been on the truck. Geoffrey got to know Roberts' wife, Atie, well in later years, because she was very involved with the Airborne Association. Atie told Geoffrey that her deceased husband had told her that Anthony had been in a very bad way. However, Roberts was not a particularly reliable man. Jim Flavell, who also knew Roberts well, not only from 2nd Parachute Battalion but in reunions after the war, said that Roberts was 'a liar and a rascal'.[664] Jim Flavell was a very reliable witness. There is, in fact, considerable doubt whether Roberts was on the truck at all.

Perhaps most telling of all are the last words which Anthony spoke to Gough, 'If you get back before me, tell Vansittart he has another disciple in me'. If Anthony had seriously felt in danger of his life (and with his medical training at Guy's and research with the RAMC, he would have had a well-informed view of his own condition), he would surely have sent back a message of love to his family rather than making a characteristic joke. Gough would have been honour-bound to remember such a message, and it is most improbable that he would have forgotten it.

It can therefore be assumed that Anthony was in no immediate danger late that evening at Rozenhoflaan. This does not, of course, preclude a sudden collapse, particularly if, after Gough and Etter left, he was transported with the other wounded to Enschede, a nightmare journey of many miles made in a basic army lorry. Etter told Geoffrey that Drs Saniter and Lathe had said that 'they would not move to Enschede that night anyone for whom the journey might be unwise'. This was a somewhat hollow promise, given the dire state of McNabb whom Gough described as 'in a very bad condition which was almost entirely due to the exposure and shock'. Nonetheless, the poor man survived the journey and only succumbed to his injuries four days later. Tannenbaum also made the journey and survived.

Anthony's journey to Enschede remains hypothetical. No evidence of any kind was ever discovered to back up the idea that he was taken there. Tannenbaum specifically says in his testimony that Anthony did not travel with him to Enschede – 'Major Cotterell was the person who was left behind'.

Hermann Thomson, the medical orderly at Rozenhoflaan, told Geoffrey that he had taken the wounded to Enschede and that no one was left behind; however, he also said that there were some Englishmen in the next room at Rozenhoflaan who were taken away earlier. This was probably Gough and the lightly wounded soldiers, but possibly also Anthony (though clearly Anthony was not moved with Gough because Gough would have remembered it).

Thomson also told Geoffrey that two men had died on the way to Enschede, a statement he later retracted, saying that he was referring to 'the two besides Tannenbaum whom he delivered as good as dead'. These were almost certainly McNabb and McCracken, although Etter spoke of McCracken as dying at the dressing station and Gough described his condition there as being 'beyond help'. There were already other bodies on the lorry, those of the three men who had died at Brummen, and Thomson may have remembered the numbers incorrectly.

There is no evidence in the records at St Joseph's to suggest that Anthony ever arrived there, either in Thomson's lorry or a later one. Interviews of hospital staff and examination of the hospital records turned up no mention of Anthony. In fact, Geoffrey saw the hospital records very early on in the search, noting: 'I saw the list of names of the Arnhem boys, as written at the time by a nurse. Tannenbaum and McNabb were included. I took a complete copy.'

If Anthony's wounds had been so severe that he died on the journey to Enschede, there is a possibility that he was never entered in the hospital records because he was taken straight to the morgue. However, he does not appear in the cemetery records either. If Anthony is indeed in Enschede cemetery, the way in which he was buried simply does not fit in with what happened with the other victims of the shooting.

McCracken would be buried at Enschede General Cemetery with his dog tags and Army uniform, even if the name in the cemetery records was incorrect. The men who had died at Brummen – Kenneth Mills, Horace Platt, and Sydney Allen – were all entered in the cemetery records correctly (though Platt is spelt Plath), and their dog tags and uniforms were also buried with them. The only body marked down as 'unknown' was the one which, at various times, was thought to be Anthony's. Clearly this body had no dog tags to identify it, nor apparently any kind of uniform.

In late January/early February 1946, this unknown body was exhumed by an American unit, attached to ETOUSA, so that the teeth could be checked. The dental chart obtained for the body did not fit with Anthony's dental records. To make doubly sure, the chart was forwarded to Anthony's father, Graham, who had performed his son's dental treatment. He found no match.

Not long afterwards, in March 1946, a far more rigorous check of the graves at Enschede was made, probably by the Search Bureau's Graves division. They checked nine graves altogether, the six thought to be connected with the Brummen shooting and three more, presumably to be quite certain that no other victims of the war crime were buried there. These additional three graves were for a shot-down RAF officer, Alan William Benting, who had been buried at the same time as all but one of the Brummen victims (McNabb), and Jean Ferdinand Huard and George Stratton Purves, airborne soldiers buried in early October 1944.[665]

Some discrepancies were sorted out by this second set of exhumations. McCracken was discovered to be in Benting's supposed grave. It was concluded that instead Benting was in a grave with a wooden cross which bore the name of Ernest Hughes (incidentally, McCracken's middle name was Ernest). There was a number of pieces of evidence that Benting was buried in the cemetery, including his name on the wooden cross on the wrong grave, which Geoffrey had noted down as 'R. Will-Bentinck', whilst in the cemetery records he appeared as 'Sold. [soldier] Binting William'. The Graves Registration Unit had him down as W. Bingteng.[666]

When Geoffrey had visited the cemetery on his first visit to Holland in October 1945, he had noted that underneath the list of names was written in English handwriting, 'C.E.M. Graham 23/27 Sep 44'. Flying Officer Clyde Euan Miles Graham was an RAF navigator, a member of the same Lancaster crew as Benting. Like their pilot, Flight Lieutenant Geoffrey Stevenson Stout, Graham was killed on 23 September after the crew's Lancaster bomber crashed near Lochem. Benting, the flight engineer, suffered critical injuries and was presumably treated for them at St Joseph's before dying there on 26 September. As for Flying Officer Graham, today he is recorded in the Commonwealth War Graves Commission records as being buried at the Arnhem Oosterbeek Cemetery. The handwriting on the Enschede register is unexplained. Perhaps Graham or Benting's families were seeking them just as Geoffrey was seeking Anthony, and someone had made the note in the register which Geoffrey referred to in his letter.

Despite the confusion with the Benting and McCracken graves, the March 1946 exhumations clearly found nothing on any of the bodies which suggested that Anthony was amongst them. The original unknown body had been ruled out on dental evidence in January, and the March exhumation report for that particular grave added nothing new except the odd information that there were no lower teeth and that a 'middle front tooth' was stopped. Anthony had all his lower teeth. 'Middle front tooth' is a very imprecise way of defining a dental condition. The ETOUSA chart which had been used in January was, in contrast, extremely detailed. In its instructions for use, it noted: 'The dental chart is very important and should be filled in with great care. There are 32 teeth to be accounted for, as shown by the numbers on the chart.' It then defined incisors, cuspids or canines, bicuspids, and molars, together with an array of dental conditions. 'Middle front tooth stopped' compares very badly, but its layman's language does at least suggest that what was meant was not the two front teeth (clearly there is no such thing as a middle front tooth) but somewhere between them and the molars. This does provide a positive match with the ETOUSA chart as Tooth 4 for the upper jaw of that chart has a silver filling, thus apparently confirming that the same man was examined in both exhumations.

This would seem to doubly prove that it is not Anthony in the original unknown grave at Enschede. Can he then be in the grave which once bore the wooden cross with the name of Ernest Hughes and which is now thought to be the grave of Alan Benting? As Anthony was such an important part of the War Crimes Group's and Search Bureau's caseload, it seems highly unlikely that those which exhumed the bodies in March 1946 would not have been extremely alert to this possibility. So much time and expense had been expended and would continue to be expended on finding Anthony that it is not credible that the primary identifying factor would have been missed. That Anthony's dental details were well known to the various search agencies is confirmed by the preliminary report in May 1946 of the investigating officer for the War Crimes Group, Captain H.P. Kinsleigh. Kinsleigh, having stated that Anthony's front upper teeth were 'porcelain', concluded that 'his body could easily be recognised therefore'.[667]

What are now numbered as Joint Graves 200-201 contain the original unknown body and that now thought to be Alan Benting's, it not having been possible to identify which body was Benting's. Although the March 1946 exhumation reports are closed to the public, it is clear that the body thought to be Alan Benting's was not found with an RAF uniform because that would have made it very easy to differentiate it from a soldier's – RAF uniforms were distinctively different in colour and design to the Army's.

As neither body could positively be identified as being that of a man from the RAF or the Army, this suggests that there was no uniform with either body in the joint grave.

In Benting's case there are potentially good reasons for him not being in his RAF uniform. His Lancaster was almost certainly on fire when it was abandoned in mid-air, and his uniform may have been partially burnt, or lost during the descent – for example, parachuting airmen almost always lost their footwear. In any case, it would have been necessary to remove his uniform in order for him to be treated. Later, during his two days of medical care, presumably he was in a hospital bed in some sort of hospital gown.

There are no good reasons for Anthony to be without his uniform. Rozenhoflaan was not a hospital where patients would be given a bed and hospital clothing. If Anthony had been transported to Enschede, he would still have been wearing his uniform. If he was in so bad a state as to die on the journey, clearly he would still be wearing his uniform when the truck arrived at Enschede. Why should anyone have then gone to the trouble of removing the uniform before he was buried?

Anthony should also have been wearing his dog tags. It seems most unlikely that at some time between his capture in Arnhem and his arrival in Brummen on the truck, he would have deliberately thrown away his dog tags. They gave only his name, rank and serial number, and were his only means of being identified if he was killed. The only possible reason for throwing them away would have been to conceal his name from the Germans, but it was a very high risk policy and argues a degree of paranoid self-importance which Anthony did not possess. Once he had been shot in Brummen, he may have been physically incapable of getting rid of the dog tags. Also, they probably would have been the last thing on his mind; he would have been under constant observation; and in any case there was no point in getting rid of the dog tags, as by now the Germans knew who he was.

If it is Anthony in the second unknown grave at Enschede, either his dog tags and uniform were lost accidentally after his death or someone deliberately removed them. As McCracken, McNabb, Mills, Platt, and Allen, all had means of identification with them, the marked absence of any identification on the unknown body at times thought to be Anthony's seems unusual to say the least.

The Search Bureau clearly felt that the March 1946 exhumations had provided the definitive answer to who was in the graves at the cemetery and that Anthony was not amongst them. Kinsleigh's report of September that year stated that no trace of Anthony's grave could be found 'in the cemetery of Enschede where other British PWs are buried. A very thorough search has been made, so far without result.'

So if the trip to Enschede and the Enschede grave are ruled out, what else might have happened to Anthony?

Very late in the search, in May 1947, information was obtained by the indefatigable Kamp about the transport which went to Enschede:

Obersturmführer Schlueter at Hamburg declared to have heard about the Brummen incident. He states to have issued the order that the injured British officers after their treatment at Zutphen Field Dressing Station were to be taken to the hospital at Enschede [...] It was reported to Obersturmführer Schlueter that at Enschede one of the German guards discovered that one of the prisoners had been hiding himself under some tarpaulin sheets. This prisoner was taken back to Zutphen PoW collecting centre.[668]

The prisoner would probably have arrived back in Zutphen some time on the Sunday. If this man was Anthony, he probably required further medical treatment, and thus the timescale fits very well with the reported sighting of Anthony at the X-ray department of Zutphen hospital on the Monday morning. That Anthony concealed himself under the tarpaulin in the lorry seems very plausible.[669]

Alternatively, he may never have left the dressing station, and just walked round the corner to the hospital on that Monday. In the reports he was accompanied by a fair-haired parachutist, also wounded, and the pair of them were guarded by three German soldiers. Anthony was limping, and his left shoulder was clearly painful, though not acutely.

It may be remembered that Anthony was positively identified as being at the hospital on that Monday morning not only by Joanna Sollman and Mrs Etterman, but also by the British airborne soldier, Sergeant Atkinson. If their stories are correct, why was Anthony still in Zutphen? In this particular scenario, the answer must be that he was not sick enough to be moved to Enschede and yet not well enough to be moved elsewhere (if he had followed the usual channels, this would have been to Oberürsel). Instead he was being kept at a dressing station under the tight control of the Germans as opposed to at the nearby civilian hospital.

The last piece of evidence gathered on this particular trail was an alleged sighting of Anthony being escorted under guard to the office of the Ortskommandantur, which was in the road adjoining Rozenhoflaan. Geoffrey wrote to his mother about this on 13 January 1946:

> The main news is that we are ten minutes further on. The procession with the limping British officer disappeared into the office of the German Town Major when they returned from the hospital. Naturally we are now looking for the Town Major whose name we have.

There is no material in Geoffrey's letters to suggest that anyone succeeded in taking this particular trail any further.

If Anthony had indeed gone into this office, then some unknown Germans might easily have taken him somewhere else, unobserved. They could have been Wehrmacht, SS, SD – there is simply no knowing.

Was Anthony of sufficient interest to the Germans to have been singled out for special treatment? The answer is definitely yes. A considerable amount of information was gathered post-war about Wehrmacht and SS policy towards captured journalists. Amongst other details, it was confirmed that Goebbels' Propaganda Ministry knew all about Anthony's work. The chief German reporter at 10 German News Service, who had once worked for Goebbels, told Geoffrey that *What No Morning Tea* in particular was discussed at great length.[670] Further confirmation that Anthony would have been of great interest to the Germans came from the affidavits of Dr Hans Fritzsche, interrogated at the Nuremberg Trials, and of Dr Paul Schmidt, interrogated whilst in American captivity. Geoffrey reported Schmidt's comments in a letter home:

> Dr Schmidt, the press chief of the Propaganda Ministry, said that Anthony did NOT go to Berlin: but what is very important is that if Anthony <u>had</u> gone to Berlin, Dr Schmidt would have seen him at once. Dr Schmidt knew all about him, books, newspaper, and everything. Dr Schmidt

then heard the circumstances of the incident and said, 'Well, then we wouldn't have seen him.'The SS had their own fiercely jealous propaganda system and under no circumstances, he said, would have handed him over to the Ministry, but kept him to themselves.[671]

The fact that Anthony was mentioned by name in the Radio Hilversum broadcast also lends credence to the idea that Anthony was considered a notable catch. In his affidavit, Gough mentioned Etter's suspicious interest in Anthony, 'I was [..] somewhat concerned about the interest taken by the Oberleutnant in him'. Etter, when he made his report to the various authorities, must have passed on what he had learned about Anthony. Thus other people would have known fairly quickly that a British war reporter, as Anthony was now being described, had been captured at Arnhem.

Dr Schmidt was certain that Anthony did not go to Berlin through Wehrmacht channels, which left only the SS (or possibly the SD) in the frame, as in fact Schmidt suggested himself.

> Since Major Cotterell was captured by the SS, there is a possibility that I may not have heard about it, because there was enmity between the Propaganda Organisation of the Waffen SS and the Propaganda Ministry. Günther d'Alquen, Chief of the Propaganda Organisation of the Waffen SS, in that case would be the man to interrogate. I would also suggest interrogating Schwarz van Berk, who was Chief Editor of *Das Schwarze Korps* [*The Black Corps*].[672]

For a while, the War Crimes people became interested in the possibility that Anthony might have fallen into the hands of an SS propaganda unit called Skorpion West. Independently of the search for Anthony, Major Reade of JAG knew that 5 Company Skorpion West, which he described as 'a unit of the Standarte Kurt Eggers, a war correspondents' brigade', had been in Arnhem at the relevant time.[673] The commander of the Standarte Kurt Eggers was that same Günther d'Alquen whom Schmidt had mentioned. D'Alquen was also the one-time editor of the SS weekly, *Das Schwarze Korps*.[674]

Schwarz van Berk was interrogated in April 1946, and said that Anthony, to his knowledge, had not been taken to Berlin. He suggested interrogating d'Alquen, who, it turned out, was being held in a prisoner of war camp in Britain, as was Pilstikker, the Interrogation Officer at Zutphen, another man wanted in connection with Anthony's disappearance. Arrangements were made for Freddie Gough to interrogate both men.[675] There appears to be no surviving record of these interrogations, and they were evidently inconclusive because they led to no further developments in the search.

Reade's interest in Skorpion West had arisen from his investigations into the murder of Captain Brian Brownscombe, a British Medical Officer. Brownscombe had been shot in Arnhem on 24 September 1944 by a member of Skorpion West. The completely gratuitous killing had been carried out by SS-Oberscharführer Karl Lerche who had simply – for no apparent reason – come up behind Brownscombe and shot him in the head. This was after Brownscombe and other British PoWs, in a spirit of fraternisation, had had several drinks with members of Skorpion West, including Lerche. Ironically, one of the Skorpion West men, Knud Helweg-Larsen, a Dane, had then invited Brownscombe back to the billet for a last drink 'to show that 'the SS were not as bad as English propaganda made out'.[676] It was after this that the killing had taken place.

The Skorpion West men were an unsavoury bunch. Helweg-Larsen was executed in Denmark in January 1946 for war crimes during the Occupation. Another non-German was De Vries, a Dutchman who had turned against his own country and thrown his lot in with the SS. As for Lerche, the killer of Captain Brownscombe, his initial defence at his trial in 1955 was the standard 'I shot him whilst he was trying to escape'. He was found guilty of murder and, due to some mitigating circumstances, received a ten year prison sentence.[677]

In the process of following up on Skorpion West, Etter was interviewed again. He said that as an interpreter with Army Group B he had little knowledge of Skorpion:

I knew that Skorpion issued from time to time to the troops a propaganda paper with the title, 'What do you want to know, Comrade? Ask the Skorpion.'

I was also informed that the Skorpion provided pamphlets which were dropped or shot to the enemy. So far as my knowledge is concerned, this pamphlet was printed by the SS Standarte Kurt Eggers. [...]

In my opinion, the work of the Skorpion was to make propaganda for the Army, their own and enemy soldiers. The normal propaganda came from Berlin (Goebbels) and was more generally subjected in form and specially for military groups. I think Skorpion was co-operating with Army Group B.[678]

The killing of Brownscombe by Lerche, not to mention the track record of Helweg-Larsen, show Skorpion West in an entirely different light from the innocuous portrait of them painted by Etter.

There remains the very grim possibility that soon after 23 September Anthony was murdered in cold blood, probably because of who he was. Someone then went to enormous lengths to cover up not only the crime but the identity of the body. As the first War Crimes report in February 1946 observed:

As it is evident that Major COTTERELL received proper medical treatment (X-ray etc) it is difficult to understand why the Germans should not have announced his death if he did die of wounds, seeing that they had already been at pains to broadcast their version of how he came to be wounded; nor could this omission be attributable to battle confusion having regard to the fact that that part of the front became relatively stabilised for several months after the failure of the ARNHEM operation, and that HOLLAND was spared any serious aerial bombardment. There therefore seems to be a certain possibility that Major COTTERELL may have been spirited away and murdered by the SS who had their own reasons for not wanting to risk the publicity which might be given by a former member of the *Daily Express* staff to the circumstances in which they had shot up the truck.[679]

Etter, it must be remembered, had observed to Finlay Wilson on the day of the shooting that he thought that the *Daily Express* would make an atrocity story out of the killings.

The Burgomeister at Enschede was told by the German authorities that the victims of the Brummen shooting who were to be buried at Enschede had been shot whilst trying to escape on the road from Enschede to Gronau.[680] Gronau was in Germany, over the border from Enschede, and many miles from Brummen. Perhaps this was a casual error, perhaps something more sinister. The German explanation always was that the British prisoners were to blame for their own deaths, but can this mix-up between Brummen and Gronau have concealed a second, more calculated and cold-blooded crime? Was Anthony executed somewhere on the way to Gronau, and later buried with the others at Enschede? Yet again one has to consider the March 1946 exhumations, which surely would have discovered that one of the bodies examined had suffered injuries consonant with an execution.

No evidence was ever found that Anthony had been executed, but then the Germans had a very long record of murdering inconvenient people in conditions of great secrecy. With his uniform and tags removed, it would have been very difficult to identify Anthony's body. He could have been buried anywhere, and no one discovering the body would have known who he was.

What is so very strange about Anthony's disappearance is precisely the extraordinary lack of evidence about what happened to him. After Gough reluctantly left him at the Zutphen dressing station, Anthony effectively entered a ghost world. There is nothing which tells us for definite what became of him, no infallible eyewitness report, no official notification through the Red Cross or other channels, no Dutch or German administrative paperwork of any sort – not even the merest scrap. Given the extreme thoroughness of the search, the huge number of people involved, both official and unofficial, the newspaper appeals in Zutphen, and the impassioned cooperation of the Netherlands War Crime Commission and the Dutch people, there is something truly odd about that lack of evidence. It is precisely because there is no evidence where the searchers expected to find it that the very real possibility exists that someone deliberately covered up all traces of his fate.

Can Kamp have had anything to do with this? He was accused in 1947 of being a former member of the NSB, who had retained sympathy for the cause of National Socialism and had acted as an informant for the SD. Can he have played the deepest of double games in so fanatically pursuing evidence about what had happened to Anthony? Can he, in fact, have destroyed evidence? It seems a most far-fetched possibility. If evidence about Anthony was intentionally destroyed, by far the greatest likelihood is that the culprit was a German.

The Radio Hilversum broadcast, which reported Anthony as saying that he was dying, need not necessarily be tied in with the possibility of his having been murdered. It did indeed provide a ready-made excuse for his death, by blaming the entire shooting incident on the British prisoners, and setting up the scenario for then – in great innocence – reporting his death. But as has already been seen, Anthony's death was never reported by the Germans, however convenient an explanation it now had.

Had there been a plot to murder Anthony, the broadcast was not necessarily implicated. The journalist Dr Tigges, when he was finally discovered and interrogated, did not state that he had been told what to say about Anthony. It is quite possible that Anthony was only mentioned to add drama to a routine propaganda piece. The program's main focus was given in its title, 'Spotlight on Invasion'. Anthony may simply have been 'copy'. As a journalist himself, Anthony, had he known that this would be his fate, may well have found the scenario a source of macabre amusement.

In the end what all the evidence – or the lack of it – boils down to is the following three possibilities. The first of these is that Anthony died shortly after Gough left him on 23 September, and his body could not later be identified because his dog tags and uniform were missing. The second is that he was considered a propaganda prize by the Germans and taken to some unknown destination. The third possibility, and perhaps the most likely, is that within two to three days of the Brummen shooting he managed to escape. As Geoffrey wrote to his mother in May 1946:

> Perhaps too little credit has been given to Anthony's intelligence and initiative: his being quite unobtrusive, in view of the fact that he could walk, was as you know immense and it is quite on the cards that ... he swallowed himself up with the men ... Other ranks are not documented as carefully as officers. And in that case he could have travelled with any bunch of men quite anonymously.[681]

At that particular point in the search, it was thought that Anthony might have been passing under the name of Atkinson. Alhough the Atkinson theory would later be disproved, nonetheless there remains the very real possibility that Anthony did manage to escape at some point, perhaps having taken off his badges of rank and assumed a different identity. In order to carry this off successfully, he may also at this point have ditched his dog tags. This could explain why his body was never identified after he met whatever fate befell him.

Anthony undoubtedly had a genius for passing unnoticed when he wanted to, and might have put this to good effect by discarding his identity as Anthony Cotterell, the name which was leading the Germans to take an unhealthy interest in him. His chameleon-like adaptability, however, would only have been of use when he was blending in with a group of British soldiers.

If he had struck out on his own, his chances would have been very much poorer. He could not speak Dutch or German, and had only a smattering of very poor French. In addition, there is no known record of the Dutch resistance aiding him, or of Dutch people having knowledge of the death of a man answering his description. Had he been shot when trying to pass as a civilian, it is almost certain that someone would have known. The resting places of those executed by the Germans were as a rule well-known to the Dutch population, who were very sharp observers of what was being perpetrated in their own country.

The investigating officer for the War Crimes Group, Captain H.P. Kinsleigh, in his report of September 1946, clearly believed that Anthony had escaped at Zutphen. What had befallen him afterwards can only be speculation, but Kinsleigh summarised the likeliest scenarios.

> The investigating officer is of the opinion that Major COTTERELL either died of exhaustion, was shot when trying to cross the Rhine, or any other line of defence, or drowned when trying to cross the Rhine. The latter fact seems to be the most likely one, as according to the information received from the Search Bureau (Graves) no unidentified grave which fits the description of COTTERELL is in the area.[682]

That many men died in trying to cross the Rhine is known from other sources. In Allard Martens' book *The Silent War*, he summarises the difficulties of crossing the river, 'at least fifteen machine-gun nests with their attendant searchlights [...] as well as numerous enemy patrol boats'. He writes that one resistance group known as 'Albrecht' specialised in smuggling airborne soldiers back to British lines, and carried out no less than 444 crossings. But the dangers were immense.

> The average crossing – in the Biesbosch area – consisted of a great deal more than the few hundred yards from one bank to the other. In order to travel from an unguarded place on the northern shore to the Allied positions on the southern side, it was necessary to go downstream for about nine miles; which meant a journey of about four hours by boat – the return journey lasting longer. On innumerable occasions the occupants were killed or wounded by a hail of machine-gun bullets.[683]

Perhaps it was in this way that Anthony lost his life.

The balance of probability is that it is not Anthony at Enschede General Cemetery, but as a place to remember him the cemetery is perfect. It is immaculately kept, with long paths, verdant grass, beautiful shrubs, and tall stately trees. In front of the little plot of British war graves there is a white memorial cross. Alan Benting's gravestone separates Anthony's from those of the five other men who were shot by the SS guard at Brummen.

And strangely, Anthony has a small common link with Benting. On the day that he was shot down, Benting had flown out of Woodhall Spa in Lincolnshire. It was the one RAF station that Anthony knew really well, and from which he too had flown out on a Lancaster bombing raid. He had spent three days in Woodhall Spa in December 1943, and had greatly enjoyed the comforts of the Officers' Mess at the Petwood Hotel. It was there that he enjoyed his last birthday – his 27th.

EPILOGUE

Amersfoort, Province Of Utrecht, Holland, September 1944

Late in the official search, not long before it began to wind down for good, there appeared a rather appealing though inconsequential story about a possible sighting of Anthony. Geoffrey had been back at Ham Frith for just over a year when Sergeant Kamp phoned him one Saturday in July to tell him about a Major, seen in September 1944, who closely resembled Anthony. The dates for the sighting were between 22 and 25 September, and the details were given by five different witnesses. No name was given for the Major. His job description – Staff Officer (IA) of 1st Airborne Division – was not exactly accurate for Anthony but would have been extremely good cover if Anthony had reinvented his identity.

The details are a little confusing but it seems that the Major was in Hilversum, the town where Radio Hilversum was sited; he was due to be taken to Amersfoort for interrogation by the Intelligence Officer of Wehrmachtsbefehlshaber, Niederlande. Wehrmachtsbefehlshaber was the supreme headquarters of the Wehrmacht in the Netherlands; its commander, Frederick Christiansen, was later charged with war crimes against the Dutch people.[684]

Geoffrey was convinced by the story, and he and Kamp seem to have followed it up. It was in August of that year that Kamp himself was charged with a war crime, and it was in helping with his case that Geoffrey wrote in November to the British Embassy in the Hague.[685] Most of the short letter was taken up with his support for Kamp, but as the man to whom Geoffrey was writing, Captain Springett, knew all about the search for Anthony, Geoffrey told him almost as a postscript, 'Incidentally, we think we have now traced Anthony's PW career as far as Amersfoort'.

A copy of the letter, forwarded by Springett, wound its way through the labyrinthine maze of JAG, Search Bureau and War Crimes bureaucracy to arrive at the Legal Section of the War Crimes Group (North West Europe) in January 1948. It then travelled a little farther to the Field Investigation Section. Lieutenant-Colonel Nightingale, the man in charge, replied in the time-honoured, sniffy, patronising way which countless officials had used when dealing with the Cotterells:

> Reference your letter WCG/15228/2/C.55/Legal, dated 8 January 1948
> Major Cotterell's movements as far as Amersfoort have already been covered in our investigations. I do not think it is likely that his brother has any information which we have not been able to obtain ourselves.[686]

And there the matter appears to have ended.

But the story itself has an odd kind of persuasiveness. The description of the Major was written down in Kamp's memorandum of his phone call with Geoffrey:

Medium built, 30 years, very intelligent, very dark blonde, cheerful, wounds about left-underarm (Stechchuss) [gun shot wound], lean face, chin a little pointed, slowly speaking (cut off) or 'abgehackt' [clipped] as Germans put it, wife and little daughter in Scotland, Staff Officer (I.A.) of 1st Airborne Div., taken to air-raid shelter (Bunker) in Hilversum, collected the following day by Oberleutnant of Feldgendarmerie, Hilversum, then probably taken to Amersfoort. There are rumours, that on the way from Hilversum to Amersfoort, the Oberleutnant was persuaded by his PoW to let him escape.[687]

Geoffrey thought the description amazingly accurate except for the wife and little daughter in Scotland, but told Kamp that he had a very good theory to account for this inaccuracy. The theory, sadly, has been lost in the mists of time, but it was probably that Anthony had invented the wife and daughter in order to win the sympathy of his captor.

Of course, the Amersfoort story is probably a case of mistaken identity. Nonetheless, it seems as happy a way to end this book as is possible under the circumstances. It has such an appealing resonance of what we have known of Anthony in happier days: a young man in the prime of life, cheerful, resourceful, focused, charming, manipulative, who just before he vanishes forever from our sight uses his brilliant gift for words one last time – to talk himself free.

ACKNOWLEDGEMENTS

This book would not have been possible in this form without the involvement of Geoffrey Cotterell, Anthony's brother. When I first got to know him, Geoffrey was in his late eighties and had had a major operation to replace his hip, yet during the course of the next two years we enjoyed two phenomenally successful research trips to Holland together. Geoffrey gave me many photographs and all the surviving Cotterell family documents which related to Anthony. The latter included not only the incredible sequence of letters which Geoffrey wrote to his mother in 1945–46, and those between his mother and his aunt Jane of the same period, but also all Anthony's surviving unpublished typescripts, including the wonderful D-Day and Normandy material.

Geoffrey, a novelist who had had a string of best-sellers in the first twenty-five or so years after the war, took a huge interest in the projected book. He had a phenomenal memory, and what he told me about the search for Anthony was invariably verified when that particular facet of the search was covered by official documents. This was also the case with his correspondence with his mother in 1945–46. It is obvious that he was always truthful and scrupulously accurate with her, never hiding the worst potential explanations for Anthony's disappearance.

The trips to Holland included exciting, amusing and, occasionally, rather harrowing times. The most moving experience of all was visiting No.12 Rozenhoflaan, the house in Zutphen in which Anthony's wounds had been medically treated just before he vanished forever. After we got back to England, Geoffrey sent me the following email:

> Re my impression of Rozenhoflaan I did send you an email which I've just failed to find under 'sent', so just possibly it didn't get to you. I know what I said was similar to your own feelings, that there is a tremendous atmosphere, I said like the feeling you have when you enter an old enormous cathedral, full of immanence and history, with the space on the right of the front door a special very holy chapel, and I thought of Tone there being a sort of Christ figure from many an old master oil painting, down from the cross and attended by Mary etc. And looking towards the second door on the left, amazed that it was all just as Tannenbaum had described it to me. And therefore real. A haunted, awesome place.

Geoffrey had never ceased to grieve deeply over the loss of his brother, and even in old age still felt responsible for never having managed to find him or discover his fate. In his eighties, he once again began to make enquiries in Holland, hoped that perhaps the passage of time and the opening up of archives might shed light on Anthony's disappearance. When I joined forces with him, I also had great hopes that I might solve the mystery, but a mystery it remains. I greatly regret this, but most of all I am sad that Geoffrey did not live to see this book published, one to which he contributed so much.

I would also especially like to thank Frits and Jeanne Slijkoord, who not only made the trip to No.12 Rozenhoflaan possible but also gave many details of life under the Occupation in Holland.

Frits with great kindness translated some Dutch documents for me and helped in numerous other ways. Jeanne was the most invaluable eyewitness; as a child, she had seen the shooting in Brummen marketplace, and the horror of that event had made an indelible impression upon her.

An equally important helper in Holland has been Bob Gerritsen. Bob has an unrivalled knowledge of the battle of Arnhem and a stupendous archive of material, all of which he shared with me with the most perfect generosity, simply in the interests of establishing the truth. Several of the photographs in this book were sourced by Bob, including the astonishing picture of the British prisoners in Saint Eusebius in Arnhem. Bob thoroughly read the manuscript of this book and made many detailed and helpful comments. Bob also helped Geoffrey a great deal when Geoffrey first opened up the new enquiries about Anthony at Arnhem.

I owe a great deal to a number of other Dutch people. The owners of No.12 Rozenhoflaan, Rene Schepers and Renske Boersma, could not be there when we visited due to a sudden death in the family. However, with the greatest kindness they did not cancel the visit, but instead asked a kind neighbor to show us round their house.

I also owe a debt to Ymi Ytsma whose father-in-law, Police Detective Jan Arend IJspeerd of the Almelo Investigation Department, had been involved in the search for Anthony in 1945–46. Ymi shared with me the Kamp documents from The Hague and other material relevant to the search.

I would like to thank the following: Dick Schlüter of the Airborne Museum, Oosterbeek; Dirk Jan Dolfing of the Regionaal Archief, Zutphen; Adrie Roding of the Stadsarchief Enschede; and Ton Wientjen, a historian living at Enschede, who checked the Dutch archives to make sure that I had not missed vital information about Anthony's disappearance. Ton also read the manuscript and made very helpful comments.

I must not leave out Wim Brekveld, who did such a marvellous job of driving me and Geoffrey around Holland, and who helped to make our two trips so enjoyable.

So far as English helpers are concerned, my grateful thanks go to Tony Hibbert, not only for talking to me at length about Anthony and Arnhem, but also for giving me a copy of his Arnhem and post-Arnhem diaries and allowing me to quote extensively from them. Another great source of information was Jim Flavell, who shared with me his memories of Arnhem and the paratroopers.

Roy Hemington at the Commonwealth War Graves Commission gave invaluable information about the British prisoners' graves at Enschede. Rosemary Mcgrath, Anthony and Geoffrey's cousin, filled in details of the family background. Graham Page, who is writing a biography of Barbara Skelton, notified me of the fascinating connection between Barbara and Anthony, revealed in her diaries. I thank them all.

I would also like to thank the following: Mark Hickman of the Pegasus Archive for helping with my enquiries and for permission to quote from the Pegasus Archive website, including the 1st Airborne Reconnaissance Squadron war diary (Crown Copyright). Thanks also go to Simon Middleton-Briggs for sharing Bernard Briggs' document of the British prisoners' wanderings after the shooting at Brummen; Kevin Bending, who helped identify the RAF station from which Anthony flew in December 1943 as Woodhall Spa; and Fred Preller, Webmaster for 384th Bomb Group in the Second World War, who supplied documents relating to Anthony's flights with the 8th Air Force on bombing missions.

The Robert Graves connection to Anthony, through his daughter Jenny Nicholson, was a rich source of information. I would like to thank Caroline Shaw, the archivist at the St John's College Robert Graves Trust, and Lucia Graves, Sam Graves, and Richard Graves. A useful letter from Anthony to Robert Graves also surfaced in the Robert Graves archive of the Poetry Collection, the University of Buffalo, and I thank James Maynard, the assistant curator, for finding it.

An incredibly rich seam of knowledge was found in the University of Calgary's Special Collections, where Ernest Watkins' papers are deposited. Watkins knew Anthony extremely well because he worked with him at *WAR* for two years. Having the greatest admiration for Anthony, he wrote extensively about him and their work for ABCA in his unpublished autobiography. I would like to thank Ernest Watkins' sons, Tim and Nick, for permission to quote from their father's writings, and for the picture of Ernest on his motorbike in Iceland. I would also like to thank the archivist Apollonia Steele of the Special Collections, for her great help in tracking down the relevant material.

I am very grateful to the following for the permission to quote from key texts: Judy Urquhart (Major General R.E. Urquhart, *Arnhem*); Jeremy Lewis (*Tears Before Bedtime*, estate of Barbara Skelton); Bob Gerritsen and Niall Cherry (*Red Berets and Red Crosses: The Story of the Medical Services in the 1st Airborne Division in World War II*); The History Press (Stuart Mawson, *Arnhem Doctor*); The Second World War Experience Centre (Sir John Killick, interviews with Peter Liddle and John Hutson); Pen and Sword Publishing (Major General John Frost, *A Drop Too Many*); Random House Group Ltd (Stephen Watts, *Moonlight on a Lake in Bond Street*). My best efforts have been made to obtain permission for certain other quotations, but it has not been possible to make contact.

Lastly, my thanks go to Helen Chapman, who was an enormous help in transcribing Geoffrey's letters and following various leads, and to Professor Andrew Thorpe of the University of Exeter, who supervised my dissertation on Anthony and *WAR*, and gave me a great deal of encouragement at a time when the scale of this project looked somewhat daunting.

APPENDIX

THE GRAVES AT ENSCHEDE GENERAL CEMETERY

Original Cemetery List

Grave Number	Name in Original Records	Date Buried	Exhumations January and March 1946
502	Unknown	26/9/44	Teeth checked by US unit January 1946, not Anthony Cotterell
503	Hughes, Ernest	26/9/44	Wooden cross, but no identification details found in grave at March 1946 exhumations; grave is then reallocated to Benting as it was known that he was in the cemetery
504	Mills	26/9/44	
505	Capt. Plath	26/9/44	
506	Allen, Sydney	26/9/44	
507	Sold [soldier?] Binting William	26/9/44	McCracken's dog tags and army uniform discovered in March 1946 exhumation
508	Capt. Mac.Nabb	29/9/44	
509	Huard	8/10/44	identity verified in March 1946 exhumation, checked to see if victim of Brummen shooting
510	Purves	12/10/44	identity verified in March 1946 exhumation, checked to see if victim of Brummen shooting

Graves at Enschede Today – Commonwealth War Graves Commission (CWGC) Records

Grave Number	Name in CWGC Records	Details	Regiment
201	John Anthony Cotterell	joint grave	Royal Fusiliers (City of London Regiment)
200	Alan William Benting	joint grave	617 Squadron, RAF, Flight Engineer of Lancaster aircraft
199	Kenneth Stanley Mills		Glider Pilot Regiment, died at Brummen
198	Horace Anthony Platt		Reconnaissance Corps, 1st Airlanding Squadron, died at Brummen
197	Sydney Allen		2nd Battalion. Parachute Regiment, died at Brummen
196	George Ernest McCracken		2nd Battalion. Parachute Regiment, died at 12 Rozenhoflaan, Zutphen
195	Trevor Victor McNabb		Reconnaissance Corps, 1st Airlanding Squadron, died at Enschede Hospital
194	Jean Ferdinand Huard		Glider Pilot Regiment, part of *Market Garden* force
193	George Stratton Purves		King's Own Scottish Borderers, 7th (Airborne) Battalion, part of *Market Garden* force

Sources: Geoffrey Cotterell correspondence; National Archives WO 309/847; Roy Hemington, CWGC; original cemetery list courtesy of Dick Schlüter.

Note: The unknown airman in grave 202 was recovered from east of Enschede in December 1947; his date of death is listed as 21 November 1944 (CWGC records).

NOTES

1 Abbreviations
   A.C./1944/DD   Anthony Cotterell, 1944 Diary and typescripts in run-up to D-Day
   A.C./1944/N   Anthony Cotterell, 1944 Normandy typescripts
   Ernest Watkins, SC/UCL Ernest Watkins Papers, Special Collections, University of Calgary
                       Library
   SJ/RGT   The Library, St John's College, and St John's College Robert Graves
                       Trust
   All Cotterell family correspondence and Anthony's unpublished work are from the Cotterell
   family archive unless otherwise stated. All family and official texts have, where necessary, had
   minor corrections in terms of punctuation, spelling, obvious missed words and so on. All military
   abbreviations have been filled in where it enhances readability as have full names when the identity is only given by rank, e.g. the Brigade Major at 1st Parachute Brigade HQ was Tony Hibbert.
   Very minor changes, of the same type, have been made to Tony Hibbert's Arnhem Diary.

1 All the information in this prologue is found in more detailed form in Chapter 22.
2 Anthony Cotterell, *What! No Morning Tea?* (Victor Gollancz, London, 1941), p.11.
3 Geoffrey Cotterell, *Then a Soldier* (Eyre and Spottiswoode, London, 1944) p.147. Geoffrey refers
   to Wanstead using the pseudonym 'Watham Heath', a name he used in other novels. In *The
   Strange Enchantment* he refers to Wanstead as 'just beginning the relentless going-down process but [it] was very convenient for the city' *The Strange Enchantment* (Eyre and Spottiswood,
   London, 1956), p.264.
4 Rosemary McGrath, Anthony's cousin, conversation with the author, 15 November 2009.
5 Ibid.
6 Anthony Cotterell, *What! No Morning Tea?* pp.9–10.
7 Ibid, p.10.
8 Ibid, p.12.
9 Graham Cotterell was, at that time, a lieutenant and dental surgeon on the training ship,
   HMS *Powerful*. Graham Geoffrey's book, *The Strange Enchantment*, is loosely based on the relationship between the two sisters; Isabel is modelled on Janie, and Sarah on Mintie.
10 Anthony Cotterell, *What! No Morning Tea?* pp.11–12. Geoffrey, possessed of a phenomenal
   memory in his late eighties, corrected Anthony's spelling of Alan to Allan. Anthony could
   sometimes be a little slapdash in checking his work.
11 Ibid, p.13.
12 Ibid, 'No less ardent old school boy than I' – 1941 typescript diary; 'From the point of view of
   personal happiness' – *Oh, It's Nice to be in the Army!* (Victor Gollancz, London, 1941) p.46.
13 Ibid, *What! No Morning Tea?* p.14.
14 Ibid, p.15.
15 Ibid, p.11. Osbert Lancaster was soon to become very famous for his huge output of morale-
   boosting cartoons. Anthony calls him 'that rising old debunker'.
16 R. Allen with John Frost, *Voice of Britain, The Inside Story of the Daily Express* (Patrick Stephens,
   Cambridge, 1983), pp.54–70.

17   Anthony Cotterell to Mintie Cotterell and Graham Cotterell, letter, 17 March 1940. The aver-
      age conscript's wages are also mentioned in *What! No Morning Tea?* where Anthony qualifies
      the figure by saying that there was a 6*d* rise in the autumn of 1940.
18   Anthony Cotterell, *What! No Morning Tea?* p.15.
19   Arthur Christiansen, *Headlines all my Life* (Heinemann, London, 1961), p.172.
20   Ibid, p.189.
21   Anthony Cotterell, *What! No Morning Tea?* p.14.
22   Ibid, p.15.
23   Ibid, p.17.
24   Ibid, undated private paper.
25   It is noticeable that it is not listed amongst Anthony's other books in *An Apple for the Sergeant*,
      published once he had become a well-established writer.
26   Anthony Cotterell, *The Expert Way of Getting Married* (T. Werner Laurie, London, 1939), p.84.
27   John Everard, *Portrait of a Model* (George Routledge and Sons, London, 1939).
28   Anthony Cotterell, *What! No Morning Tea?* p.54.
29   Ibid, *An Apple for the Sergeant* (Hutchinson and Co, London 1944), p.31.
30   The details of this lunch came from Geoffrey.
31   Geoffrey Cotterell, *Then a Soldier*, p.20.
32   Ibid, p.22.
33   Anthony Cotterell, *What? No Morning Tea*, p.50.
34   Ibid, p.151.
35   Ibid, p.151.
36   Ibid, p.17.
37   Ernest Watkins, 'It is Dangerous to Lean Out', SC/UCL, Accession no: 469/90.9, file 5.1. p.158.
38   Anthony Cotterell, *What? No Morning Tea*, p.19.
39   Ibid, p.22.
40   Ibid, p.22.
41   Ibid, p.22.
42   Ibid, pp.23–24.
43   Ibid, p.24.
44   Ibid, p.26.
45   Ibid, p.42.
46   He did not date the letter (he almost never did) but the date is obvious from the content.
47   Anthony Cotterell, *An Apple for the Sergeant*, p.21.
48   Ibid, *What? No Morning Tea*, p.32.
49   Ibid, p.82. The Greyfriars stories, written by Charles Hamilton (under one of his many pseudo-
      nyms, Frank Richards) appeared in the boys' comic *The Magnet* from 1908–1940.
50   Ibid, p.52.
51   Ibid, p.83
52   Ibid, p.47
53   Ibid, p.40.
54   Meggs' letter is quoted in *What! No Morning Tea?* p.82. There he is given his proper name,
      Uncle Alec (Crews).
55   Anthony Cotterell, *What! No Morning Tea?* p.64
56   Ibid, p.61.
57   Ibid, pp.66–67.
58   Ibid, p.71.
59   Ibid, p.80.
60   Ibid, p.88–92.
61   Anthony had misheard 'Attend B' as '10B'.
62   Anthony Cotterell, *What! No Morning Tea?* pp.117–119.
63   Ibid, *An Apple for the Sergeant*, p.8.
64   Ibid, *What! No Morning Tea?* p.128.

65 Ibid, p.143.

66 The platoon photograph would appear in Anthony's book, *An Apple for the Sergeant*.

67 Anthony Cotterell, *What! No Morning Tea?* p.150.

68 Jeremy A. Crang, *The British Army and the People's War, 1939–1945* (Manchester University Press, 2000), p.2.

69 Anthony Cotterell, *What! No Morning Tea?* p.151.

70 The first 29 chapters of *An Apple for the Sergeant* carry on Anthony's story after initial training camp, and like *What! No Morning Tea?* were adapted from a diary.

71 Anthony Cotterell, *An Apple for the Sergeant*, p.18.

72 Ibid, pp.9–13.

73 Anthony Cotterell to Mintie Cotterell, letter, undated, summer 1940.

74 Presumably Graham was helping with the local anti-aircraft defences.

75 Anthony Cotterell to Mintie Cotterell, letter, undated, summer 1940.

76 Like Anthony, Geoffrey utilised his diaries and letters in his fiction.

77 Mintie Cotterell to Anthony Cotterell, letter, undated, probably late 1940/early 1941.

78 Anthony Cotterell, *An Apple for the Sergeant*, p.83.

79 Ibid, p.20.

80 Geoffrey Cotterell, *Then a Soldier*, p.14.

81 Ibid, p.35.

82 Anthony Cotterell, *An Apple for the Sergeant*, pp.20–21.

83 Ibid, p.27.

84 Ibid, p.26.

85 Ibid, p.27.

86 Geoffrey Cotterell, *Then a Soldier*, p.45.

87 Ibid, pp.54–55.

88 Anthony Cotterell to Mintie Cotterell, letter, undated, summer 1940.

89 Ibid.

90 Anthony Cotterell, *An Apple for the Sergeant*, p.28.

91 Jeremy A. Crang, *The British Army and the People's War*, p.62.

92 Anthony Cotterell, *An Apple for the Sergeant*, pp.28–29.

93 Ibid, p.29.

94 Emrys Jones and Cesar Romero were famous actors.

95 Anthony Cotterell, *What! No Morning Tea?*

96 Anthony Cotterell to Geoffrey Cotterell, letter, one leaf only (pp. 5–6, the rest are missing). The information on who Langman was and what he was like came from Geoffrey.

97 Stephen Watts, *Moonlight on a Lake in Bond Street* (The Bodley Head, London, 1961), p.111.

98 Anthony Cotterell, *An Apple for the Sergeant*, p.30.

99 Ibid, p.31.

100 Anthony Cotterell service records, Company Commander's Report, Army Personnel Centre, Historical Disclosures Section, Glasgow.

101 Geoffrey Cotterell, unpublished notes on his military career, 18 October 2008. The date of his going into the Army is based upon a letter to Mintie Cotterell of 18 April 1945.

102 Anthony Cotterell to Janie Pool, undated letter but October 1940 as it mentions his passing out date from OCTU as 18 October.

103 In *An Apple for the Sergeant*, Anthony places his return home in the Blitz between his leaving the OCTU and starting his first officer posting, which would put it as mid October, some five-six weeks after the onset of the Blitz. This is likely to have been a misdating, particularly in view of the second sentence of the account, saying it was nearly a year since he had gone away to war. A more likely date would be January-February 1941. Anthony Cotterell, *An Apple for the Sergeant*, pp.32–34.

104 Geoffrey Cotterell, *Then a Soldier*, p.139.

105 Ibid, the account of the visit runs from pp.145–157.

106 Anthony Cotterell, *An Apple for the Sergeant*, pp.33–34.

107 Ibid, p.34.
108 Anthony Cotterell to Mintie Cotterell and Graham Cotterell, undated but October 1940. Geoffrey commented at some length on this letter on 25 March 2009: 'Jennie – I so enjoyed that letter. Although he didn't care for his fellow officers, he must have had a good time there. Tenby. Tone had a running title he was fond of 'We always went to Tenby', but never used. I was there myself later on because there was a rocket practice camp nearby. It would have been a very long journey for mother to visit him, but of course she would have. I am thrilled to be able to give you an answer to a query, since I usually can't. Kenneth Kove was an actor we liked, he always performed in the famous Aldwych farces, played at the Aldwych Theatre, written by Ben Travers and starring Tom Walls and Ralph Lynn. I think the most famous was 'Rookery Nook'. Kove was a light comedian, ideal for playing a clueless curate. Also in the cast was always Mary Brough, who would be a formidable landlady or tyrannical wife. We loved these shows and so did everybody.'
109 Anthony Cotterell, *An Apple for the Sergeant*, pp.37–38.
110 Anthony Cotterell to Mintie Cotterell, undated letter, late 1940–early 1941.
111 Anthony Cotterell, *An Apple for the Sergeant*, p.39.
112 As Geoffrey would comment in 2009, using one of Anthony's family pet-names: 'The Count was in his glory – the plan he had had when he was conscripted to put a hard-backed note-book in his battledress trousers and note down everything and then make a book of it had come off magnificently.'
113 Anthony Cotterell, *An Apple for the Sergeant*, pp.56–57.
114 Ibid, p.40.
115 Ibid, p.41.
116 Geoffrey knew Zoe Farmer very well. After her marriage to Bernstein ended, she married Geoffrey's loyal friend Robin Barry, and they all remained very close. Anthony was always mentioned with great affection by Zoe. Zoe's real surname was Farmar but as a journalist she was known as Farmer.
117 Quentin Reynolds, *By Quentin Reynolds* (New York McGraw-Hill Book Company, New York, 1963), p.205, digitised by the Internet Archive, San Francisco: http://www.archive.org/stream/byquentinreynold001597mbp/byquentinreynold001597mbp_djvu.txt.
118 Anthony Cotterell, 1941 typescript diary, p.3. *An Apple for the Sergeant* was largely based upon this diary, and in the published version Anthony substitutes Teheran for the rather more contentious 'BugBug'.
119 Ibid, pp.3–9.
120 Ibid, pp.2–3.
121 Ibid, p.6.
122 See Julian Maclaren-Ross 'I Had to Go Absent', and Paul Willetts' commentary on this statement, *Times Literary Supplement*, 27 June 2008.
123 Anthony Cotterell, 1941 typescript diary, pp.8–14.
124 Ibid, *An Apple for the Sergeant*, p.71.
125 John Steinbeck, the American writer best-known for his novel of the Depression, *The Grapes of Wrath*.
126 Anthony Cotterell, 1941 typescript diary, p.10.
127 Ibid, pp.19–20.
128 Ibid, *An Apple for the Sergeant*, pp.74–75.
129 Ibid, 1941 typescript diary, p.6.
130 Ibid, *An Apple for the Sergeant*, p.77.
131 DSO: Distinguished Service Order; DFC: Distinguished Flying Cross, both highly prestigious RAF decorations.
132 Anthony Cotterell, 1941 typescript diary, p.16.
133 Ibid, 1941 handwritten diary, entry for Friday, 25 April 1941.
134 Ibid, *An Apple for the Sergeant*, p.87.
135 Hess flew to Scotland on May 10 1941.
136 Anthony Cotterell, 1941 handwritten diary, entry for Thursday, 29 May 1941.

137   Ibid, entry for Saturday, 31 May 1941.
138   Ibid, *She Walks In Battledress* (Christophers, London, 1942). Anthony acknowledges at the
      beginning of the book that the title came from a lightly satirical poem published in *Punch*.
139   Ibid, pp.7–8.
140   Ibid, 1941 handwritten diary, entry for Sunday, 1 June 1941.
141   Ibid, entry for Saturday, 7 June 1941.
142   Ibid, entry for Tuesday, 17 June 1941.
143   Ibid, *An Apple for the Sergeant*, p.27.
144   Stephen Watts, *Moonlight on a Lake in Bond Street*, p.105.
145   Anthony Cotterell, *What! No Morning Tea?* p.113.
146   Ibid, *An Apple for the Sergeant*, p.93.
147   Stephen Watts, *Moonlight on a Lake in Bond Street*, p.106.
148   Anthony Cotterell, *An Apple for the Sergeant*, pp.93–4.
149   Stephen Watts, *Moonlight on a Lake in Bond Street*, p.107.
      The book Anthony was writing must have been the early drafts of *An Apple for the Sergeant*.
150   Anthony Cotterell, *An Apple for the Sergeant*, p.95.
151   Ibid, pp.95–96.
152   Stephen Watts, *Moonlight on a Lake in Bond Street*, pp.107–8.
153   Alanbrooke's diaries contain references to Churchill's attempts to get rid of Adam, for example
      on 17 January 1944 he writes, 'he wants again to get Adam out of AG job, and wishes to
      send him to Gibraltar'. Field Marshal Lord Alanbrooke, *War Diaries, 1939–45* (Weidenfeld and
      Nicolson, London, 2001), p.514.
154   T.H. Hawkins and L.J.E. Brimble, *Adult Education, the Record of the British Army* (Macmillan,
      London, 1947), pp.119–120.
155   Pamphlet of August 1941, quoted at length in the *ABCA Handbook, A Manual designed for the
      guidance of all officers in the conduct of talks and discussions on Current Affairs. With Preface by the
      Secretary of State for War* (Army Bureau of Current Affairs, The War Office, August 1942).
156   William Emrys Williams, Secretary of the British Institute of Adult Education, executive
      member of the Workers' Educational Association, and the inspiration behind the Penguin
      Specials of the 1930s. He was reputed to be left-wing, which led to mistrust of ABCA in con-
      servative circles.
157   Army Film Unit, *The Story of the Army Bureau of Current Affairs*, black and white film (Ministry
      of Information, 1943), Imperial War Museum, London, ref: MGH 56.
158   Stephen Watts, *Moonlight on a Lake in Bond Street*, p.111. Watts was in the bath because at that
      stage the *WAR* office was in a bedroom of the requisitioned Hotel Victoria in Northumberland
      Avenue, London.
159   Ibid, pp.114–5.
160   Army publications were often quite outspoken and sometimes much more controversial than
      their civilian counterparts. The difference with *WAR* was that most Army papers sprung from
      below rather than being organised from above by the Army Council. See S.P. Mackenzie's arti-
      cle: 'Vox Populi: British Army Newspapers in the Second World War', *Journal of Contemporary
      History*, vol. 24, No 4 (Sage Publications Ltd, October 1989).
161   *CURRENT AFFAIRS* was written by contributors from outside the Army, but was edited within
      the War Office by Major Guy Chapman, a former Workers' Educational Association tutor and
      editor with Jonathan Cape. He was thus a man with a very different background to Anthony,
      Stephen Watts and Ernest Watkins. His tone in the Editorial is much more worthy and school-
      masterish than the equivalent in *WAR*; for example, in issue Number 50, 'You are Going to
      Europe', even the title, 'Ponder This First', is, well, appropriately ponderous in tone.
162   Ernest Watkins, 'Inherent suspicion of vaguely liberal ventures' – from the Epilogue of the
      draft titled 'Out of My Wits', p.3. SC/UCL, Accession no: 469/90.9, file 6.4.3.
163   Stephen Watts, *Moonlight on a Lake in Bond Street*, p.115.
164   Ernest Watkins, 'It Is Dangerous to Lean Out', Accession no: 469/90.9, file 5.2., p.167.
165   Stephen Watts, *Moonlight on a Lake in Bond Street*, p.110.
166   Ernest Watkins, 'It is Dangerous to Lean Out', p.159.

167   Stephen Watts, *Moonlight on a Lake in Bond Street*, p.115.
168   Ernest Watkins, 'ABCA I, Inception', p.8. SC/UCL, Accession no: 469/90.9, file 6.1.
169   Ibid, *No Depression in Iceland* (George Allen and Unwin Ltd, London, 1942), pp.70–71.
170   Ibid, 'It is Dangerous to Lean Out', p.162.
171   Ibid, p.206.
172   Ernest Watkins, From 'ABCA I, Inception', handwritten notes on ABCA, no page number. Ernest Watkins, SC/UCL, Accession no: 469/90.9, file 6.1.
173   Ibid.
174   Geoffrey Cotterell, 'Rockets for the Home Guard', WAR, issue 70, 13 May 1944, pp.7–10.
175   Ernest Watkins, 'It Is Dangerous to Lean Out', p.169.
176   Ibid, p.159.
177   Ernest Watkins, 'Hard and shrewd' – from the Epilogue of the draft titled 'Out of My Wits', p.3; 'surprised at the charm he could conjure up', 'It is Dangerous to Lean Out', p.209.
178   Ibid, 'It is Dangerous to Lean Out', p.160.
179   Ibid, 'ABCA I, Inception', p.5.
180   The Ministry of Information, *Roof Over Britain: the Official Story of the A.A. Defences, 1939–42* (HM Stationery Office, London, 1943).
181   *Horizon*, June 1994, under the title 'Completely in the Air'.
182   The assumption that Anthony was a medical officer has also been made by the modern historian, Mark Harrison, in his book *Medicine and Victory: British Military Medicine in the Second World War* (Oxford University Press, Oxford, 2004).
183   Anthony Cotterell to George Edinger, letter, 5 April 1944.
184   The girlfriend was Barbara Skelton. See the next chapter, 'Shubb's War, Jenny Nicholson, and Anne'.
185   Ernest Watkins, Epilogue, 'Out of My Wits', p.3.
186   Geoffrey Cotterell to author, 'addicted to nobility', email 9 April 2009.
187   R.J. Adam, Adjutant-General, 'The End of 'War', WAR, issue 97, 23 June 1945.
188   Ernest Watkins, 'It is Dangerous to Lean Out', p.173.
189   Ibid, pp.185–6.
190   Ernest Watkins, 'ABCA I, Inception', p.6.
191   Anthony Cotterell, *An Apple for the Sergeant*, p.14.
192   Ibid, 'Ships that Pass in the Day', *An Apple for the Sergeant*, p.112.
193   Ibid, 'Did I Ever Tell You About My Operation?'. The account runs over pp.174–185 of *An Apple for the Sergeant*. It is the last chapter in the book.
194   Geoffrey Cotterell, notes on his military career, 18 November 2008.
195   Geoffrey Cotterell to Mintie Cotterell, letter, Dover, 9 August 1942.
196   Geoffrey Cotterell, 'We Bag our First', WAR, issue 5, 15 November 1941, pp.7–10.
197   Ibid, 'Factory Guard', in Anthony Cotterell, *Oh, It's Nice to be in the Army!*, p.123.
198   Ibid, 'Rockets for the Home Guard', WAR, issue 70, 13 May 1944, pp.7–10.
199   Geoffrey Cotterell, notes on his military career, 18 November 2008.
200   Geoffrey Cotterell to Janie Pool, letter, 24 August 1943.
201   Geoffrey Cotterell to Janie Pool, letter, 27 October 1943.
202   Geoffrey Cotterell to Mintie Cotterell, letter, 22 May 1945.
203   Barbara Skelton, *Tears Before Bedtime* (Hamish Hamilton, London, 1987), p.35.
204   Anthony Cotterell, 'Ships that Pass in the Day', *An Apple for the Sergeant*, p.110.
205   Barbara Skelton, *Tears Before Bedtime*, p.34.
206   Richard Perceval Graves website, *Robert Graves and the White Goddess 1940–1985*, Book Three: *The Shout*, Chapter 3: *Wife to Mr Milton*: http://www.richardgraves.org/html/gravchap.htm#shout
207   Alan Moorehead, *A Late Education, Episodes in a Life* (Hamish Hamilton, London, 1970), p.142.
208   Geoffrey Cotterell, conversation with the author, September 2009.
209   Anthony Cotterell to Robert Graves, letter, 20 November 1942, SJ/RGT.
210   Ibid, 21 May 1943, SJ/RGT.

211 Ibid, 7 June 1943, the Poetry Collection, University at Buffalo, the State University of New York.

212 Geoffrey, on reading Anthony's letters to Graves after I obtained them in 2009, observed that Anthony was very good at 'arse-licking', and had always been far better at this than himself. Conversation with the author, Arnhem. September 2009.

213 Anthony Cottcrell to Robert Graves, letter, 5 November 1943, SJ/RGT.

214 Geoffrey Cotterell to Robert Graves, letter, 8th January 1944. Geoffrey thanks Graves for all the trouble he has taken, and also thanks Beryl, Graves's wife 'I hate to think how many evenings I have ruined'. SJ/RGT.

215 Jenny Nicholson to Robert Graves, letter, undated, probably 1944. SJ/RGT.

216 The details of the relationship between Jenny and the Cotterells came from Geoffrey.

217 Geoffrey Cotterell to the author, June 2008.

218 Anthony Cotterell, 'A Sergeant in Tow', WAR, issue 72, 10 June 1944.

219 E.W.C. Flavell, 'British Parachutists', WAR, issue 7, 13 December 1944, pp.9–11.

220 Ibid, p.10.

221 Anthony Cotterell, 'The Airborne Forces', WAR, issue 32, 28 November 1944, pp.1–10.

222 Editorial, WAR, issue 39, 6 March 1943.

223 Anthony Cotterell, An Apple for the Sergeant, p.145.

224 Ibid, p.159.

225 Ibid, p.161.

226 Ibid, p.163.

227 Ibid, p.167.

228 Ibid, p.172.

229 Ernest Watkins, 'ABCA I, Inception', p.9.

230 Geoffrey Cotterell to Mintie Cotterell, letter, 14 May 1946.

231 Ernest Watkins, 'It Is Dangerous to Lean Out', p.181.

232 Ibid, fragment, SC/UCL, Accession no: 469/90.9, file 3.4.

233 Ibid, 'With the connivance of medical authorities' – from the Epilogue of the draft titled 'Out of My Wits', p.4.

234 Ibid, 'It is Dangerous to Lean Out', p.205.

235 Ibid, typescript unnumbered fragment, SC/UCL, Accession no: 469/90.9, file 3.4.

236 Watkins has two rather different versions of their arrest. See Accession no: 469/90.9, file 3.4., and 469/90.9, file 5.1., 'It is Dangerous to Lean Out', pp. 206–10.

237 Ernest Watkins, 'It is Dangerous to Lean Out', p.209.

238 Anthony Cotterell, 'Is This the Way to the Second Front?' p.3, A.C./1944/DD.

239 Ibid, diary, entry for 21 May 1944, A.C./1944/DD.

240 Anthony's base unit was still the Royal Fusiliers, to whom he had been posted after officer training; he was only on attachment to the War Office and ABCA.

241 Anthony Cotterell, diary, entry for 22 May 1944, A.C./1944/DD.

242 Ibid, entry for 23–24 May, 1944.

243 A Short History of the 8th Armoured Brigade, foreword by Lieutenant-General B.G. Horrocks, 30 Corps, March 1946, Warlinks website:
http://www.warlinks.com/armour/8th_armoured/index.php

244 The Sherwood Rangers Yeomanry was usually known simply as the Sherwood Rangers.

245 Laycock was killed by a direct shell hit on the regimental HQ. There is now a memorial to him and the other officers who were killed with him at Tilly sur Seulles.

246 A Short History of the 8th Armoured Brigade, chapter IV, 'D-Day to the Island'.

247 Anthony Cotterell, diary, entry for 29 May 1944, A.C./1944/DD.

248 Ibid.

249 Ibid.

250 Ibid, entry for 31 May 1944.

251 Ibid, entry for 27 May 1944.

252 Ibid, 'Is This the Way to the Second Front?' p.11.

253   Ibid, 'Sitting on the Fence', *WAR*, issue 73, 24 June 1944, p.9.

254   Ibid, diary, entry for 1 June 1944, A.C./1944/DD.

255   Ibid.

256   Ibid.

257   Ibid.

258   Ibid, entry for 2 June 1944.

259   Ibid, entry for 5 June 1944.

260   The description and quotations about D-Day itself, unless otherwise indicated, come from Anthony's account in *WAR*, Part 2: 'Going on Shore', *WAR*, issue 74, July 8th 1944.

261   Anthony Cotterell, 'On A Steamer Going Over', A.C./1944/DD.

262   Details from the information Anthony was given by the Brigade's Intelligence Officer at some stage after Anthony joined his tank crew. There seems to be a likelihood that his tank crew did actually not come ashore on D-Day, but the following day. Anthony Cotterell, description of 8th Armoured Brigade's initial progress, A.C./1944/N.

263   Anthony Cotterell, entry for 7 June 1944, A.C./1944/N.

264   Bofors: anti-aircraft guns.

265   Anthony Cotterell, entry for 7 June 1944, A.C./1944/N.

266   Ibid, entry for 8 June 1944.

267   Anthony Cotterell, pages beginning: 'The taking of Fontenay was typical of the early stages of the Normandy campaign', A.C./1944/N.

268   Anthony Cotterell, entry for 7 June 1944, A.C./1944/N.

269   Ibid, entry for 9 June 1944.

270   Ibid.

271   Quotations throughout this chapter, unless otherwise specified, are taken from Anthony Cotterell's Normandy typescript, no title, unnumbered pages beginning: 'The taking of Fontenay was typical of the early stages of the Normandy campaign.'

272   In his typescript, Anthony crosses out 'B' and writes 'C' in in pencil. However, he also added the information at another point that his tank, X-ray twelve, was transferred to C squadron, so it seems that X-ray twelve was in both.

273   Information given in separate section of Anthony Cotterell's Normandy typescript, untitled unnumbered pages, A.C./1944/N.

274   Anthony Cotterell, unnumbered pages beginning: 'Down by the beaches where the minefields lay', A.C./1944/N.

275   Anthony Cotterell, unnumbered pages but with a title: 'An Operation was Performed', A.C./1944/N.

276   Geoffrey Cotterell to author, email, 3 August 2009.

277   Ernest Watkins, 'It Is Dangerous to Lean Out', p.238

278   Ibid, p.240.

279   Ibid, p.247.

280   Ernest Watkins, SC/UCL, Accession no:120/77.8, file 37.3.

281   Anthony Cotterell to Robert Graves, letter, undated but clearly after the liberation of Brussels on 3 September and before Anthony left for Arnhem on 17 September 1944, SJ/RGT.

282   Geoffrey Cotterell to author, email, 9 April 2009.

283   John Paddy Carstairs, *Hadn't We the Gaiety?* (Hurst and Blackett, 1945), p.33.

284   Ibid, p.34. That it was the *News Chronicle* is obvious from family letters after Anthony went missing.

285   David Astor would eventually have a stable of people with distinguished war records, including Terence Kilmartin, the literary editor, who had helped to rescue him in France.

286   Dwight D. Eisenhower, *Crusade in Europe* (London, 1948), cited by Paul Latawski, *Battle Zone Normandy: Falaise Pocket* (Sutton Publishing, Stroud, 2004) p.92.

287   Anthony Cotterell, 'Jumping to a Conclusion: Part One', 1944 pencil/typescript.

288   Tony Hibbert, Arnhem diary, entry for 8 July 1944, Tony Hibbert private papers.

289   Anthony Cotterell, 'Airborne Worries: Waiting to Be Scrubbed', *WAR*, issue 79, 14 October 1944.

290 Jenny Nicholson, 'Fair Women and Brave Men', *WAR*, issue 82, 25 November 1944, pp.8–11.

291 Cited by Toby Thacker, *The End of the Third Reich: Defeat, Denazification and Nuremberg, January 1944 – November 1946* (Tempus, London, 2006), p.57.

292 Tony Hibbert, 'I remember this very well, childish letting off steam, miracle no-one blinded'. Undated notes written just prior to the Brummen service in September 2008.

293 Major-General R.E. Urquhart with William Greatorex, *Arnhem* (Cassell, London, 1958), p.18.

294 'The three battalion commanders' – Lieutenant-Colonels Dobie, Frost and Fitch.

295 Ernest Watkins, 'It is Dangerous to Lean Out', p.248.

296 Anthony Cotterell to Robert Graves, letter, undated but clearly after the liberation of Brussels on 3 September and before Anthony left for Arnhem on 17 September 1944, SJ/RGT.

297 Tony Hibbert, Arnhem diary, entry for 16 September 1944,

298 Major-General John Frost, *A Drop Too Many* (Leo Cooper, London, 1994), p.203.

299 Major-General R.E. Urquhart with William Greatorex, *Arnhem*, p.38.

300 Major-General John Frost, *A Drop Too Many*, p.203.

301 James Simms, *Arnhem Spearhead, a private soldier's story* (Imperial War Museum, London, 1978), p.31.

302 Arthur Christiansen, the Editor of the *Daily Express*, wrote in his autobiography of how Wood had got to Arnhem. He had put his name into the the hat with men from other newspapers, had it drawn, and was thus 'one of the two 'lucky' ones, if you can use the term, to have the honour to represent the entire Allied Press on the operation'. Arthur Christiansen, *Headlines All my Life*, pp.204–5.

303 Ian Grant, *Cameramen at War* (Patrick Stephens, Cambridge, 1980), p.123.
Details of Mike Lewis's equipment are from the above book; Anthony took a typewriter with him to D-Day, so probably also took one to Arnhem.

304 Stuart Mawson, *Arnhem Doctor* (Spellmount, Stroud, 2007), p.13.

305 Major-General John Frost, *A Drop Too Many*, p.207.

306 Tony Hibbert, Arnhem Diary. All quotations from Tony Hibbert are from this diary unless otherwise specified.

307 Anthony Cotterell, *An Apple for the Sergeant*, p.143.

308 The circumstantial evidence for Anthony being with Brigade HQ/2nd Battalion for the entire operation is that the timeframe was exceedingly tight for anyone getting to the bridge. Nearly all those who followed the other two routes to Arnhem failed to get there. From first light on Monday, 18 September, no one could get through to or leave the bridge area, and these conditions persisted for the entire battle. Anthony would be captured close to the bridge on Thursday 21 September.

309 Captain C.A. Harrison, *The Great Battle of Arnhem, a personal account*, Imperial War Museum Ref: 4488, 82/33/1, p.4.

310 James Simms, *Arnhem Spearhead*, pp.39–40.

311 Ibid, p.40.

312 Anthony Cotterell, entry for 7 June 1944, A.C./1944/N.

313 Tony Hibbert is the anonymous Brigade Major quoted in Ernest Watkins' article 'Arnhem: The Landing and the Bridge', *WAR*, issue 83, 9 December 1944, pp.8–9.

314 Major-General John Frost, *A Drop Too Many*, p.210.

315 James Simms, *Arnhem Spearhead*, p.45.

316 In September 2009, I visited the old church at Oosterbeek with Geoffrey Cotterell, and as soon as he saw the St Eusebius tower this was his immediate observation about his brother, made with a smile.

317 Captain C.A. Harrison, *The Great Battle of Arnhem*, p.5.

318 1st Airborne Reconnaissance Squadron War Diary recorded that Freddie Gough, with Lieutenant McNabb, left the Squadron on 17 September at 16.45 to report to Divisional HQ. Captain Allsop then took command in his absence. Gough was then unable to return, or to get news through to the Squadron. On 20 September at 16.30 the diary reported: 'News that Major Gough M.C. is with 1 Para Bde and holding main bridge, which is still intact, cheers the troops. Lieutenant McNabb who is with the CO is assumed to be alright.' Allsop kept the com-

mand for the rest of the battle, and though wounded got back across the Rhine to British lines. 1st Airborne Reconnaissance Squadron War Diary, courtesy of the Pegasus Archive (Arnhem Archive, http://www.pegasusarchive.org/arnhem/frames.htm), see War Diaries page.

319   Lieutenant-General Frederick Browning, commander of 1st Airborne Corps and thus to large degree responsible for the Arnhem operation, would actually use Gough as an alibi in his extra-marital affairs, possibly without the knowledge of Gough. See comments by Browning's son 'Kits', Christopher Browning, in Jane Wheatley's article 'The Real Rebecca' in *The Times*, 11 September 2005.

320   Captain C.A. Harrison, *The Great Battle of Arnhem*, p.5.

321   Tony Hibbert, Arnhem diary.

322   Captain C.A. Harrison, *The Great Battle of Arnhem*, p.5.

323   Tony Hibbert, Arnhem diary.

324   The figures given for Frost's force are variable according to source, but generally are thought to be around the 740 mark.

325   Tony Hibbert, conversation with the author, 11 June 2008.

326   Ibid, Arnhem diary.

327   'Contrary to orders', see William F. Buckingham, *Arnhem 1944, a Reappraisal* (Tempus, 2002), p.160. Different accounts give different figures of the number of dead, but 70 dead seems to be the usual figure, see for example Niall Cherry's *With Nothing Bigger than a Bren Gun: the story of the defence of the Schoolhouse at the Arnhem Road Bridge, September 1944* (Brendon Publishing, 2007), p.14.

328   Major-General John Frost, *A Drop Too Many*, p.220.

329   Jim Flavell, conversations with the author, August 2008.

330   Jim Flavell in David G. van Buggenum's *B Company Arrived, The Story of B Company of the 2nd Parachute Battalion at Arnhem, September 1944* (Sigmond Publishing, Renkum, Holland, 2003), p.100.

331   Major Douglas Edward Crawley of 'B' Company, 2nd Battalion, 1st Parachute Brigade, biography on the Pegasus Archive: http://www.pegasusarchive.org/arnhem/frames.htm

332   *A Drop Too Many*, Major-General John Frost, p.224.

333   Ibid, p.224.

334   Ibid, p.227.

335   Major-General R.E. Urquhart with Wilfred Greatorex, *Arnhem*, p.178.

336   Major Freddie Gough, letter copied into a letter fromMintie Cotterell to Janie Pool, 28 May 1945.
      The unattributed words were used in an 'In Memoriam' notice by the Cotterell family, which is evidently quoting Gough, perhaps from the Cotterells' meeting with him at his City office after the war.

337   Tony Hibbert, conversation with the author, 11 June 2008.

338   'Indomitable', Leo Heaps, *The Grey Goose Of Arnhem, The Story Of The Most Amazing Mass Escape Of World War II* (Weidenfeld and Nicholson, London, 1996), p.60.

339   When the time came to evacuate the wounded, someone carried James Simms out of the darkness of the cellar into the open air. 'A huge Canadian press photographer was in the cellar with us. He had already smashed his camera and plates. He lifted me as though I were a child and carried me upstairs [to safety].' James Simms, *Arnhem Spearhead*, p.85.

340   Anthony Cotterell, 'Did I ever Tell You About My Operation?', *An Apple for the Sergeant*, p.184.

341   Major-General R.E. Urquhart with Wilfred Greatorex, *Arnhem*, p.114.

342   Tony Hibbert, Arnhem diary.

343   Sir John Killick, interviews with Peter Liddle (October 2001) and John Hutson (February 2002), Leeds World WAR II Experience Centre, http://www.war-experience.org/.

344   Major-General John Frost, *A Drop Too Many*, p.230.

345   David Wright quoted in Niall Cherry's *Red Berets and Red Crosses, The story of the Medical Services in the 1st Airborne Division in World War II* (Sigmond Publishing, Renkum, Holland, 2005), p.110.

346   James Simms, *Arnhem Spearhead*, p.86.

347   Major-General John Frost, *A Drop Too Many*, p.233.

348   James Simms, *Arnhem Spearhead*, p.87.

349   Reuters Report, *The Times*, 22 September 1944.

350   This chapter is based upon Tony Hibbert's Arnhem Diary unless otherwise stated, and any unattributed quotations are from the diary.

351   H.E. Trinder, typescript on the Arnhem battle, Imperial War Museum, Ref:3530 85/8/1, p.5.

352   Jim Flavell, letter to the author, 27 September 2008.

353   Major Freddie Gough, 1st Airborne Reconnaissance Squadron, biography on the Pegasus Archive: http://www.pegasusarchive.org/arnhem/frames.htm

354   Tony Hibbert, conversation with the author, 11 June 2008.

355   Anthony Cotterell, diary 23 May 1944, A.C./1944/DD.

356   Anthony Cotterell, *What! No Morning Tea*, p.136.

357   The Dutch civilian population were well aware that, if caught, the penalty for helping the British was death. As Piet Kamphuis writes, 'Although the German military authorities generally acted in accordance with the Geneva Convention, several civilians were, nevertheless, summarily executed'. Piet Kamphuis, 'Caught Between Hope and Fear, Operation *Market Garden* and its Effects on the Civilian Population in the Netherlands', in M.R.D. Foot (editor), *Holland at War Against Hitler: Anglo-Dutch relations 1940–1945* (Frank Cass, London, 1990), p.172.

358   Sir John Killick, interviews with Peter Liddle (October 2001) and John Hutson (February 2002), Leeds World WAR II Experience Centre. Sir John gives an explanation of his slightly complex attachment to 89th Parachute Field Security Section and why he was not wearing the unit's badges.

359   Jim Flavell, who would be on the truck with Anthony at the time of the Brummen shooting, thought that Anthony was just another officer from the very mixed groups at the bridge. Flavell met Geoffrey several times post-war, and such details as this became fixed in his memory. Other officers, who later give testimony about the Brummen shooting referred to Anthony as 'Major Cotterell, Royal Fusiliers'.

360   The St Eusebius photograph, published in *Buczacz – Caen – Nimwegen: Der Kampf der 10.SS-Division-Frundsberg im Jahre 1944*, was identified in a brilliant piece of detective work by David van Buggenum. He realised the similarities between the photograph in the German book with one taken in 1945 after Arnhem was liberated, which showed the same fallen bench lying in exactly the same position in front of exactly the same pews on which the prisoners had been sitting. No one had replaced the bench because Arnhem was cleared of the Dutch population after the battle.
      Geoffrey on seeing this photo, commented, 'Well, if Tone is there he will be at the back, because that is what he did'.

361   Sir John Killick, interviews with Peter Liddle (October 2001) and John Hutson (February 2002), Leeds World WAR II Experience Centre.

362   Major-General John Frost, *A Drop Too Many*, p.233.

363   Anthony Deane-Drummond, *Return Ticket* (Collins, London, 1953), p.183.

364   Ibid, pp.216–217.

365   Ibid, pp.220–222.

366   Jac Janssen, later a distinguished professor, in his contribution to a discussion in M.R.D. Foot (editor), *Holland at War Against Hitler*, p.179.

367   Letter, Finlay Wilson to Mintie Cotterell, 3 July 1945.

368   Anthony Cotterell, 'Ships that Pass in the Day', *An Apple for the Sergeant*, p.113.

369   Sir John Killick, interviews with Peter Liddle (October 2001) and John Hutson (February 2002), Leeds World WAR II Experience Centre.
      Though some people recalling the Brummen shooting thought that Killick was on that particular truck, Killick himself categorically stated in 2001 'I wasn't there fortunately'. Sir John Killick, interview with Peter Liddle.

370   Like many other eyewitness details, there are slight variants in the number of the guards, but this tally is the most usual one.

371   Major Freddie Gough, statement in Sergeant Gerrit Kamp's papers, certified a true copy of the original statement taken on 21 June 1947, copy dated 28 June 1947, transcribed at Herford (office of 33 Netherlands War Crime Commission) and signed by Kamp. Dutch National Archives at The Hague, copy lent by Ymi Ytsma.

372   The earliest descriptions of the SS guards given by witnesses are to be found in JAG file MD/JAG/FS/61/4(D), CASE 'K', report dated 11 April 1945. Both Captain Gell and Captain Livesey used the word 'Jewish'. Gemeente Archief Enschede, copy courtesy of the Airborne Museum, Oosterbeek.

373   Tony Hibbert, conversation with the author, 11 June 2008.

374   Donkersgoed was, very fortunately for him, allowed to go when he reached Zutphen. For this and other details of the airborne soldiers passing through Brummen see Piet Willemsens' *Oorlog in een Dorp aan de IJssel, Brummen-Eerbeek 1940–1945* (P.H.L. Willemsens, Brummen, 1994), pp.68–75.

375   Janie Pool to Mintie Cotterell, letter, 14 May 1945.

376   Jeanne Slijkoord (née Veldkamp), eyewitness account, October 2008.

377   Major Freddie Gough, statement in Sergeant Gerrit Kamp's papers, certified a true copy of the original statement taken on 21 June 1947.

378   Captain John D. White, Officer Commanding, 137 Town Major, Zutphen, summary of the investigations already made before the matter was taken up by Sergeant Gerrit Kamp, dated 11 September 1945. The information about the Dutch girls came from a Mr D.W.J. Detmar of Rijksstraatweg A-62, possibly the same Mr Detmar who tried to give one of the prisoners (probably Anthony) a glass of water. Dutch National Archives at The Hague, copy lent by Ymi Ytsma.

379   Cecil Byng-Maddick statement, National Archives, WO 309/1951.

380   Douglas Murray statement, National Archives, WO 309/1951.

381   JAG, London, National Archives, WO 311/377.

382   Wilfred Morley statement, National Archives, WO 309/1951.

383   Trevor Livesey, statement, National Archives, WO 309/1951.

384   Major Freddie Gough, 'Particulars Regarding War Crime at Arnhem on September 23 1944', National Archives, WO 309/847.

385   Ibid.

386   Jim Flavell, account of the Brummen Incident, written 10 March 1990, private papers.

387   Jim Flavell in David G. van Buggenum's *B Company Arrived, The Story of B Company of the 2nd Parachute Battalion at Arnhem, September 1944* (Sigmond Publishing, Renkum, Holland, 2003), p.137.

388   Jim Flavell, account of the Brummen Incident, written 10 March 1990, and conversations with the author, August 2008.

389   Major Freddie Gough, 'Particulars Regarding War Crime at Arnhem on September 23 1944'.

390   Korteweg was awarded The King's Medal for Courage in the Cause of Freedom on 23 April 1947.

391   Major Freddie Gough, 'Particulars Regarding War Crime at Arnhem on September 23 1944'.

392   Finlay Wilson to Geoffrey Cotterell, letter, 11 November 1945.

393   Deposition of Gustav Etter, 15 January 1946, National Archives, WO 309/2035.

394   Jim Flavell, and Piet Willemsens' *Oorlog in een Dorp aan de IJssel*, p.70.

395   Mintie Cotterell to Janie Pool, letter containing transcript of John Cairns' letter to Mintie Cotterell, 6 May 1945.

396   Eyewitness account of Jaap Detmar in Piet Willemsens' *Oorlog in een Dorp aan de IJssel*, p.73. Translation by Frits Slijkoord. The exact details of the wounds suffered by Anthony and his fellow prisoners are discussed in Part Four, *The Search for Anthony*.

397   Geoffrey Cotterell to Mintie Cotterell, letter, diary-style entry for 27 October in letter dated 30 October 1945.

398   Deposition of Gustav Etter, 15 January 1946.

399   Statement of Dr Ernst Tigges, 3 July 1946, National Archives, WO 309/847.

400   Jeanne Slijkoord, eyewitness account, October 2008.

401   Geoffrey Cotterell to Mintie Cotterell, letter, 17/18 January 1946. The witness was Hermann Thomson, the orderly.

402   Some witnesses say that a different truck was used to the one which they had arrived at Brummen in. This is possibly because, as another witness, Cecil Byng-Maddick, stated, one of the shots had damaged the right-hand back wheel of the first truck.

403   Janie Pool to Mintie Cotterell, letter, 14 May 1945.

404   Eyewitness account of Jaap Detmar in Piet Willemsens' *Oorlog in een Dorp aan de IJssel*, p.73. Translation by Frits Slijkoord.

405   After the war, Etter would specifically enquire after Gough and Arnold, 'Please give [the fellow officers of your brother] my best regards, especially Major Gough and Major Arnold'. Geoffrey Cotterell to Mintie Cotterell, letter, 15 January 1946, which contains a transcript of the letter from Etter.

406   The witness was Bernard Briggs. Statement in Sergeant Gerrit Kamp's papers, certified a true copy of the original statement taken on 21 November 1945, copy dated 28 June 1947, transcribed at Herford (office of 33 Netherlands War Crime Commission) and signed by Kamp, Dutch National Archives at The Hague, copy lent by Ymi Ytsma.

407   Details as given in the deposition of Gustav Etter, 15 January 1946.

408   'Staubwasser would later say he had no recollection of the conversation with Etter.' See Part Four.

409   'Q: Did the Unteroffizier assist you in caring for the wounded?
      A: Yes, of course he did, especially at Zutphen.' Deposition of Gustav Etter, 15 January 1946.

410   The back room was sometimes described by the Dutch as the inner room – 'it is certain that [Anthony] first was admitted into the inner room described by you as the place where Major Gough left him'. Aps Tjeenk Willink to Mintie Cotterell, letter, 21 November 1945.

411   Geoffrey Cotterell to Mintie Cotterell, letter, 20 November 1945.

412   There are many small details of the dressing station scattered through Geoffrey Cotterell's letters home in 1945–46. For example, the details of the air raid and Etter ordering the medical orderly to give the British cigarettes came from his meeting with one of these medical orderlies, Hermann Thomson. Geoffrey Cotterell to Mintie Cotterell, letter, 21 January 1946.

413   Geoffrey and I were able to visit No.12 Rozenfhoflaan in September 2009. It was an extremely moving visit. See Acknowledgements.

414   'I was ... somewhat concerned about the interest taken by the Oberleutnant in him.' Major Freddie Gough, 'Particulars Regarding War Crime at Arnhem on September 23 1944'.

415   Gerard Schutt, a member of the Dutch resistance, would always credit Aps with saving his life in the last days of the war. 'The SS were rounding people up and she knew this and got on her bike and cycled to Eerbeek where I lived and told me, so when the SS came I wasn't there.' Gerard Schutt, conversation with the author at Oosterbeek, September 2009.

416   'Stretching all the way back to Paracelsus probably' – Geoffrey Cotterell, conversation with author, 18 June 2008.

417   See 'How Dutch Resistance Was Organized' in M.R.D. Foot (editor), *Holland at War Against Hitler: Anglo-Dutch relations 1940–1945* (Frank Cass, London, 1990), pp.68–119.

418   The word 'Moffen' was the equivalent of the English words 'Hun', 'Boche' or 'Kraut', an insulting epithet which was forbidden by law.

419   Geoffrey Cotterell to Mintie Cotterell, diary letter, 26–30 October 1945

420   Ibid.

421   Tony Hibbert, Arnhem diary, entry for Tuesday, 26 September 1944.

422   Tony Hibbert, 'Disconnected Notes: Wireless News and Newspapers', written whilst in hiding in Holland, September-October 1944, and diary entry for Thursday, 28 September 1944.

423   1st Airborne Reconnaissance Squadron War Diary, courtesy of the Pegasus Archive (Arnhem Archive, http://www.pegasusarchive.org/arnhem/frames.htm), see War Diaries page.

424   Major-General R.E. Urquhart with Wilfred Greatorex, *Arnhem*, pp.166–7.

425   Stanley Maxted, quoted in Ernest Watkins' article '1 Airborne Div at Arnhem (cont)', *WAR*, issue 84, 23 December 1944, pp.12–14.

426   Alan Wood was an Australian leader writer, whom Arthur Christiansen, Anthony's old boss at the *Daily Express*, characterised as 'a rangy, difficult sour-puss, a man with a permanent load of grievances'. Wood's chief grievance was that Christiansen did not pay him enough. 'Even so, I did not expect to get a radio message from his [Oosterbeek] fox-hole, the last he was able to send, which said: "How about a rise now, Mister Christiansen?"' Woods never recovered from the ordeal of Arnhem and eventually committed suicide. Christiansen concluded his account of him by writing, 'I salute the memory of this brave, awkward man who told no one at the *Express* office of his troubles but went his own lonely way'. Arthur Christiansen, *Headlines all my Life*, pp.204–5.

427   Tony Hibbert, Arnhem diary, entry for Thursday, 28 September 1944.

428   Edith Menzies to Anthony Cotterell, letter dated 14 October 1944.

429   Ernest Watkins, 'Better Water than Blood', *WAR*, issue 87, 3 February 1945, p.2.

430   Ed Beattie, an American journalist captured on 12 September 1944, notes Limburg as being the place where PoWs were finally allowed to send the first postcard. Edward W. Beattie, *Diary of a Kriegie* (Thomas Y. Crowell Co, New York), p.84.

431   Bernard Briggs, handwritten record, courtesy of Simon Middleton-Briggs.

432   However, it seems certain that the death toll which Beattie quotes was added from his post-war knowledge of the incident, because Bernard Briggs' group could only have been aware of the deaths of Tony Platt, Kenneth Mills, and Sydney Allen, and possibly (through Freddie Gough, if he was travelling with them) of George McCracken.
      Edward W. Beattie, *Diary of a Kriegie*, pp.77–82.

433   Ibid, p.87.

434   Major Freddie Gough, statement in Sergeant Gerrit Kamp's papers, certified a true copy of the original statement taken on 21 June 1947.

435   The War Office to Mintie Cotterell, letter, 10 April 1945.

436   The War Office to Geoffrey Cotterell, letter, 12 July 1945.

437   BBC to War Crimes Investigation Unit, BAOR, letter, 22 May 1946. National Archives, WO 309/847.

438   Kamp transcript of 'Spotlight on the Invasion', 33 Netherlands War Crimes Commission files, Dutch National Archives at The Hague, copy lent by Ymi Ytsma.

439   Tony Hibbert, Arnhem Diary, entry for Tuesday, 3 October 1944.

440   Tony Hibbert's first words to the author about Anthony Cotterell were: 'I was responsible for his death and I have carried that burden all my life.' TH conversation with the author, June 2008.

441   Janie Pool to Mintie Cotterell, diary letter commencing 14 May 1945.

442   The Germans lifted the ban at the beginning of November, but by then it was too late. Piet Kamphuis, 'Caught Between Hope and Fear, Operation *Market Garden* and its Effects on the Civilian Population in the Netherlands', *Holland at War Against Hitler*, pp.174–176.

443   Gerard Schutt, a member of the Dutch resistance, was once going through the woods at Ede in the middle of the night with a parachutist on his bicycle when he was stopped by two Germans. They were lost and asked him the way. 'They knew all sorts of things were going on in the woods and wanted to get out.' They asked him to show them to way and he did so. 'Then they said "Thank you very much, goodbye" and were off. Schutt laid great emphasis on the word "goodbye."' In other words, the Germans were just as relieved to get away as he was. Conversation with the author, Oosterbeek, September 2009.

444   Editorial, *WAR*, issue 83, 9 December 1944, p.ii.

445   Geoffrey Cotterell to Robert Graves, letter, 17 October 1944, SJ/RGT.

446   In a letter to Mintie of 21 May 1946, Geoffrey describes Watkins as working on *The Haymarket* with a part-time secretary.

447   Ernest Watkins, 'It Is Dangerous to Lean Out' (incomplete draft), Ernest Watkins, SC/UCL, Accession no: 469/90.9, file 5.2., p.275.

448   *WAR*, issue 87, 3 February 1945.

449   Ibid, issue 97, 23 June 1945.

450 The 49th Infantry Division, Ernest Watkins' old unit, had supported the liberation of Arnhem by the 1st Canadian Army.

451 The London Ballet Group program in the family archives is for the India tour which Janie embarked on soon after the European tour ended. That it is the same company she was travelling with is evident from the many signed messages on the farewell program, some from performers who had been with Janie for fifteen months. It seems likely that the basics of the repertoire had not changed.

452 Janie Pool to Mintie Cotterell, diary letter commencing 14 May 1945.

453 Janie Pool to Mintie Cotterell, letter, 28 May 1945. Janie says she did not go to Enschede as it was too far away, but that Dick Tjeenk Willink did make the trip and she gives the details of what he found there.

454 Freddie Gough, obituary notice in *The Times*, 22 September 1977, and Major Freddie Gough, statement in Sergeant Gerrit Kamp's papers, certified a true copy of the original statement taken on 21 June 1947.

455 Captain Frank to Mintie Cotterell, 30 April 1944.

456 Janie Pool to Mintie Cotterell, letter, 26 May 1945.

457 Mintie Cotterell to Janie Pool, letter, 23 May 1945.

458 Ibid, 24 May 1945.

459 Freddie Gough letter, transcribed in letterMintie Cotterell to Janie Pool, 28 May 1945.

460 'A Farewell Message from the Adjutant-General', *WAR*, issue 97, 14 June 1945.

461 Geoffrey Cotterell to Mintie Cotterell, letter, 8 December 1945.

462 Geoffrey Cotterell to Janie Pool, letter, 25 August 1945.

463 Geoffrey Cotterell to Mintie Cotterell, letter, 22 August 1945.

464 'The technique is similar to countering planes, but it is rather closer.' Geoffrey Cotterell to the author, June 2009.

465 He has written or remembered the date wrongly, and writes 8 June rather than 6th.

466 This was indeed what happened with the captured American journalist, Ed Beatty, who was liberated by the Russians, though not subsequently detained by them. See Chapter 10, 'Etter', and in more detail Chapter 15, 'What Happened to Anthony Cotterell?'

467 Geoffrey Cotterell to Mintie Cotterell, letter, 25 May 1945.

468 Geoffrey Cotterell to Graham Cotterell, letter, 25 October 1945.

469 Geoffrey Cotterell to Mintie Cotterell, letter, 27 July 1945.

470 The War Office to Geoffrey Cotterell, letter, 12 July 1945.

471 Geoffrey Cotterell to Robert Graves, letter, 22 September 1945, SJ/RGT.

472 Brian Spray to Graham and Mintie Cotterell, letter, 11 September 1945.

473 Geoffrey Cotterell to Robert Graves, letter, 22 September 1945, SJ/RGT.

474 Friends of the Cotterell family in Wanstead. Mr Townley was Graham's golfing partner.

475 Geoffrey Cotterell to Mintie Cotterell, letter, 15 January 1946. In a later letter, Geoffrey, obviously answering a question of his mother, told her 'C.E.M. Graham was a signature, no resemblance at all'. The identity of C.E.M. Graham is discussed in Chapter 15.

476 Kamp is always referred to as a sergeant by Geoffrey, though on the Eberhard Taubert statement, which he certified, of 28 June 1946, his full rank and job title are given as Sergeant Major G.J. Kamp, HQ Investigating Team.

477 At some stage IJspeerd must have wanted references of his good character from the British, as in his family papers there is a 'Certificate' from BAOR of 10 July 1945, testifying to his 'cheerful disposition', adding that the 'cooperation between the corps of Military Police and the indigenous Police of Almelo may be called splendid'. There is also a reference from Major A. MacGregor, of the Search Bureau at Bünde, 17 December 1945, saying that the information that IJspeerd gathered on Anthony's case 'has been of a great help indeed'. Also included in the family papers is a personal note from Geoffrey, dated January 1946, giving IJspeerd his grateful thanks. Family papers, courtesy of Ymi Ytsma.

478 Geoffrey Cotterell to Captain Springett, British Embassy, The Hague, letter, 12 November 1947.

479 See Coen Hilbrink, *De Illegalen, Illegaliteit in Twente & het aangrenzende Salland, 1940–1945* (SDU, 1989) and C.B. Cornelissen *Sipo en SD in Twente, 1940–1945* (Cornelissen, 2010).

480   Further details of the accusations against Kamp and his court trial are given in Chapter 14, 'Demob and Afterwards'.

481   Geoffrey Cotterell to Mintie Cotterell, letter, 15 January 1946.

482   Further details of this office are given in Kamp's report of 26 January 1946. He writes that he called in at 'Zutphen Detachment CMP (VP), 603 Company, and says he can be contacted on the Zutphen Town Major's phone: 1499. 33 Netherlands War Crimes Commission files. Dutch National Archives at The Hague, courtesy of Ymi Ytsma.

483   The War Office to the British Section of the Control Commission for Germany, letter, 27 September 1945. 33 Netherlands War Crimes Commission files. Dutch National Archives at The Hague, courtesy of Ymi Ytsma.

484   Captain John D. White, Officer Commanding, 137 Town Major, Zutphen – his extensive local enquiries had been thoroughly supported by the Dutch. A copy of his findings, dated 11 September 1945, is in 33 Netherlands War Crimes Commission files. Dutch National Archives at The Hague, courtesy of Ymi Ytsma.

485   Geoffrey Cotterell to Mintie Cotterell, letter, 10 January 1946.

486   Ibid, 20 November 1945.

487   Undated handwritten note, not signed, National Archives, WO 309/847.

488   Dick Tjeenk-Willink to Mintie Cotterell, letter, 5th January 1946.

489   Toby Thacker, *The End of the Third Reich: Defeat, Denazification and Nuremberg, January 1944–November 1946* (Tempus, Stroud, 2006), p.17.

490   Ibid, p.130.

491   Patricia Meehan, *A Strange Enemy People, Germans Under the British, 1945–50* (Peter Owen, London, 2001), p.13.

492   Geoffrey Cotterell, *Randle in Springtime* (Eyre and Spottiswoode, London, 1949), p.86.

493   Ibid, pp.5–7.

494   Geoffrey Cotterell to Mintie Cotterell, letter, 4 November 1945.

495   He is referring to gun sites on which he served in England.

496   Max Schmeling was heavyweight boxing champion of the world in the early 1930s.

497   William Joyce was found guilty of treason and hanged in 1946. The recording of his drunken final broadcast still exists, and is thoroughly chilling.

498   See Patricia Meehan, *A Strange Enemy People*, pp.180–181.

499   Geoffrey Cotterell to Mintie Cotterell, letter, 25 January 1946.

500   Geoffrey Cotterell, *Randle in Springtime*, p.97.

501   Ibid, p.218.

502   Randle was a lieutenant, and thus on a junior officer's pay. See *Randle in Springtime*, p.189.

503   See for example Geoffrey Cotterell to Mintie Cotterell, letter, 26 November 1945.

504   Geoffrey Cotterell to Mintie Cotterell, letter, 7 November 1945.

505   Geoffrey Cotterell, *Randle in Springtime*, p.166.

506   Geoffrey Cotterell to Mintie Cotterell, letter, 12 December 1946.

507   Churchill did not use this phrase until March 1946, but permutations of the phrase seem to have been in existence earlier. Geoffrey certainly used something very similar in a letter of 2 November 1945, when writing about permission to go to the Russian Zone 'Permission has occasionally been granted: but of course there is this complete curtain'.

508   Geoffrey Cotterell to Mintie Cotterell, letter, 8 December 1946.

509   Ibid, 28 November 1945.

510   Albert Speer's *Inside the Third Reich*, p.509, quoted by Toby Thacker, *The End of the Third Reich*, p.54.

511   Franz von Papen was one of the defendants at the Nuremberg trial. A mannered aristocrat, he was acquitted on the grounds that he had committed minor immoralities rather than major war crimes.

512   Geoffrey adds in brackets that the meaning is that Anthony must have already left, i.e. left the Arnhem district.

513   James Owen, *Nuremberg, Evil on Trial* (Headline Publishing, London, 2006), pp.360–2.

514   Geoffrey Cotterell to Mintie Cotterell, diary letter, ending 30 October 1945.

515 Immediately after the war, the main body for collecting evidence of war crimes had been attached to SHAEF (Supreme Headquarters Allied Expeditionary Force), well known for its CROWCASS list of people suspected of committing war crimes. However, the files in the Brummen case originate from the solely British organization, the War Crimes Group (North West Europe) or from the military department of the Judge Advocate General's office, simply called JAG on most letterheadings or memos.

516 Patricia Meehan, *A Strange Enemy People*, p.60.

517 War Crimes Group memo, National Archives, WO 311/377.

518 JAG, London, National Archives, WO 311/377.

519 To the Officer Commanding, 603 Coy CMP (VP). Handwritten date of 29 October 1945, but covers research done up to 31st October. There is also a corrected and augmented version of three pages of the report, hand-dated 26/11/45. 33 Netherlands War Crimes Commission files. Dutch National Archives at The Hague, courtesy of Ymi Ytsma.

520 Dirk Dolfing, Regionaal Archief Zutphen, email to the author, 28th August 2009.

521 Kamp report, 26 November 1944. 33 Netherlands War Crimes Commission files. Dutch National Archives at The Hague, courtesy of Ymi Ytsma.

522 The number is very badly typed, having been corrected. It has the word 'hrs' after it, but as it was dark at the time this cannot actually have meant 9.30am. The rest of the report confirms that she meant 9.30pm.

523 There is an account of this incident in Kamp's papers for 26 November 1945. This says that the murdered officers were buried in the garden of the burgomaster's house and that they had subsequently been identified as Lieutenant R. Roussel, 156 Parachute Regiment, and Lieutenant A. Michael Cambridge of the same regiment. 33 Netherlands War Crimes Commission files. Dutch National Archives at The Hague, courtesy of Ymi Ytsma.

524 This appears in the corrected and augmented version of three pages of Kamp's original report, hand-dated 26/11/45.

525 This nurse's name is given in several different ways – in Kamp's initial report as Mrs Holman Disbergen in line with the Dutch custom of giving a woman's married name followed by her birthname; in War Crimes 1 as Mrs F.R. Vossevelde; in War Crimes 2 as Sollmann, née Disbergen, Johanna. I have adopted the Johanna Sollman format as it is the one which appears on her deposition.

526 Geoffrey Cotterell, *Randle in Springtime*, pp.251–252.

527 These names and the interrogations made can be read in Kamp's 'Summary of Investigations re case Major J.A. Cotterell', 26 November 1945.

528 This almost certainly refers to Geoffrey's visit to Captain Cranford in Bünde just before Geoffrey was posted to Hamburg.

529 Aps Tjeenk Willink to Mintie Cotterell, letter, 21 November 1945.

530 Geoffrey Cotterell to Mintie Cotterell, letter, 11 November 1945.

531 Criminal Investigation Department, County Borough of Bolton Police, memo dated 15 October 1945, National Archives, WO 309/1951.

532 Criminal Investigation Department, County Borough of Bolton Police, report dated 7 December 1945, National Archives, WO 309/1951.

533 Gerritt Kamp, 'Summary of Investigations re case Major J.A. Cotterell', 26 November 1945.

534 Geoffrey Cotterell to Mintie Cotterell, letter, 5 December 1945.

535 See, for example, Geoffrey's note to Captain Peter Kinsleigh of 20 July 1946, which tells of Conroy's telephone conversation with Mintie. National Archives, WO 309/847.

536 Possibly Lieutenant Colonel A.J.M. Harris or Lieutenant Colonel R.A. Nightingale, whose names appear on several items of correspondence.

537 Ed Beattie, *Diary of a Kriegie*, pp.114–127.

538 Deposition of Gustav Etter, 18 December 1945, National Archives, WO 309/847.

539 Bob Gerritsen has pointed out that 'haltung', meaning conduct or behaviour, is a positive word and that by it Etter shows his admiration for Anthony.

540 Geoffrey means the nurse at the Zutphen General Hospital, Joanna Sollman, who had supposedly recognised Anthony. Geoffrey Cotterell to Mintie Cotterell, letter, 6 January 1946.

541   See Geoffrey Cotterell letter of 28 January 1946 when these details were given to him by Etter. 'Two weeks ago he was taken away to be grilled by the War Crimes commission, complete with electric lights and six hours of questioning.' Years later, Geoffrey would write: 'My abiding memory [of Etter] was his constant grievance at his tough interrogations by British officers, which he found outrageous since in his view he had prevented catastrophe, rather than being part of causing it'. Geoffrey Cotterell to author, email, 2 September 2009.

542   Major T.P.A. Davies, circulated memo attached to Etter deposition, 17 January 1945, National Archives, WO 309/2035.

543   Major T.P.A. Davies to Lieutenant-Colonel Hill, letter, copied to Lieutenant-Colonel Harris, 19 March 1945. Gemeente Archief Enschede, copy courtesy of the Airborne Museum, Oosterbeek.

544   Lieutenant-Colonel A.J.M. Harris to Major T.P.A. Davies, letter, 11 May 1946. National Archives, WO 309/1951.

545   Major A.E.E. Reade to Major T.P.A. Davies, office memo, 12 April 1946, National Archives, WO 309/1951.

546   Patricia Meehan, *A Strange Enemy People*, p.108.

547   See National Archives, WO 311/377.

548   Geoffrey Cotterell to Mintie Cotterell, letter, 15 January 1946.

549   Ibid, 4 February 1946.

550   Ibid, 27 December 1945.

551   Zhukov was very shortly to fall from grace with Stalin and lose the post.

552   Dr Robert Ley, former head of the Labour Front, one of the accused at Nuremberg, committed suicide in his cell on 25 October 1946.

553   Janie Pool to Mintie Cotterell, letter, 12 January 1946.

554   Ibid, 4 January 1946.

555   Mintie Cotterell to Janie Pool, letter, 17 January 1946.

556   Janie Pool to Mintie Cotterell, letter, 20 January 1946.

557   Ibid, 28 January 1946.

558   Telephone conversation reported in letter,Mintie Cotterell to Janie Pool, 23 May 1945.

559   Albert Tannenbaum, affidavit, 19 April 1946. Gemeente Archief Enschede, copy courtesy of the Airborne Museum, Oosterbeek.

560   Geoffrey Cotterell to author, email, 5 September 2009. Geoffrey did not go to Wembley, but probably met Tannenbaum in London, venue no longer remembered – 'A likely place would have been the RAC in Pall Mall.'

561   Kamp, Netherlands War Crimes Commission report, dated 12 November 1945. 33 Netherlands War Crimes Commission files. Dutch National Archives at The Hague, courtesy of Ymi Ytsma.

562   Ibid.

563   Copy of statement by James Flynn, National Archives, WO 309/847.

564   Will-Bentinck was a Dutch corruption of the name of Alan William Benting, who is buried at Enschede General Cemetery. Another corruption of the name was Binting William, which appears in the cemetery register. See Chapter 15, 'What Happened to Anthony Cotterell?'

565   Geoffrey Cotterell to Mintie Cotterell, letter, 22 January, 1946.

566   'Brief for Investigation', 19 February 1946, National Archives, WO 309/847.

567   Kamp, Netherlands War Crimes Commission report, dated 15 March 1946. 33 Netherlands War Crimes Commission files. Dutch National Archives at The Hague, courtesy of Ymi Ytsma.

568   Geoffrey Cotterell, conversation with the author, Arnhem, September 2009.

569   Anthony himself refers fleetingly to his teeth in *What! No Morning Tea*, when the Army dentist who is examining him calls out, 'Artificial crowns one and two'. *What! No Morning Tea?* p.30.

570   These two graves seem to have been identified at the time of the January exhumations (or perhaps the one which followed in March) because in the end only one unknown grave remained. They may have been the graves of Purves and Huard, who were buried in October 1944, see Chapter 15, 'What Happened to Anthony Cotterell?'

571   Geoffrey Cotterell to Mintie Cotterell, letter, 5 February 1946.

572 It may possibly have been a copy, or there may have been another form attached, as the one in the family archives only shows the details of the teeth and Geoffrey writes of the papers he sent, 'you will see that [the jacket caps] are mentioned on the form'.

573 Geoffrey Cotterell to Mintie Cotterell, letter, 5 March 1946.

574 Ibid, 20 January 1946.

575 33 Netherlands War Crimes Commission report, addendum to original report, hand-dated 26/11/45, Dutch National Archives at The Hague, courtesy of Ymi Ytsma.

576 Geoffrey Cotterell to Mintie Cotterell, letter, 26 January 1946.

577 Ibid, 20 January 1946.

578 Ibid, 5 February 1946.

579 'Translation of a Document Established by Dr Lathe', Essen, 6 February 1946, National Archives, WO 309/847.

580 Ibid. SS-Obertruppführer was a rank which did not exist by 1944,

581 Geoffrey Cotterell to Mintie Cotterell, letter, 25 January 1946.

582 Ibid, 15 January 1946.

583 Ibid, 20 January 1946.

584 This letter is on Anthony's case file with 33 Netherlands War Crime Commission, Dutch National Archives at The Hague, copy lent by Ymi Ytsma. Translation by Frits Slijkoord.

585 National Archives, WO 309/847.

586 Geoffrey Cotterell to Mintie Cotterell, letter, 5 March 1946.

587 'We have had no news at all and I am afraid that there is little for us to hope for. A Catholic priest said he heard Anthony was taken to Apeldoorn and in a very bad way, so you can imagine our feelings.' Mintie Cotterell to Janie Pool, letter, 21 May 1945.

588 Geoffrey Cotterell to Mintie Cotterell, letter, 10 March 1946.

589 Ibid, 23 March 1946.

590 Ibid, 17/18 March 1946.

591 Ibid, 23 March 1946.

592 Ibid, 2 June 1946.

593 Opel was a make of car. Juliana was the Princess Royal of the Netherlands. The MP (Military Police) corporal was another Englishman; Aps Willink gives his name as Hill in her letter of 31 March 1946.

594 Geoffrey Cotterell to Mintie Cotterell, letter, 1 April 1946.

595 Ibid, 3 April 1946.

596 Albert Deuss to Mintie Cotterell, letter, 31 March 1946.

597 Geoffrey Cotterell to Mintie Cotterell, letter, 4 April 1946.

598 Kamp Report, 26 November 1945.

599 This letter is on Anthony's case file with 33 Netherlands War Crime Commission. Dutch National Archives at The Hague, copy lent by Ymi Ytsma. Translation by Frits Slijkoord.

600 Geoffrey Cotterell to Mintie Cotterell, letter, 25 April 1946.

601 The Unteroffizier was thought to be Dr Eberhard Taubert, whom the Dutch were very eager to locate because he was indeed chief of Radio Hilversum. It was not actually him who had been present at Brummen, although this mistake was not cleared up for some time.

602 Geoffrey Cotterell to Mintie Cotterell, letter, 2 April 1946.

603 The possible connection of Günther d'Alquen's organisation to Anthony is examined in Chapter 15, 'What Happened to Anthony Cotterell?' Affidavit of Dr Paul Karl Schmidt, National Archives, WO 309/847.

604 Affidavit of Dr Hans Fritzsche, National Archives, WO 309/847.

605 See for example 'Case of Major Cotterell', 21 June 1946, signed by Lieutenant Colonel R.A. Nightingale. National Archives, WO 309/847.

606 Preliminary report by Captain H.P. Kinsleigh, dated 14 May 1946. National Archives, WO 309/847.

607 Geoffrey Cotterell to Mintie Cotterell, letter, 8 April 1946.

608   Geoffrey Cotterell, conversation with the author, Arnhem 2009: 'The Dr Lathe incident was revolting, I wished I could have shot myself there and then, but Sergeant Kamp was implacable.'

609   Dr Heinrich Lathe swore his deposition before de Ferrare at Essen in March 1946. See Deposition of Heinrich Lathe, National Archives, WO 309/1951.

610   Geoffrey Cotterell to Mintie Cotterell, letter, 14 April 1946.

611   Ibid, 8 April 1946.

612   Ibid, 21 April 1946.

613   Ibid, 20 May 1946.

614   'From Our Own Correspondent in London', article in *The Argus*, Tuesday 15 May 1945, p.16, Australia Trove, http://trove.nla.gov.au/ndp/del/article/1108881

615   Geoffrey Cotterell to Mintie Cotterell, letter, 30 April 1946.

616   Gemeente Archief Enschede, copy courtesy of the Airborne Museum, Oosterbeek.

617   Geoffrey Cotterell to author, email, 4 August 2010.

618   National Archives, WO 309/2035.

619   Ibid.

620   Staubwasser deposition, 20 September 1946. Gemeente Archief Enschede, copy courtesy of the Airborne Museum, Oosterbeek. Translation Helen Chapman.

621   National Archives, WO 311/377.

622   Ibid, WO 309/2035.

623   Kinsleigh Report, 23 September 1946, National Archives, WO 309/21.

624   This fact was discovered during Geoffrey's researches in Holland, see letter to Mintie Cotterell 3 April 1946.

625   BBC to War Crimes Investigation Unit, BAOR, letter, 22 May 1946, National Archives, WO 309/847. Captain H.P. Kinsleigh, report, 23 September 1946, National Archives, WO 309/21.

626   Major A.E.E. Reade to No 3 Team, Field Investigation Section, letter, 24 February 1947, National Archives, WO 309/847.

627   Major A.E.E. Reade, memo, 3 June 1947, National Archives, WO 309/847.

628   Janie Pool to Mintie Cotterell, letter, 25 March 1946.

629   Ibid, 28 March 1946.

630   Janie's flat was No. 11, Amhurst Court, in Amhurst Park.

631   Geoffrey Cotterell to Mintie Cotterell, letter, 16 May 1946.

632   Ibid, 10 April 1946.

633   Ibid, 9 April 1946.

634   Ibid, 2 April 1946.

635   Ernest Watkins to Mintie Cotterell, letter, 9 May 1946.

636   Geoffrey Cotterell to Mintie Cotterell, letter, 15 May 1946.

637   Ibid, 22 May 1946.

638   Ibid, 24 May 1946.

639   Marcowitz – 'The final orderly in the dressing station has been located in Vienna and the Field Security there have been briefed on the case and told to interrogate him thoroughly.' Geoffrey Cotterell to Mintie Cotterell, letter, 3/4 May 1946.

640   Aps Tjeenk Willink to Mintie Cotterell, letter, 27 May 1946.

641   Geoffrey Cotterell to Mintie Cotterell, letter, 1 June 1946.

642   Sergeant E.E.G. Atkinson to Geoffrey Cotterell, 10 July 1946, and statement by Sergeant E.E.G. Atkinson included in a letter from Geoffrey Cotterell to Captain Kinsleigh, 5 August 1946. National Archives, WO 309/847.

643   Major A.E.E. Reade to War Crimes Investigation Unit, letter, 11 July 1946, National Archives, WO 309/847.

644   Major David Conroy to Major A.E.E. Reade, letter, 11 July 1946, National Archives, WO 309/847.

645   Geoffrey Cotterell to Mintie Cotterell, letter, 30 May 1947.

646   Ibid, 26 May 1947.

647   The story of this prisoner is told in Chapter 15, 'What Happened to Anthony Cotterell?'

648 Geoffrey Cotterell to Mintie Cotterell, letter, 30 May 1947.

649 War Crimes Group progress report 25 August 1947, National Archives, WO 309/21.

650 The village of Putten in Gelderland was targeted by the Germans in retaliation for the Dutch resistance shooting up a Wehrmacht car on the night of 30 September/1 October 1944, injuring two soldiers and killing an officer. 110 houses were burned down and 661 men of the village transported to concentration camps, where they were so badly maltreated that only forty-eight of them returned after the war.

651 See Coen Hilbrink, *De Illegalen, Illegaliteit in Twente & het aangrenzende Salland, 1940–1945* (SDU, Netherlands, 1989) and C.B. Cornelissen *Sipo en SD in Twente, 1940–1945* (Cornelissen, Netherlands, 2010).

652 War Crimes Commission correspondence, 29 December 1947, NA: WO 309/21; Geoffrey Cotterell to Captain Springett, British Embassy, The Hague, letter, 12 November 1947; Geoffrey Cotterell to the author, email, 12 October 2008.

653 Conspiracy theories surfaced in the United States in the 1990s that American, and thus by extension probably also British, soldiers had been abandoned in the Soviet gulags. Careful historical research has proved that this was nonsense. See Timothy K. Nenninger's 'United States Prisoner of War and the Red Army, 1944–45: Myths and Realities', *The Journal of Military History*, 6, 3 (July 2002), pp.761–781.

654 Letter from the War Office to Messrs Elliott and Gill, Graham Cotterell's solicitors, 1 January 1963.

655 In November 2008, Geoffrey clarified why he had revised his view on the unknown grave at Enschede. He had previously told me that Minty died in 1982 and that she therefore did not know Enschede was where Anthony was – there was one unknown grave from those buried in September 1944 (the one whose teeth were checked and it was not Anthony) and then there was another unknown grave. This seemed a rather difficult explanation to follow, and I asked for clarification. Geoffrey then explained that this man had turned up alive after the war, which ruled him out of being in the unknown grave; however Geoffrey did not know about the man's reappearance until after 1982. Geoffrey, not knowing about or having forgotten about the March 1946 exhumations which had checked all the graves, came to the conclusion that the man in the unknown grave had to be Anthony. It was then that he 'gave up the thought that Tone was still alive, but Mother had gone by then so she didn't have to be presented with that'. Geoffrey could no longer remember the man's name.

656 Geoffrey Cotterell, conversation with the author, Arnhem, September 2009.

657 Mintie Cotterell to Janie Pool, letter, 25 May 1945.

658 Ibid, 17 May 1945.

659 Freddie Gough letter transcribed by Mintie Cotterell, Mintie Cotterell to Janie Pool, letter, 28 May 1945.

660 Deposition of Gustav Etter, 18 December 1945.

661 Geoffrey Cotterell to Mintie Cotterell, 24 March 1946.

662 'Brief for Investigation', 19 February 1946, National Archives, WO 309/847.

663 Bernard Briggs to Captain C.R. Miller, HQ, 1st Airborne Division, letter, 21 November 1945.

664 Jim Flavell, conversation with the author, August 2008.

665 I am indebted to Roy Hemington of the Commonwealth War Graves Commission for all information regarding the March 1946 exhumations (sent by email on 22 September 2009).

666 Ibid.

667 Captain H.P. Kinsleigh, Preliminary Report, 14 May 1946, National Archives, WO 309/847.

668 Preliminary Report dated 19 May 1947, 33 Netherlands War Crime Commission. Dutch National Archives at The Hague, copy lent by Ymi Ytsma.

669 There is, of course, no evidence of who this prisoner actually was. One concern about this story is that John Killick also tried to escape by hiding under tarpaulin sheets, was discovered, and returned to Zutphen, probably on 24 September. However, Killick was definitely not on the truck to Enschede.

670 Geoffrey Cotterell to Mintie Cotterell, letter, 12 November 1945.

671 Ibid, 2 April 1946.

672   Affidavit of Dr Paul Schmidt, NA WO 309/847.

673   Letter, Major A.E.E. Reade to Major T.P.A. Davies, War Crimes Liaison Officer at Baden-Baden, 19 February 1946, National Archives, WO 309/1951.

674   All these new leads were confusing, and in May 1946, Geoffrey wrote to give Mintie a much needed explanation of all the new names who were being followed up, 'You say you wonder who the names are'. Geoffrey Cotterell to Mintie Cotterell, letter, 5 May 1946.

675   D.A. Conroy, 'Cotterell Case – VIP 140, April Progress Report', National Archives, WP 309/847.

676   R.M. Gerritsen, *For No Apparent Reason: the Shooting of Captain Brian Brownscombe GM, RAM.C.* (Sigmond Publishing, Renkum, Holland, 2000), pp.14–15.

677   Ibid, pp.28–29.

678   No date is given for the testimony but it is attached to a letter dated 19 May 1946. National Archives, WO 309/1951.

679   'Brief for Investigation', 19 February 1946, National Archives, WO 309/847.

680   Jan A. Hey, *Files on the Shooting of Prisoners of War at Brummen, Holland*, typescript report, July 1991, Gemeente Archief Enschede, p.2.

681   Geoffrey Cotterell to Mintie Cotterell, letter, 15 May 1946.

682   Kinsleigh Report, 23 September 1946, National Archives, WO 309/21.

683   Allard Martens, with Daphne Dunlop, *The Silent War: Glimpses of the Dutch Underground and Views on the Battle of Arnhem* (Hodder and Stoughton, London, 1961), p.208.

684   Christiansen was tried after the war as a war criminal and given a twelve-year sentence. It was he who had ordered the infamous retaliatory raid on the village of Putten in Gelderland in October 1944.

685   Geoffrey Cotterell to British Embassy, The Hague, letter, 12 November 1947.

686   Memo dated 8 January, National Archives, WO 309/847.

687   Kamp, paperwork of 33 Netherlands War Crimes Commission, Investigation Team 3, HERFORD 2815, placed on file 22 July 1947. Dutch National Archives at The Hague, copy lent by Ymi Ytsma.

BIBLIOGRAPHY

Archival Sources

33 Netherlands War Crimes Commission papers, Dutch National Archives, The Hague, Netherlands

Airborne Museum, Oosterbeek, Netherlands

Army Personnel Centre, Historical Disclosures Section, Glasgow

Commonwealth War Graves Commission

Gemeente Archief, Enschede, including: Jan A. Hey, Files on the Shooting of Prisoners of War at Brummen, Holland, typescript report, July 1991

Imperial War Museum
Harrison, Captain C.A., *The Great Battle of Arnhem, a personal account*, Ref: 4488, 82/33/1
Trinder, H.E., *Untitled account*, Ref: 3530, 85/8/1

National Archives, Kew, London
WO 309/1951
WO 309/2035
WO 309/21
WO 309/847
WO 309/848
WO 311/377
WO 311/884

Regionaal Archief, Zutphen

Robert Graves archive, The Library, St John's College, and St John's College Robert Graves Trust

Robert Graves archive, the Poetry Collection, University at Buffalo, the State University of New York

Cotterell Family Correspondence

Cotterell, Anthony
Cotterell, Geoffrey
Cotterell, Mintie
Deuss, Albert
Pool, Janie
Tjeenk Willink, Aps
Tjeenk Willink, Dick

Internet Sources

Capture of Helen Sensburg, 'From Our Own Correspondent in London', *The Argus*, Tuesday 15 May 1945, Australia Trove, http://trove.nla.gov.au/ndp/del/article/1108881

Horrocks, Lieutenant-General B.G., *A Short History of the 8th Armoured Brigade*, foreword by Lieutenant-General B.G. Horrocks, 30 Corps, March 1946, Warlinks website: http://www.warlinks.com/armour/8th_armoured/index.php

Sir John Killick, interviews with Peter Liddle (October 2001) and John Hutson (February 2002), Leeds World WAR II Experience Centre, http://www.war-experience.org/

Reynolds, Quentin, *By Quentin Reynolds*, (New York McGraw-Hill Book Company, New York, 1963), the Internet Archive, San Francisco

http://www.archive.org/stream/byquentinreynold001597mbp/byquentinreynold001597mbp_djvu.txt

Richard Perceval Graves website, *Robert Graves and the White Goddess 1940–1985*, Book Three: *The Shout*, Chapter 3:*Wife to Mr Milton*: http://www.richardgraves.org/html/gravchap.htm#shout

The Pegasus Archive, http://www.pegasusarchive.org/arnhem/main.htm
    1st Airborne Reconnaissance Squadron War Diary
    1st Airlanding Anti-Tank Battery, RA War Diary
    1st Parachute Brigade HQ War Diary
    1st Parachute Squadron War Diary
    2nd Parachute Battalion War Diary
    Major Douglas Edward Crawley biography
    Major Freddie Gough biography

Published Sources

ABCA, *The ABCA Handbook, A Manual Designed for the Guidance of all Officers in the Conduct of Talks and Discussions on Current Affairs*, Preface by the Secretary of State for War (ABCA, The War Office, August 1942)

ABCA, *The ABCA Song Book* (ABCA, The War Office, 1944)

Adam, Sir Ronald, 'A Farewell Message from the Adjutant-General', *WAR*, issue 97, 14 June 1945

Alanbrooke, Field Marshal Lord, *War Diaries, 1939–45* (Weidenfeld and Nicolson, London, 2001)

Allen, R., with Frost, John, *Voice of Britain: The Inside Story of the Daily Express* (Patrick Stephens, Cambridge, 1983)

Altes, A. Korthals, Margry, K., Thuring, G., Voskuil, R., *September 1944, Operation Market Garden* (De Haan, Netherlands, 1987)

Anon, *Arnhem Lift, Diary of a Glider Pilot* (Pilot Press, 1945)

Army Film Unit, *The Story of the Army Bureau of Current Affairs*, black and white film (Ministry of Information, 1943), Imperial War Museum, London, ref: MGH

Beattie, Edward W., *Diary of a Kriegie* (Thomas Y. Crowell Co, New York, 1946)

Beaumont, Joan, 'Protecting Prisoners of War, 1939–45', in Moore, Bob and Kent Fedorowich (eds), *Prisoners of War and Their Captors in World War II* (Berg, Oxford, 1996)

Biddiscombe, Perry, *The Denazification of Germany, A History 1945–1950* (Tempus, Stroud, 2007)

Buckingham, William F., *Arnhem 1944, a Reappraisal* (Tempus, 2002)

Buggenum, David G. van, *B Company Arrived, The Story of B Company of the 2nd Parachute Battalion at Arnhem, September 1944* (R.N. Sigmond Publishing, Renkum, Netherlands, 2003)

Carstairs, John Paddy, *Hadn't We the Gaiety?* (Hurst and Blackett, 1945)

Cherry, Niall, *Red Berets and Red Crosses, The Story of the Medical Services in the 1st Airborne Division in World War II* (R.N. Sigmond Publishing, Renkum, Netherlands, 2005)

Cherry, Niall, *With Nothing Bigger than a Bren Gun: the story of the defence of the Schoolhouse at the Arnhem Road Bridge, September 1944* (Brendon Publishing, 2007)

Christiansen, Arthur, *Headlines All my Life* (Heinemann, London, 1961)

Churchill, Winston Spencer, *The Second World War, 'Closing the Ring'*, Volume 5 (Folio Society, London, 2000)

Clark, Lloyd *Arnhem, Operation Market Garden, September 1944* (Sutton Publishing, Stroud, 2002)

Clifford, Alexander and Jenny Nicholson, *The Sickle and the Stars* (Peter Davies, London, 1948)

Cornelissen, C.B., *Sipo en SD in Twente, 1940–1945* (Cornelissen, Netherlands, 2010)

Cotterell, Anthony, 'A Day at the Seaside: Going on Shore', *WAR*, issue 74, 8 July 1944

___ 'Airborne Worries: Waiting to Be Scrubbed', *WAR*, issue 79, 14 October 1944

___ *An Apple for the Sergeant* (Hutchinson and Co, London, 1944)

___ 'A Sergeant in Tow', *WAR*, issue 72, 10 June 1944

___ 'Completely in the Air', *Horizon*, June 1944

___ *Oh, It's Nice to be in the Army!* (Victor Gollancz, London, 1941)

___ *RAMC, An Authoritative Account Prepared with the Assistance of the Army Medical Department of the War Office and the RAMC* (Hutchinson, London, 1942)

___ *Roof Over Britain: the Official Story of the A.A. Defences, 1939–42* (The Ministry of Information, HM Stationery Office, London, 1943)

___ *She Walks In Battledress* (Christophers, London, 1942)

___ 'Sitting on the Fence', *WAR*, issue 73, 24 June 1944

___ 'The Airborne Forces', *WAR*, issue 32, 28 November 1944

___ *The Expert Way of Getting Married* (T Werner Laurie, London, 1939)

___ 'Tiger, Tiger, Burning Bright', *WAR*, issues 76 and 77, 19 August and 2 September 1944

___ *What! No Morning Tea?* (Victor Gollanz, London, 1941)

Cotterell, Geoffrey, 'Factory Guard', *Oh, It's Nice to be in the Army!* (Victor Gollancz, London, 1941)

___ *Randle in Springtime*, (Eyre and Spottiswoode, London, 1949)

___ 'Rockets for the Home Guard', *WAR*, issue 70, 13 May 1944

___ *Then a Soldier* (Eyre and Spottiswoode, London, 1944)

___ *The Strange Enchantment* (Eyre and Spottiswoode, London, 1956)

___ 'We Bag our First', *WAR*, issue 5, 15 November 1941

Crang, Jeremy A., *The British Army and the People's War, 1939–1945* (Manchester University Press, 2000)

Current Affairs, issues 50 and 54, 28 August 1943 and 23 October 1943

Deane-Drummond, Anthony, *Return Ticket* (Collins, London, 1953)

Doherty, Richard, *Normandy 1944: The Road to Victory* (Spellmount, Staplehurst, 2004)

Fabricius, Johan, *A Tribute to the Men*, transcript of broadcast on BBC Home Service on 27 September 1944, *WAR*, issue 83, 9 December 1944

Flavell, E.W.C., 'British Parachutists', *WAR*, issue 7, 13 December 1944

Foot, M.R.D. (editor), *Holland at War Against Hitler: Anglo-Dutch relations 1940–1945* (Frank Cass, London, 1990)

Foray, Jennifer L., *Visions of Empire in the Nazi-Occupied Netherlands* (Cambridge University Prsss, Cambridge, 2012)

Frost, Major General John, *A Drop Too Many* (Leo Cooper, 1994)

Gerritsen, R.M., *For No Apparent Reason: The Shooting of Captain Brian Brownscombe GM, RAMC* (R.N. Sigmond Publishing, Renkum, Holland, 2000)

Gerritsen, Bob and Revell, Scott, *Retake Arnhem Bridge, An Illustrated History of Kampgruppe Knaust, September–October 1944* (R.N. Sigmond Publishing, Renkum, Netherlands, 2010)

Grant, Ian, *Cameramen at War* (Patrick Stephens, Cambridge, 1980)

Harrison, Mark, *Medicine and Victory: British Military Medicine in the Second World War* (Oxford University Press, Oxford, 2004)

Hawking, Desmond (ed), *War Report, D-Day to VE-Day, Dispatches by the BBC's War Correspondents with the Allied Expeditionary Force 6 June 1944–5 May 1945* (BBC, London, 1985)

Hawkins, T.H. and L.J.F. Brimble, *Adult Education: The Record of the British Army* (Macmillan and Co, London, 1947)

Heaps, Leo, *Escape from Arnhem: A Canadian Amongst the Lost Paratroops* (The Macmilllan Company of Canada, 1945)

___ *The Grey Goose of Arnhem, The Story Of The Most Amazing Mass Escape Of World War II* (Weidenfeld and Nicholson, London, 1996)

Hibbert, Tony, *Trebah, My Story* (Trebah Publications, Cornwall, 2005)

Hilbrink, Coen, *De Illegalen, Illegaliteit in Twente & het aangrenzende Salland, 1940–1945* (SDU, Netherlands, 1989)

Horne, Alistair with David Montgomery, *The Lonely Leader: Montgomery 1944–45* (Pan Books, London, 1995)

Latawski, Paul, *Battle Zone Normandy: Falaise Pocket* (Sutton Publishing, Stroud, 2004)

Lewis, Jeremy, *Cyril Connolly: A Life* (Pimlico, London, 1998)

MacKenzie, S.P., *Politics and Military Morale* (Oxford University Press, 1992)

___, 'The Treatment of Prisoners of War in World War II', *Journal of Modern History*, 66, 3 (September 1994)

___, 'Vox Populi: British Army Newspapers in the Second World War', *Journal of Contemporary History*, vol 24, No 4 (Sage Publications Ltd, October 1989)

Maclaren-Ross, Julian, 'I Had to Go Absent', *Times Literary Supplement*, 27 June 2008

Martens, Allard with Daphne Dunlop, *The Silent War: Glimpses of the Dutch Underground and Views on the Battle of Arnhem* (Hodder and Stoughton, London, 1961)

Mawson, Stuart, *Arnhem Doctor* (Spellmount, Stroud, 2007)

Meehan, Patricia, *A Strange Enemy People: Germans Under the British, 1945–50* (Peter Owen, London, 2001)

Maxted, Stanley, *The Withdrawal*, transcript of broadcast on BBC, *WAR*, issue 83, 9 December 1944

Ministry of Information, *By Air to Battle: The Official Account of the British First and Sixth Airborne Divisions* (HM Stationery Office, London, 1945)

Moorehead, Alan, *A Late Education, Episodes in a Life* (Hamish Hamilton, London, 1970)

Nenninger, Timothy K., 'United States Prisoner of War and the Red Army, 1944–45: Myths and Realities', *The Journal of Military History*, 6, 3 (July 2002)

Nicholson, Jenny, 'Fair Women and Brave Men', *WAR*, issue 82, 25 November 1944

Overmans, Rüdiger, 'The Repatriation of Prisoners Once Hostilities are Over: A Matter of Course?' in Moore, Bob and Barbara Hately-Broad (eds), *Prisoners of War, Prisoners of Peace: Captivity, Homecoming and Memory in World War II* (Berg, Oxford, 2005)

Owen, James, *Nuremberg, Evil on Trial* (Headline Publishing, London, 2006)

Reinders, Philip, *Major J. Anthony Cotterell, War Correspondent* (self-published booklet, Holland, 2008)

Reuters Report, *The Times*, 22 September 1944

Rose, Norman, *Vansittart, Study of a Diplomat* (Heinemann, London, 1978)

Ryan, Cornelius, *A Bridge Too Far* (Hamish Hamilton, London, 1974)

Seymour, Miranda, *Robert Graves: Life on the Edge* (Doubleday, London, 1995)

Simms, James, *Arnhem Spearhead: A Private Soldier's Story* (Imperial War Museum, 1978)

Skelton, Barbara, *Tears Before Bedtime* (Hamish Hamilton, 1987)

Taylor, A.J.P., *Beaverbrook* (History Book Club, 1972)

Thacker, Toby, *The End of the Third Reich: Defeat, Denazification and Nuremberg, January 1944 – November 1946* (Tempus, Stroud, 2006)

Urquhart, Major General R.E. with Wilfred Greatorex, *Arnhem* (Cassell, London, 1958)

van Roekel, C., *Who was Who during the Battle of Arnhem, The Order of Battle of Airborne Officers and Warrant Officers who Fought at Arnhem in 1944* (The Society of Friends of the Airborne Museum, Oosterbeek, 1996)

Vansittart, Lord Robert, *Black Record: Germans Past and Present* (Hamish Hamilton, London, 1941)

___ *Lessons of My Life* (Hutchinson & Co, London, 1943)

Vourkoutiotis, Vasilis, 'What the Angels Saw: Red Cross and Protecting Power Visits to Anglo-American POWs, 1939–45', *Journal of Contemporary History*, 50, 4 (October 2005)

Waddy, John, *A Tour of the Arnhem Battlefields* (Leo Cooper, London, 2001)

Walters, Guy, *Hunting Evil, How the Nazi War Criminals Escaped and the Hunt to Bring Them to Justice* (Bantam Press, London, 2009)

Watkins, Ernest, '1 Airborne Div at Arnhem, Inside the Perimeter', *WAR*, issue 84, 23 December 1944

___ '1 Airborne Div at Arnhem, The Landing and the Bridge', *WAR*, issue 83, 9 December 1944

___ 'Arnhem Revisited', *WAR*, issue 97 (23 June 1945)

___ 'Lines of Thought'; 'Better Water than Blood', *WAR*, issue 87, 3 February 1945

___ *No Depression in Iceland* (George Allen and Unwin Ltd, London, 1942)

___ (With Michael Bratby) *Iceland Presents* (J nsson and safoldarprentsmi ja, Reykjavik, 1941)

Watts, Stephen, *Moonlight on a Lake in Bond Street* (The Bodley Head, London, 1961)

Wheatley, Jane, 'The Real Rebecca', *The Times*, 11 September 2005

Willemsens, Piet, *Oorlog in een Dorp aan de IJssel, Brummen-Eerbeek 1940–1945* (P.H.L. Willemsens, Brummen, Holland, 1994)

Willetts, Paul (ed), *Julian Maclaren-Ross: Collected Memoirs* (Black Spring Press, London, 2004)

Unpublished Sources

Briggs, Bernard, handwritten record, courtesy of Simon Middleton-Briggs

Cotterell, Anthony, 1941 Diary, handwritten

___ 1941 Diary, typescript

___ 1943 Parachute course typescripts

___ 1944 Diary and typescripts in run-up to D-Day

___ 1944 Normandy typescripts

___ 1944 'Jumping to a Conclusion: Part One', pencil/typescript

Flavell, Jim, personal account

Hibbert, Tony, Arnhem and post-Arnhem diary

McGrath, Rosemary, personal account

Slijkoord, Jeanne, personal account

Watkins, Ernest, Ernest Watkins Papers, Special Collections, University Of Calgary, Accession Number: 469/90.9

___ 'ABCA I, Inception', file 6.1

___ 'It Is Dangerous to Lean Out' (incomplete draft), file 5.1–5.2

___ 'Out of My Wits', files 6.3.1–7.1.2

___ Fragment inside novel *Irregardless*, file 3.4

Ytsma, Ymi, family papers

INDEX